Cindy Levine

Meta-Analysis, Decision Analysis, and Cost-Effectiveness Analysis

Monographs in Epidemiology and Biostatistics
Edited by Jennifer L. Kelsey, Michael G. Marmot,
Paul D. Stolley, Martin P. Vessey

MONOGRAPHS IN EPIDEMIOLOGY AND BIOSTATISTICS
VOLUME 31

Meta-Analysis, Decision Analysis, and Cost-Effectiveness Analysis

Methods for Quantitative Synthesis in Medicine

SECOND EDITION

DIANA B. PETITTI

New York   Oxford
OXFORD UNIVERSITY PRESS
2000

Oxford University Press

Oxford   New York
Athens   Auckland   Bangkok   Bogotá   Buenos Aires   Calcutta
Cape Town   Chennai   Dar es Salaam   Delhi   Florence   Hong Kong   Istanbul
Karachi   Kuala Lumpur   Madrid   Melbourne   Mexico City   Mumbai
Nairobi   Paris   São Paulo   Singapore   Taipei   Tokyo   Toronto   Warsaw
and associated companies in
Berlin   Ibadan

Published by Oxford University Press, Inc.,
198 Madison Avenue, New York, New York, 10016

Library of Congress Cataloging-in-Publication Data
Petitti, Diana B.
Meta-analysis, decision analysis, and cost-effectiveness analysis :
methods for quantitative synthesis in medicine /
Diana B. Petitti.
— 2nd ed.
p.   cm. — (Monographs in epidemiology and biostatistics : v. 31)
Includes bibliographical references and index.
ISBN 0-19-513364-1
1. Medicine—Decision making.   2. Statistical decision.
3. Meta-analysis.   4. Cost effectiveness.
I. Title.   II. Series.
R723.5.P48   2000   614.4'07'2—dc21   99-13213

9 8 7 6 5 4 3 2 1

Printed in the United States of America
on acid-free paper

Preface

It was difficult to undertake a second edition of this book. The first edition achieved its aims and, with only a few exceptions (a few mistakes in formulae), nothing in the first edition is dead wrong, even today. I know of more than one second edition that is worse than the first edition. The fear of failure that I experienced in writing the first edition returned upon contemplating a second edition. I finally agreed (with myself) to write the second edition only when I agreed (with myself) that the second edition would not be much different from the first and would not be a lot longer. Once the mental block was overcome, I became enthusiastic about the second edition, because its preparation allowed me to update some of the examples, correct some errors in Chapter 7, and add material describing the few substantive advances in each field.

The second edition project became a bit more extensive than I had anticipated. Although not much has changed, I felt compelled to "modernize" the examples. I found that I needed to make some material more advanced, to reflect advances in the field. So, the second edition is the same, but a lot different.

The second edition deemphasizes meta-analysis of observational studies, because meta-analysis of observational studies has been disappointing. The second edition more clearly defines as one the most important goals of meta-analysis the identification and exploration of heterogeneity. Meta-analysis of individual level data is discussed.

Material on cost-effectiveness analysis has been brought into alignment with the recommendations of the U.S. Public Health Services Panel on Cost-Effectiveness in Health and Medicine. The chapters on cost-effectiveness analysis in the first edition were not far off the mark, but the availability of an authoritative source of recommendations on how to "standardize" cost-effectiveness analysis improves this book as an introduction to this complex subject.

Literature on the methodology for measurement of quality-adjusted life expectancy has exploded since the first edition. This edition adds some detail to its discussion of this topic and describes how health-related quality of life is measured and incorporated into utility analysis and cost-utility analysis. It would not possible cover this topic comprehensively.

Web-o-philes will perhaps be disappointed that this textbook is a traditional textbook. Much as I love the Web, I love paper and ink better. No apologies.

I would not have overcome my inertia if Jeff House had not so strongly encouraged me to prepare a second edition. Drummond Rennie must also be thanked for helping me see that a second edition did not have to be a total rewrite of the first edition. Selene Hausman, my daughter, did much of the work of retrieving articles from the library. The second edition would never have been completed if she had not spent many weekends and holidays wrestling with the truly archaic copy machine at the University of Southern California library.

Sierra Madre, Cal.   D. B. P.

Contents

Meta-Analysis, Decision Analysis, and Cost-Effectiveness Analysis

1

Introduction

The rapid accumulation of medical information makes decisions about patient management more and more difficult for the practicing physician. Increasing numbers of medical technologies and the availability of several different technologies for the management of the same condition greatly complicate decision making at both the individual and the policy level. The need to develop guidelines for clinical practice and to set funding priorities for medical interventions is pressing, but the volume and the complexity of medical information thwarts attempts to make firm recommendations about what should and should not be done and what should and should not be paid for. It is in this context that the three related research methods—meta-analysis, decision analysis, and cost-effectiveness analysis—have been developed and have gained popularity. The overall objective of this book is to show how these research methods can be used to meet the growing challenge of making sense of what is known in order to maximize the usefulness of medical knowledge.

Section 1.1 presents three problems that illustrate the need for these research methods; it describes the reasons for considering the three methods in a single text. Section 1.2 defines the three methods and shows their application to the three illustrative problems. Section 1.3 describes the history of the application of each method in medicine. Section 1.4 gives an example of how the methods can be used together to comprehensively address a single medical problem, illustrating the value of the methods used together. Section 1.5 briefly describes the organization of the book.

1.1   THREE ILLUSTRATIVE PROBLEMS

A physician must decide whether to recommend primary coronary angio-plasty or intravenous thrombolytic therapy for patients with acute myocardial infarction.

A committee charged with developing guidelines on the management of prostate cancer must decide whether to recommend radical prostatectomy, radiation, or watchful waiting as the initial therapy for men with localized prostate cancer.

The Health Care Financing Administration must decide whether Medicare will pay for beneficiaries to receive pneumococcal vaccine.

Each of these problems is a real problem, either past or present. Each problem requires a policy solution—a solution for the patients of one physician, for a group of patients, or for an organization. Like almost all other contemporary medical problems, these three problems cannot be addressed by looking at only one piece of information. There are many different studies of angioplasty compared with thrombolysis in patients with myocardial infarction, and no single study is definitive. A decision to recommend prostatectomy, radiation, or watchful waiting must consider the morbidity of the treatments, the likelihood of metastases in men with localized cancer and the consequences of metastases, and the age and life expectancy of the individual. Deciding to pay for pneumococcal vaccine must take into account the effectiveness of the vaccine and its cost in relation to competing demands for Medicare resources. Addressing each problem requires the synthesis of information.

Synthesis is the bringing together of parts or elements to form a whole (Webster's New Collegiate Dictionary 1982). Meta-analysis, decision analysis, and cost-effectiveness analysis have in common that they synthesize knowledge. Each method takes parts of the medical literature or of clinical experience and attempts to create from this information a whole answer to a defined problem.

Each of the three methods is quantitative, using statistical and numerical analysis in the attempt to create the whole. Each of the methods aims to resolve uncertainty. For meta-analysis, the uncertainty is in what conclusions to draw from a body of research studies on the same topic. For decision analysis, the uncertainty is in what to recommend for a single patient or for a group of similar patients. For cost-effectiveness analysis, the uncertainty is in the value of a medical procedure, treatment, or service. Each method aims to facilitate decision making, particularly decision making at the policy level, and each has come to play a prominent role in the formulation of clinical and public policy in health care.

1.2   DEFINITIONS

1.2.1   Meta-Analysis

Meta-analysis is a quantitative approach for systematically assessing the results of previous research in order to arrive at conclusions about the body of research.

Studies of a topic are first systematically identified. Criteria for including and excluding studies are defined. In traditional meta-analysis, data from the eligible studies are abstracted or collected from the investigators in the study. The data are then analyzed. The analysis includes statistical tests of the heterogeneity of the study results, and, if the results are homogeneous, estimation of a summary estimate of the size of the effect of treatment. If the studies are not homogeneous, clinically or statistically, the heterogeneity is explored.

> *EXAMPLE:* The question of whether to recommend angioplasty or thrombolytic therapy for patients with myocardial infarction is controversial. By 1997, ten randomized trials had compared angioplasty with thrombolytic therapy to treat patients with acute myocardial infarction, but many of the studies were small, and their results were contradictory. A meta-analysis of these studies by Weaver et al. (1997) concluded that there was a reduction in the estimated relative risk of death or nonfatal reinfarction in patients treated with primary angioplasty as well as a significant reduction in the relative risk of total and hemorrhagic stroke.

Pooled analysis of individual level data from different studies is also called meta-analysis. In this form of meta-analysis, the individual data from participants in a systematically ascertained group of studies are obtained and then analyzed. Pooled analysis of individual level data from multiple studies is conceptually the same as meta-analysis (Friedenreich 1993; Lau, Ioannidis, and Schmid 1998) and has the same aims.

1.2.2 Decision Analysis

Decision analysis is a quantitative approach that assesses the relative value of different decision options (Weinstein and Fineberg 1980; Pauker and Kassirer 1987). The information from decision analysis is used to decide how to manage an individual patient,[1] to formulate policy recommendations about a group of similar patients, and as information to help individuals make decisions about therapies. Decision analysis begins by systematically breaking a problem down into its components and, in most cases, creating a decision tree to represent the components and the decision options. Outcomes of the decision options are defined. Uncertainties in the components are identified, and review of the medical literature and expert opinion are used to estimate probabilities for the uncertainties. Values of the outcomes are measured or inferred.[2] Last, the decision tree is analyzed using statistically based methods. Decision analysis yields an estimate of the net value of the different decision options in relation to each other.

> *EXAMPLE:* The best initial treatment of patients with localized prostate cancer is controversial. In 1997, there were no studies that definitively proved the benefit of either prostatectomy or radiation over watchful waiting. Both prostatectomy and radiation have high rates of morbidity, including impotence and incontinence. A decision analysis by Fleming et al. (1997) con-

cluded that watchful waiting was a reasonable alternative to invasive treatment for most men with localized prostatic cancer.

1.2.3 Cost-Effectiveness Analysis

Cost-effectiveness analysis compares decision options in terms of their monetary cost. In medical applications, a decision analytic model is usually the conceptual basis for the analysis of the effectiveness of the decision options. Cost-effectiveness analysis involves, in addition, identification of the costs of the decision options and valuation of these costs and, in many cases, determination of the preferences of society or individuals for the health outcomes of the decision options. Once the problem has been framed, the effectiveness determined and data on costs and outcomes gathered, the costs of the decision options per unit of outcome are compared.

In 1986, Doubilet, Weinstein, and McNeil pointed out the terms "cost effective" and "cost-effectiveness analysis" were frequently misused in medicine (Doubilet, Weinstein, McNeil 1986). This situation has not changed. The terms are properly used only when formal analysis comparing the cost of alternative strategies has been done.

> *EXAMPLE:* Sisk and Riegelman (1986) did a cost-effectiveness analysis of vaccination against pneumococcal pneumonia in persons over 65 from the point of view of Medicare.[3] They estimated that the net Medicare expenditures for pneumococcal vaccination of the elderly would be $4400 to $8300 (1983 dollars) per year of healthy life gained. They also estimated that vaccination would save money for the Medicare program if it were administered in a public program, where the cost per vaccination would be low. The analysis supported Medicare reimbursement for pneumococcal vaccine. Further, it suggested that a public program to administer the vaccine would be the most efficient and financially desirable method for vaccinating the elderly.

1.3 HISTORICAL PERSPECTIVE

Attempts to synthesize knowledge are very old. Narrative reviews of the scientific literature have been around for as long as there has been a scientific literature. Quantitative approaches to the synthesis of information appear to be mostly twentieth-century inventions. Over the past two decades, quantitative synthesis has become more popular and more influential. Figure 1-1 shows the number of publications that used these methods or discussed the methods editorially or in reviews that were published from 1975 through 1997 and indexed in MEDLINE. Taken together, the growth has been exponential. The growth in publications that deal with meta-analysis or report the results of a meta-analysis is particularly striking.

1.3.1 Meta-Analysis

The term "meta-analysis" was coined by Glass in 1976 from the Greek prefix "meta," which means "transcending," and the root, analysis. Glass sought to

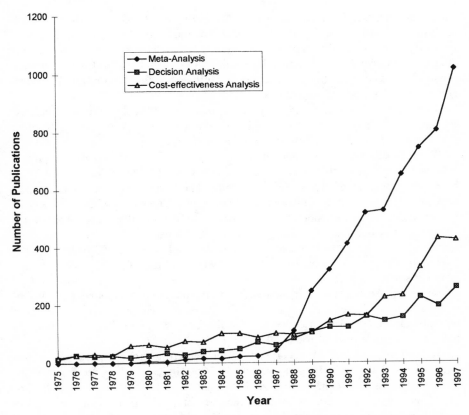

Figure 1-1   Number of publications 1975–1997 indexed in MEDLINE that used meta-analysis, decision analysis, and cost-effectiveness analysis or discussed the methods editorially or in a review.

distinguish meta-analysis from primary analysis—the original analysis of data from a research study—and secondary analysis—the reanalysis of data to answer new research questions (Glass 1976; Glass, McGaw, Smith 1981). However, the statistical combination of data from multiple studies of the same topic began long before a word for it was coined. In the 1930s, Tippett (1931), Fisher (1932), Cochran (1937), and Pearson (1938) each described statistical techniques for combining data from different studies, and examples of use of these techniques in the agricultural literature of the 1930s are numerous.

The need for techniques to combine data from many studies of the same topic became especially acute in the social sciences in the mid-1970s, when literally hundreds of studies existed for some topics. Development of meta-analysis was driven by the perception that narrative literature reviews were selective in their inclusion of studies and subjective in their weighting of studies.

During the late 1970s and early 1980s, social scientists, including Rosenthal (1978), Glass, McGaw, and Smith (1981), Hedges (1982, 1983), Hunter, Schmidt, and Jackson (1982), Light (1983), and Light and Pillemar (1984), popularized meta-analysis and further developed the statistical methods for its application. Equally important, they expanded the goal of studies that combine data to include the attempt to systematically identify the studies to be combined, and they made estimation of effect size, not just statistical significance, and exploration of heterogeneity primary aims of meta-analysis.

The first use of meta-analysis in medicine is difficult to date precisely. Winkelstein (1998) identified a use of the meta-analytic approach by Goldberger that dated to 1907, but this use was not called meta-analysis.

Widespread use in medicine of meta-analysis (called meta-analysis) quickly followed its popularization in the social sciences. Starting in 1978, meta-analyses began to appear in the biomedical literature. The early published meta-analyses were done by social and behavioral scientists and addressed psychological topics. In the late 1980s, descriptions of the method of meta-analysis appeared almost simultaneously in three influential general medical journals, the *New England Journal of Medicine, Lancet,* and the *Annals of Internal Medicine* (L'Abbe, Detsky, O'Rourke 1987; Sacks et al. 1987; Bulpitt 1988), and use of the method has been growing since.

More widespread use of meta-analysis in medicine has coincided with the increasing focus of medical research on the randomized clinical trial, and it has undoubtedly benefited from concern about the interpretation of small and individually inconclusive clinical trials.

Interest in, and use of, meta-analysis of data from nonexperimental studies began at about the same time as meta-analysis of clinical trials (Greenland 1987). Meta-analysis of non-experimental studies makes up a high proportion of all published meta-analyses. Table 1-1 shows the percentage of all publications indexed with the publication type ''meta-analysis'' that were based solely on non-

Table 1-1 Number and percentage of 1997–1998 publications on meta-analysis in general medical and specialty clinical journals that reported meta-anaylsis of nonexperimental studies

Type of Journal	Total Publications	Nonexperimental Studies	
		N	%
General medical[a]	35	11	31.4
Specialty clinical[b]	33	17	51.5
Total	68	28	41.2

[a] *New England Journal of Medicine, Lancet, British Medical Journal, Journal of the American Medical Association.*

[b] *Obstetrics and Gynecology, Cardiology, Pediatrics, Neurology, Urology, Gastroenterology, Annals of Internal Medicine.*

experimental studies in 1997 for two kinds of journals—general medical journals and seven selected specialty society journals.

1.3.2 Decision Analysis

Decision analysis is a derivative of game theory, which was described by von Neumann in the 1920s and applied on a widespread basis in economics by the late 1940s (von Neumann and Morgenstern 1947). As early as 1959, Ledley and Lusted (1959) described the intellectual basis for the application of decision analysis to medical problems, but it was not until 1967 that a published application of decision analysis to a specific clinical problem appeared. In that year, Henschke and Flehinger (1967) published a paper that used decision analysis to address the question of whether to do radical neck dissection in patients with oral cancer and no palpable neck metastases.

More attention to decision analysis followed publication of articles by Lusted (1971) and Kassirer (1976) that described again the application of decision theory in medicine. Since the 1970s, the use of decision analysis has grown slowly but steadily.

Decision analysis encompasses the use of decision-analytic techniques by clinicians at the bedside as a way to guide the management of individual patients. The application of decision theory to questions of how to manage individual patients has become less prominent than the use of decision analysis to address policy questions about the use of treatments for groups of patients. Decision analytic models are the conceptual framework for most cost-effectiveness and cost-utility analyses, and decision models are increasingly influential in decision making because of their use in cost-effectiveness analysis. The information in Figure 1-1 underestimates the use and influence of decision analysis in medicine because cost-effectiveness analyses based on decision analytic models are not separately represented.

1.3.3 Cost-Effectiveness Analysis

The commonsense principles of cost-benefit and cost-effectiveness analysis have been promoted for centuries (Warner and Luce 1982). Formal use of the techniques in fields other than medicine date to the beginning of the twentieth century. Cost-benefit analysis has been used on a widespread basis in business for at least several decades.

Examples of the systematic analysis of costs in relation to benefits in the medical arena began to appear with some frequency in the mid 1960s. Cost-benefit and cost-effectiveness analysis were particularly prominent in the discussions about treatment of end-stage renal disease that took place in the mid to late 1960s (Warner and Luce 1982).

Cost-effectiveness analysis has gained rapidly in prominence since the mid-1990s, as evidenced by the growing number of publications that use the method shown in Figure 1-1. Cost-benefit analysis remains a seldom used technique in economic assessments of health care in the United States.

1.4   LINKAGES OF THE THREE METHODS

The linkage of meta-analysis, decision analysis, and cost-effectiveness analysis to address a single problem is illustrated in two studies of adjuvant chemotherapy in women with early breast cancer, one by the Early Breast Cancer Trialists' Collaborative Group (1988) and the second by Hillner and Smith (1991). After surgical treatment of early breast cancer, a physician must decide whether to recommend treatment with adjuvant chemotherapy—either tamoxifen or cytotoxic chemotherapy. To make this decision, it is important to know how much adjuvant chemotherapy prolongs life and whether it is equally useful in all patients with early breast cancer. The cost of adjuvant chemotherapy needs to be considered in relation to other available therapies for breast cancer.

By 1988, fifty-nine different randomized clinical trials of adjuvant chemotherapy following surgical treatment for breast cancer had been done—28 involving tamoxifen and 31 cytotoxic chemotherapy. These trials involved more than 28,000 women. A meta-analysis by the Early Breast Cancer Trialists' Collaborative Group (1988) showed a highly significant 20% reduction in the annual odds of death within 5 years for women 50 years of age or older who had been treated with tamoxifen, even though none of the 28 trials had individually shown a significant reduction in the odds of dying. Data from these 28 trials are shown in Figure 1-2. There was also a highly significant 22% reduction in the annual odds of death among women under 50 years who had been treated with combination cytotoxic chemotherapy, despite the fact that only 1 of the 31 trials was itself statistically significant. These data are shown in Figure 1-3.

The meta-analysis by the Early Breast Cancer Trialists' Collaborative Group (1988) led the National Cancer Institute to issue a Clinical Alert to all United States physicians. The information showing the benefits of adjuvant chemotherapy for women with early breast cancer was intended to help physicians decide whether to recommend the chemotherapy to their patients with early breast cancer. The analysis strongly suggested that tamoxifen would be useful in women 50 years of age or older with early breast cancer and that cytotoxic chemotherapy would be useful in younger women.

Hillner and Smith (1991) used this meta-analysis (along with data from several of the largest clinical trials) and decision analysis to examine the benefits of adjuvant chemotherapy considering length of life and taking into account other patient and tumor characteristics. Using an assumption that adjuvant chemotherapy reduced the odds of death by 30%, close to the value suggested in the Early Breast Cancer Trialists' Collaborative Group meta-analysis (1988), Hillner and Smith showed that the benefit of adjuvant chemotherapy was highly dependent on the likelihood of having a recurrence of breast cancer, itself a function of age and certain features of the tumor (e.g., size, estrogen receptor status). In a woman with an annual probability of recurrent breast cancer of 1%, as expected with very small, estrogen receptor positive tumor in a 60-year-old woman, treatment was estimated to increase quality-adjusted life expectancy[4] by only 1 month. In contrast, in a woman with an 8% annual probability of recurrent breast cancer, as expected in a large, estrogen receptor negative tumor in a 45-year-old woman, treatment was estimated to increase quality-adjusted life expectancy by 8 months.

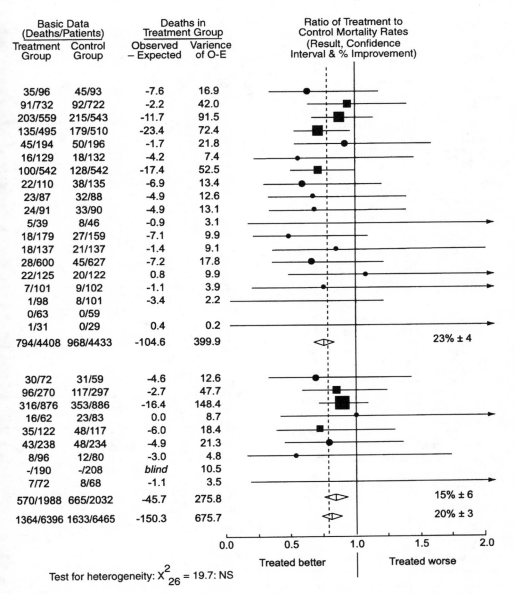

Figure 1-2 For women 50 or more years of age, odds ratio of mortality in women treated with tamoxifen compared with women who were not treated with tamoxifen and 99% confidence interval for this ratio. Each line represents one study. The solid vertical line represents no association with treatment (odds ratio of 1.0). When the line for a study does not cross the solid vertical line, there is no statistically significant association of treatment with a lower risk of death in that study.

The diamonds represent the summary odds ratio for death in treated women and their 95% confidence intervals. When the diamond does not touch the solid vertical line, the summary estimate of the odds ratio of death in treated women is statistically significantly different from 1.0 when based on all of the studies combined. For all studies, there is a highly significant 20% reduction in the odds ratio of death in women 50 years of age or more who were treated with tamoxifen. References to individual studies are as cited in Early Breast Cancer Trialists' Collaborative Group (1988). (Reproduced with permission from Early Breast Cancer Trialists' Collaborative Group, *New England Journal of Medicine,* 1988;319:1685.)

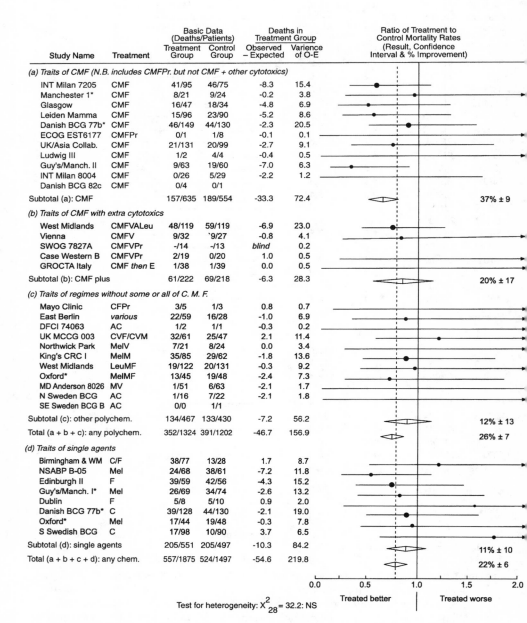

Figure 1-3 For women less than 50 years of age, odds ratio of mortality in women treated with cytotoxic chemotherapy compared with women who did not have chemotherapy and 99% confidence interval for this ratio. Each line represents one study. The symbols are interpreted in the same way as the symbols in Figure 1.2.

For all studies, there is a highly significant 22% reduction in the odds ratio of death in women less than 50 years who were treated with cytotoxic chemotherapy. References to individual studies are as cited in Early Breast Cancer Trialists' Collaborative Group (1988). (Reproduced with permission from Early Breast Cancer Trialists' Collaborative Group, *New England Journal of Medicine,* 1988;319:1686.)

The decision analysis suggested that women at low risk of recurrence have little to gain by adjuvant chemotherapy, whereas high-risk women have much to gain. By expressing the benefit in terms of life expectancy, the decision analysis translates the results of the meta-analysis into units that are more intuitively accessible to patients and to physicians. The delineation of underlying risk of breast cancer recurrence as an important determinant of the benefit of adjuvant chemotherapy allows some women to be spared the inconvenience and discomfort associated with chemotherapy. Thus, recommendations by physicians about adjuvant chemotherapy can be tailored more carefully to the individual patient.

Hillner and Smith (1991) also used cost-effectiveness analysis to estimate the cost of adjuvant chemotherapy overall and for the subgroups defined by their risk of breast cancer recurrence. As shown in Figure 1-4, the estimated cost of adjuvant chemotherapy for a woman with a 1% annual probability of recurrent breast cancer was about $65,000 (1989 dollars) per quality-adjusted life year. For a woman with an 8% annual probability of recurrence, the estimated cost of adjuvant chemotherapy was only $9,000 (1989 dollars) per quality-adjusted life year.

The cost-effectiveness analysis allows choices between adjuvant chemotherapy and competing therapies to be made. It also allows for comparison of adjuvant chemotherapy with other life-enhancing interventions that might be offered to the same woman.

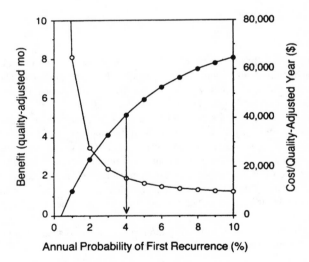

Figure 1-4 In 45-year-old women with node-negative breast cancer, estimated benefit of adjuvant chemotherapy compared with no treatment, according to the annual probability of recurrence of breast cancer. The left vertical axis shows the benefit in terms of quality-adjusted life months; the line with solid circles shows the benefit by this measure. The right vertical axis shows the benefit in terms of cost per quality-adjusted life year; the line with the open circles shows the benefit by this measure. The greater the probability of recurrence the greater the benefit in terms of gain in quality-adjusted life months and the less the cost per quality-adjusted life year gained. (Reproduced with permission from Hillner and Smith, *New England Journal of Medicine*, 1991;324:164.)

Taken together, the meta-analysis, the decision analysis, and the cost-effectiveness analysis for this topic provide a rational framework for counseling patients with early breast cancer, setting clinical policies about use of adjuvant chemotherapy, and aiding in policy decisions about funding of these therapies. The integration of the three research methods illustrates the power of the three techniques as clinical and policy tools.

1.5 ORGANIZATION OF THE BOOK

Chapter 2 gives an overview of each method as applied in its simplest form. The subsequent three chapters describe three elements—planning, information retrieval, and data collection—that inhere to common principles. Chapters 6, 7, and 8 present the advanced features of meta-analysis. Chapters 9 and 10 cover advanced topics in decision analysis. Chapter 11 describes the measurement of preferences. Chapter 12 discusses cost-effectiveness analysis. Chapter 13 describes utility and cost-utility analysis. Chapter 14 discusses the exploration of heterogeneity as a common goal of all three methods. Chapter 15 describes sensitivity analysis as it applies to all three methods. Chapter 16 suggests ways to present effectively the results of studies using each method. Chapter 17 describes the most critical limitations of the methods and identifies the situations in which the methods are the most and least useful.

NOTES

1. The term "clinical decision analysis" is used to refer to decision analysis as applied to management of individual patients at the bedside. This book addresses decision analysis as it applies to formulation of policy decisions for groups of patients. The reader interested in clinical decision analysis is referred to Sox et al. (1988).

2. Measures of preference are referred to broadly as measures of "utility." Decision analysis that incorporates utility measures is "utility analysis." When utilities are incorporated into cost-effectiveness analysis, it is cost-utility analysis. The most common outcome measure in utility analysis and cost-utility analysis is the quality-adjusted life year (QALY).

3. An updated cost-effectiveness analysis of pneumococcal vaccine has been done by Sisk et al. (1997). The 1986 analysis is discussed because it was the basis for the decision by Medicare to pay for this service. The overall conclusions of the earlier and later analyses are broadly the same.

4. Quality adjustment of life expectancy attempts to take into account not only the length of life but also the quality of life during the period of extended life.

2

Overview of the Methods

Doing a study that involves meta-analysis, decision analysis, or cost-effectiveness analysis is complex for most real-life applications, reflecting the complexity of the problems that the methods are used to address. However, each method involves a limited number of discrete, fairly simple steps.

The three sections of this chapter give an overview of meta-analysis, decision analysis, and cost-effectiveness analysis and describe the steps in applying the methods in their simplest form. In later chapters, advanced issues in application of the three methods are discussed in depth.

2.1 META-ANALYSIS

2.1.1 Overall Goals, Main Uses, and Description of Steps

The overall goal of meta-analysis is to combine the results of previous studies to arrive at summary conclusions about a body of research. It is used to calculate a summary estimate of effect size, to explore the reasons for differences in effects between and among studies, and to identify heterogeneity in the effects of the intervention (or differences in the risk) in different subgroups.

Meta-analysis has historically been useful in summarizing prior research based on randomized trials when individual studies are too small to yield a valid conclusion.

EXAMPLE: In 1982, use of thrombolytic agents after acute myocardial infarction was controversial. At that time, eight randomized clinical trials examining the effect of a loading dose of at least 250,000 international units of intravenous streptokinase on mortality given a short time after an acute myocardial infarction had occurred (Stampfer et al. 1982). As shown in Table 2-1, two of the trials found a higher risk of mortality in treated patients, five found a lower risk, and one found essentially identical mortality in the treated and the control patients. The trials were all fairly small, and the difference in mortality between treated and control patients was statistically significant in only one trial. These studies were interpreted as inconclusive about the benefit of early treatment with intravenous streptokinase.

In a meta-analysis based on these trials, Stampfer et al. (1982) estimated the relative risk of mortality in patients treated with intravenous streptokinase to be 0.80 with 95% confidence limits of 0.68 and 0.95. A subsequent study of intravenous streptokinase after acute myocardial infarction involving thousands of patients (GISSI 1986) confirmed the conclusion based on the meta-analysis of early studies—that intravenous treatment with streptokinase reduces mortality following acute myocardial infarction.

Because randomized trials reduce the effects of confounding on study results and because randomized trials are more homogeneous in their design, meta-analysis is applied most appropriately to randomized trials. However, there are many topics for which randomized trials are impossible. For example, smoking, alcohol use, use of contraceptive methods, and family history cannot be assigned at random. Meta-analysis of observational studies of such topics is useful to explore dose-response relationships, to understand the reasons for discrepancies among the re-

Table 2-1　Results of randomized trials of effect on mortality of intravenous streptokinase following acute myocardial infarction published before 1982

Reference	N Deaths/Total		Mortality (%)		Estimated Relative Risk	95% Confidence Interval
	Treated	Control	Treated	Control		
Avery et al. (1969)	20/83	15/84	24.1	17.9	1.35	0.74–2.45
European Working Party (1971)	69/373	94/357	18.5	26.3	0.70	0.53–0.92[a]
Heikinheimo et al. (1971)	22/219	17/207	10.0	8.2	1.22	0.67–2.24
Dioguardia et al. (1971)	19/164	18/157	11.6	11.5	1.01	0.55–1.85
Breddin et al. (1973)	13/102	29/104	12.7	27.9	0.46	0.26–0.81
Bett et al. (1973)	21/264	23/253	8.0	9.1	0.88	0.50–1.54
Aber et al. (1976)	43/302	44/293	14.2	15.0	0.95	0.64–1.40
European Cooperative Study Group for Streptokinase in Acute Myocardial Infarction (1979)	18/156	30/159	11.5	18.9	0.61	0.36–1.04
			Summary relative risk		0.80	0.68–0.95

[a]$p < 0.01$.
Source: Stampfer et al. (1982); table references cited there.

sults of different studies, and to assess the possibility of differences in the effects of the exposure in subgroups by taking advantage of the larger number of subjects upon which such the meta-analysis is based.

There are four steps in a meta-analysis. First, studies with relevant data are identified. Second, eligibility criteria for inclusion and exclusion of the studies are defined. Third, data are abstracted. Fourth, the abstracted data are analyzed statistically. This analysis includes formal statistical tests of heterogeneity and exploration of the reasons for heterogeneity.

2.1.2 Identifying Studies for the Meta-Analysis

A critical feature of the proper application of the method of meta-analysis is development of systematic, explicit procedures for identifying studies with relevant data. The systematic, explicit nature of the procedures for study identification distinguishes meta-analysis from qualitative literature review. In being systematic, the procedures reduce bias. In being explicit, the procedures help to ensure reproducibility. No matter how sophisticated the statistical techniques used to aggregate data from studies, a review does not qualify as meta-analysis unless the procedures to identify studies are both systematic and explicit.

Identification of published studies usually begins with a search of personal reference files and is followed by a computerized search of MEDLINE and of other computerized literature databases. The title and abstract of studies identified in the computerized search are scanned to exclude any that are clearly irrelevant. The full text of the remaining articles is retrieved, and each paper is read to determine whether it contains information on the topic of interest. The reference lists of articles with information on the topic of interest are reviewed to identify citations to other studies of the same topic, and publications that were not identified in the computerized literature search are retrieved and reviewed for presence of relevant information. Reference lists of review articles are also reviewed to check for completeness of the assembled list of relevant publications. In many cases, the list of studies identified by computer literature search and reference checks is submitted for review to a knowledgeable expert, who is asked to identify studies of the topic that have not been included on the list.

EXAMPLE: Dupont and Page (1991) set out to identify publications that presented information on menopausal estrogen replacement therapy and breast cancer. They used MEDLINE to identify 556 articles indexed with a MeSH heading of ''breast neoplasms'' and either ''estrogens'' or ''estrogens, synthetic'' and were also classified under the MeSH category ''occurrence,'' ''etiology,'' ''epidemiology,'' or ''chemically induced'' and in the MeSH category ''human'' and ''female.'' Thirty-five publications identified in the MEDLINE search provided an estimate of breast cancer risk in women who took estrogen replacement therapy. The reference lists of these 35 publications and those in a review article led to identification of 15 more publications with information on breast cancer risk in women using estrogen replacement therapy.

Details of procedures for identifying studies for a meta-analysis are discussed in Chapter 4.

2.1.3   Defining Eligibility Criteria for the Meta-Analysis

After studies with relevant information have been identified, the next step in the meta-analysis is to define eligibility criteria for the meta-analysis. Just as not all people are eligible for a randomized trial, not all studies can or should be included in the meta-analysis. For example, nonexperimental studies usually are not eligible for a meta-analysis of randomized trials; studies of stroke should not be eligible for a meta-analysis of coronary heart disease; and studies of a nontherapeutic dose of a drug should not be included in a meta-analysis of the efficacy of the drug.

> *EXAMPLE*: The meta-analysis of intravenous streptokinase and mortality after acute myocardial infarction by Stampfer et al. (1982) excluded four studies because a careful reading of the methods sections for these four studies showed that allocation to the treatment and control groups was not strictly random.

The goals of defining eligibility criteria are to ensure reproducibility of the meta-analysis and to minimize bias in selection of studies for the meta-analysis. Another analyst faced with the same body of literature applying the same eligibility criteria should choose the same set of studies. The studies chosen for the meta-analysis should be unbiased with respect to their results and their conclusions.

> *EXAMPLE*: Early studies of intravenous streptokinase used loading doses that ranged from several thousand to over 1 million international units. If dose is an important determinant of the effect of streptokinase on mortality, inclusion of studies with very low doses might bias the meta-analysis toward finding no effect of the drug. Recognizing this, Stampfer et al. (1982) restricted their meta-analysis to studies that used a loading dose at least 250,000 international units of streptokinase.

Additional detail on defining the eligibility criteria for a meta-analysis appears in Chapter 6.

2.1.4   Abstracting Data

In a meta-analysis, there are usually two levels of data abstraction. First, data that document whether or not identified studies are eligible for the meta-analysis study need to be abstracted for all of the studies identified. Next, for all eligible studies, data on the relevant outcomes of the study and the characteristics of the study, such as number of patients, are abstracted. The procedures for abstracting data in a meta-analysis should be similar to procedures to abstract data from a medical record or other administrative document. That is, data should be abstracted onto structured forms that have been pretested, and an explicit plan to ensure reliability of abstraction should be in place.

Greater detail on development of forms and on ensuring reliability of data abstraction appears in Chapter 5.

2.1.5   Analyzing the Data

The last step in a meta-analysis is to analyze the data. Analysis appropriately includes tests of homogeneity of the effect sizes. If the results are homogeneous, a summary estimate of effect size can be appropriately estimated. The meta-analysis should also explore heterogeneity. The exploration of heterogeneity should attempt to determine whether there are features of the study or the study population that are related to effect size. Exploration of heterogeneity also includes examination of subgroup results in the aggregate of studies.

When it is appropriate to present a summary estimate of effect size, this estimate should include a measure of its variance and its 95% confidence interval.

Models of dose-response may also be developed, and the predictors of effect size may be explored in multivariate models.

Chapters 7 and 8 describe the statistical methods to derive summary estimates of effects based on both fixed-effects and random-effects models. Chapter 14 discusses the exploration of heterogeneity.

2.2   DECISION ANALYSIS

2.2.1   Overall Goals, Main Uses, and Description of Steps

Decision analysis is a systematic quantitative approach for assessing the relative value of one or more different decision options. Historically, it was developed as a method to help clinicians make decisions on how to manage individual patients (Weinstein and Fineberg 1980; Sox et al. 1988). It is increasingly used to help develop policies about the management of groups of patients by providing information on which of two or more strategies for approaching a medical problem has the "best" outcome or the most value. Decision analysis often is the conceptual model used for cost-effectiveness analysis, and it is used increasingly for this purpose.

Decision analysis is useful when the clinical or policy decision is complex and information is uncertain.

EXAMPLE: Gallstones are often detected in persons who have no symptoms of gallstone disease. In such persons, a decision must be made on whether to do a "prophylactic" cholecystectomy or to wait until symptoms develop to operate. Ransohoff et al. (1983) did a decision analysis to compare the effect on life expectancy of prophylactic cholecystectomy and expectant waiting.

If a person has a prophylactic cholecystectomy, an immediate consequence is the possibility of operative death. If a person does not have a prophylactic cholecystectomy, possible consequences are death from other causes before the gallstones cause symptoms or development of pain or another complication of biliary disease before death from another cause, events that would require a cholecystectomy. Operative mortality after cholecystectomy is influenced by the age of the patient and by the presence during the operation of complications of gallstone disease, such as acute cholecystitis. The decision about whether to do a prophylactic cholecystectomy or to wait is complex at least in part because the consequences of waiting are far removed in time from the decision about whether or not to operate.

The analysis by Ransohoff et al. (1983) showed that a decision to do prophylactic cholecystectomy would result in an average loss of 4 days of life for a 30-year-old man and 18 days for a 50-year-old man. The analysis supports a decision to forgo prophylactic cholecystectomy.

There are five steps in a decision analysis (Weinstein and Fineberg 1980). First, the problem is identified and bounded. Second, the problem is structured, a process that usually includes construction of a decision tree. Third, information necessary to fill in the decision tree is gathered. Fourth, the decision tree is analyzed. Last, a sensitivity analysis is done.

2.2.2 Identifying and Bounding the Problem

The first step in a decision analysis is to identify and bound the problem (Weinstein and Fineberg 1980). Problem identification consists of stating the main issue concisely. Identifying and bounding the problem consists of breaking the problem down into its components. The first component of a problem is always identification of the alternative courses of action.

EXAMPLE: Fifteen new cases of measles are reported in a small urban area. This is the first report of measles in the area in several years. All of the cases are in children age 8 through 15 who previously received only one measles vaccination. This schedule was recommended at the time these children were infants, but it is now known not to confer complete and lifelong immunity to measles in all persons who are vaccinated. The problem is deciding whether to recommend that children who were vaccinated only once be revaccinated. The first component of the problem is identification of the alternative courses of action. One course of action is to recommend revaccination for all children 8 through 15; the alternative is not to recommend revaccination.

Other components of the problem are then identified. These are usually events that follow the first course of action and its alternative. The final component of the decision problem is identification of the outcome.

EXAMPLE: The relevant event that follows revaccinating or not revaccinating children is exposure to an infectious case of measles. Upon exposure to an infectious case, children either contract or do not contract measles. If they contract measles, the outcome of interest (for the purpose of this example) is death from measles.

2.2.3   Structuring the Problem

To structure the problem in a decision analysis, a decision tree is constructed. The decision tree depicts graphically the components of the decision problems and relates actions to consequences (Schwartz et al. 1973).

The building of a decision tree is guided by a number of conventions. Thus, by convention, a decision tree is built from left to right. When time is an issue, earlier events and choices are depicted on the left and later ones on the right.

A decision tree consists of nodes, branches, and outcomes. There are two kinds of nodes—decision nodes and chance nodes. Decision nodes are, by convention, depicted as squares. Chance nodes are depicted as circles. Outcomes are depicted as large rectangles. Branches are conventionally drawn at right angles to nodes; they connect nodes with nodes and nodes with outcome.

EXAMPLE: Figure 2-1 is the skeleton of a decision tree with nodes, branches, and outcomes labeled.

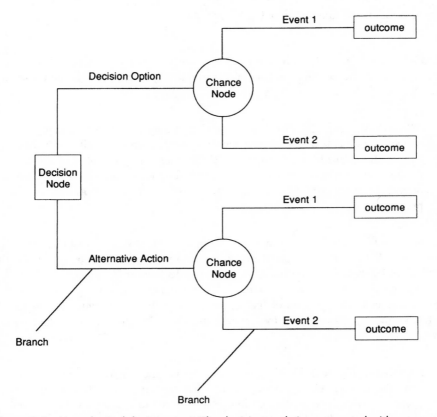

Figure 2-1   Hypothetical decision tree. The decision node is represented with a square. Chance nodes are represented with circles. Outcomes are represented with rectangles. Branches are drawn at right angles to the decision and chance nodes.

Re-vaccinate

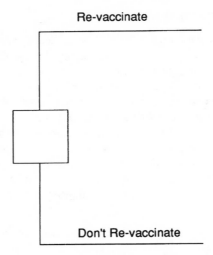

Don't Re-vaccinate

Figure 2-2   The first step in construction of a decision tree for the measles revaccination problem. The decision node is drawn as a square. The two alternatives—revaccinate and do not revaccinate—are represented as branches.

Decision nodes identify points where there are alternative actions that are under the control of the decision maker. In the simplest problem, the decision node describes the problem.

> *EXAMPLE:* Figure 2-2 shows the beginning of a decision tree for the problem of whether or not to recommend measles revaccination of children 8 to 15. The square decision node at the left of the diagram represents the decision; the alternative courses of action—to recommend revaccination or not to recommend revaccination—are labeled on the horizontal portions of the branches.

Chance nodes identify points where one or more of several possible events that are beyond the control of the decision maker may occur. Chance nodes for the same events should line up horizontally in the decision tree.

Probabilities are associated with the events depicted at chance nodes. At any given chance node, the sum of the probabilities of the events must be equal to 1. That is, the chance node defines events that are mutually exclusive and jointly exhaustive.

> *EXAMPLE:* Figure 2-3 is a decision tree for the measles revaccination problem. The circular chance nodes identify the first event that follows the decision to revaccinate—either children are exposed to measles or they are not exposed to measles. This event is out of the control of the decision maker. The sum of the probabilities of being exposed or not being exposed to measles is 1.

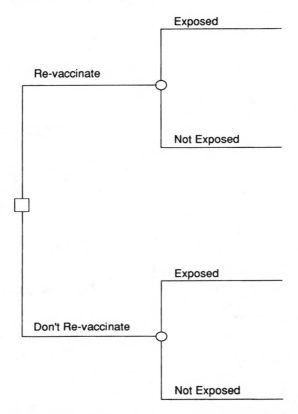

Figure 2-3   The second step in construction of a decision tree for the measles revaccination problem. Chance nodes that represent the likelihood of being exposed to measles are drawn.

> *EXAMPLE:* Figure 2-4 is a decision tree for the measles problem with circular chance nodes to also identify events that follow the exposure to measles. Children exposed to measles either get measles or they do not get measles. Again, this is an event that is out of the control of the decision maker, and it is depicted by a chance node. The sum of the probabilities of getting or not getting measles is 1.

In the decision tree, outcomes are the consequences of the final events depicted in the tree. Outcomes may include life or death; disability or health; or any of a variety of other risks or benefits of the treatment.

> *EXAMPLE:* The rectangular boxes in Figure 2-5 identify the outcome of getting and of not getting measles. For this example, the outcomes of interest are death or nondeath from measles.

Most current decision analyses do not focus simply on the comparison of decision options in terms of their effect on life and death. They focus on the amount of

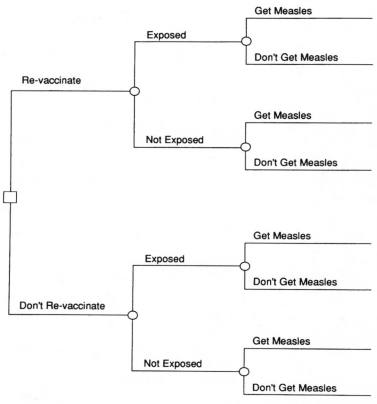

Figure 2-4 The third step in construction of a decision tree for the measles revaccination problem. For each branch of the exposed/not exposed dichotomy represented in the prior step, the chance of getting or not getting measles is represented with a chance node.

extension in life and on measures of the quality of life. This focus recognizes the use of medical care to do things other than prevent death. Moreover, everyone dies, and analyses of medical interventions can reasonably expect only to delay death, not to prevent it. The outcome measures used in many current decision analyses is life expectancy or quality adjusted life expectancy. Estimation of quality adjusted life expectancy involves the measurement of utilities. A utility is a measure of the preference for the outcome to society or to an individual. Chapter 11 is devoted to a description of the concept of utilities and the methods for measuring utilities. Chapter 13 discusses incorporation of measures of utility into decision analysis and cost-effectiveness analysis.

2.2.4 Gathering Information to Fill in the Decision Tree

The next step in the decision analysis is to gather information on the probabilities of each chance event. Information gathering for decision analysis almost always

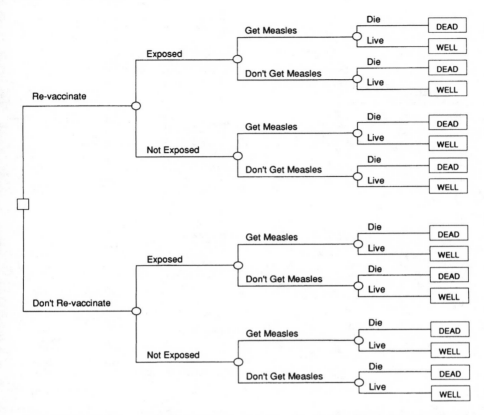

Figure 2-5   Final decision tree for the measles revaccination problem. The chances of dying or remaining alive after getting or not getting measles are represented with chance nodes, and the outcome is represented as a rectangle. In this problem, the outcome is death or remaining well, which is the same as the final event.

uses one or more of the following: literature review, including meta-analysis; primary data collection; consultation with experts. After the information on the probabilities and the outcome is obtained, it is recorded on the decision tree.

EXAMPLE: In the context of an epidemic of measles in an inner-city population, experts estimate that 20 out of every 100 children age 8 through 15 will come in contact with an infectious case of measles each year. Literature review reveals that the probability of getting measles if exposed to an infectious case is 0.33 in a child who has had only one measles vaccination and 0.05 in a child who is revaccinated (Mast et al. 1990). The probability of getting measles in children who are not exposed to measles is, of course, zero. During the current epidemic, the probability of dying from measles if a child gets measles is 23 per 10,000 cases, or 0.0023 (Centers for Disease Control 1990). It is assumed that the probability of dying from measles in

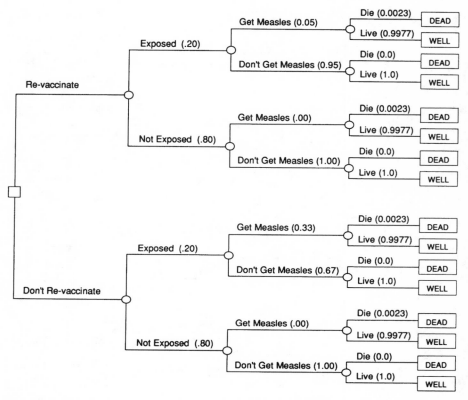

Figure 2-6   Measles decision tree showing all of the probabilities used in the analysis.

children who don't get measles is zero. Figure 2-6 shows the decision tree on which these probability estimates are shown.

2.2.5   Analyzing the Decision Tree

The decision tree is analyzed by a process called folding back and averaging. The final result is an estimate of the probability of the expected outcome of each of the decision alternatives.

Specialized computer software for analyzing decision trees is available. However, the computations necessary to analyze decision trees are simple arithmetic operations that can be done with widely available spreadsheet programs. Here, the mechanics of the process of folding back and averaging are illustrated by analyzing the decision tree as if it were two spreadsheets. Showing these computations as spreadsheet computations facilitates an understanding of the mechanics of decision analysis.

The decision tree is considered to consist of spreadsheets, one for each of the decision alternatives. The number of rows in each spreadsheet is equal to the number of outcome boxes in the decision tree. The spreadsheet has a column for each probability estimate and a column for the estimated probability of the outcome.

> *EXAMPLE:* Table 2-2 recasts the measles problem as two blank spreadsheets—one for the revaccination decision option and one for the no-revaccination option. For each spreadsheet, there are eight rows, because there are eight outcome boxes in the decision tree. There are three columns, one for each probability estimate and one for the outcome.

After the spreadsheets are set up, the probabilities are filled in.

> *EXAMPLE:* Table 2-3 shows the spreadsheet for the revaccination arm of the decision tree with the relevant probabilities in their proper columns.

The next step is to carry out the process of folding back and averaging. For each row, all of the probabilities in the row are multiplied together. This is folding back the decision tree. The products of the rows that represent the same outcome (die or don't die) are summed for each decision option. This is averaging. The sum

Table 2-2 Measles decision analysis as a spreadsheet

	Revaccination		
Probability of Exposure	Probability of Getting Measles	Probability of Outcome	
			die
			don't die
			die
			don't die
			die
			don't die
			die
			don't die

	No Revaccination		
Probability of Exposure	Probability of Getting Measles	Probability of Outcome	
			die
			don't die
			die
			don't die
			die
			don't die
			die
			don't die

Table 2-3 Measles decision analysis as a spreadsheet

Revaccination

Probability of Exposure	Probability of Getting Measles	Probability of Outcome	
0.2	0.05	0.0023	die
0.2	0.05	0.9977	don't die
0.2	0.95	0.0000	die
0.2	0.95	1.0000	don't die
0.8	0	0.0023	die
0.8	0	0.9977	don't die
0.8	1	0.0000	die
0.8	1	1.0000	don't die

No Revaccination

Probability of Exposure	Probability of Getting Measles	Probability of Outcome	
0.2	0.33	0.0023	die
0.2	0.33	0.9977	don't die
0.2	0.67	0.0000	die
0.2	0.67	1.0000	don't die
0.8	0	0.0023	die
0.8	0	0.9977	don't die
0.8	1	0.0000	die
0.8	1	1.0000	don't die

of the products is the expected value of that outcome for the specified decision option.

> *EXAMPLE:* Table 2-4 shows the measles problem with a column labeled "product" for each row. The number in the column labeled "product" is the product of the probabilities for the corresponding row. For example, the value in the first row of the column labeled "product" is 0.000023, which is

$$0.2 \times 0.05 \times 0.0023$$

The expected probability of death from measles in the example is equal to the sum of the values in the product column for the rows that correspond to the outcome "die." For the revaccination option, this is

$$0.000023 + 0.000000 + 0.000000 + 0.000000 = 0.000023$$

For the no-revaccination option, it is

$$0.000152 + 0.000000 + 0.000000 + 0.000000 = 0.000152$$

Table 2-4 Measles decision analysis as a spreadsheet

	Revaccination			
Product	Probability of Exposure	Probability of Getting Measles	Probability of Outcome	
0.000023	0.2	0.05	0.0023	die
0.009977	0.2	0.05	0.9977	don't die
0.000000	0.2	0.95	0.0000	die
0.190000	0.2	0.95	1.0000	don't die
0.000000	0.8	0	0.0023	die
0.000000	0.8	0	0.9977	don't die
0.000000	0.8	1	0.0000	die
0.800000	0.8	1	1.0000	don't die

Sum for death
0.000023

	No Revaccination			
Product	Probability of Exposure	Probability of Getting Measles	Probability of Outcome	
0.000152	0.2	0.33	0.0023	die
0.065848	0.2	0.33	0.9977	don't die
0.000000	0.2	0.67	0.0000	die
0.134000	0.2	0.67	1.0000	don't die
0.000000	0.8	0	0.0023	die
0.000000	0.8	0	0.9977	don't die
0.000000	0.8	1	0.0000	die
0.800000	0.8	1	1.0000	don't die

Sum for death
0.00152

Difference between Revaccination and No Revaccination

Death   0.000129

Difference Expressed as Events per 100,000

Death   12.9

The final step is to compare the two strategies by subtracting the results of the preceding calculations for the revaccination arm from the result for the alternative arm.

EXAMPLE: The difference in the expected probability of death from measles between a strategy of revaccination and a strategy of no-revaccination is

$$0.000152 - 0.000023 = 0.000129$$

This is interpreted to mean that 12.9 deaths from measles are prevented per 100,000 children revaccinated.

2.2.6 Sensitivity Analysis

Analysis of a decision tree virtually always includes sensitivity analysis. Sensitivity analysis is described in detail in Chapter 13. The overall goal of sensitivity analysis is to assess the stability of the conclusion of the analysis to assumptions made in the analysis. Sensitivity analysis also may identify crucial areas of information deficiency and may guide further research.

Assumptions about the probabilities used in the analysis are among the most important assumptions made in the analysis. A sensitivity analysis varying these probabilities one at a time while holding all of the other variables in the analysis constant is almost always done.

EXAMPLE: The probability of being exposed to an infectious case of measles varies according to the area of the county. It is 1 per 100 in the suburban areas, whereas it is 45 per 100 in one inner-city area where an epidemic is in progress. The results of a sensitivity analysis varying the probability of exposure to an infectious case of measles between 0.01 and 0.45 is shown in Table 2-5. The number of deaths from measles prevented per 100,000 children revaccinated is highly dependent on the assumption about the probability of being exposed to an infectious case. Revaccination is estimated to prevent less than 1 death from measles per 100,000 children revaccinated in the low-risk area and 29 in the highest risk area.

Table 2-5 Results of sensitivity analysis varying probability of exposure to measles

Assumed Probability of Exposure	Net Number of Lives Saved per 100,000 Children Revaccinated
0.01	0.6
0.05	3.2
0.10	6.4
0.15	9.7
0.20[a]	12.9
0.25	16.1
0.30	19.3
0.35	22.5
0.40	25.8
0.45	29.0

[a] Probability in baseline analysis.

2.3 COST-EFFECTIVENESS ANALYSIS

2.3.1 Overall Goals, Main Uses, and Description of Steps

Cost-effectiveness analysis compares the outcome of decision options in terms of their monetary cost per unit of effectiveness. It is used to help in the setting of priorities for the allocation of resources and to decide among one or more treatments or interventions based on their value, as expressed in monetary terms.

EXAMPLE: Patients with nonvalvular atrial fibrillation are at high risk of ischemic stroke. Ischemic stroke can be prevented using either warfarin or aspirin. The efficacy of warfarin in preventing ischemic stroke is higher than that of aspirin, but warfarin is more likely than aspirin to cause bleeding, sometimes fatal, and it is more expensive, especially when the cost of monitoring prothrombin time is considered.

Gage et al. (1995) did a cost-effectiveness analysis comparing warfarin and aspirin for stroke prophylaxis in patients with nonvalvular atrial fibrillation. They showed that warfarin was preferred to aspirin in patients at high risk for stroke but that aspirin was preferred to warfarin in patients at low risk for stroke. In this example, the question posed is not whether to treat patients with nonvalvular atrial fibrillation, but how to treat them.

Table 2-6 describes the steps in a cost-effectiveness analysis.

The first step is the same as in a decision analysis. The problem is identified and the intervention and its alternatives are defined.

The second step in a cost-effectiveness analysis is to describe the conceptual model for the analysis. The conceptual model for a cost-effectiveness analysis outlines the full range of events stemming from the intervention and guides the analysis. Decision analytic models are used most often as the conceptual framework for cost-effectiveness analysis. Decision analysis has become so closely linked with cost-effectiveness as to be an almost integral part of it. This book describes decision analysis as the cornerstone of cost-effectiveness analysis and discusses conduct of cost-effectiveness analysis solely within the decision analytic framework. Thus, in the second step in the cost-effectiveness analysis, a decision tree is constructed and information to estimate the probabilities in the decision tree is gathered.

Next, the perspective of the analysis is defined. Based on this perspective, costs

Table 2-6 Steps in a cost-effectiveness analysis

State the problem
Describe the conceptual model
Define the perspective
Identify costs and gather data to value costs
Identify outcomes and gather data to value outcomes
Estimate cost-effectiveness
Do sensitivity analysis

are identified and valued. The outcomes are identified and data are gathered to value the outcomes. The data are analyzed to estimate net cost of each decision option per unit of the outcome measure, and the decision options are compared in relation to net cost per unit of outcome. Finally, a sensitivity analysis is done.

2.3.2 Defining the Perspective

Costs are seen differently from different points of view. For example, the cost of hospitalization from the perspective of an insurance company is the amount of money that the company pays the hospital for that illness under the coverage plan for the individual who is hospitalized. The cost from the perspective of the hospital is the true cost of providing the service, which includes the labor costs, the costs of the building in which the services are provided, and other overhead costs.

It is important to state explicitly the perspective of a cost-effectiveness analysis, since the perspective determines which costs should be included in the analysis and what economic outcomes are considered as benefits. Usual perspectives in cost-effectiveness analysis are the societal perspective and the program perspective.

> *EXAMPLE:* The decision about whether to revaccinate children against measles could be made based on considerations of cost. A county health department might decide to undertake a cost-effectiveness analysis of revaccinating versus not revaccinating taking the program perspective, since the question addressed is how many deaths from measles an investment in revaccination might prevent. Taking the program perspective, the costs that will be considered are the costs that are born directly by the program.

2.3.3 Identifying Cost and Gathering Data to Value Costs

The contributors to the cost of the intervention must first be identified. Contributors to cost include direct health care cost, such as the cost of vaccine or drug, as well as costs to people to partake of the intervention, such as the cost of travel and the cost of lost wages. Induced costs, such as the cost to take care of side effects of the intervention, and averted costs, due, for example, to averted future illness, are also direct health care costs that should be counted as contributors to cost. Chapter 12 discusses the identification of costs in detail.

Once the contributors to cost have been identified, data on these costs must be gathered. Cost data can be obtained by primary data collection (i.e., in a special study) or from secondary sources. In practice, cost data are most often gathered either from administrative sources, such as Medicare fee schedules or insurance company payments.

> *EXAMPLE:* The costs of vaccination from the perspective of the program consist of the cost of purchasing the vaccine and the cost of administering it.
>
> By doing a survey of pharmaceutical suppliers, the county determines that the measles vaccine can be purchased in bulk quantities for $4.44 per dose (Mast et al. 1990). An expert estimates that it will take 15 minutes for

a nurse to vaccinate each child. Based on a nurse's salary of $36,000 per year and considering the cost of space for the waiting room, the nurses' office, and the room in which the vaccine will be administered of $2.00 per child revaccinated, it is estimated that the total cost of revaccination is $9.44 per child.

2.3.4   Gathering Data to Value Outcomes

The next step in a cost-effectiveness analysis is to identify the relevant outcomes and to value the outcomes.

In the measles example, the outcome of interest to the health department is prevention of death due to measles. It is assumed that prevention of death due to measles has value to society.

2.3.5   Estimating Cost-Effectiveness

In the simplest case, the decision analysis proceeds as described in the section on decision analysis, yielding an estimate of the net benefit of one decision option compared with the other. The net cost of the intervention in relation to its alternative is calculated by subtracting of the total costs of the alternative from the cost of the intervention. The cost-effectiveness of the intervention relative to its alternative is the ratio of the net cost to the net benefit.

> *EXAMPLE:* Based on the estimate that it will cost $9.44 to revaccinate each child, the cost to the county of a program revaccinating 100,000 children is $944,000; the cost to the county of not revaccinating 100,000 children is $0. The net cost of a program of revaccination compared with no program of revaccination is $944,000. The net number of deaths from measles prevented per 100,000 children revaccinated, estimated in the decision analysis, is 12.9. Thus, compared with a strategy of no-revaccination, a school-based program of measles revaccination costs $73,178 per death prevented, or ($944,000 − $0)/12.9.

When costs and monetary benefits of an intervention are spread over time, it is necessary to discount costs and benefits and to consider inflation. These issues are discussed in detail in Chapter 12.

2.3.6   Sensitivity Analysis

As in decision analysis, sensitivity analysis is almost always done in a cost-effectiveness analysis. It has the same goal in cost-effectiveness analysis as it does in decision analysis—to assess the effect of the various assumptions made in the analysis on the conclusion.

> *EXAMPLE:* The sensitivity analysis from the decision analysis in which the probability of being exposed to measles was varied is used to do a sensitivity analysis for the cost-effectiveness analysis. The number of deaths prevented

Table 2-7   Results of sensitivity
analysis varying probability of
exposure to measles

Assumed Probability of Exposure	Cost per Life Saved
0.01	$1,573,333
0.05	295,000
0.10	147,500
0.15	97,320
0.20[a]	73,178
0.25	58,634
0.30	48,912
0.35	41,956
0.40	36,589
0.45	32,552

[a] Probability in baseline analysis.

by a program, compared with no program, was estimated in Section 2.2.6 for several estimates of the probability of being exposed to measles. The net cost of the program compared with no program is divided by each of these estimates to estimate the cost per death prevented for several estimates of the probability of exposure to measles. These results are shown in Table 2-7. The estimated cost per death prevented is highly variable, depending on the assumption about the probability of exposure to measles. In low-risk areas, the analysis shows that the cost of the program is over $1.5 million per death prevented; in the highest risk area, it is $32,552 per death prevented.

3
Planning the Study

Studies that involve synthesis seem seductively simple to do. The impression of simplicity has several consequences. First, data may be collected without a formal plan and analyzed in an ad hoc fashion. Second, resource needs for the study may be underestimated. Last, administrative obstacles may not be anticipated. In reality, it is as important to carefully plan a study that involves synthesis as it is to carefully plan a clinical trial, a cross-sectional survey, and a case-control or cohort study. Documentation of all aspects of study design and conduct is a crucial and often overlooked step in carrying out studies that involve meta-analysis, decision analysis, and cost-effectiveness analysis.

The four steps common to the planning all three types of synthetic studies are definition of the problem; development of a protocol; acquisition of resources; and procurement of administrative approvals. The four sections of this chapter describe these four steps.

3.1 DEFINING THE PROBLEM

The first step in planning the study is to define the problem. The problem definition is a general statement of the main questions that the study addresses.

EXAMPLES: Chapter 1 described a meta-analysis of primary coronary angioplasty or intravenous thrombolytic therapy for patients with acute myocardial infarction, a project to develop guidelines on initial therapy for men with localized prostate cancer, and a cost-effectiveness analysis on pneumococcal vaccination in persons over 65 years of age. The problems addressed in these three studies are the following.

Meta-Analysis

What are the quantitative effects on mortality and reinfarction of primary coronary angioplasty compared with thrombolytic therapy in patients with acute myocardial infarction? Are there differences in these effects for different kinds of thrombolytic therapy?

Decision Analysis

What are the estimated effects of radical prostatectomy, external-beam radiation therapy, and watchful waiting on life expectancy and quality of life for men with localized prostate cancer? Are there differences in these effects by tumor grade or by age?

Cost-Effectiveness Analysis

What is the estimated cost of pneumococcal vaccination in persons over 65 per year of life saved?

3.2 DEVELOPING A STUDY PROTOCOL

3.2.1 Overview

A protocol is the blueprint for conduct of the study. It also serves as a permanent record of the original study objectives and of the study methods and procedures. A study protocol should be prepared before the study begins, and it should be freely available for others to review after the study has been completed.

For all three types of study, the protocol should have a section on objectives, background, information retrieval, data collection, and analysis. There are some unique requirements of a protocol for a cost-effectiveness analysis. The specific elements of each of these sections, listed in Table 3-1, differ among the three study types.

3.2.2 Objectives

The protocol should begin with a statement of the main objectives of the study. The statement should be concise and specific. For decision analysis and cost-effectiveness analysis that will incorporate utilities, the statement of objectives should specify the utility measure for the analysis. For cost-effectiveness analysis, the statement of the main objectives should state the perspective of the analysis.

EXAMPLES:

Meta-Analysis

Problem: What is the effect on mortality and reinfarction of primary coronary angioplasty compared with thrombolytic therapy in patients with acute myocardial infarction? Are there differences in these effects for different kinds of thrombolytic therapy?

Objective: To identify all randomized trials comparing primary coronary angioplasty with intravenous thrombolytic therapy and use data from these studies to derive a quantitative estimate of the odds ratio for mortality and reinfarction comparing the two therapeutic approaches; to determine whether there is heterogeneity in the study results, and to examine possible differences between angioplasty and thrombolytic therapy for different kinds of thrombolytic therapy.

Decision Analysis

Problem: What is the effect of radical prostatectomy, external-beam radiation therapy, and watchful waiting on life expectancy and quality of life for men with localized prostate cancer? Are there differences in these effects by tumor grade or by age?

Objective: To do a decision analysis that uses information on the complications of prostatectomy, radiation, and watchful waiting and their effect on progression to metastatic disease and death to estimate the effect of the therapies on quality-adjusted life expectancy according to tumor grade and age at diagnosis of prostate cancer.

Cost-Effectiveness Analysis

Problem: What is the cost of pneumococcal vaccination per year of life saved?

Objective: To estimate the effect of pneumococcal vaccination and the costs associated with its adminstration in order to determine the cost-effectiveness analysis of pneumococcal vaccination from the perspective of Medicare.

If there are secondary objectives, these should also be presented in the protocol. Subgroup analysis is frequently a secondary objective of meta-analysis and of decision analysis. Describing plans for secondary analyses in the protocol is important because the subgroup analyses are documented as a priori aims of the study.

3.2.3 Background

The protocol should include a few paragraphs on the background of the study with enough citations to the literature so that the reader can form an accurate picture of the state of knowledge on the topic of the study. Key references to prior work should be cited; a complete review of the world's literature on the topic of the study is not necessary.

3.2.4 Information Retrieval

3.2.4.1 Meta-analysis

Systematic procedures for searching the literature are the centerpiece of meta-analysis, and the protocol for meta-analysis should describe these procedures in

Table 3-1 Elements of a study protocol for meta-analysis, decision analysis, and cost-effectiveness analysis

Section	Meta-Analysis	Decision Analysis	Cost-Effectiveness Analysis
Objectives	State main objectives Specify secondary objectives	State main objectives Specify secondary objectives Specify utility measure (if applicable)	State main objectives Specify secondary objectives Specify utility measure (if applicable) State perspective of the analysis
Background	Give brief review of pertinent literature	Give brief review of pertinent literature	Give brief review of pertinent literature
Information Retrieval	Describe overall strategy Specify Medline search terms Explain approach to unpublished reports and "fugitive" literature	Give sources and explain these choices	Give sources and explain these choices
Primary Data Collection	Describe procedures for abstracting data from publications (blinding, reliability checks, handling of missing data.) Describe quality rating scheme and procedures for assessing quality	Describe methods to measure utilities (if applicable) Describe how expert opinions will be solicited (if applicable)	Describe methods to measure utilities (if applicable) Describe how expert opinions will be solicited (if applicable)

Analyis	State methods for estimating variance for individual studies State model to be used and explain choice Specify approach to missing data Describe how quality rating scheme will be used in the analysis Specify sensitivity analyses Specify subgroup analyses	Specify sensitivity analyses Specify subgroup analyses	Specify sensitivity analyses Specify subgroup analyses
Other		Describe any human subjects considerations	Provide rationale for choice of perspective Describe any human subject considerations State discount rate and explain choice
Appendices	Copies of data collection forms	Copies of data collection forms Copies of informed consent documents	Copies of data collection forms Copies of informed consent documents

detail. The protocol section on literature search should begin with a statement of whether the meta-analysis will include only published studies or whether an attempt will be made to also identify and include unpublished studies. All of the computer databases that will be searched should be listed. If there are computer databases with possibly relevant information that will not be searched, a rationale for this decision should be provided. The exact search terms and the search algorithm for each computer database should be presented in the protocol. If the literature search will include an attempt to retrieve unpublished studies, this section of the protocol should include a description of the procedures for identifying these studies. If investigators will be contacted to clarify data or to obtain information that was not presented in the published reports, this should be stated.

"Fugitive" literature is a term applied to studies published in documents that either are difficult to identify because they are not abstracted or are difficult to retrieve because of their limited circulation. The fugitive literature includes dissertations, conference proceedings, and some government reports. If studies published in the fugitive literature will not be included, a rationale for this decision should be presented in the protocol.

3.2.4.2   Decision Analysis and Cost-effectiveness Analysis

Decision analysis and cost-effectiveness analysis also rely heavily on published data as a source of information on probabilities. When known ahead of time, the sources that will be used to estimate probabilities should be stated. If these are unknown, the criteria for deciding how to identify relevant literature should be specified. Where there are alternative sources of information about probabilities, the criteria for choosing among the alternatives should be stated explicitly.

Just as in a decision analysis, a protocol for a cost-effectiveness analysis should include information on how probabilities will be assessed. It should also give the sources for data on cost. Alternative sources of cost data and the reasons they were not chosen should be described. The protocol should provide a rationale for use of charge data to estimate cost when this is the plan of the study.

3.2.5   Primary Data Collection

3.2.5.1   Meta-Analysis

For meta-analysis, the section on data collection should begin with a statement of the inclusion and exclusion criteria that will be used to decide which of the studies identified in the literature search will be abstracted. The procedures for abstracting data should be presented in detail.If reliability checks will be made, the frequency for these checks should be specified along with a plan for using the information. The rules for choosing from among several estimates of effect should be given. The procedures for handling missing data should be described.

If studies will be rated on quality, the protocol should describe how the rating scheme was developed. The procedures for abstracting information on quality should be specified. If the information to rate quality will be collected with the raters blinded to any aspect of the study, the manner of ensuring blinding should be described.

3.2.5.2 Decision Analysis and Cost-Effectiveness Analysis

Decision analysis and cost-effectiveness analysis increasingly incorporate measures of utility, and utilities are often measured as part of the study. The protocol should state what utility measure will be used. The methods for gathering data to estimate utilities should be described in detail.

Expert opinion is often used to estimate probabilities in decision analysis and cost-effectiveness analysis. Experts may be the source of estimates of utilities. When experts are used, the composition of the expert group and the rationale for the choice of experts should be described. The methods for obtaining information from the experts (e.g., interview, survey, focus group) should be described.

When "guesses" of probabilities will be used in a decision analysis or cost-effectiveness analysis in place of estimates from the literature or empiric studies, the protocol should define who will make the guess, and it should give the framework for the guess.

3.2.6 Analysis

3.2.6.1 Meta-Analysis

For a meta-analysis, the analysis section of the protocol should state whether the calculation of a summary estimate of effect size will be based on a fixed-effects model or a random-effects model. If variances will be estimated directly from data presented in publications or reports, the methods used should be stated and appropriate references to the methods should be cited. If there are a priori hypotheses about the sources of heterogeneity that will be examined as part of the analysis, these hypotheses should be specified.

3.2.6.2 Decision Analysis and Cost-effectiveness Analysis

For decision analysis and cost-effectiveness analysis, plans for sensitivity analysis should be given, to the extent that these can be anticipated. If a stochastic estimate of uncertainty of the outcome will be made (see Chapter 9), the methods for this estimate should be described.

3.2.7 Other

The protocol for a decision analysis or cost-effectiveness analysis that will involve primary data collection from patients or normal volunteers should address any human subjects issues, including protection of confidentiality, assurance of voluntarism, and informed consent.

The rationale for the perspective of the cost-effectiveness analysis should be explained. The discount rate used in the analysis should be given along with the reason for choosing it. The protocol should state whether or not benefits will also be discounted and specify the rate of discount for benefits.

3.3   ACQUIRING RESOURCES

Planning a study that uses meta-analysis, decision analysis, or cost-effectiveness analysis should include a realistic assessment of resource needs for the study. All three types of studies can require a substantial investment in personnel resources. It is easy to underestimate these needs.

> *EXAMPLE:* A computer literature search for meta-analysis of menopausal estrogen replacement therapy and breast cancer (Dupont and Page 1991) iden-tified 565 published studies that were potentially relevant to the topic of the meta-analysis. If it were necessary to retrieve each article from a library to determine whether it was eligible for inclusion in the meta-analysis and if retrieval took only 10 minutes per article, 94 hours of personnel time would be required to retrieve all 565 articles. If as many as 80% of articles identified through the computer search could be eliminated from consideration based on reading the title and the abstract, which might take only 2 minutes per article, the task of identification and retrieving relevant articles would still take almost 34 hours of personnel time.

After articles are retrieved, information from them must be abstracted. Abstraction also is time-consuming, especially when it is done systematically onto structured forms and when an attempt is made to blind the abstractor to various aspects of the study. Computer resources will be needed for most analyses that use these three methods. It also may be desirable to purchase special-purpose software for some of the studies, and this may be costly.

3.4   PROCURING ADMINISTRATIVE APPROVALS

Virtually all clinical trials, surveys, and case-control and cohort studies require some administrative approvals. These approvals include such things as approval to recruit patients from a clinic, approval to have access to medical records, and approval to use a certain desk for the project recruiter. Fewer administrative ap-provals are necessary for a synthetic study, but failure to anticipate those that are necessary may delay the study or even prevent its completion. Some of the kinds of administrative approvals that might be needed in a meta-analysis, a decision analysis, or a cost-effectiveness analysis are listed in Table 3-2.

Studies that rely solely on data from reports and publications do not require review and approval by an institutional review board for the protection of human subjects. Some studies that use decision analysis or cost-effectiveness analysis will fall within the scope of review by an institutional review board for the protection of human subjects. If patients or volunteers will be asked to provide information

Table 3-2 Examples of types of administrative approvals that might be needed in a synthetic study

---

Meta-Analysis

Approval to use unpublished data
Approval to obtain original data[a]

Decision Analysis

Approval to review medical records
Approval to involve human subjects in measurement of utilities
Approval to use administrative databases

Cost-Effectiveness Analysis

Approval of access to Medicare or other cost databases
Approval to review patient billing records
Approval to involve human subjects in measurement of utilities or in
surveys to determine utilization, out-of-pocket costs, lost wages

---

[a] Applies to meta-analysis of individual-level data.

that is used to estimate utilities for a decision analysis or a cost-effectiveness analysis, review by an institutional review board will be required.

Sometimes such studies involve collecting data that would potentially allow individuals to be identified. An example is a study that will use medical records to estimate probabilities for a decision analysis when information on the relevant probabilities is not available from a published source. Such studies fall within the scope of review by an institutional review board, and they should be submitted for review and approval to the committee early, to avoid delays in study completion. Access to large administrative databases that contain data that allow individuals to be identified requires institutional review board review and approval. It is not uncommon to use either medical charts or billing records to gather data to estimate resource utilization and cost, and this requires review and approval.

EXAMPLE: The most important effect of cigarette smoking during pregnancy on the infant is its effect on birth weight. Smoking increases the chances of being low birth weight and preterm (before 37 weeks) by a factor of about 1.3, and it increases the likelihood of being low birth weight and term by about 4.0. The cost of caring for an infant who is low birth weight and preterm is much higher than the cost of caring for one who is low birth weight but term, because preterm infants are much sicker. In our study of the cost-effectiveness of smoking cessation programs during pregnancy (Shipp et al. 1992), published information on the cost of hospitalization for low birth weight infants who are preterm and term was not available, and administrative databases that would allow this classification were not available. To obtain it, a special study involving primary data collection was carried out. Delivery logs at two hospitals were reviewed to identify infants who were low birth weight. The infants were classified according to whether they were preterm or term by reviewing the mothers' medical records. Copies of the billing records of these infants were then retrieved and abstracted.

Since linkage of information from the delivery logs with the maternal medical records and with the billing records required individuals to be identified, it was necessary to submit this study to review by an institutional review board for the protection of human subjects.

4

Information Retrieval

Because of the rapidity of growth of knowledge, the task of identifying and retrieving information for a study that uses any of these methods is formidable. The problem of information retrieval has received a great deal of attention in meta-analysis. Development of the field of meta-analysis has highlighted the importance of a systematic approach to information retrieval as a means of obtaining information that is free from bias. The importance of a systematic and unbiased approach to information retrieval is not restricted to meta-analysis, since many of the probabilities used in a decision analysis, and, by extension, cost-effectiveness analysis, are estimated based on existing published information.

Section 4.1 describes an overall strategy for comprehensive retrieval of published information for a specific topic. Section 4.2 discusses computerized searches of MEDLINE as a method for retrieving published studies, while Section 4.3 describes other computer-stored databases of information. Section 4.4 discusses the limitations of searches of computerized databases and some ways to overcome these limitations. Section 4.5 describes the problem of publication bias and some ways to assess and handle it.

4.1 OVERALL STRATEGY FOR RETRIEVING INFORMATION FROM PUBLISHED STUDIES

Decisions about what studies should be eligible for a meta-analysis and what information should be used to estimate probabilities or costs must be scientifically defensible and free of bias. Only when all information on the given topic is identified is the investigator in a position to achieve this goal. Ideally, the search for information for a decision analysis or a cost-effectiveness analysis would identify all of the relevant information and decide which information to use in the analysis based on its freedom from bias.

The existence of registers of clinical trials has made it possible to attain this ideal for many topics for which data derive from randomized trials. The Cochrane Collaboration is international network of individuals and institutions committed to preparing, maintaining, and disseminating systematic reviews of health care using explicitly defined methods (Bero and Rennie 1995). The Collaboration has stimulated the preparation of comprehensive registries comprising completed, on-going, and unpublished trials. When registries of trials exist, they should be used as a source of information for a meta-analysis.

There are no registries of unpublished nonexperimental studies. Data from non-experimental studies are often analyzed to address questions that were not specified when the study was designed. The questions may have been asked on a questionnaire because of interest in the variable as a confounder, not because assessing the relationship between the exposure and the disease were of primary interest.

It is not possible to know all of the studies that collected data that could be used to address a given question. For this reason, the retrieval of information from nonexperimental studies has usually been limited to retrieval of published information. Growing interest in, and conduct of, meta-analysis of individual-level data may change this. This topic is discussed in more detail in Chapter 6.

Table 4-1 lists the steps generally used to retrieve published information for a meta-analysis. These steps also should be followed to retrieve information for decision analysis or cost-effectiveness analysis whenever there is a need to estimate a probability and this estimate is going to be based on published data.

The first step in comprehensive retrieval of information is almost always a search of the personal files of the investigator or knowledgeable colleagues to identify materials that are already in hand. This search is followed by a computerized search of one or more computer databases, virtually always including MEDLINE. The titles of publications identified in the computer search and their abstracts, when available, are scanned to eliminate articles that are obviously irrelevant. The full text of the remaining articles is then retrieved. These articles

Table 4-1 Usual steps for comprehensive retrieval of published information on a specific topic

---

Step 1 Search personal files
Step 2 Do computerized literature search of computer-stored databases
      A. Search titles and abstracts and eliminate obviously irrelevant ones
      B. Retrieve remaining articles
      C. Review articles systematically and eliminate those that don't contain needed information
Step 3 Review reference lists of articles and review articles to find new articles
Step 4 Retrieve newly identified articles and review them for relevance
Step 5 Consult experts

Table 4-2 Other strategies for retrieval of published studies

Hand search *Index Medicus* for period prior to MEDLINE (1966)
Hand search journals known to publish material in subject area of interest

are read quickly, and those that clearly are not relevant are put aside. The remaining publications are then systematically reviewed to determine whether they are eligible for the meta-analysis based on predetermined criteria for eligibility.

The reference lists of the articles that contain useful information are reviewed to identify publications on the same topic that have not yet been identified. When new articles are identified by this procedure, these articles are retrieved and the process of reading them to ascertain whether they are eligible continues. The reference lists of reviews articles are reviewed.

Simultaneously, other information sources are explored (Table 4-2). The abstracts of published doctoral dissertations should be searched by computer if there is any possibility that information on the topic may be contained in them. A hand search of the journals that are known to publish papers on the subject matter of the analysis may identify studies that otherwise remain unknown.

When a list of all of the articles identified by the foregoing methods is complete, it is often submitted to an expert for review. The expert is asked to identify other publications that may contain information on the topic of interest. These articles are retrieved and reviewed systematically to determine eligibility for the meta-analysis.

4.2 COMPUTERIZED SEARCHES OF MEDLINE

4.2.1 Overview

MEDLINE is a computerized bibliographic database that is the primary source of information on publications in the biomedical literature. MEDLINE contains information on publications in over 3,200 biomedical journals. It covers the period from 1966 to the present.

MEDLINE does not contain everything that is published in the journals that are indexed. Editorials, commentaries, and letters to the editor have been subject to special rules about indexing. These rules have changed over time. When the rules for indexing change, there is no attempt to correct or change information from years prior to the change. Indexing of letters in the early years of the database is very incomplete. Published abstracts are selectively indexed. With only a few recent exceptions, MEDLINE is not a full-text database. That is, the complete text of publications is not available in computer-stored form. Rather, for each indexed publication, MEDLINE contains the title, the authors, and the source of publication; the author abstract, if one is available; and a number of "medical subject headings" (MESH) terms and other "tags" that provide information about the publication.

Table 4-3 Selected "tags" used to index articles in MEDLINE

	Selected Categories
Publication type	Journal article
	Review
	Meta-analysis
	Editorial
	Letter
	Randomized controlled trial
	Comment
Language	English
	Foreign
	Specific Languages
Affiliation	—

4.2.3 Structure of MEDLINE

The National Library of Medicine assigns each publication that it indexes with medical subject headings (MESH headings) and a number of "tags." These tags include the publication type, the language, and the affiliation of the authors of the research. Selected tags that can be important in retrieving information from MEDLINE are listed in Table 4-3.

"Medical subject headings," called MESH headings, are assigned to publications in MEDLINE by expert indexers working under a set of highly structured rules. MESH terms are chosen from a limited vocabulary that was developed by the National Library of Medicine and is periodically updated. The number of MESH terms assigned to a publication varies. Most articles are assigned between 8 and 15 MESH terms. The tags are also assigned by the expert indexer.

The assignment of MESH terms to publications is a special feature that allows the searcher to identify relevant published material even when the author might not have used the subject term in the title or the abstract. The use of MESH heading in conjunction with the other tags allows searches of this large and complex database to be focused and specific. Careful and knowledgeable searches using MESH headings and other tags can greatly reduce the amount of material that needs to be retrieved while simultaneously achieving completeness in the information retrieval process.

Indexing of publications in MEDLINE began in 1966. There are now millions of indexed publications in the MEDLINE database. To comprehensively identify publications for a period from the inception of MEDLINE to the present, all years should be searched.

4.2.2 Access to MEDLINE Through the Internet

Access to MEDLINE is free through the internet (www.ncbi.nlm.nih.gov). Free access to MEDLINE through the internet greatly enhances the ability to conduct searches. The online availability of abstracts reduces the effort of reviewing the results of a search. Documents can also be ordered on-line through free MEDLINE, which makes retrieval of the results of a search easier, although the cost of retrieving articles through the online service is high.

Free internet searches of MEDLINE can use either Grateful Med or PUBMED. PUBMED (www.ncbi.nlm.nih.gov/PubMed) permits customized use of the National Library of Medicine's advanced search language. PUBMED, unlike Grateful Med, has "expert" features, which are described in more detail later in this chapter.

Because of its expert features and its flexibility in the conduct of advances searches, PUBMED is the search engine that is likely to be of greatest interest to those conducting literature searches for meta-analysis and decision analysis. The National Library of Medicine has made a commitment to further development of PUBMED as the main search engine for MEDLINE. For this reason, only searches of MEDLINE using PUBMED will be discussed further in this chapter.

4.2.3 Basic Search Strategy

The overall goal of any search of MEDLINE is to identify all of the relevant material and nothing else. This ideal is very difficult to achieve in practice. Sensitivity and precision are the terms that are used to describe the results of a search of MEDLINE (Dickersin, Scherer and Lefebvre 1994). The sensitivity of a search is its ability to identify all of the relevant material. Precision (which is the positive predictive value of the search) is the amount of relevant material among the materials retrieved by the search. The overall strategy in a MEDLINE search is to maximize sensitivity and precision (positive predictive value). However, the MEDLINE search, no matter how well conducted, is only a small piece of the total information retrieval process.

A strategy for use of MEDLINE is as follows. First, identify two or more publications that are known to be eligible for the meta-analysis—one published recently and one less recently. The MESH terms for each publication would be examined, and those that would have identified both publications would be included in a preliminary MEDLINE search.

EXAMPLE: A meta-analysis of published randomized trials of warfarin or aspirin for the treatment of atrial fibrillation is being done. Two studies, one by the European Atrial Fibrillation Trial Study Group and published in 1993 in the *Lancet* and another by Peterson et al. and published in the *Lancet* in 1989, are known to be eligible for the meta-analysis. Both publications are indexed with either the MESH term "anticoagulants" or "warfarin" and both are indexed with either the term "cerebrovascular disorders" or "thromboembolism." Both are indexed with the MESH term "atrial fibrillation." A search using the terms "anticoagulants or warfarin" and "cerebrovascular disorders or thromboembolism" and "atrial fibrillation" yields 481 publications. A quick check of the search strategy is done to make sure that both of the index publications are identified by the search strategy. Both are.

4.2.4   Limiting Searches to Make the Work of Information
Retrieval Manageable

Searches generally return too many publications, most of which are irrelevant. Sorting through a large number of publications to try to determine whether they contain pertinent information is often an arduous undertaking. Ways to limit searches include identification of only those publications that are of randomized clinical trials or have another specified design (e.g., comparative study).

> *EXAMPLE:* Limiting the search for randomized trials of warfarin in patients with nonvalvular atrial fibrillation to those with a publication type of "clinical trial" or "randomized clinical trial" reduces the number articles retrieved in a MEDLINE search from 481 to 64. The strategy continues to identify the two index publications upon which the search strategy was based.

Searches can be narrowed by excluding certain publication types.

> *EXAMPLE:* Exclusion of publications with a publication type of "meta-analysis," "comment," "editorial," or "letter" further reduced the number of publications of warfarin and atrial fibrillation to 54.

Conducting searches that are narrow enough to reduce the number of publications retrieved to some manageable number requires use of the National Library of Medicine's structured search capability. Effective use of the power of the structured search capability of PUBMED requires knowledge of the system for indexing articles. The MESH vocabulary undergoes constant revision and the rules for assigning MESH terms and tags are periodically updated, making MESH searches of the entire database from 1966 to the present a complex undertaking. Effectively searching MEDLINE has been made easier with the advent of PUBMED, with its expert features. However, using the advanced search features available through PUBMED requires training and experience.

It is difficult to develop search strategies that do not return large amounts of irrelevant material even when what is sought by the search seems to be highly specific and well within the capabilities of the search language.

4.2.5   Using the Expert Features of PUBMED to Do Better Searches

Publications in PUBMED can be identified by simply specifying the words that define the overall goal of the search. PUBMED will search for these words in the title and the abstract. The expert feature of PUBMED will "infer" the MESH and identify all of the publications that map to the inferred MESH heading. This allows more complete searches to be conducted without a detailed knowledge of the MESH headings.

> *EXAMPLE:* "Stroke" is not a MESH term, although it has a precise meaning and is commonly used to refer to all forms of cerebrovascular disease. Before the implementation of the expert feature of PUBMED, a search of MEDLINE

using the term "stroke" as a MESH term would not return any publications, because "stroke" is not a MESH heading. Until the institution of expert features, search of MEDLINE using the term "stroke" as a text word would identify only publications that specifically used this term. Both searches would miss publications about subarachnoid hemorrhage that did not describe the condition as a kind of stroke. Without these expert features, a search of MEDLINE that would take full advantage of indexing required detailed knowledge of the MESH vocabulary. Since there are more than 17,000 MESH terms, searches were often conducted well only by librarians with special training.

With the addition of expert features, a search that specifies simply "stroke" is automatically mapped to the MESH term "cerebrovascular disorders," and the database is searched for publications that are indexed with the MESH term "cerebrovascular disorders" as well as publications that contain "stroke" as a text word. Since subarachnoid hemorrhage is mapped as a cerebrovascular disorder, the search would identify studies of this condition.

PUBMED also identifies "links" of publications to related publications. The links can be displayed online. The links are arranged displayed in order of relatedness to the initial article. Reviewing the links can be useful in identifying other information on the same topic and other studies that are eligible for a meta-analysis or of interest in a decision analysis or cost-effectiveness analysis.

EXAMPLE: PUBMED was used to try to identify studies of stroke and hormone replacement therapy for a meta-analysis of this topic. A prior comprehensive literature review had been conducted, and it was known that there were 19 publications that reported the results of a case-control or cohort study examining this topic and thus would be eligible for a meta-analysis on this topic. The publications spanned the years 1977 through 1998.

The PUBMED search was done using the terms "stroke" AND "estrogen." This search identified 50 publications that met both of these two conditions. On-line review of the abstracts yielded 13 publications that appeared to be relevant. Only 10 of the 19 relevant studies were among the 50. However, examination of the top 10 links to related articles for these 10 publications identified all of the publications that were known a priori to be eligible for the meta-analysis. The process of conducting the initial search, reviewing the abstracts based on the search, and reviewing the top 10 links from the possibly eligible publications based on the initial search took only a few hours and was done entirely using information available on-line.

4.2.6 Other Ways to Reduce the Work of Retrieving Documents

PUBMED has a feature, called citation matcher, that can be used to retrieve the information available in MEDLINE so that this information can be reviewed online, thus obviating the need to retrieve the document in its full text form. Using this feature of PUBMED can be especially useful when a publication appears in a reference list and needs to be reviewed to see if it is eligible for a meta-analysis.

4.2.7 Finding Additional Relevant Published Studies

PUBMED can be used to search MEDLINE by author. That is, all of the publications with a certain person as one of the authors can be identified. In an author search, it is necessary only to specify the last name of the author in question. For example, all of the publications written by a person with the last name "Smith" can be identified. By also specifying the first and last initial of the author, the number of publications by authors with the specified last name identified will be limited. For example, all publications by "AB Smith" can be identified; this is obviously fewer than the number of publications with any "Smith" as author.

An author search may be useful in comprehensive retrieval of information for a given topic when it is known that certain people regularly publish studies in a given subject area.

> *EXAMPLE:* Decision analysis is done by only a few authors. To identify publications that might be used as examples of recent, well-conducted decision analysis for the second edition of this book, a search was done for publications by the author for the five year period prior to July, 1998. "MC Weinstein" and "BE Hillner" are known to publish regularly on decision analysis. The search for publications in 1996–1998 with these people as authors identified 20 articles that were potential examples to be used in this book.

4.3 OTHER COMPUTER-STORED DATABASES

MEDLINE is just one of several computer-stored databases operated by the National Library of Medicine and subsumed under the term MEDLARS (Medical Library Information Retrieval System). Other computer databases that might contain information that would be of use in a meta-analysis, a decision analysis, or a

Table 4-4 Computer-stored bibliographic databases other than MEDLINE that might be searched in a meta-analysis, decision analysis, or cost-effectiveness analysis

Database	Description of Contents
AIDSLINE	AIDS-related records from journal articles, government reports, meeting abstracts, special publications, and theses (1980 to present)
CANCERLIT	Cancer literature from journal articles, government and technical reports, meeting abstracts, published letters, and theses (1963 to present)
Dissertation Abstracts Online	American and Canadian doctoral dissertations (1861 to present)
TOXLINE	Effects of drugs and other chemicals from journal articles, monographs, theses, letters, and meeting abstracts

cost-effectiveness analysis are listed in Table 4-4. Procedures for searching these databases are not covered in this book.

4.4 LIMITATIONS OF COMPUTERIZED SEARCHES OF COMPUTER-STORED DATABASES

4.4.1 Overview

The availability of MEDLINE and other computer-stored bibliographic databases has greatly aided the identification of potentially relevant published material for studies involving meta-analysis, decision analysis, and cost-effectiveness analysis. Access to computer bibliographic databases has by no means solved the problem of information retrieval. The databases are incomplete. Indexing and search algorithms are imperfect. Practical constraints on retrieval of articles can lead to incompleteness of even perfect searches. Most important, computer-stored bibliographic databases contain only part of the literature of medicine.

4.4.2 Incomplete Databases

No single computerized database covers all periodicals, even for a defined, broad subject area like medicine. MEDLINE, for example, contains information on original research reported in less than one third of all biomedical journals.

Journals that are not included in MEDLINE are described as highly specialized journals on topics considered to be of limited interest, journals of low circulation, and journals in which articles have not been peer-reviewed. These criteria do not ensure that important data have not been published in them.

4.4.3 Imperfect Search Algorithms

Even if the computerized data sources contained every journal, it is not always possible to search the database in such a way that every pertinent article is retrieved. Developing a search algorithm that identifies all of the pertinent material that appears in a computer-stored database takes considerable expertise even for simple problems. Even algorithms developed by experts fail.

EXAMPLE: The National Perinatal Epidemiology Unit at Oxford University has compiled a register of controlled trials in perinatal medicine using a variety of methods, including contact of individual investigators, hand searches of the perinatal journals, and perusal of meeting reports. This publication list was considered the "gold standard" in a comparison with a search of the MEDLINE database by Dickersin et al. (1985). The investigators chose two topics—neonatal hyperbilirubinemia and intraventricular hemorrhage. Without knowledge of the contents of the register, a medical librarian experienced in computer searches developed a search strategy designed to identify all pertinent published articles reporting the results of randomized trials of neonatal hyperbilirubinemia or intraventricular hemorrhage

Table 4-5   For two topics, the number of randomized trials eligible for a meta-analysis that were registered in perinatal trials database and the number found in MEDLINE search

Topic	Number of Studies Registered in Perinatal Database	Number of Studies Found in MEDLINE Search	
		Expert Searcher	Amateur Searcher
Neonatal hyperbilirubinemia	88	28	17
Intraventricular hemorrhage	29	19	11

Source: Dickersin et al. (1985).

indexed in the MEDLINE database for the period of operation of the MED-LINE database, 1966–1983.

In the register, there were 88 English-language publications on neonatal hyperbilirubinemia that were confirmed to be randomized trials and 29 on intraventricular hemorrhage. The MEDLINE search identified only 28 English-language publications on neonatal hyperbilirubinemia and only 19 on intraventricular hemorrhage, as shown in Table 4-5.

Table 4-6 shows that 81 of the 88 published trials of neonatal hyperbilirubinemia registered in the Perinatal Database and 27 of the 29 published trials of intraventricular hemorrhage registered were indexed in MEDLINE and potentially retrievable. Thus, the failure to retrieve some of the articles was strictly due to the search strategy, which was imperfect despite the fact that it was done by an expert.

The MEDLINE search identified some pertinent articles that had not been included in the "gold standard" register. The ability of a search algorithm to identify all of the pertinent literature can be improved by consultation with an expert searcher.

EXAMPLE: In the comparison of the Perinatal Trials Database with the MEDLINE search described above (Dickersin et al. 1985), an "amateur"

Table 4-6   For two topics, the number of published studies in the perinatal trials database and the number that were indexed in MEDLINE

Topic	Number of Published Studies in the Perinatal Database	Number of Those Published Studies Indexed in MEDLINE
Neonatal hyperbilirubinemia	88	81
Intraventricular hemorrhage	29	27

searcher, Dr. Thomas Chalmers, developed a search strategy independently. His strategy identified only 17 studies of neonatal hyperbilirubinemia and only 11 of intraventricular hemorrhage, as shown in Table 4-5.

Even when an expert searcher is used, a MEDLINE search is not enough to identify all relevant publications. Dickersin, Scherer and Lefebvre (1994) reported on an evaluation in which 15 different groups compared a MEDLINE search for randomized trials done by an expert searcher with a "gold standard" list of trials. The sensitivity of the search (ability of the search to find all trials) was on average only 0.51.

Dickersin, Scherer and Lefebvre (1994) also showed that the number of articles that need to be retrieved in order to identify relevant trials can be very large even when the search strategy has been developed by an expert. Their data are summarized in Table 4-7. The number of articles retrieved in the search and in need of review for 10 meta-analyses ranged from 21 to 9,643.

4.4.4 Indexing

The success of searches that are based on use of index terms depends on both the accuracy of indexing and on the ability of the medical subject heading terms, or other indexing procedure, to capture relevant information. Dealing with the large number of irrelevant articles retrieved in what appear to be specific searches that take advantage of the indexing is a particularly vexing problem in computerized searches of MEDLINE.

EXAMPLE: A search of MEDLINE was done using PUBMED to evaluate the outcome of a search for publications that report the results of randomized

Table 4-7 Number of publications retrieved for MEDLINE search by expert searcher and number of relevant randomized trials for ten topics

Reference	Topic	Number of Retrieved Publications	Number of Relevant Trials
Dickersin (1985)	Intraventricular hemorrhage	36	19
	Hyperbilirubinemia	39	18
Bernstein (1988)	Liver disease	9,643	155
Ohlsson (1989)	Pregnancy	125	10
Gøtzsche (1991)	Rheumatoid arthritis	738	128
Kleijner (1992)	Homeopathy	52	18
	Vitamin C	81	22
	Gingko	46	14
Dickersin (1994)	Ophthalmology	1,520	193
Lacy (Unpublished)	Newborn	21	8

Source: Dickersin, Scherer, and Lefebvre (1993); table references cited there.

clinical trials for stroke. Only 1997 was searched. The search specified "cerebrovascular disorders" and "randomized clinical trials" as MESH terms and excluded "review," "editorial," "letter" and "meta-analysis" as publication types and "meta-analysis" as a MESH term. Twenty-one publications were identified in the search. Table 4-8 categorizes these 21 publications. Only one publication reported the primary results of a randomized trial of a treatment for stroke. One described the design of a randomized trial. Four publications were comparisons of results of observational studies with randomized trials in terms of patient selection or results, and one publication reported an observational analysis of data from a randomized trial. Ten retrieved publications, or almost 50% of the total search, were comments on trials or on treatments studied in trials but were not indexed as editorials or letters.

Indexing itself is limited by the low quality and inaccuracy of the descriptions of the research in some source documents.

EXAMPLE: One of the publications identified in the search described above was a "failed meta-analysis." That is, it met all of the criteria as a meta-analysis but did not present a summary estimate of effect size and did not describe itself as a meta-analysis. It was not indexed with meta-analysis as either publication type or MESH heading and was not excluded in the MEDLINE search. One publication was clearly a formal meta-analysis that was described in this term and was indexed incorrectly.

The National Library of Medicine continues to try to improve indexing and the ability of researchers to conduct both sensitive and specific searches. But the large number of publications being indexed, the complexity of the indexing rules, and

Table 4-8 Final classification of 21 publications identified in MEDLINE search for randomized trials of stroke treatments

Classification	Number of Publications
Comment	10
Formal meta-analysis	1
"Failed" meta-analysis	1
Consensus statement on RCT results	1
Comment or methods in RCT	1
Observational analysis of data from an RCT	1
Comparison of RCT data with population data or observational data	4
Description of design of RCT	1
Results of an RCT	1

the inherent difficulty of the task of categorizing publications render illusive the goal of perfect indexing.

4.4.5 Restriction of Literature Retrieval to English-language Publications

Publications published in languages other than English are included in MEDLINE. Their titles are usually provided in English. However, deciding whether an article is relevant by perusing the translated title is difficult. In MEDLINE, an English-language abstract is available only if the author provided one and it was published in the journal. Thus, if a publication cannot be judged to be definitely relevant or definitely not relevant based on its title, there may not be other clues to relevance.

Retrieval of the full text of foreign-language journals can be difficult, and getting a translation of an article is expensive, if it can be obtained at all. For all of these reasons, information retrieval for research synthesis is often limited to studies published in English.

Moher et al. (1996) have shown that there is no difference in the quality of randomized trials published in English and in other languages.

Egger et al. (1997) did a study that compared pairs of reports of randomized clinical trials of the same topic, matched for author and time of publication, with one publication in English and one in German. They were able to identify 40 pairs in which an author had published one randomized trial in a German language publication and one in an English-language publication. There were no differences between the randomized trials published in German or in English for a number of measures of the quality of the trial, including parallel group versus crossover design, masking, and use of a placebo. The mean number of subjects was the same in the trials published in German and in English. Table 4-9 shows the p values for the main endpoints in the trials published in German and in English. Of the trials published in German, 65% had a p value greater than or equal to 0.05 compared with 38% of trials published in English. This study provides convincing evidence for a bias of publication of trials with "positive" results in English language journals.

Table 4-9 Probability values for the results of two different randomized trials by the same author, one published in a German language publication and one in an English language publication.

p for Main Endpoint	German Language		English Language	
	N	%	N	%
$p > 0.05$	26	8	15	38
$0.01 \leq p < 0.05$	8	20	14	38
$0.001 \leq p < 0.01$	3	8	4	8
$p < 0.001$	3	8	7	18
All	40	100	40	100

Source: Egger et al. (1997).

Gregoire et al. (1995) showed that exclusion of trials published in foreign language journals could produce different results from those that would have been obtained if the exclusion had not been used.

Limiting meta-analysis to publications in English-language journals decreases the completeness of information retrieval. Studies published in English-language journals are not of higher quality than studies published elsewhere. Limiting information retrieval to English-language journals can cause bias. There is no justification for limiting meta-analyses to studies published in English. This is a practice that must be condemned.

4.4.6 Fugitive Literature

Government reports, book chapters, the proceedings of conferences, and published dissertations are called "fugitive" literature because the material published in them is difficult to identify and because the documents or their contents may be difficult to retrieve. Studies published in conference proceedings, as book chapters, and in government reports are not identified in searches of MEDLINE and most other computer databases. Information in the fugitive literature should be included in meta-analysis.

The fugitive literature is often the source of probability estimates for decision analysis and cost-effectiveness analysis.

> *EXAMPLE:* Danese et al. (1996) did a decision and cost-effectiveness analysis of screening for mild thyroid failure at the periodic health examination. The analysis required estimates of the probability of cardiovascular disease by age. The source for these estimates were three government reports on the results of the Framingham study published in 1973, 1987, and 1988.

The amount of material on a given topic that may appear in the fugitive literature is highly variable, depending on the topic.

> *EXAMPLE:* Elbourne, Oakley, and Chalmers (1989) did a meta-analysis of the effect of social support on the rate of low birth weight. Table 4-10 lists the nine randomized trials of the topic that they identified after an exhaustive search for studies, along with the place of publication, if published. Of the five published studies on this topic, only three were published in periodicals that would have been identified in a search of MEDLINE.

In contrast, Table 4-11 shows the number of studies that were published in the fugitive literature for six meta-analyses that were selected because of the presumed rigor of identification of pertinent material. For two of the meta-analyses (Collins, Yusuf, Peto 1985; Longnecker et al. 1988), none of the studies included in the meta-analysis had been published in the fugitive literature. For each of the other five meta-analyses, the number of studies published in the fugitive literature was very small.

Unfortunately, it is not possible to know ahead of time whether the number of

Table 4-10 Studies included in meta-analysis of effect of social support on likelihood of low birthweight, the place of publication, the number of subjects, and the estimated relative risk

Reference	Place of Publication	Number of Subjects	Estimated Relative Risk
Blondel et al.	Unpublished	152	1.43
Oakley et al.	Unpublished	486	0.84
Heins et al.	Unpublished	1346	0.91
Spencer and Morris (1986)	*Prevention of Preterm Birth* (book)	1183	1.05
Elbourne et al. (1987)	*British Journal of Obstetrics and Gynaecology*	273	0.82
Lovell et al. (1986)	*Pediatric and Perinatal Epidemiology*	197	0.48
Reid et al. (1983)	*Report to Health Services Research Committee*	155	0.60
Olds et al. (1986)	*American Journal of Public Health*	308	2.09
Dance	Unpublished	50	0.72

Source: Elbourne, Oakley, and Chalmers (1989); table references cited there.

Table 4-11 Number of eligible studies published as abstracts or doctoral dissertations or in books, government reports, or conference proceedings for six meta-analyses chosen for the presumed rigor of identification of publications

Reference	Topic	Total Number of Eligible Studies	Number Published as Abstracts or Doctoral Dissertations or in Books, Reports, or Proceedings
Collins, Yusuf, Peto (1985)	Diuretics during pregnancy[a]	11	0
Law, Frost, Wald (1991)	Salt reduction and blood pressure[a]	70	1
Littenberg (1988)	Aminophylline for acute asthma[a]	13	1
Longnecker et al. (1988)	Alcohol and breast cancer[b]	16	0
Stampfer and Colditz (1991)	Estrogen and coronary heart disease[b]	32	2
Yusuf et al. (1985)	Fibrinolytic therapy in acute myocardial infarction[a]	33	3

[a] Meta-analysis of randomized clinical trials.

[b] Meta-analysis of observational studies.

studies published in the fugitive literature will be large or small, and the attempt to identify them must be vigorous.

Experts may be a good source of information about publications in the fugitive literature. Writing to persons who have published in the field of interest and specifically asking them if they have published relevant material in a report or a book chapter or if they know of any reports or book chapters with information may be fruitful.

It is possible to find appropriate published dissertations by searching Dissertation Abstracts, and this is a step in any literature search that strives to be entirely complete.

Unpublished studies are the ultimate example of fugitive literature. The existence of large numbers of unpublished studies has the potential to cause bias in meta-analysis. Publication bias is discussed in detail in the next section of this chapter.

Retrieval of the ultimately fugitive literature in the form of unpublished data is an important consideration in decision analysis and cost-effectiveness analysis since these analyses can be highly reliant on such information.

EXAMPLE: Chapter 1 discussed a cost-effectiveness analysis of pneumococcal vaccination among the elderly (Sisk and Riegelman 1986) and an update (Sisk et al. 1997). In the 1997 update, ''unpublished'' was the source of data for nine estimates used in the analysis. An additional source of information in the analysis was a report of United States Council of Economic Advisors.

4.5   PUBLICATION BIAS

4.5.1   Definition

The term publication bias'' is usually used to refer to the greater likelihood of research with statistically significant results to be submitted and published compared with nonsignificant and null results. More generally, publication bias is the systematic error induced in a statistical inference by conditioning on the achievement of publication status (Begg and Berlin 1988). Publication bias occurs because published studies are not representative of all studies that have ever been done.

4.5.2   Evidence for Publication Bias

Existence of a bias in favor of publication of statistically significant results is well documented (Sterling 1959; Simes 1986; Easterbrook et al. 1991; Ioannidis 1998). The most extreme example comes from the social science literature and is provided by Sterling (1959), who found that 97% of a series of consecutive articles that used significance testing published in the mid 1950's in four prestigious psychology journals reported results that were statistically significant. His findings are shown in Table 4-12.

In the medical literature, Easterbrook et al. (1991) documented less extreme, but nonetheless serious, bias in favor of publication of statistically significant re-

Table 4-12 Number and percentage of articles using significance testing that reported statistically significant ($p < 0.05$) results by journal

Journal	Year	Total Reports Using Tests of Significance	Reports That Were Statistically Significant[a]	
			N	%
Experimental Psychology	1955	106	105	99.1
Comparative and Physiological Psychology	1956	94	91	96.8
Clinical Psychology	1955	62	59	95.2
Social Psychology	1955	32	31	96.9
All		294	286	97.3

[a] Reject H_0 with $p \leq 0.05$.
Source: Sterling (1959).

sults. Examining the publication status of 285 analyzed studies for which institutional review board approval had been obtained between 1984 and 1987 at Oxford, the investigators found 154 studies had statistically significant results and 131 did not. Of the 154 studies with statistically significant results, 60.4% had been published, whereas only 34.4% of the studies that did not have statistically significant results had been published. These findings are shown in Table 4-13.

More recently, Ioannidis (1998) did a follow-up of 66 completed randomized phase 2 and phase 3 trials examining the efficacy of treatments for human immunodeficiency virus infection that had been sponsored by the National Institutes of Health. The time to the start of enrollment to publication was substantially longer for negative trials than for trials that favored an experimental treatment (median

Table 4-13 Publication status in 1991 for 285 analyzed studies reviewed by the Central Oxford Research Ethics Committee in 1984–1987

Publication Status	Study Result			
	Statistically Significant[a]		Not Statistically Significant[b]	
	N	%	N	%
Published	93	60.4	45	34.3
Presented only	38	24.7	31	23.7
Neither published nor presented	23	14.9	55	42.0
Total	154	100.0	131	100.0

[a] $p < 0.05$.
[b] $p \geq 0.05$.
Source: Easterbrook et al. (1991).

6.5 versus 4.3 years, respectively). Most of the difference was due to differences in the time from trial completion to publication (median 3.0 for negative trials versus 1.7 years for positive trials). This publication lag has the potential to cause larger treatment effects in early meta-analyses (Ioannidis 1998).

Simes (1986) showed that a conclusion based on meta-analysis about the effect of an alkylating agent alone compared with combination chemotherapy on survival in patients with advanced ovarian cancer would be different depending on whether the meta-analysis was based on published studies or on studies registered with the International Cancer Research Data Bank. Table 4-14 shows that when only published studies were used, there was overall a statistically significant increase in median survival in patients treated with combination chemotherapy. When a group of studies noted in a registry at their initiation, before the results were known, was used in the meta-analysis, there was no significant advantage of treatment with combination chemotherapy.

There are no comparable concrete examples of bias toward publication of null results, as opposed to statistically significant results, for any topic. Begg and Berlin (1988), however, speculate that historically a bias toward publication of null results may have characterized the study of asbestos and cancer. When there are adverse financial or regulatory consequences of a positive result, a bias in favor of publication of null or negative results is a theoretical possibility.

It is common to attribute publication bias to editorial policies that favor publication of positive results and to bias of journal reviewers against negative results. Dickersin, Min, and Meinert (1992) did a follow-up of studies that were either approved or ongoing in 1980 by the two institutional review boards that serve the Johns Hopkins Health Institutions. As in the study of Easterbrook et al. (1991), completed studies with statistically significant results were more likely to have been published than studies with nonsignificant results. Over 90% of the unpublished studies had not been submitted for publication, and only 6 of the 124 unpublished studies had been submitted for publication and rejected by a journal.

Table 4-14 Results of meta-analysis of published and registered studies of treatment with an alkylating agent alone compared with combination chemotherapy in patients with advanced ovarian cancer[a]

Results	Published Studies ($N = 16$)	Registered Studies ($N = 13$)
Median survival ratio[b]	1.16	1.06
95% confidence interval	1.06–1.27	0.97–1.15
p value	0.02	0.24

[a] Adjusted for sample size.

[b] Median months of survival in patients treated with combination chemotherapy/median survival in patients treated with alkylating agent alone.

Source: Simes (1986).

Table 4-15 Contributions to publication lag for completed positive and negative randomized trials of treatments for human immunodeficiency virus infection

Trial Result	Median Time (years)		
	Enrollment to Publication	Completion to Submission	Submission to Publication
Positive[a]	4.3	1.0	0.8
Negative	6.5[b]	1.6[b]	1.1[b]

[a] Statistically significant ($p > 0.05$) finding in favor of an experimental arm for a main efficacy end point defined in the protocol.

[b] Difference between positive and negative trials statistically significant ($p > 0.05$).

Source: Ioannidis (1998).

Ioannidis (1998), in his study of randomized trials of treatments for human immunodeficiency virus infection, found evidence that both investigator decisions and journal policy contribute to the lag in the time from trial completion to publication. Table 4-15 shows data on the median time completion to first submission for publication and from submission to publication for the 45 completed trials that had been submitted for publication. Both the time from completion to submission and the time from submission to publication were significantly (both p's < 0.05) for negative trials than for positive trials. Of the 45 trials, 4 negative trials were rejected 2 or 3 times, whereas no positive trial was rejected multiple times.

4.5.3 Effects of Publication Bias on Decision Analysis and Cost-Effectiveness Analysis

Publication bias is a concern in decision analysis and cost-effectiveness analysis as well as in meta-analysis, since these methods also rely on published information to derive the probabilities of various events. In decision analysis and cost-effectiveness analysis, the assumption about the overall effectiveness of the intervention being studied often derives from an aggregation of published studies, and publication bias can affect conclusions.

EXAMPLES: Table 4-16 shows the results of a decision analysis that compared treatment of patients with advanced ovarian cancer with an alkylating agent alone or with combination chemotherapy (Simes 1985). Therapy with combination chemotherapy has more serious side effects than therapy with an alkylating agent alone. When the difference in survival associated with combination chemotherapy was assumed to be 1.08, a value that is close to the value found in the meta-analysis based on all registered studies described above (Simes 1986), 9 of 9 women would favor the alkylating agent over combination chemotherapy. When the difference in survival with combination chemotherapy was assumed to be 1.23, a value close to the value

Table 4-16 Results of a decision analysis: Number of women who would favor alkylating agent alone over combination chemotherapy according to assumptions about median survival ratio by method used to assess utility of treatment

Utility Method	Median Survival Ratio[a]			
	1.08[b]	1.23[c]	1.58	1.75
Time trade-off	9/9	3/9	1/9	0/9
Standard gamble	9/9	2/9	1/9	0/9

[a] Median months survival in patients treated with combination chemotherapy/median months survival in patients treated with alkalating agent alone.

[b] Estimate close to result of meta-analysis of all registered studies.

[c] Estimate close to result of meta-analysis of published studies only.

Source: Simes (1985).

found in the meta-analysis of all published studies (Simes 1986), only 2 or 3 of 9 women would favor the alkylating agent.

The effect of publication bias on decision analysis and cost-effectiveness analysis has not received much attention in the literature describing the conceptual basis for the methods. Decision analysis and cost-effectiveness analysis are beginning to rely more on meta-analysis to estimate probabilities for both decision analysis and cost-effectiveness, putting the results of the analyses on firmer scientific footing.

4.5.4   Solutions to the Problem of Publication Bias

The problem of publication bias will be solved completely only when investigators submit and editors accept all well-conducted studies of important questions irrespective of the statistical significance of their results. Changes in journal policies that cause lag in publication of negative results must also occur. Until the time that this ideal is achieved, there are three choices: ignore the problem; attempt to retrieve all study results, whether published or unpublished; or use statistical or quasi-statistical methods to assess or overcome it.

4.5.4.1   Ignore the Problem

Because the existence of publication bias is so well documented, it is impossible to ignore. At a minimum, the potential for publication bias to explain a study finding should be acknowledged explicitly. Documented examples of publication bias all show a tendency for preferential publication of statistically significant results. In the face of a null result, it may be useful to point this out. When unpublished studies have not been sought, it may be useful to discuss the incentives and disincentives for publishing results that are not statistically significant.

4.5.4.2 Attempt to Retrieve All Studies

Retrieval of information from all studies, not just published studies, is the theoretically ideal solution to the problem of publication bias. Searches for unpublished trials are required for the preparation of Cochrane Reviews (Bero and Rennie 1995). Whenever possible, an attempt should be made to identify all studies, published and unpublished.

Identification of unpublished as well as published studies is most feasible when studies are registered in their planning stages or when they begin. When there is a registry of trials, all investigators in the registered trials should be contacted and asked to provide the results of the trial, even when it has not been published.

Retrieving unpublished studies is laborious. Investigators may fail to respond to queries about the trial or choose to withhold the results of completed trials that are in the process of being submitted for publication. In these cases, the possibility of publication bias remains. On the other hand, if the number of unpublished studies is known and can be reported, concern about publication bias may be diminished when this number is small.

Registers of nonexperimental studies have not yet been created. The obstacles are formidable, since many nonexperimental studies are based on secondary analysis of data collected for a purpose other than the original goal of the study. Retrieval of information from all of the observational studies of a given topic may be infeasible, because the data on the topic may not even have been analyzed. For example, a meta-analysis of coffee drinking and coronary heart disease based on unpublished as well as published studies would require identification of all the studies that have collected data on coffee and coronary heart disease, requiring review of original questionnaires for a large number of studies.

The problem of publication bias would be mitigated by changes in policy and thinking that place higher value on studies that report ''statistically significant'' associations. Greater reliance on interval estimation and decreased emphasis on significance testing should continue to be encouraged as one way of decreasing barriers to publication of negative trials.

4.5.4.3 Statistical and Quasi-Statistical Approaches

Several statistical and quasi-statistical approaches to assessing and dealing with publication bias have been described. The statistical approaches developed to date lack a firm footing in formal statistical theory and make assumptions that are dubious or untenable. These statistical approaches are not recommended, for reasons that are discussed in detail in Chapter 8.

Light and Pillemer (1984) describe a graphical, quasi-statistical technique for assessing the possibility of publication bias, the funnel plot.

They suggest plotting the effect measure on the horizontal (x) axis and the sample size (or a measure that reflects the precision of the effect size estimate) on the vertical (y) axis. Small and large studies (or precise and less precise studies) should be symmetrically distributed around the summary estimate of effect size. The effect size from large, more precise studies will be close to the true effect size. The effect size estimates from small, less precise studies will have more ''spread'' than those from large, more precise studies. In the absence of publication bias, the data from all studies should take the shape of a funnel with the large opening (mouth of the funnel) down and the tip of the funnel pointed up and centered on the true effect size. If there is bias against the publication of small studies with null results or results showing an adverse effect of the treatment, the pyramidal corners of the funnel will be distorted or missing.

In statistics, it is customary to plot the independent variable on the horizontal (x) axis and the dependent variable on the vertical (y) axis. For studies, sample size (or precision) is the independent variable and effect size is the dependent variable in studies. Some funnel plots follow the statistical convention of plotting the sample size (or the precision) on the horizontal (x) axis and the effect size on the vertical (y) axis. In this case, the data will lie within a funnel that is laid on its side, with the mouth of the funnel to the left and the tip of the funnel to the right. (This funnel would fall over, and it is easy to understand why funnel plots were described as they were by Light and Pillemer).

EXAMPLES: Light and Pillemer (1984) provide an example of distortion of the expected funnel shape of a plot of sample size and a measure of effect

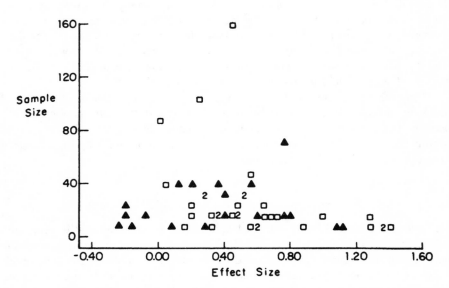

Figure 4-1 Traditional funnel plot of sample by effect size for all studies, published (squares) and unpublished (triangles), of psychoeducational interventions and hospital stay in surgical patients. The plot has the expected funnel shape. (Reproduced with permission from Light RJ and Pillemer DB: *Summing Up: The Science of Reviewing Research.* Harvard University Press, Cambridge, Massachusetts, 1984, p. 69.)

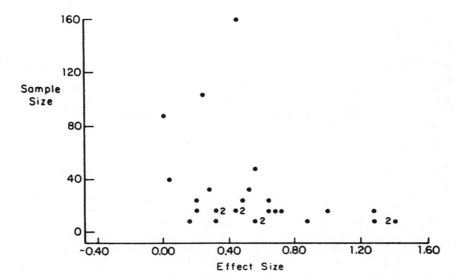

Figure 4-2 Traditional funnel plot of sample size by effect size for published studies only. The left corner of the funnel, which should contain the results of small studies with negative and null results, is missing. (Reproduced with permission from Light RJ and Pillemer DB: *Summing Up: The Science of Reviewing Research.* Harvard University Press, Cambridge, Massachusetts, 1984, p. 68.)

in a situation where there was evidence of publication bias. The data were drawn from a meta-analysis of the effect of psychoeducational interventions on hospital length of stay in surgical patients (Devine and Cook 1983). The meta-analysis of published studies showed a statistically significant association of the invention with a reduction in hospital length of stay, whereas an analysis of published studies plus studies reported in dissertations showed no statistically significant association and an estimated effect of 0.0. A plot of sample size against effect size for the whole group of published and unpublished studies, shown in Figure 4-1, was in the expected funnel shape. A plot of sample size against effect size for the published studies only, shown in Figure 4-2, shows that the left corner of the funnel, which should contain small studies reporting negative or null results, is missing.

Midgley et al. (1996) prepared a non-traditional funnel plot (tip of the funnel to the right) based on randomized trials of the effect of sodium reduction on blood pressure. Figure 4-3 shows the data. In this funnel plot, the estimates of the effect of sodium restriction on blood pressure are plotted on the y-axis. The effective sample size is plotted on the x-axis. The funnel plot shows evidence of publication bias. The upper left corner of the funnel plot, which would be expected to contain estimates from small studies with no effect on blood pressure or an increase in blood pressure, has no data. Confronted with weak data or data showing an effect of sodium reduction in increasing blood pressure, and faced with a near unanimity of belief that

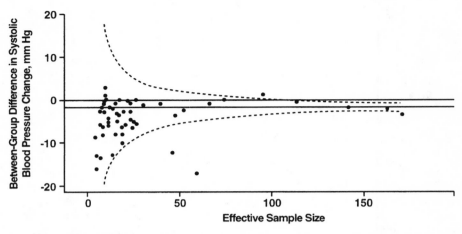

Figure 4-3 For randomized trials of the effect of sodium reduction on blood pressure, non-traditional funnel plot showing the difference in blood pressure between those with and without sodium reduction (y-axis; a measure of effect size; studies that found a reduction in blood pressure in association with lower sodium intake have negative effects) by the effective sample size (x-axis; a measure of precision). The results of studies with small effective sample sizes are concentrated in the left corner of the funnel. They show large effects of sodium reduction in lowering blood pressure. There are no studies of small size that show an increase in blood pressure with sodium reduction. Studies with large effective sample size show only a small reduction in blood pressure with reduction in sodium. The funnel plot provides strong evidence of publication bias. (Reproduced with permission from Midgley et al., *Journal of the American Medical Association,* 1996;275:1595.)

sodium reduction decreases blood pressure, authors might fail to submit, or reviewers reject, small studies that show an increase in blood pressure with sodium reduction.

In medical applications, a funnel plot should be scaled to ensure that negative effects and positive effects are equally spaced. For studies that measure effects on a ratio scale (relative risk or odds ratio), this can be accomplished either by plotting the measure on a logarithmic scale or, more easily, by taking the logarithm of the measure and plotting it on a linear scale. For studies that use ratio measures of effect size, the measure of statistical precision of the effect measure should be plotted in preference to the sample size, since total sample size for case-control and cohort studies does not provide information about the precision of the effect measure.

The sensitivity of funnel plots as a method for detecting the existence of publication bias has not been assessed systematically. When a funnel plot is distorted, publication bias should be suspected. But even when a funnel plot does not provide clear-cut evidence of publication bias, this possibility cannot be ruled out.

EXAMPLE: Figure 4-4 shows traditional funnel plot (tip of the funnel up) for the published studies of an alkylating agent alone compared with com-

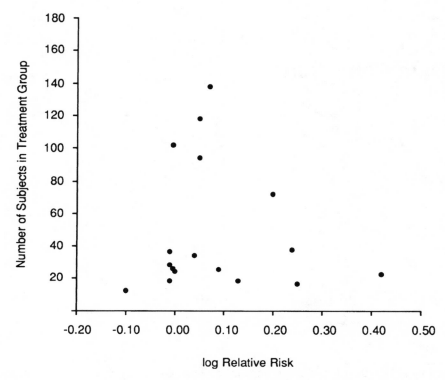

Figure 4-4   Plot of sample size by logarithm of the relative risk for published studies only. The plot is not selectively missing small studies with negative and null results even though there is other evidence to suggest that there is publication bias for this topic. Data are from Simes (1987).

bination chemotherapy in patients with advanced ovarian cancer that was discussed earlier. For these studies, Simes (1987) provided clear evidence of publication bias, and the funnel plot would be expected to demonstrate this. For these data, it is difficult to say with certainty that the funnel plot is distorted.

5

Data Collection

Meta-analysis, decision analysis, and cost-effectiveness analysis all rely on abstraction of information from written, usually published, reports. Decision analysis and cost-effectiveness analysis may involve, in addition, primary data collection. Data collection in synthetic studies should adhere to the same standards of quality assurance that guide data collection in other types of research studies. It is no more acceptable to collect data on scraps of paper in a meta-analysis, a decision analysis, or a cost-effectiveness analysis than it would be to collect data on scraps of paper in a clinical trial.

Section 5.1 describes the overall goals of the process of data collection in synthetic studies. Section 5.2 discusses reliability of data collection and ways of enhancing the reliability of collection of data from written reports. Section 5.3 discusses the concept of validity as applied to abstraction of data from written reports. Section 5.4 discusses bias in the collection of data from written reports and ways to minimize it.

5.1 OVERALL GOALS

The main goal of data collection in any study is the collection of information that is reliable, valid, and free of bias. In addition, the data collection process should create a permanent record of the information that was used in the study so that others can review it. The requirement for a permanent record of data used in the study applies equally to information collected for use in meta-analysis, decision analysis, and cost-effectiveness analysis. In the absence of a permanent, well-organized record of the results of data collection, it is impossible for others to be sure even that the work was done. When information has been collected from written reports, the record of data collection makes it possible to recheck the information used in the study, and it facilitates bookkeeping.

5.2 RELIABILITY

5.2.1 Definition

A measure is reliable if it is free of measurement error. Reliability is assessed by determining the extent to which the measurement is consistent—whether the measurement is the same when made a second time. Reliability is a concept that applies both to individual items of data and to scales composed of an aggregation of items.

Intrarater reliability is a single rater's consistency in rating an item when it is presented more than once. Test-retest reliability is consistency of values when rated twice by the same person, with some interval of time between the independent ratings. Interrater reliability is consistency in rating by different persons.

Reliability is a matter of concern in abstraction of information from written reports. This includes the abstraction of information about the number of subjects and the year of publication, as well as information on the summary measure of effect and information used to rate the quality of the study. In decision analysis and cost-effectiveness analysis, reliability of information about the probabilities used in the analysis is a concern, as well as the reliability of measures of utility and cost.

5.2.2 Reliability of Data Abstracted from Written Reports

Superficially, it would seem that information abstracted from written publications ought to be inherently reliable. After all, the information is written down in black and white. Reliability of information abstracted from written reports cannot be assumed for several reasons. First, data collection from written reports is subject to simple human error. The numbers given in the publication may be recorded incorrectly. These simple human errors lead to unreliability. Second, in most written reports, measures of the same quantity are cited more than once. For example, a measure of the overall association of the treatment with the outcome may be presented in the abstract, in the narrative section of the results, in a table, and again in the discussion. A simple instruction to record the measure of association may lead one abstractor to record the number reported in the abstract, whereas another abstractor might record the number reported in the results section.

EXAMPLE: In a publication reporting on mortality follow-up of women in the Walnut Creek Contraceptive Drug Study (Petitti, Perlman, Sidney 1987), the estimated relative risk of death from cardiovascular disease in ''ever users'' of noncontraceptive estrogens compared with ''never users'' after adjustment for age and other cardiovascular disease risk factors was cited as 0.5 in the abstract but was given as 0.6 in the relevant table in the text of the article. The discrepancy between the two citations arose because a correction to the abstract made to the galley proofs was not incorporated into the published manuscript. This fact cannot be known to a person abstracting information on cardiovascular disease from the written report, and it leads to unreliability in the measure of risk of cardiovascular disease in non–contraceptive users abstracted from this publication unless an instruction is given to consistently abstract information from one or the other section of the published paper.

Last, the information from a written report may not be presented exactly in the form in which it is needed. In this case, the abstractor must make assumptions about the material presented in the text. The assumptions made from one reading of the text to the next by the same abstractor, or by different abstractors reading the same text, may not be identical, and the data may be unreliable for this reason.

There are few formal evaluations of the reliability of data abstraction for meta-analysis. The most thorough examination of the issue of reliability for meta-analysis is a study of interrater reliability by Stock et al. (1982). A random sample of 30 documents was selected from a list of sources of information on the topic of the meta-analysis. A statistician and two postdoctoral educational researchers coded 27 items from the 30 studies. The items included judgments such as whether or not a study should be coded, as well as calculations from the original data sources such as the median age of subjects in the study. Correlations between pairs of coders ranged from 0.57 for quality of the study to 1.00 for median age and the standard deviation of age. The low level of reliability for some items suggests that specific procedures to maximize reliability are necessary.

5.2.3   Enhancing Reliability

5.2.3.1   General Procedures for Abstraction from Written Reports

Table 5-1, adapted from Stock et al. (1982), lists several ways to enhance the reliability of abstraction of information from written reports. Most of these pro-

Table 5-1   Ways to enhance the reliability of data collection for studies involving abstraction from published literature

---

Develop and pilot test forms before the study begins
Develop a detailed book of abstracting instructions and rules for each form.
Provide training to abstractors based on the rule book and forms
Assess interabstractor reliability
Revise the rule book and forms and retrain abstractors as needed
Develop procedures for adding new abstractors
Encourage abstractors' involvement in discussions and decisions about abstracting instructions
    and rules

Source: Stock et al. (1982).

cedures apply to data collection in all kinds of studies, not just studies that rely on abstraction of data from written reports. The general procedures for abstracting information include development of data collection forms before the study begins, pilot testing of the forms, and revision of the forms based on the results of the pilot test.

When information on a topic is available only from a single source, as is often the case in a decision analysis, a single form may need to be developed for a single piece of information. Alternatively, a single form that documents the source of data on each of the probabilities may be developed.

When data will be abstracted from multiple reports, a detailed book of abstracting instructions must be prepared. This book should include rules for each of the forms and for all items on the forms that are not entirely self-explanatory. The abstracting book should be updated when decisions to change rules, procedures, or forms are made.

Abstractors should be formally trained. In training sessions, as described by Stock et al. (1982), the principal investigator should meet with the abstractor, describe each item, and go through the process of abstracting a report with the abstractor observing. Graduate students and fellows who are doing their own data abstraction also need to be trained.

The early forms abstracted by the newly trained abstractor should be reabstracted to assess formally the reliability of the abstraction process. A sample of forms should be periodically abstracted as part of ongoing quality control. When new abstractors are hired, they should also be trained and the reliability of their work monitored closely during the early stages of the study.

Stock and colleagues (1982) emphasize the importance of involvement of abstractors in discussions about the instructions and rules for abstraction. Implicit is the notion that those closest to the data are most knowledgeable about the problems and their solutions.

For some items of information, it may be useful to have two or more independent abstractions. Discrepancies in the judgments of the two readers can then be adjudicated by a master reader or by a consensus of the study investigators meeting as a committee.

EXAMPLE: Littenberg (1988) did a meta-analysis of aminophylline treatment in severe, acute asthma. To assign a quality score to each study, he developed a nine-point scale in which the presence or absence of nine characteristics of a well-designed study was assessed for each study. To determine the quality score, each report was reviewed by two board-certified internists with training in clinical epidemiology.

5.2.3.2   Format and Organization of Data Collection Forms

Attention to the format and organizational structure of the standardized data collection form is important. Good forms used to abstract information from written reports have features in common with all good survey instruments and data collection forms. Table 5-2, modified from Meinert (1986), lists the features that are especially important in the design of forms for abstraction from written reports.

Table 5-2 Important features of forms for abstraction from published literature

---

Each item should have a unique identifying number
Each item should require a response, regardless of whether information is or is not available.
Skip and stop instructions should be clear; they should be printed on the form
The language should be simple
The layout should be pleasant; it should facilitate data entry by standardizing the location of
  check items
The pages should be numbered sequentially and the total number of pages in the form should be
  indicated on each page
The sequence of items should be logically related to the format of most scientific publications

---

Source: Meinert (1986).

Each item on the form should have a unique identifying number. This facilitates data entry and data analysis. Each item should require a response, regardless of whether information on the item is or is not available. This allows missing information to be distinguished from an incomplete abstraction. Skip and stop instructions should be clear, and these instructions should be printed on the form. Doing this makes it possible for others to understand how data collection flows. The language used on the form should be simple. Use of esoteric terms, unnecessary words, and double negatives should be avoided, for reasons that are obvious. The pages of the forms should be numbered sequentially, and the total number of pages in the form should be indicated on each page. In this way, missing pages can be spotted and the abstractor will know when the form has been completed. The sequence of items on the form should be logically related to the material to be abstracted. For example, items related to information that is likely to be presented in the methods section should precede items related to information likely to appear in the results section.

5.3 VALIDITY

Information collected by data abstraction from a written report, by polling experts, or in a survey is valid if it measures what it is intended to measure. In a meta-analysis, the information on the estimate of effect is valid to the extent that the original study results are valid. In measuring study quality, a valid measure is a measure that adequately represents the quality of the study. An estimate of the probability of a certain outcome provided by experts is valid if it is an accurate estimate of that probability. A scale that assigns a preference value to a health state is valid if it is a true measure of the preference of individuals or society for that health state. An estimate of cost used in a cost-effectiveness analysis is valid if it is a true measure of cost.

Measures that are not reliable are not valid. That is, reliability is the sine qua non of validity. The prior section described some of the ways to assure that measures derived from abstraction from written reports are reliable.

Chapter 11 discusses reliability and validity of measures of preference.

5.4 BIAS

5.4.1 Definition and Origins

Bias is systematic error that distorts the truth. While measurement error makes it more difficult to find true associations, bias leads to erroneous conclusions. It is very difficult to detect biased data collection from reading the results of a study. When data collection is biased, the problem is almost impossible to overcome analytically.

Bias in data collection from written reports can arise in many ways, some of them quite subtle. The abstractor who believes strongly that one treatment is better than another may select the data from the report most favorable to this position. The knowledge that the study is "positive" or is "negative" may lead this biased abstractor to search harder for information that would ensure that the study is excluded from or included in a meta-analysis. Knowledge that a study was published in a prestigious journal may cause the abstractor to rate the paper more highly on measures of quality, when these measures are being used, and this will ultimately result in bias.

5.4.2 Reducing Bias in Data Collection from Written Reports

5.4.2.1 Blinding

Chalmers et al. 1981 suggested that the abstraction of information for a meta-analysis should be done with the abstractor blinded to information that would allow the author, the journal, and the funding source to be identified. These were aspects of the study that were believed to possibly influence the judgment of the abstractor. The practice of blinding abstractors has been followed on occasion.

> EXAMPLE: In the quality rating that Littenberg (1988) did for his meta-analysis of aminophylline treatment in severe, acute asthma, identifying information—authors, titles, journal, institution, and country of origin—were removed from the report before they were given to the internists for abstraction.

Berlin et al. (1997) conducted a formal study to assess the effect of blinding on the results of meta-analysis. They selected five published meta-analyses of randomized clinical trials at random. Every study of every meta-analysis was read by each of four readers, working in two pairs. One of the pairs was blinded to information in the papers. The other pair read the unblinded copies of the papers. Blinding was complete. It involved use of a computerized page scanner to transfer each printed article to a word processing program and then removal of all references to authors, institutions, and journal, as well as to treatment groups.

Berlin et al. (1997) found considerable disagreement between blinded and unblinded reviews about which papers should be accepted for the meta-analysis. Table 5-3 shows summary odds ratios from the blinded and unblinded reviews. In spite of the disagreement about the eligibility of individual studies, the blinded and

Table 5-3   Summary odds ratios from blinded and unblinded review of five published meta-analyses

Topic	Blinded Review		Unblinded Review	
	Odds Ratio	95% Confidence Interval	Odds Ratio	95% Confidence Interval
Steroids for otitis media	0.09	0.03–0.23	0.36	0.18–0.74
Ateplase and APSAC for acute MI	0.63	0.53–0.75	0.73	0.48–1.11
Adjuvant therapy for head and neck cancer	0.91	0.78–1.00	0.91	0.78–1.07
Corticosteroids to prevent preterm birth	0.51	0.41–0.63	0.53	0.43–0.66
Interferon for non-A, non-B hepatitis	0.06	0.04–0.11	0.05	0.03–0.08
Weighted average	0.63	0.57–0.70	0.64	0.57–0.72

Source: Berlin (1997).

unblinded summary estimates of effect are very close. The process of blinding was labor intensive, requiring almost 10 hours per paper.

Blinding may not affect conclusions when rules for abstraction are well-defined. It is cumbersome and costly. It is not recommended as a general strategy. For some limited tasks (e.g., rating of study quality), it may be feasible and useful, although there are no empiric data to prove this.

5.4.2.2 Task Separation

Chalmers et al. (1981) also suggested that knowledge of the results of the study might influence the perception of the methods. This led to a suggestion to abstract information from the methods section separate from the results section to reduce bias. Other suggestions for reducing bias in data abstraction (Chalmers et al. 1981) were use of two separate forms, one for methods and one for results. These were to be abstracted by the same person on separate occasions or by two abstractors, with the task of abstracting the methods section assigned to one of them and that of abstracting the results section to the other.

These approaches to data abstraction have not been assessed empirically to determine whether they reduce bias. Careful attention to construction of data collection forms, training of abstractors, and formal assessment of the reliability of data collection are probably more important than task separation as methods for reducing bias in the abstraction of data for a meta-analysis.

6

Advanced Issues in Meta-Analysis

The principles of protocol development, comprehensive identification of information, and data collection that were described in earlier chapters apply to each of the three methods of quantitative synthesis. This chapter begins the presentation of advanced issues pertinent only to meta-analysis.

Having developed a strategy for identifying studies using the methods described in Chapter 4 and data collection forms as described in Chapter 5, the next steps in a meta-analysis are to define eligibility criteria for the meta-analysis, to apply these criteria to the selection of studies, and to select the data from the studies that are deemed eligible for the meta-analysis. These topics are covered in this chapter. Chapter 7 describes statistical methods for meta-analysis of data from comparative studies, and Chapter 8 describes other statistical aspects of meta-analysis and meta-analysis of individual subject data. Chapter 14 is a detailed discussion of approaches to exploring heterogeneity in meta-analysis.

Section 6.1 discusses the goals, timing, and process of defining eligibility criteria and determining the eligibility of studies for the meta-analysis. Sections 6.2 through 6.8 discuss the rationale for basic eligibility criteria. Section 6.9 discusses the choice of estimates of effect from studies with more than one estimate. Section 6.10 discusses the measurement of study quality in meta-analysis.

6.1   DEFINING ELIGIBILITY CRITERIA AND DETERMINING ELIGIBILITY OF INDIVIDUAL STUDIES

6.1.1   Overall Goals

The overall goals of the process of defining eligibility criteria for a meta-analysis are to ensure reproducibility of the meta-analysis and to minimize bias. The selection of studies is reproducible if another person arrives at the same conclusion about which studies will be included in the meta-analysis. If the eligibility criteria are well described, the selection of studies will be reproducible. Bias in the selection of studies for the meta-analysis can arise when selection is influenced by knowledge of the results or by other aspects of the study design. Defining eligibility criteria reduces bias by assuring that decisions about eligibility are systematic.

Defining eligibility criteria of studies for a meta-analysis is analogous to defining eligibility criteria for entry to a randomized trial or for inclusion of subjects in a case-control or cohort study. The decision to include or exclude a person from a study of any design should not be arbitrary, and it should not be based on convenience. It should be based on sound scientific reasoning. Similarly, the decision to include or exclude a study from a meta-analysis should be based on sound scientific reasoning.

6.1.2   When to Define Eligibility Criteria and Determine Eligibility

Eligibility criteria for the meta-analysis should be defined before the abstraction of data from the studies begins. The criteria should be described in a protocol that has been prepared in advance of the conduct of the study. Developing eligibility criteria ahead of time and describing them in a protocol documents the intent of the analyst and protects the meta-analysis from allegations that the choice of studies in the final analysis was influenced by investigator bias. Documentation is particularly important when the investigator has a previously stated position on the topic, when the investigator has published one or more studies on the topic that are in conflict with other studies, and when the results of the meta-analysis have beneficial or adverse monetary consequences for the investigator or for the sponsor of the research.

It is especially important to determine whether a study is eligible for the meta-analysis before carrying out the statistical analysis of the studies. Doing this minimizes bias. When the effect estimates from each study are known, it may be possible to pick and choose from among them and arrive at just about any conclusion.

EXAMPLE: Table 6-1 presents the estimates of the relative risk of sepsis in preterm infants treated with intravenous immunoglobulin (IVIG) from randomized clinical trials that Jenson and Pollock (1998) identified as eligible for a meta-analysis of this topic. The summary estimate of relative risk of sepsis in infants treated with IVIG based on all of the studies considered eligible is 0.68 (95% C.I. 0.58–0.80). A statistical test of homogeneity yields a very high chi-square value, and the hypothesis of homogeneity of effect is

Table 6-1   Estimates of the realtive risk of sepsis in preterm infants treated with intravenous immune globulin

Reference	Double-Blind, Placebo-Controlled	Estimated Relative Risk	95% Confidence Interval
Haque and Zaidi (1996)	No	0.37	0.08–1.53
Chirico et al. (1987)	No	0.18	0.03–0.79
Stabile et al. (1988)	No	1.37	0.26–7.78
Clapp et al (1989)	Yes	0.00	0.00–0.46
Bussel (1990)	Yes	0.49	0.19–1.24
Conway et al. (1990)	No	0.32	0.10–1.02
Magny et al. (1991)	Yes	2.15	1.02–4.65
Kinney et al. (1991)	Yes	0.94	0.24–3.62
Baker et al. (1992)	Yes	0.62	0.41–0.93
van Overmeire et al. (1993)	No	0.99	0.41–2.38
Weisman et al. (1994)	Yes	0.94	0.59–1.51
Fanaroff et al. (1994)	Yes	0.87	0.70–1.10

Summary relative risk: all eligible studies 0.68 (0.58–0.80)
Summary relative risk: studies published before 1991 0.12 (0.08–0.19)
Summary relative risk: studies published 1991$^+$ 0.88 (0.74–1.04)
Summary relative risk: double-blind, placebo controlled 0.86 (0.76–1.01)

Source: Jenson and Pollock (1998); table references cited there.

rejected ($p < 0.001$). After inspecting the estimates of relative risk, it is easy to see that omission of the studies published before 1991 would eliminate most of the studies that found an effect of IVIG on sepsis. The summary estimate of the relative risk of sepsis in infants treated with IVIG after excluding the six studies published before 1991 is 0.88 (95% C.I. 0.74–1.04). A test of the hypothesis of homogeneity of effect is not rejected ($p > 0.05$).

Studies done before 1991 might be of lower quality than later studies. In this example, only four of the six studies done before 1991 were double-blind and placebo-controlled, whereas all but one of the six studies done in 1991 or after were double-blind and placebo controlled. A cogent argument for excluding the early studies might be made based on the grounds that the earlier studies were less rigorous. If there are a priori plans to explore heterogeneity and to try to explain it, and if study quality is one of the factors to be explored, then excluding them is justifiable. If the argument is made after inspecting the relative risk estimates, the critical reader might suspect investigator bias.

6.1.3   The Process of Assessing Eligibility

The process of determining whether studies are eligible for inclusion in the meta-analysis should be systematic and rigorous. Each potentially eligible study should be scanned in a specified order. The determination of whether or not a study meets the predetermined eligibility criteria should be made by personnel who have been trained and who work from a set of written instructions. The goal of each of these procedures is to ensure reliability of determinations of eligibility and to minimize bias.

The reasons why a study is deemed ineligible should be recorded, and a log of ineligible studies needs to be maintained (Chalmers et al. 1981). Studies that are directly pertinent but are not included in the meta-analysis should be cited in the published report on the meta-analysis or the information made readily accessible. The reasons for rejecting studies should be recorded for each study presented in the publication describing the results of the meta-analysis. These procedures allow others to assess the completeness of the literature review process and the accuracy of the application of the stated eligibility criteria. Keeping a log of ineligible studies is analogous to keeping a log of patients who were screened for a clinical trial but were not enrolled, and the goals are the same.

Chalmers et al. (1981) suggested blinding the abstractor to the results of the study, to the source of publication, and to the authors as a way to reduce bias in data abstraction (Chalmers et al. 1981). Chapter 5 described the results of randomized trial that assessed the effect of blinding on the results of five meta-analyses. This formal study did not show any value in blinding and it is costly and difficult to blind abstractors. Blinding is not recommended as a general strategy. For some limited tasks (e.g., rating of study quality), it may be feasible and useful.

It is desirable to have the decisions about eligibility reviewed independently by another abstractor. It may be especially important to re-review rejected studies. When there are discrepancies between the judgments of two independent reviewers, they should be resolved using a predetermined procedure, such as a conference or adjudication by an expert.

6.1.4 General Eligibility Criteria

Table 6-2 lists seven basic considerations about eligibility that should be addressed in almost all meta-analyses. First, the designs of eligible studies should be specified. Second, the inclusive dates of publication, presentation, or conduct of studies eligible for the meta-analysis should be given. Third, the eligibility of studies whose results are not available in English should be addressed. Fourth, the criteria for choosing among results of multiple publications from the same study population should be defined. Fifth, any restrictions on eligibility due to sample size or length

Table 6-2 Basic considerations in defining eligibility for a meta-analysis

Study designs to be included
Years of publication or study conduct
Languages
Choice among multiple publications
Restrictions due to sample size or follow-up
Similarity of treatments and/or exposure
Completeness of information

of follow-up should be stated. Sixth, eligibility or ineligibility based on the similarity of treatments or exposure should be considered. Last, the eligibility or ineligibility of incomplete and unpublished reports should be addressed.

6.2 STUDY DESIGN

The average effect of a new treatment has generally been found to be larger in nonrandomized than in randomized studies (Chalmers, Block, Lee 1972; Sacks, Chalmers, Smith 1983; Wortman and Yeatman 1983; Colditz, Miller, Mosteller 1989; Miller, Colditz, Mosteller 1989). When both randomized and nonrandomized studies are available for a topic, estimates of effect size should be made separately for the randomized and the nonrandomized studies.

When all available studies are nonexperimental, it is difficult to make a rule about similarity of study design as an eligibility criterion for the meta-analysis. The study design that is likely to yield the most valid conclusion may be different for different topics. There may be conflict between the results of studies of different designs, and it may not be possible to say which study design yields the correct conclusion.

EXAMPLE: Table 6-3 shows estimates of the relative risk of osteoporotic fracture in female smokers according to whether the study was a case-control study or a cohort study. All of the case-control studies found a higher risk

Table 6-3 Estimated relative risk of osteoporotic fracture in female smokers by study type

Reference	Estimated Relative Risk
Case-control studies	
Daniell (1976)	4.2
Aloia et al. (1985)	3.2
Paganini-Hill et al. (1981)	1.96[a]
Kreiger et al. (1982)	1.29
Kreiger and Hildreth (1986)	
Williams et al. (1982)	6.5[b]
Alderman et al. (1986)	13.5[c]
Cohort studies	
Jensen (1986)	0.7
Hemenway et al. (1988)	1.0[d]
Holbrook, Barrett-Connor, Wingard (1988)	1.1

[a] >11 cigarettes/day.

[b] Hip fracture in average weight smoker compared with obese nonsmoker.

[c] Hip fracture in thin smoker compared with obese nonsmoker.

[d] ≥25 cigarettes/day.

Source: United States Department of Health and Human Services (1990); table references cited there.

of osteoporotic fracture in smokers, whereas all of the cohort studies found a relative risk of 1 or less.

In almost all of the case-control studies, response rates were higher in cases than in controls. Response rates in smokers are lower than in non-smokers in most population-based surveys, and response bias may explain the higher relative risk observed in case-control studies of smoking and fracture. Case-control studies are also subject to recall bias, which would spuriously increase the estimates of relative risk of fracture in smokers. Considering these issues, it would seem that cohort studies yield the more correct conclusion. On the other hand, information about smoking in many cohort studies is defined at entry to the study and is not updated thereafter. The absence of an association of smoking with osteoporotic fracture in cohort studies may be due to nondifferential misclassification of smoking status and a bias to the null that would result from failure to update smoking status.

In the interest of completeness, it may be prudent to consider studies of all designs to be eligible for a meta-analysis of nonexperimental studies. If there is statistical evidence of heterogeneity in the estimate of effect, the possibility of study design as an explanation for the discrepancy in estimates of effect can be examined. This topic is covered in more depth in Chapter 14.

6.3   INCLUSIVE DATES OF PUBLICATION

Because of the availability of MEDLINE as a method for identifying published literature, it has become common to define 1966, the date when MEDLINE began, as the starting date for identification of studies eligible for a meta-analysis. The fact that MEDLINE began in 1966 is not an adequate justification for defining 1966 as the starting date for eligibility for a meta-analysis. The inclusive dates of publication should be chosen based not simply on convenience but on consideration of the likelihood of finding important and useful information during the period that is chosen.

> *EXAMPLE:*   Table 6-4 showed the results of an exhaustive review done by Mahomed and Hytten (1989) to identify studies of the effect of routine iron supplementation during pregnancy. Eight studies were identified; only four of them were published in 1966 or later. Two of the three largest randomized trials of this topic were done before 1966. Of the 643 subjects who had participated in randomized studies, 337 had participated in studies whose results were published before 1966.

The meta-analysis should be as up-to-date as possible. The cutoff date for identification of eligible studies should be specified in the report on the meta-analysis so that material published after the cutoff date will not be assumed to have been missed in the literature search.

Table 6-4 Studies included in meta-analysis of effect of routine iron supplementation on anemia at 36–40 weeks, year of publication, journal, and total number of subjects

Reference	Year of Publication	Journal	Number of Subjects
Holly	1955	*Obstetrics and Gynecology*	149
Pritchard and Hunt	1958	*Surgery, Gynecology, and Obstetrics*	123
Morgan	1961	*Lancet*	65
Chisholm	1966	*Journal of Obstetrics and Gynaecology of the British Commonwealth*	144
Fleming et al.	1974	*Medical Journal of Medical Science*	60
Batu et al.	1976	*Israel Journal of Medical Science*	55
Taylor et al.	1982	*British Journal of Obstetrics and Gynaecology*	46

Source: Mahomed and Hytten (1989); table references cited there.

6.4 ENGLISH-LANGUAGE PUBLICATIONS

The potential problems with inclusion only of publications in English were discussed in Chapter 4. There is no justification for doing a meta-analysis based on only English-language publications, and the common practice of relying only on English-language publications has been shown to have the potential to cause bias. It is not valid to conduct a meta-analysis based solely on the publications and reports that are easily found and understood.

6.5 MULTIPLE PUBLICATIONS FROM THE SAME STUDY POPULATION

Multiple published reports from the same study are very common. The summary estimates of effect from reports on the same study population are not independent, and including more than one estimate of effect from the same study population violates the statistical assumptions that underlie the procedures for aggregating data. Information from the same study population should contribute only once to the summary estimate of effect. Failure to exclude multiple reports from the same study population has the potential to cause bias in the summary estimate of effect.

EXAMPLES: Grady et al. (1992) conducted a meta-analysis of observational studies of stroke in users of estrogen replacement therapy. They found information on the relative risk of stroke in users of estrogen replacement therapy in three publications based on follow-up of women living in Leisure World, in two publications based on women in the Walnut Creek Contraceptive Drug Study, and in two publications from the National Health and Nutrition Examination Survey (NHANES) Follow-up Study. Although the period of follow-up and the number of events differ, the estimates of effect are not independent, and information from each study should be included only once in computing the summary estimate of relative risk.

Table 6-5 shows estimates of the relative risk of stroke for all of the publications of stroke in estrogen users. In this table, information from multiple publications from the Leisure World cohort, the Walnut Creek Contraceptive Drug Study, and the NHANES cohorts is listed separately. The summary estimate of relative risk in current users of estrogen replacement therapy based on use of only one estimate per study is 0.96 (0.82–1.13). The summary estimate of the relative risk of stroke for estrogen replacement therapy is 0.89 (95% C.I. 0.77–1.03) when based on all publications.

Although the overall conclusion about the effect of estrogen on stroke risk is not different between the two analyses, use of all publications would overestimate the public health benefit of estrogen use for stroke. Tramer et al. (1997) did an analysis of 84 randomized trials of the effect of ondansetron for the treatment of postoperative emesis published between 1991 and 1996. They found that 17% of published full reports were duplicated. Trials with a greater treatment effect were more likely to be duplicated. Inclusion of duplicated data in a meta-analysis of ondansetron to prevent emesis led to a 23% overestimation of efficacy.

Table 6-5   Estimated relative risk of stroke in users of estrogen replacement therapy from all publications

Study Population	Reference[a]	Estimated Relative Risk	95% Confidence Interval
Leisure World	Pfeffer (1976)	1.12	0.79–1.57
	Paganini-Hill, Ross, Henderson (1988)[b]	0.53	0.31–0.91
	Henderson, Paganini-Hill, Ross (1991)[b]	0.63	0.40–0.97
Northern California Kaiser-Permanente Health Plan	Rosenberg et al. (1980)	1.16	0.75–1.77
Oxford, England	Adam, Williams, Vessey (1981)[b]	0.64	0.06–6.52
Walnut Creek Study	Petitti et al. (1979)	1.19	0.67–2.13
	Petitti, Sidney, Perlman (1987)[b]	0.6	0.2–2.2
Framingham	Wilson, Garrison, Castelli (1985)	2.27	1.22–4.23
Lipid Research Clinics	Bush et al. (1987)[b]	0.40	0.01–3.07
Denmark	Boysen et al. (1988)	0.97	0.50–1.90
Nurses' Health Study	Stampfer et al. (1991)	0.97	0.65–1.45
National Health and Nutrition	Finucane et al. (1991)[b]	0.35	0.14–0.88
Examination Survey	Finucane et al. (1992)	0.65	0.45–0.95
Summary relative risk		0.89	0.77–1.03

[a] Table references are as cited in Grady et al. (1992).
[b] Studies of fatal stroke.

6.6   RESTRICTIONS ON SAMPLE SIZE OR LENGTH
OF FOLLOW-UP

Some of the statistical methods for meta-analysis are asymptotic methods. Asymptotic methods will tend to overestimate the precision of small studies (Greenland 1987). When the precision of a study is overestimated, it will carry too much weight in the meta-analysis. To avoid the problem of weighting small studies inappropriately in the meta-analysis, it is reasonable to make sample size an eligibility criterion for the meta-analysis. Small studies are excluded.

For some topics, the length of follow-up may influence the likelihood of observing a true association. For example, a treatment for breast cancer probably will not have an effect on the likelihood of breast cancer recurrence in the first year after treatment. Including studies with only one year of follow-up of breast cancer patients in a meta-analysis of treatments for breast cancer would bias the estimate of the effect of treatment to the null. Similarly, there are many situations where exposure would not affect the risk of disease until after a latent period. For example, screening mammography would not be expected to affect the risk of death from breast cancer in the first 5 years after the test. Including studies with less than 5 years of follow-up of women who have undergone screening mammography in a meta-analysis of randomized trials of screening mammography and death from breast cancer would bias the result to the null. To avoid these problems, length of follow-up could be a criterion for eligibility for the meta-analysis.

Restrictions based on sample size or length of follow-up should be specified in advance and documented in the protocol.

An alternative to making study size or length of follow-up an eligibility criterion is to estimate effect with and without small studies or with and without studies with short follow-up or low-dose exposure. This is a kind of sensitivity analysis, which is discussed further in Chapter 15.

6.7   ELIGIBILITY BASED ON SIMILARITY OF TREATMENTS (OR
EXPOSURES) OR OUTCOMES

One of the most critical decisions about eligibility for a meta-analysis is the decision about how similar the treatments (or exposures) and the outcome must be to use them in the same analysis. These decisions are varied. They include deciding whether to consider together studies with different doses of the same drug; studies of chemically different drugs with the same mechanism of action; and studies of diseases in the same organ system but with a possibly different underlying pathophysiology.

EXAMPLES: Chapter 1 described a meta-analysis of randomized trials of primary coronary angioplasty compared with intravenous thrombolytic therapy in patients with acute myocardial infarction (Weaver et al. 1997). Two different intravenous thrombolytic agents—streptokinase and tissue plasminogen activator—were studied. Tissue plasminogen activator was given in two different ways in different trials—in a 3–4 hour infusion and in an "accelerated,'' 90-minute infusion. The analysis did not demonstrate any difference in outcome between the 3–4 hour and accelerated regimens, but combining results for the two ways of administering the thrombolytic therapies without considering the possibility of a difference in their effect was an important aspect of the meta-analysis.

Randomized trials of the effects of long-term beta-blocker drugs after acute myocardial infarction on mortality that were included in a meta-analysis reported by Yusuf et al. (1985) included studies of propanolol, metoprolol, atenolol, sotalol, timolol, practolol, alprenolol, oxprenolol, and pindolol.

The studies of stroke and estrogen replacement therapy used in the meta-analysis by Grady et al. (1992) described in Table 6.5 and discussed in Section 6.5 included studies of hospitalized ischemic stroke, fatal subarachnoid hemorrhage, hospitalized stroke (including both ischemic and hemorrhagic stroke) only, and fatal ischemic stroke only.

When the treatments evaluated in different studies do not have the same effect on outcome, including all of the studies in the meta-analysis may bias the meta-analytic summary estimate of effect.

EXAMPLE: In the meta-analysis of beta-blocker drugs after acute myocardial infarction by Yusuf et al. (1985), the overall odds ratio of death in persons treated long-term with a beta-blocker drug was 0.77 (95% C.I. 0.70–0.85) when based on all trials. The odds ratio for death based on the 11 trials of long-term treatment with the beta blockers with intrinsic sympathomimetic activity (practolol, alprenolol, oxprenolol, pindolol) was 0.90 (95% C.I. 0.77–1.05). The odds ratio was 0.69 (95% C.I. 0.61–0.79) when based on the 14 trials of drugs without intrinsic sympathomimetic activity (metoprolol, atenolol, propranolol, sotalol, timolol). The inclusion of treatments with drugs with sympathomimetic activity, which appear not to have much effect on mortality, biased the overall summary estimate toward the null.

When a treatment has an effect on one outcome but not on another, including all of the studies may also bias the summary estimate of effect.

EXAMPLE: The summary estimate of the relative risk of stroke in users of estrogen replacement therapy based on all of the studies in Table 6-5, taking only one estimate from each study, is 0.96 (95% C.I. 0.82–1.13). The summary estimate of relative risk based only on studies of fatal stroke is 0.50 (95% C.I. 0.39–0.82). There are different interpretations of this observation. It is possible that estrogen use protects only against fatal stroke. Alternatively, estrogen users may be different from nonusers in ways that influence the likelihood that they will die from stroke but not their chances of suffering a stroke. In either case, the conclusions differ depending on the outcomes that are used to define eligibility for the meta-analysis.

Including disparate treatments or outcomes in the same meta-analysis may result in overgeneralization of the results of the meta-analysis.

EXAMPLE: A conclusion about beta blockade based on a meta-analysis of all 24 trials of long-term treatment and mortality would be that beta blockade is beneficial. The analysis is, however, more consistent with the conclusion that the benefit of long-term treatment is confined to use of beta blockers that are without intrinsic sympathomimetic activity.

Decisions about eligibility based on the similarity of the outcome or the treatment must balance strictness, which enhances the homogeneity of the studies, against all-inclusiveness, which enhances completeness. Highly restrictive eligibility criteria tend to give the meta-analysis greater face validity. But criteria may be so restrictive and require so much homogeneity that they limit the eligible studies to only one or two studies, thus defeating one of the goals of meta-analysis as a method to increase statistical power. Nonrestrictive criteria may lead to the accusation that the meta-analysis "mixes apples and oranges." For example, given the differences in the underlying pathophysiology of various stroke syndromes, it seems unlikely that estrogen use would have the same effect on both hemorrhagic stroke and ischemic brain infarction. Including studies with both these stroke endpoints in the same analysis does not make sense based on an understanding of the pathophysiology of the diseases.

6.8 COMPLETENESS OF INFORMATION

6.8.1 Inclusion of Abstracts and Brief and Preliminary Reports

Information from a study may be available only as an abstract, which may or may not have been published, or in preliminary form, as a letter to the editor or a brief report. These types of reports are all examples of incomplete or summary reports. A decision must be made on whether studies with information available only in an incomplete or summary form are eligible for inclusion in the meta-analysis or how they should be handled.

Research in several fields shows that only about 35% to 40% of abstracts are followed by a full report within four to five years (Dudley 1978; Goldman and Loscalzo 1980; Meranze, Ellison, Greenhow 1982; McCormick and Holmes 1985; Chalmers et al. 1990). Incomplete reports may contain information on a large proportion of all studies undertaken. Studies whose results are reported only in incomplete form do not appear to be of lower quality than studies whose results are reported in full form.

Chalmers et al. (1990), for example, rated the quality of 16 controlled trials originally published in summary form, which included abstracts, brief reports, and letters to the editor. Only 36% were followed by publication of a complete report within four years. Table 6-6 shows that publication as a full report was not associated with higher quality. Callahan et al. (1996) reported similar results about the quality of studies submitted for presentation at a meeting of the Society for Academic Emergency Medicine.

Cook et al. (1993) conducted a survey that involved 214 authors of published meta-analyses or methodologists. A high proportion (>90%) believed that infor-

Table 6-6 For controlled trials originally published in summary form,[a] percent published in full form by quality score assigned to study

Quality Score	Number of Trials	Trials Published in Full Form	
		N	%
High (6+)	10	3	30.0
Medium (3–5)	114	43	37.7
Low (<3)	52	18	34.6

[a] As an abstract, brief report, or letter to the editor.

Source: Chalmers et al. (1990).

mation from journal supplements, published symposia, dissertations, book chapters, published abstracts, and non-peer-reviewed articles should be included in a meta-analysis. These findings argue for the inclusion of incomplete reports in a meta-analysis.

Incomplete reports often describe the design, analysis, and results of the study in sketchy terms. It may be impossible to determine from the material in the publication whether the study meets the eligibility criteria that have been applied to more complete reports. Studies presented in incomplete form have generally not been subjected to rigorous peer review. Most important, there is evidence that both the submission and acceptance of abstracts is biased toward those with positive results. Callahan et al. (1996), in an analysis of 492 research abstracts submitted for consideration for the Society for Academic Emergency Medicine, reported that the odds ratio for acceptance was 2 for abstracts reporting a positive outcome, defined as either a finding of benefit for the intervention studied or a statistically significant result. Koren et al. (1989) found that acceptance of abstracts reporting on the effects of exposure to cocaine during pregnancy was biased toward acceptance of those that reported positive outcomes. DeBellefeuille, Morrison, and Tannock (1992) reported that abstracts submitted to a cancer meeting were more likely to be accepted if they reported positive results.

These latter considerations, and especially the evidence for positive-outcomes bias, argue for exclusion of incomplete reports from the meta-analysis.

An attempt should be made to identify published abstracts and other published incomplete reports in the information identification phase of a meta-analysis. Studies that report findings in these formats studies should be considered eligible or ineligible for the meta-analysis by applying the same criteria to them as to full reports. Analysis with and without the results of the eligible incomplete reports should be done (Cook et al. 1993). When analyses including and excluding incomplete reports point to the same conclusion, the inference is strong. This is sensitivity analysis, which is discussed in detail in Chapter 15. If results differ when incomplete reports are included, possible explanations should be sought. This is exploration of heterogeneity, which is discussed in Chapter 14.

6.8.2   Inclusion of Unpublished Data

A decision must also be made whether to seek to identify data from studies that have not yet been published or presented anywhere. Although publication bias is a serious threat to the validity of meta-analysis, the practical difficulties of identifying unpublished studies are large, except when there is a register of studies. Schesselman (1997) points out the problems that arise even if unpublished studies can be identified. How, he asks, should the work be described and cited? What should be done if the investigators refuse to allow its publication? How can the information be scrutinized?

Expert opinions about inclusion of information that had never been published anywhere are mixed. Only 60% of the 214 authors of published meta-analyses and methodologists surveyed by Cook et al. (1993) believed that methodologically adequate material that had never been published anywhere should be included in a meta-analysis. This was despite the fact that these survey respondent were no doubt aware of the importance of publication bias as a source of bias in meta-analysis.

The difficulty of identifying unpublished studies, the practical problems in retrieving their results once identified, and the absence of a strong consensus among methodologists that unpublished studies should be included in a meta-analysis argues against attempts to identify and include unpublished studies as a standard procedure in meta-analysis. When registers exist to allow identification of analyzed, unpublished clinical trial results, they should be used.

6.8.3   Inclusion of Published Studies with Incomplete Data

Published reports of studies that meet all of the eligibility criteria for a meta-analysis may not present an estimate of effect size, and the raw data that would allow an estimate to be calculated may not be available in the study report. These studies cannot contribute to the summary estimate of effect. They are analogous to dropouts in a clinical trial, nonresponse in a case-control study, and loss to follow-up in a cohort study. Based on this analogy, it is probably best not to consider these studies ineligible for the meta-analysis. Rather, the study should be identified as eligible. It should appear in the table of eligible studies with a blank to indicate the absence of usable information. In this way, readers will recognize that these studies were not missed in the literature search. If the number of eligible studies that could not be used to estimate the summary measure of effect is large, the reader will be alerted to the possibility of bias.

6.9   CHOOSING ESTIMATES OF EFFECT WITHIN ELIGIBLE STUDIES

It is rare for studies to present one and only one estimate of effect. Crude and adjusted estimates, estimates of effect in several subgroups, and estimates of effect including and excluding subjects who did not comply with treatment or complete the trial are often reported. The presentation of numerous estimates of effect is a particular problem in reports of nonexperimental studies, because extensive multivariate analysis is often done.

EXAMPLE: Table 6-7 presents the estimates of relative risk of fatal cardiovascular disease in estrogen users from the Lipid Research Clinics study
(Bush et al. 1987), which is one of the studies included in a meta-analysis
of estrogen and coronary heart disease (Stampfer and Colditz 1991). The results of eight different multivariate analyses were described in the publication.
Although all of the estimates of the relative risk of disease in users of estrogen are less than 1.0 and all analyses yield the same overall conclusion about
the association of estrogen use with cardiovascular disease, it is uncertain
which estimate is the most appropriate one to include in the meta-analysis.

For a meta-analysis, one and only one estimate of effect from each eligible study
should be used in the calculation of the summary estimate of effect, because using
more than one would inappropriately weight studies with many estimates of effect.
When all of the studies are randomized, controlled trials, the estimate used in the
meta-analysis should be the estimate that is based on the "once randomized, always
analyzed" rule. Alternative analyses that use estimates that take into account loss
to follow-up or compliance can also be done, but these analyses should be interpreted cautiously, just as analyses of the data from the individual trials that are not
intention-to-treat analyses should be interpreted cautiously.

For nonexperimental studies, rules to choose from the estimates should be established before the analysis begins. The rules should be documented in the protocol. Table 6-8 lists some rules that could be used to choose from among effect
estimates in nonexperimental studies. The abstractor should be trained to apply the
rules, and the reliability of application of the rules should be evaluated.

When some of the variables included in a multivariate model are not true confounders, the model will be overfitted. The precision of the estimate of effect is

Table 6-7   Estimates of the relative risk of fatal cardiovascular disease in estrogen
users presented in one publication by Bush et al. (1987)

Estimated Relative Risk	95% Confidence Interval	Subgroup	Variables Adjusted
0.34	0.12–0.81	All	Age only
0.37	0.16–0.88	All	Age, blood pressure, smoking
0.44	0.19–1.03	All	Age, blood pressure, smoking, total cholesterol
			Age, blood pressure, smoking, LDL cholesterol, HDL choles-terol
0.44	0.19–1.03	All	Age, blood pressure, smoking, total cholesterol, education
0.47	0.20–1.12	All	Age, blood pressure, smoking, total cholesterol body mass index
0.21	0.00–0.51	Randomly selected	Age only
0.48	0.00–1.00	Elevated lipids	Age only
0.42	0.13–1.10	No history of heart disease	Age only

Table 6-8 Possible rules for choosing from among several estimates of effect for studies where more than one is presented

---

Choose the estimate adjusted only for age
Choose the estimate adjusted for age and a specified set of confounders that are widely agreed to be true confounders
Choose the "most adjusted" estimate; that is, the estimate with the largest number of variables in the model
Choose the estimate presented in the abstract

---

reduced in overfitted models, and the 95% confidence intervals for all variables in the model will be wider than for the appropriately fitted model. Many of the statistical methods for estimating effect in nonexperimental studies use estimates of the 95% confidence intervals to assign a weight to the study (see Chapter 7). Studies with wider confidence intervals are weighted less, and when the model is overfitted, the study will be weighted too little in the analysis. The same problem occurs when intermediate variables are included in the multivariate model. These problems should be taken into account when making rules about the choice of estimates to use in the meta-analysis. The model with the most variables may not be the best model.

> *EXAMPLE:* It is believed that part of the reason why estrogen use prevents coronary heart disease is because it lowers total cholesterol and LDL cholesterol and raises HDL cholesterol. Cholesterol is an intermediate variable. Table 6-7 shows that including total cholesterol or LDL cholesterol or HDL cholesterol in the multivariate model aimed at estimating the effect of estrogen on the risk of cardiovascular disease changes the estimated relative risk of disease in estrogen users from 0.37 to 0.44. The 95% confidence limit is wider when cholesterol is included in the model. Use of an estimate of relative risk from a model with cholesterol in a meta-analysis weights the study less than it would be if the estimate from the model without cholesterol is used.

6.10 STUDY QUALITY

6.10.1 Overview

An estimate of the effect of treatment in a clinical trial or the magnitude of association in a nonexperimental study is valid if it measures what it was intended to measure. Studies of poor quality may yield information that is not valid. Including studies with invalid information in a meta-analysis may render the conclusion of the meta-analysis invalid. For example, a study that calls itself a randomized trial but permits the investigator to tamper with the randomization by placing sicker patients selectively in the treatment arm will yield an estimate of the effect of treatment that is not valid. Including such a study in a meta-analysis would bias the summary estimate of the effect of treatment, and may lead to an invalid conclusion about the effect of the treatment. Similarly, a case-control study of cancer that includes patients whose diagnosis is not confirmed and who may not truly have had cancer will bias the estimate of the association of exposure with disease to the null and may lead to an invalid conclusion about the association of exposure with disease.

Studies that allow the investigator to tamper with the randomization or that enroll patients whose diagnosis is not confirmed are of lower quality than studies that protect against tampering and ensure the accuracy of diagnosis of disease. Taking the quality of studies into account in a meta-analysis has the potential to enhance the validity of meta-analysis because quality is implicitly a measure of validity. Rating study quality and using the ratings to interpret the meta-analysis assumes that studies of higher quality scores yield more valid information than studies with lower quality scores. At the extreme, a study that is excluded from the meta-analysis because it is of such low quality has a weight of zero and thus contributes no information to the meta-analysis (Laird and Mosteller 1990).

6.10.2 Assessing Study Quality and Using the Information

Attempts to measure study quality and use the measures of quality are generally carried out as follows. First, criteria that measure study quality are defined. A scoring system to weight the criteria is developed and a scale is constructed. A data collection form to record the assessments of the study in terms of the criteria is prepared. Information about the criteria is abstracted for each eligible study, and the study's quality score calculated. Last, the information on study quality is used to interpret the results of the meta-analysis.

The information on study quality can be used in a number of ways. Most straightforward is defining a threshold for quality and excluding from the analysis any study that does not exceed this threshold. As described above, this approach gives studies of poor quality no weight in the analysis.

The measure of quality can be used to define categories of study quality. Summary estimate of effects can then be calculated within each stratum.

> *EXAMPLE:* Steinberg et al. (1991) did a meta-analysis examining the risk of breast cancer in users of estrogen replacement therapy. Table 6-9 shows the mean proportional increase in the relative risk of breast cancer for each year of use of estrogen for case-control studies in three strata of quality score—high, moderate, and low. There was a statistically significant association of breast cancer risk with increasing years of estrogen use in studies with high quality scores, but no association or a negative association in studies with moderate and low scores. The authors interpreted these findings as suggestive of a true association of long duration of estrogen use with increased risk of breast cancer.

The quality scores can be used to weight the study-specific estimates of effect size.

Table 6-9   Estimates of the proportional increase in the relative risk of breast cancer per year of estrogen use by quality rating of study for 15 case-control studies eligible for meta-analysis

Reference	Quality Score	Mean Proportional Increase in Risk	95% Confidence Interval
High-Quality Score: 71–83			
Wingo et al. (1987)	83		
Bergkvist et al. (1989)	82		
Ross et al. (1980)	75		
Hoover et al. (1981)	72		
Hiatt et al. (1984)	71		
Summary estimate of proportional increase		0.040	0.030–0.050
Moderate-Quality Score: 40–57			
Nomura et al. (1986)	57		
Brinton et al. (1986)	51		
Kaufman et al. (1984)	45		
LeVecchia et al. (1986)	43		
Kelsey et al. (1981)	40		
Summary estimate of proportional increase		−0.008	−0.002–0.000
Low-Quality Score: 15–38			
Hulka et al. (1982)	38		
Jick et al. (1988)	38		
Ravnihar et al. (1979)	26		
Wynder et al. (1978)	25		
Sartwell et al. (1977)	15		
Summary estimate of proportional increase		0.006	0.000–0.012

Source: Steinberg et al. (1991); table references cited there.

EXAMPLE: Moher et al. (1998) selected 12 meta-analyses from a database of 491 meta-analyses of randomized trials. The quality of the report of each trial for each meta-analysis was assessed using a validated quality rating scale. The summary measure of effect was estimated by weighting each study by the product of the precision of the effect estimate and the quality score, instead of the precision of the estimate alone.

Using the measure of study quality to change the weight of the study in the meta-analysis reduces the contribution of any study with a score of less than 1.0 to the summary estimate of effect (Detsky et al. 1992). For example, weighting by a quality score of 0.5 makes the study equivalent to an unweighted study of half the sample size. When quality scores are used to adjust the weights, the confidence interval for the summary estimate of effect will be wider. Both of these consequences of weighting by study quality are intuitively appealing. It seems logical for lower quality studies to "count less" and for inclusion of poor quality studies to make the summary estimate of effect size more uncertain.

Detsky et al. (1992) state that the use of quality scores as weights is "without empiric support and somewhat arbitrary.'' They point out that the amount of widening of the confidence interval can be modified by multiplying the quality score by a constant. Further, there is no a priori reason why study quality should affect the Type I or Type II error rates, which is the consequence of widening the confidence interval (Detsky et al. 1992).

On balance, statistical weighting of studies by measures of quality is not recommended.

6.10.3 Other Limitations

Quality is difficult to define (Ioannidis and Lau 1998). Translating intuition about quality into a valid scoring system is a complex undertaking (Dickersin and Berlin 1992).

Quality rating is based on the report of the study, but the report of the study may not be an accurate measure of the truth about some elements of quality. For example, if a study report does not state that the patients were blinded to treatment, it does not necessarily mean that the study was unblinded. The study will likely be rated as lower in quality than a study in which the report is explicit about whether or not patients were blinded. The lower rating of quality may not be valid.

The standards for reporting details of the methods of studies are related to the era in which they were conducted. This trend will likely intensify as standards for reporting of studies are enforced by editors. Studies published more recently will tend to be rated higher in quality simply because of changes in the quality of reporting.

EXAMPLE: Figure 6-1 shows the quality score of each of the case-control studies included in the meta-analysis of Steinberg et al. (1991) of breast cancer in users of estrogen replacement by year of publication. There is a trend of increasing quality with more recent publication.

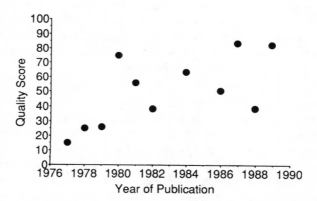

Figure 6-1   Average quality score of case-control studies of estrogen replacement therapy and breast cancer by year of publication. Data are from Steinberg et al. (1991).

The more recent studies may be noted as higher quality because of better reporting quality, but may not be truly better.

Bias is not easy to detect from reading published reports, since most authors do not draw attention to bias. If bias is not apparent based on the review of the information used to develop the quality score, the score cannot reflect poor quality.

It is especially challenging to develop scoring systems to measure the quality of nonexperimental studies. It is difficult to classify studies of different designs fairly in relation to one another. Cohort studies are not inherently of higher quality than case-control studies, and vice versa.

For nonexperimental studies, the main quality issue is bias and the possibility of uncontrolled confounding, which may be more of a problem with some studies than with others. It is inherently difficult to rate different sources of bias in relation to one another. For example, is recall bias worse than diagnostic bias? Is non-response bias worse than recall bias?

In addition to these theoretical problems with quality rating systems, there are practical problems with the implementation of the assessment of study quality. There is no consensus on a single instrument to measure quality, even for randomized trials. Moher et al. (1995) identified 25 different scales and 9 different checklists that had been used assess the quality of randomized trials in published meta-analyses.

The reliability of the quality rating scales in published meta-analyses is often not formally evaluated. Moher et al. (1995) found that less than half of scales used to rate the quality of randomized trials reported inter-rater reliability. Of those that reported on reliability, only half used an appropriate statistical measure of reliability.

6.10.4   Ways to Improve Quality

The most important advances in development of scales to rate quality will come from continued applications of psychometric principles to development of these scales. Standardization of reporting, which is becoming a reality for randomized trials (Begg et al. 1996), will lessen the contribution of poor reporting to poor perceived study quality. The real advances in meta-analysis will likely come from improvements in the source studies and not from improvements in the post hoc assessment of their quality or the quality of reporting (Ioannidis and Lau 1998). Well-conducted studies are essential to the quality of meta-analysis.

The development of valid and reliable measures of the quality of studies that are useful in assessing the validity of meta-analysis remains an illusive goal.

7

Statistical Methods in Meta-Analysis

This chapter introduces the issue of heterogeneity as it applies to the approach to meta-analysis of experimental and nonexperimental studies. It describes the statistical methods that are used most often to conduct meta-analysis of studies with dichotomous outcomes. Statistical methods for meta-analysis of data measured on a continuous scale are described in Chapter 8. Chapter 8 discusses statistical approaches to publication bias and other statistical issues in meta-analysis. Chapter 14 is devoted entirely to exploration of the reasons for heterogeneity as a goal of meta-analysis.

Section 7.1 discusses fixed-effects and random-effects models and the problem of statistical heterogeneity. Section 7.2 discusses the choice of a measure of effect in meta-analysis. Section 7.3 describes the Mantel-Haenszel method as a method for estimating a summary measure of effect size. Section 7.4 describes the Peto method. Section 7.5 describes a general variance-based method for estimated a summary measure of rate differences and rate ratios. Section 7.6 describes a general variance-based method for estimating a summary measure of effect size. Section 7.7 discusses statistical tests of heterogeneity. Section 7.8 describes the DerSimonian-Laird method for calculating summary estimates of effect based on a fixed effects model.

7.1 GOALS OF META-ANALYSIS AND THE PROBLEM OF HETEROGENEITY

7.1.1 Summary Estimates of Effect or Exploration of Heterogeneity?

Nonexperimental studies of the same topic are often diverse in their designs, the methods for collecting data, the definitions of endpoints, and the degree of control for bias and confounding. Calculating a single summary estimate of effect in the face of such diversity may give a misleading picture of the truth. There are no statistical methods that account for bias and confounding in the original studies. Exploring and accounting for heterogeneity has emerged as one of the principal, if not the principal, goal of meta-analysis of non-experimental studies.

Experimental studies of the same intervention are more homogeneous in their designs. Randomization minimizes bias and confounding as explanations of any differences between the groups being studied. Many experimental studies, especially modern studies of drugs and devices, are conducted under a rigorous set of guidelines and are monitored by the Food and Drug Administration and/or expert committees of external consultant scientists. For many topics, there is standardization of definitions of outcome variables among studies done by different groups, on different interventions, and even among studies done at different times. Because experimental studies are expensive and recruitment to experiments may be difficult, the situation in which there are many small experimental studies, all of which seek to answer the same question, occurs with increasing rarity. For these reasons, estimation of a summary estimate of effect is more defensible as a main goal of meta-analysis of experimental studies than as a goal of meta-analysis of nonexperimental studies.

On the other hand, even for randomized trials, there may differences between trials in, for example, patient selection, baseline disease severity, or follow-up between trials. The effect of the treatment may be different in different subgroups of patients. Exploration of heterogeneity is also a critically important component of meta-analysis of randomized trials (Thompson 1993; Lau et al. 1997).

Thompson (1993) has gone so far as to say that the guiding principle of meta-analysis should be to "investigate the influences of specific clinical differences between studies rather than to rely on a statistical test of heterogeneity." Because of its importance, the topic of exploration of heterogeneity is discussed in detail in a separate chapter, Chapter 14.

7.1.2 Fixed Versus Random Effects Methods and Models

The statistical methods used to combine study results when fixed effects are assumed differ from the methods used when random effects are assumed. The Mantel-Haenszel method (Mantel and Haenszel 1959), the Peto method (Yusuf et al. 1985), general variance-based methods (Wolf 1986), and the confidence interval methods described independently by Prentice and Thomas (1986) and Greenland (1987) are all methods based on the assumption of fixed effects. The methods described by DerSimonian and Laird (1986) are based on the assumption of random effects.

The choice of a method based on a fixed-effects or a random-effects model can have important consequences for conclusions based on the meta-analysis.

EXAMPLE: Berlin et al. (1989) compared the results of 22 meta-analyses using the Peto method (Yusuf et al. 1985), which is an analysis based on the assumption of fixed effects, with that using the DerSimonian-Laird method (DerSimonian and Laird 1986), which is based on the assumption of random effects. One of the meta-analyses they compared was a meta-analysis of randomized trials of interventions using nicotine gum or no gum as an adjunct to smoking cessation in patients seen by primary care physicians (Lam et al. 1987). An analysis of the eligible studies using the Peto method yielded a highly significant ($z = 2.83$, $p < 0.01$) association of treatment with better outcome, whereas the DerSimonian-Laird method yielded a nonsignificant result ($z = 1.58$, $p > 0.05$).

In an analysis based on a fixed-effects model, inference is conditional on the studies actually done. In an analysis based on a random-effects model, inference is based on the assumption that the studies used in the analysis are a random sample of some hypothetical population of studies.

Examples of results that seem counterintuitive for one method but not the other can be developed for both the fixed-effects model and the random-effects model.

EXAMPLE: Table 7-1 describes two hypothetical randomized clinical trials of the same treatment. In the first trial, 500 patients are treated with the active drug and 500 are given a placebo. The rate of cure in treated patients is 50%. In the patients given placebo, it is 10%. This difference is highly statistically significant ($p < 0.01$). The odds ratio for cure in treated patients is 9.0 (95% C.I. 6.40;–12.65). In the second trial, 1000 patients are treated with the active drug, and 1000 are given placebo. The rate of cure in treated patients is 15%. In the control patients, it is 10%. This difference is also highly statistically significant ($p < 0.01$). The odds ratio for cure in treated patients is 1.59 (95% C.I. 1.21–2.08).

Table 7-1 Hypothetical data showing how an analysis based on a random-effects model, but not one based on a fixed-effects model, gives a counterintuitive result

	Group				
Hypothetical Study	Active Treatment Cured/N of Subjects	Placebo Cured/N of Subjects	Odds of Cure in Treated Patients	95% Confidence Interval	p
1	250/500	50/500	9.0	6.40–12.65	<0.01
2	150/1000	100/1000	1.59	1.21–2.08	<0.01
	Summary estimate of odds of cure: fixed-effects model 3.27 (2.67–4.01); $p < 0.01$				
	Summary estimate of odds of cure: random-effects model 3.73 (0.58–24.07); $p > 0.05$				

The summary estimate of the odds ratio for cure in treated patients using the method of DerSimonian and Laird (1986), which is based on a random-effects model, is 3.73 (95% C.I. 0.58–24.07). The 95% confidence limit for the estimated effect of treatment includes 1.0. The conclusion based on the results of the meta-analysis is that treatment is not effective. This result is counterintuitive, because one would expect that calculating a summary estimate of effect for these two highly statistically significant results should lead to a conclusion that the treatment is effective. An analysis using the Mantel-Haenszel method, which is based on a fixed-effects model, gives an estimate of the odds ratio for cure of 3.27 (95% C.I. 2.67–4.01). The conclusion based on this analysis is that treatment is effective, as one would expect intuitively.

Fleiss and Gross (1991) give an example in which an analysis based on a fixed-effects model, but not an analysis based on a random-effects model, yields a result that is counterintuitive. Table 7-2 shows two hypothetical sets of studies. Each set has two studies. In the first set of studies, the odds ratios are 1.0 and 6.0. In the second set of studies, the odds ratios are 2.0 and 3.0. If the variance of the logarithm of the odds ratios for all four studies is the same and equal to 0.01, the summary odds ratio based on a Mantel-Haenszel analysis, which is based on a fixed-effects model, is 2.45 for both sets of studies. The confidence intervals are also identical (2.13–2.81). These findings are counterintuitive, because one would expect that the confidence interval for the first set of studies would be wider than for the second set of studies because the estimates of the odds ratio are more different. An analysis based on the method of DerSimonian and Laird (1986), which is based on a random-effects model, also yields a summary odds ratio of 2.45 for both sets of studies. The upper and lower bounds of the confidence intervals are 0.43 and 13.75

Table 7-2 Hypothetical data showing how an analysis based on the fixed-effects model, but not one based on a random-effects model, gives a counterintuitive result

Hypothetical Study	Odds Ratio	Variance of Logarithm Odds Ratio
Set 1		
1	1.0	0.01
2	6.0	0.01
Summary estimate of odds ratio: fixed-effects model 2.45 (2.13–2.81)		
95% C.I.	random-effects model 2.45 (0.43–13.75)	
Set 2		
1	2.0	0.01
2	3.0	0.01
Summary estimate of odds ratio: fixed-effects model 2.45 (2.13–2.81)		
95% C.I.	random-effects model 2.45 (1.65–3.60)	

Source: Fleiss and Gross (1991).

for the first set of studies and 1.65 and 3.60 for the second set of studies, which is in line with intuition about the amount of difference in the odds ratios.

The random-effects assumption means that the analysis addresses the question, "Will the treatment produce benefit 'on average'?" whereas the fixed-effects assumption means that the analysis addresses the question, "Did the treatment produce benefit on average in the studies at hand?" (Bailey 1987). The random-effects model is appropriate if the question is whether the treatment, or the risk factor, will have an effect. If the question is whether the treatment has caused an effect in the studies that have been done, then the fixed-effects model is appropriate.

Several statisticians have expressed a preference for the fixed-effects approach (Demets 1987; Peto 1987; Thompson and Pocock 1991); others favor the random-effects approach (Meier 1987; Fleiss and Gross 1991). Peto (1987) states that analysis using the random-effects model is "wrong" because it answers a question that is "abstruse and uninteresting." Thompson and Pocock (1991) describe as "peculiar" the premise of the random-effects model that studies are representative of some hypothetical population of studies. In contrast, Fleiss and Gross (1991) believe that question addressed by the fixed-effects model is less important than the one addressed by the random-effects model. Consideration of the differences in the questions addressed does not seem to resolve the question of which model to use.

7.1.3 Heterogeneity Is the Issue

In all the methods based on the assumption of fixed effect, the variance component of the summary estimate of effect size is composed only of terms for the within-study variance of each component study. The assumption of the random-effects model that studies are a random sample from some population of studies makes it necessary to include a between-study as well as a within-study component of variation in estimation of effect size and statistical significance (Demets 1987; Meier 1987; Lau et al. 1997).

Because the random-effects model incorporates a between-study component of variance, an analysis based on a random-effects model will generally yield a confidence interval that is at least as wide as, and usually is wider than, the confidence interval based on a fixed-effects model. When the confidence interval is used as a statistical test and the null hypothesis of no association is rejected if the confidence interval does not encompass 1.0 (which is not a recommended practice), an analysis based on a random-effects model will generally be more "conservative."

EXAMPLES: In a comparison of the results of meta-analyses using a method based on the assumption of fixed effects (the Peto method) and a method based on the assumption of random effects (the DerSimonian-Laird method) that was described earlier, Berlin et al. (1989) examined the results of 22 previously published meta-analyses of data from randomized trials. The two methods yielded the same conclusion about the statistical significance of the treatment compared with the control for 19 of the 22 meta-analyses, as shown in Table 7-3. For three meta-analyses, the method based on the fixed-effects model was statistically significant, whereas the method based on the random-effects model was not statistically significant. In this example, there

Table 7-3   Number of statistically significant results for 22
published meta-analyses analyzed using the Peto method
(fixed-effects model) and the DerSimonian-Laird method
(random-effects model)

	Fixed-Effects Model	
Random-Effects Model	Significant	Not Significant
Significant	8	0
Not significant	3	11

Source: Berlin et al. (1989).

were no cases where the random-effects analysis yielded a statistically significant result and the fixed-effects analysis did not.

Poole and Greenland (1998) give an example in which estimates of effect based
on a random-effects model but not a fixed-effects model leads to rejection of the
null hypothesis of no association. Thus, meta-analyses based on the random-effects
model are not always conservative.

   As the between-study variance becomes large (i.e., when there is heterogeneity),
the between-study variance term will dominate the weights assigned to the study
using the random-effects model, and large and small studies will tend to be
weighted equally. In this situation, the results of an analysis based on the fixed-
effects model, which weights studies according to their sample size, and the
random-effects model may differ considerably, as shown in the hypothetical example given above. When there is not much heterogeneity, the fixed-effects and
the random-effects models will both weight studies according to sample size and
will yield results that are essentially identical.

   EXAMPLE: In the Berlin et al. (1989) comparison of the Peto method,
   based on a fixed-effects model, and the DerSimonian-Laird method, based
   on a random-effects model, there were 14 meta-analyses for which there was
   no statistical evidence of heterogeneity. For these 14 meta-analyses, Table
   7-4 shows that there was complete agreement in the conclusions about statistical significance for the two methods.

Thus, while it is generally agreed that the questions addressed by analysis based
on the fixed-effects model and based on the random-effects model are different
(Bailey 1987), it has also been shown that differences in the results of meta-analysis
based on fixed-effects and random-effects models arise only when the study results
are statistically heterogeneous. Use of a random effects model does not ''control
for,'' ''adjust for,'' or ''explain away'' the heterogeneity. Greenland and Salvan
(1990) and Thompson and Pocock (1991) point out that the choice of a fixed-
effects model and a random-effects model is secondary to the examination of the
factors that contribute to heterogeneity. If studies are not statistically heterogeneous,

Table 7-4 Number of statistically significant results for 14 published meta-analyses without statistical evidence of heterogeneity analyzed using the Peto method (fixed-effects model) and the DerSimonian- Laird method (random-effects model)

	Fixed-Effects Model	
Random-Effects Model	Significant	Not Significant
Significant	5	0
Not significant	0	9

Source: Berlin et al. (1989).

then the choice between the fixed-effects model and the random-effects model is unimportant, as the models will yield results that are identical.

Greenland and Salvan (1990) argue that one shouldn't calculate a single summary estimate of effect for the disparate study results at all. Most agree that the reasons for the heterogeneity should be examined (Thompson and Pocock 1991; Thompson 1994; Colditz et al. 1995; Lau et al. 1997).

In this chapter, methods that allow comparative data to be analyzed using the random-effects model as well as methods based on fixed effects are presented. However, use of the random-effects model is not considered to be a defensible solution to the problem of heterogeneity. Meta-analysis should not be used exclusively to arrive at an average or ''typical'' value for effect size. Meta-analysis is not simply a statistical method but rather a multicomponent approach for making sense of information.

7.2 CHOICE OF EFFECT MEASURE

In randomized trials and cohort studies, the effect of treatment can be estimated as a difference in the rates of disease between the treatment (or exposed) group and the control (or unexposed) group, as the ratio of disease rates measured as incidence density (i.e., with denominators of person-time), as the ratio of rates measured as cumulative incidence (i.e., with denominators of person), or as an odds ratio. In population-based case-control studies, effect can be estimated as an odds ratio or as an attributable risk. It is usual to measure effect using either the odds ratio or a rate ratio in nonexperimental studies. Rate differences are more often used to measure effect in randomized trials. The advantages and disadvantages of ratio and difference measures of effect are discussed by Rothman (1986). These advantages and disadvantages should be considered carefully before choosing a measure of effect for the meta-analysis when more than one effect measure is possible.

The analytic method and the specific formulas used in a meta-analysis are affected by the choice of effect measure. Table 7-5 summarizes the methods that can be used to calculate a summary estimate of effect size according to the model

Table 7-5 Methods that can be used in meta-analysis according to the underlying model assumption and the type of effect measure for which the method is appropriate

Model Assumption	Methods	Effect Measures
Fixed effects	Mantel-Haenszel	Ratio (typically odds ratio; can be applied to rate ratio and risk ratio)
	Peto	Ratio (approximates the odds ratio)
	General variance-based	Ratio (all types) and difference
Random effects	DerSimonian-Laird	Ratio (all types) and difference

(fixed effects or random effects) and the choice of effect measure. The methods are described in detail in subsequent sections.

7.3 MANTEL-HAENSZEL METHOD

7.3.1 Overview

The Mantel-Haenszel method (Mantel and Haenszel 1959) is a well-known method for calculating a summary estimate of effect across strata. Since studies identified for a meta-analysis are strata, the Mantel-Haenszel method is an appropriate method for analyzing data for a meta-analysis. The method is based on the assumption of fixed effect. It can be used when the measure of effect is a ratio measure, typically an odds ratio. A summary chi-square statistic (Mantel 1963), the variance of the summary effect measure (Robins, Greenland, Breslow 1986), and a test for homogeneity of effect size across strata (Mantel, Brown, Byar 1977) have all been described.

If the data from a study are arranged as shown in Table 7-6 with table notation as shown, Table 7-7 presents the formulas for computing a summary odds ratio using the Mantel-Haenszel method. Kleinbaum, Kupper, and Morgenstern (1982) give formulas that would allow the Mantel-Haenszel method to be applied when data are of the incidence density or cumulative incidence type and the summary estimate of effect is a rate ratio or a risk ratio.

Table 7-6 Arrangement of data and table notation for application of Mantel-Haenszel and Peto methods

	Exposed[a]	Not Exposed[b]	Total
Diseased	a_i	b_i	g_i
Not diseased	c_i	d_i	h_i
Total	e_i	f_i	n_i

[a] Or treated.

[b] Or not treated.

Table 7-7 Mantel-Haenszel method: Formulas to estimate the summary odds ratio and 95% confidence interval for the summary odds ratio

Summary odds ratio

$$OR_{mh} = \frac{\text{sum}(\text{weight}_i \times OR_i)}{\text{sum weight}_i}$$

$$OR_i = \frac{(a_i \times d_i)}{(b_i \times c_i)}$$

$$\text{weight}_i = \frac{1}{\text{variance}_i}$$

$$\text{variance}_i = \frac{n_i}{(b_i \times c_i)}$$

95% confidence interval

$$95\% \text{ C.I.} = e^{\ln OR_{mh} \pm 1.96\sqrt{\text{variance } OR_{mh}}}$$

where variance OR_{mh} is calculated as shown in the appendix to this chapter using the method of Robins, Greenland, and Breslow (1986)

7.3.2 Application of the Mantel-Haenszel Method

EXAMPLE: Table 7-8 shows data from two case-control studies of passive smoking and lung cancer that have been included in a meta-analysis of this topic done by the United States Environmental Protection Agency (1991) and others. Both studies were confined to women. In both studies, cases and controls were matched on age. The odds ratio for lung cancer in women exposed to passive smoking was 1.31 in the first study (Garfinkel, Auerbach, Joubert 1985) and 1.65 in the second (Lam et al. 1987). The Mantel-Haenszel

Table 7-8   Data from two matched case-control studies of lung cancer and passive smoking in women

	Exposed	Not Exposed	Totals
Study 1. Garfinkel, Auerbach, and Joubert (1985)			
Cases	90	44	134
Controls	245	157	402
Totals	335	201	536
Odds ratio = 1.31 95% C.I. (0.85–2.02)			
Study 2. Lam et al. (1987)			
Cases	115	84	199
Controls	152	183	335
Totals	267	267	534
Odds ratio = 1.65 95% C.I. (1.14–2.39)			

method is used to estimate a summary odds ratio and its 95% confidence interval for these data as follows:

1. Estimate the variance of the odds ratios for each study where

$$\text{variance}_i = \frac{n_i}{(b_i \times c_i)}$$

Study 1: $\text{variance}_1 = \dfrac{536}{(44 \times 245)} = 0.050$

Study 2: $\text{variance}_2 = \dfrac{534}{(84 \times 152)} = 0.042$

2. Calculate the weights for each study where

$$\text{weight}_i = \frac{1}{\text{variance}_i}$$

Study 1: $\text{weight}_1 = \dfrac{1}{\text{variance}_1} = \dfrac{1}{0.050} = 20.00$

Study 2: $\text{weight}_2 = \dfrac{1}{\text{variance}_2} = \dfrac{1}{0.042} = 23.81$

3. Calculate the product of the weights and the ORs:

Study 1: $\text{product}_1 = \text{odds ratio}_1 \times \text{weight}_1 = 20.00 \times 1.31 = 26.20$
Study 2: $\text{product}_2 = \text{odds ratio}_2 \times \text{weight}_2 = 23.81 \times 1.65 = 39.29$

4. Calculate the sum of the weights:

sum of weights $= 20.00 + 23.81 = 43.81$

5. Calculate the sum of the product of the weights and the ORs:

sum of products $= 26.20 + 39.29 = 65.49$

6. Estimate the OR_{mh} by dividing the sum of the products by sum of the weights:

summary $\text{OR}_{mh} = \dfrac{65.49}{43.81} = 1.49$

7. Estimate the variance of OR_{mh} using the method of Robins, Greenland, and Breslow (1986) using the formulas in the appendix to this chapter:

variance $\text{OR}_{mh} = 0.019$

8. Estimate the 95% confidence interval where

CI $= e^{\ln \text{ OR} \pm (1.96 \times \sqrt{\text{variance OR}_{mh}})}$
upper bound $= e^{0.399 + (1.96 \times \sqrt{0.019})} = e^{0.399 + \, 0.270} = e^{0.669} = 1.95$
lower bound $= e^{0.399 - (1.96 \times \sqrt{0.019})} = e^{0.399 + \, 0.270} = e^{0.129} = 1.14$

7.3.3 Strengths and Limitations

A number of factors argue for the use of the Mantel-Haenszel method when it is applicable and the data are available. First, the test based on the Mantel-Haenszel chi-square has optimal statistical properties, being the uniformly most powerful test (Radhakrishna 1965). Second, the Mantel-Haenszel estimate of effect equals one only when the Mantel-Haenszel chi-square is equal to zero, which provides a mathematical connection of the effect estimate with the summary statistic. Third, a number of widely available computer programs (e.g., EPIINFO, EGRET, STATXACT) include programs to apply the method.

There are some problems with the Mantel-Haenszel approach that limit its usefulness in practice. First, application requires that data to complete a 2 × 2 table of outcome by treatment (or exposure by disease) for each study be available. If data that would allow construction of a 2 × 2 table for a study are unavailable, the study must be excluded. Exclusion has the potential to result in bias.

More important, the Mantel-Haenszel approach ignores confounding that is not taken into account in the design of the study. In randomized trials and in case-control studies that have been matched for confounders, as in the example, the failure of the method to control for confounding is not a problem. In a meta-analysis where some studies are case-control studies that are unmatched for age, or only coarsely matched for age, age differences between cases and controls will not be taken into account in the summary estimate of effect using this method. Highly misleading conclusions can result in this situation and in any other situation where the result of an analysis controlling for confounding is different from the crude result.

7.4 PETO METHOD

7.4.1 Overview

The Peto method (Yusuf et al. 1985) is a modification of the Mantel-Haenszel method. Like the Mantel-Haenszel method, it is based on a fixed-effects model. It is an alternative method for calculating a summary measure of effect when the effect measure of interest is a ratio measure. Like the Mantel-Haenszel method, it is computationally simple. It has been used frequently in meta-analyses of randomized trials.

Table 7-9 shows the formulas for using the Peto method for combining data to estimate a summary measure of effect, which will be called the Peto odds ratio (OR_p). The formulas are based on an arrangement of data and table notation that was shown in Table 7-6.

7.4.2 Application of the Peto Method

EXAMPLE: Table 7-10 presents data from the two largest randomized trials of antiplatelet treatment for patients with a transient ischemic attack or ischemic stroke identified by the Antiplatelet Trialists' Collaboration (1988) as

Table 7-9   Peto method: Formulas to estimate the summary odds ratio and 95% confidence interval for the summary odds ratio Summary odds ratio

---

Summary odds ratio

$$OR_p = e^{\text{sum}(O_i - E_i)/\text{sum variance}_i}$$

or

$$\ln OR_p = \frac{\text{sum}(O_i - E_i)}{\text{sum variance}_i}$$

$$E_i = \frac{(e_i \times g_i)}{n_i}$$

$$\text{variance}_i = \frac{(E_i \times f_i \times h_i)}{n_i \times (n_i - 1)}$$

95% confidence interval

$$95\% \text{ C.I.} = e^{\ln OR_p \pm 1.96/\sqrt{\text{sum variance}_i}}$$

where the variance$_i$ are calculated as shown above

---

eligible for their meta-analysis. In the first study, 14.6% of the patients treated with active drug had an important vascular event (first myocardial infarction, stroke, or vascular death) compared with 21.1% in the control group. In the second study, 22.1% of patients in the active treatment group had an important vascular event compared with 25.1% in the control group. The Peto method is used to estimate a summary odds ratio and its 95% confidence interval for these data as follows:

1. Calculate the expected number of events in the treatment group for each study where

Table 7-10   Data from two randomized trials of antiplatelet therapy for treatment of transient ischemic attack or stroke

	Treatment	Control	Total
Study 1. European Stroke Prevention Study Group (1987)			
Events[a]	182	264	446
Nonevents	1,068	986	2,054
Total	1,250	1,250	2,500
Odds ratio = 0.64			
Study 2. United Kingdom Transient Ischemic Attack Aspirin Trial			
Events[a]	348	204	552
Nonevents	1,273	610	1,883
Total	1,621	814	2,434
Odds ratio = 0.82			

[a] Important vascular events (first myocardial infarction, stroke, vascular death).

Source: Antiplatelet Trialists' Collaboration (1988); table references cited there.

$$E_i = \frac{(e_i \times g_i)}{n_i}$$

Study 1: $E_1 = \frac{(1250 \times 446)}{2500} = 223.0$

Study 2: $E_2 = \frac{(1621 \times 552)}{2435} = 367.5$

2. Calculate the difference in the observed and expected number of events in the treatment group for each study:

   Study 1: $O_1 - E_1 = 182 - 223.0 = -41.0$
   Study 2: $O_2 - E_2 = 348 - 367.5 = -19.5$

3. Estimate the variance of the observed minus expected for each study where

$$variance_i = \frac{(E_i \times f_i \times h_i)}{n_i(n_i - 1)}$$

   Study 1: $variance_1 = \frac{(223.0 \times 1250 \times 2054)}{(2500 \times 2499)} = 91.6$

   Study 2: $variance_2 = \frac{(367.5 \times 814 \times 1883)}{(2435 \times 2434)} = 95.0$

4. Calculate the sum of the values of observed minus expected:

   sum $(O_i - E_i) = -41.0 + -19.5 = -60.5$

5. Calculate the sum of the variances:

   sum $variance_i = 91.6 + 95.0 = 186.6$

6. Estimate the natural logarithm of the OR_p by dividing the sum of the sum of observed minus expected (result of step 4) by the sum of variances (result of step 5):

$$\ln OR_p = \frac{-60.5}{186.6} = -0.32$$

7. Estimate the summary odds ratio by taking e to the power of the result of step 6:

   $OR_p = e^{-0.32} = 0.72$

8. Estimate the 95% confidence interval where

$$CI = e^{\ln OR_p \pm 1.96 \div \sqrt{sum\ of\ variance_i}}$$

   upper bound $= e^{-0.32+0.14} = 0.84$
   lower bound $= e^{-0.32-0.14} = 0.63$

7.4.3 Strengths and Limitations

The Peto method, like the Mantel-Haenszel method, requires data to complete a 2 $\times$ 2 table for every study to be included in the meta-analysis. If data to complete a 2×2 table are not available, the study must be excluded. Exclusion has the potential to cause bias. The Peto method will rarely be useful in the analysis of study-level data from nonexperimental studies because appropriate data from every eligible study are rarely available. Furthermore, like the Mantel-Haenszel method, the Peto method cannot incorporate confounding that is not taken care of by design. Last, the Peto method can yield a biased summary estimate of effect when some of the individual studies are unbalanced (Greenland and Salvan 1990; Fleiss 1993). Greenland and Salvan (1990) recommend against using the Peto method to analyze data from nonexperimental studies. For nonexperimental studies, the advantages of the Peto method over the Mantel-Haenszel method in terms of computational simplicity probably do not outweigh the disadvantage due to the possibility of bias, especially since it has the same limitations as the Mantel-Haenszel method (Greenland and Salvan 1990).

7.5 GENERAL VARIANCE-BASED METHODS

7.5.1 Overview

The Mantel-Haenszel method and the Peto method generally apply to estimation of effects measured on a ratio scale. When the goal of the meta-analysis is to derive a summary estimate of a difference measure, the following general, variance-based method applies:

$$RD_s = \frac{\text{sum}(w_i \times RD_i)}{\text{sum } w_i}$$

where

$$w_i = \frac{1}{\text{variance}_i}$$

Here, RD_s is the summary estimate of the rate difference, w_i is the weight assigned to the ith study, RD_i is the rate difference from the ith study, and variance$_i$ is an estimate of the variance of the rate difference in the ith study (Prentice and Thomas 1986; Wolf 1986; Greenland 1987). The formulas for estimating the variance of the difference in two rates differ according to whether the data to be summarized are cumulative incidence or incidence density data. These formulas are provided in Kleinbaum, Kupper, and Morgenstern (1982).

A 95% confidence interval for an estimate of effect derived from the preceding general equation can be estimated as follows:

$$95\% \text{ CI} = RD_s \pm 1.96 \times \sqrt{\text{variance}_s}$$

where

$$\text{variance}_s = \frac{1}{\text{sum weight}_i}$$

When effect size is measured as an incidence density ratio (i.e., as the ratio of two incidence rates measured with person-time in the denominator) or as a risk ratio (i.e., as the ratio of two incidence rates measured as cumulative incidence), the general variance-based method given above can be applied after logarithmic transformation as follows:

$$\ln RR_s = \frac{sum(w_i \times \ln RR_i)}{sum \ w_i}$$

where

$$w_i = \frac{1}{variance_i}$$

Formulas to estimate the variance of the incidence density ratio and the risk ratio are also provided by Kleinbaum, Kupper, and Morgenstern (1982). A 95% confidence interval for the summary ratio is estimated as

$$95\% \ C.I. = e^{RR_s \pm 1.96 \times \sqrt{variance_s}}$$

where

$$variance_s = \frac{1}{sum \ weight_i}$$

7.5.2   Application of the General Variance-Based Method

7.5.2.1   Rate Difference with Cumulative Incidence Data

EXAMPLE: The data from the two studies of antiplatelet treatment shown in Table 7-10 can be expressed as the difference in the rates of disease in the active treatment group and the control group. In the first study, the difference in the rate of important vascular events between the treated and untreated patients was 6.5 events per 100 (0.065). In the second study, the difference in rates was 3.6 events per 100 (0.036). The general variance-based method can be used to estimate a summary measure of the rate difference and a 95% confidence interval as follows:

1. Estimate the variance of the rate difference for each study where

$$variance \ RD_i = \frac{(g_i \times h_i)}{(e_i \times f_i \times n_i)}$$

Study 1: $variance_1 = \dfrac{(446 \times 2054)}{(1250 \times 1250 \times 2500)} = 0.00023$

Study 2: $variance_2 = \dfrac{(552 \times 1883)}{(1621 \times 814 \times 2435)} = 0.00032$

2. Estimate weight for each study where

$$\text{weight}_i = \frac{1}{\text{variance}_i}$$

Study 1: $\text{weight}_1 = \dfrac{1}{0.00023} = 4347.8$

Study 2: $\text{weight}_2 = \dfrac{1}{0.00032} = 3125.0$

3. Calculate the sum of the weights:

sum of weights $= 4347.8 + 3125.0 = 7472.8$

4. Calculate the product of the weights and the RDs:

Study 1: $\text{product}_1 = \text{weight}_1 \times \text{RD}_1 = 4347.8 \times 0.065 = 282.6$
Study 2: $\text{product}_2 = \text{weight}_2 \times \text{RD}_2 = 3125.0 \times 0.036 = 112.5$

5. Calculate the sum of the product of weights and rate differences:

sum of products $= 282.6 + 112.5 = 395.1$

6. Divide the sum of products (result of step 5) by the sum of weights (result of step 3):

$$\text{RD}_s = \frac{395.1}{7472.8} = 0.053 \qquad \text{or} \quad 5.3 \text{ deaths per } 100$$

7. Estimate the 95% confidence interval where

$$\text{CI} = \text{RD}_s \pm 1.96 \times \sqrt{\text{variance}_s} \qquad \text{and} \quad \text{variance}_s = \frac{1}{\text{sum weight}_i}$$

lower bound $= 0.053 - \left(1.96 \times \sqrt{\left(\dfrac{1}{7472.8} \right)} \right) = 0.05 - 0.023 = 0.030$

upper bound $= 0.053 + \left(1.96 \times \sqrt{\left(\dfrac{1}{7472.8} \right)} \right) = 0.05 + 0.023 = 0.076$

7.5.2.2 *Rate Ratio with Cumulative Incidence Data*

EXAMPLE: The data in Table 7-10 from the randomized trials of antiplatelet treatment could have been analyzed to derive an estimate of the ratio of the rates of important vascular disease in the treated and untreated. In the first study, the ratio of the rate of important vascular disease in the treated group compared with the control group is 0.69. In the second study, it is 0.86. The summary measure of the rate ratio and its 95% confidence limit are estimated as follows:

1. Estimate the variance of the rate ratio where

$$\text{variance RR}_i = \frac{(h_i \times n_i)}{(e_i \times f_i \times g_i)}$$

Study 1: $\text{variance}_1 = \dfrac{(2054 \times 2500)}{(1250 \times 1250 \times 446)} = 0.0074$

Study 2: $\text{variance}_2 = \dfrac{(1883 \times 2435)}{(1621 \times 814 \times 552)} = 0.0063$

2. Calculate the weights for each study where

$$\text{weight}_i = \frac{1}{\text{variance}_i}$$

Study 1: $\text{weight}_1 = \dfrac{1}{\text{variance}_1} = \dfrac{1}{0.0074} = 135.1$

Study 2: $\text{weight}_2 = \dfrac{1}{\text{variance}_2} = \dfrac{1}{0.0063} = 158.7$

3. Calculate the sum of weights:

   sum of weights $= 135.1 + 158.7 = 293.8$

4. Calculate the natural logarithm of each rate ratio:

   Study 1: $\ln \text{RR}_1 = \ln 0.69 = -0.371$
   Study 2: $\ln \text{RR}_2 = \ln 0.86 = -0.151$

5. Calculate the product of the weights and the natural logarithm the rate ratios:

   Study 1: $\text{product}_1 = \text{weight}_1 \times \ln \text{RR}_1 = 135.1 \times (-0.371) = -50.12$
   Study 2: $\text{product}_2 = \text{weight}_2 \times \ln \text{RR}_2 = 158.7 \times (-0.151) = -23.96$

6. Calculate the sum of the product of weights and the natural logarithm of the rate ratios:

   sum of products $= -50.12 + (-23.96) = -74.08$

7. Calculate natural logarithm of the summary RR where

$$\ln \text{RR}_s = \frac{\text{sum of products}}{\text{sum of weights}}$$

$$\ln \text{RR}_s = \frac{-74.08}{298.8} = -0.248$$

8. Estimate the summary measure of effect by taking e to the power of the result of step 7:

$$\text{RR}_s = e^{-0.248} = 0.78$$

9. Estimate the 95% confidence interval where

$$CI = e^{\ln \text{ summary } RR \pm 1.96 \times \sqrt{\text{variance}_s}} \quad \text{and} \quad \text{variance}_s = \frac{1}{\text{sum weight}_i}$$

$$\text{lower bound} = e^{-0.248 - 1.96 \times \sqrt{1 \div 293.8}} = e^{-0.362} = 0.70$$
$$\text{upper bound} = e^{-0.248 + 1.96 \times \sqrt{1 \div 293.8}} = e^{-0.134} = 0.87$$

This result can be compared with the result based on the Peto method based on the same data, which yielded an estimated odds ratio 0.72 (95% C.I. 0.63–0.84).

7.5.3 Strengths and Limitations

These general variance-based methods allow meta-analysis with rate difference as the measure of effect. When the measure of effect of interest is an odds ratio, these methods have no obvious advantages over the Mantel-Haenszel method. Estimating the variances and the weights for each study is computationally more burdensome. The general variance-based approach is the basis for the confidence interval approach, a widely applicable procedure for summarizing data from nonexperimental studies that is described in the following section.

7.6 GENERAL VARIANCE-BASED METHODS THAT USE CONFIDENCE INTERVALS

7.6.1 Overview

The problem with all of the previously described methods is that they require construction of 2×2 tables for every study in the meta-analysis and they ignore confounding. Prentice and Thomas (1986) and Greenland (1987) independently described a general variance-based method for meta-analysis where the effect measures are ratio measures that require only information on each study's estimate of relative risk and its 95% confidence interval. The estimate of the 95% confidence interval from each study is used to estimate the variance of each study's effect measure. The following general formulas apply:

$$\ln RR_s = \frac{\text{sum}(w_i \times \ln RR_i)}{\text{sum } w_i}$$

where

$$w_i = \frac{1}{\text{variance } RR_i}$$

The RR_i are estimates of relative risk and may have been measured as odds ratios, rate ratios, or risk ratios.

The formula for estimating variance from the 95% confidence interval given by Prentice and Thomas (1986) is

$$\text{variance RR}_i = \left[\frac{\ln (RR_i \div RR_l)}{1.96} \right]^2$$

or, equivalent when the confidence interval is symmetric (i.e., when $RR_i \div RR_l = RR_u \div RR_i$),

$$\text{variance RR}_i = \left[\frac{\ln (RR_u \div RR_i)}{1.96} \right]^2$$

where RR_i is the estimate of the relative risk in the ith study, RR_u is the upper bound of the 95% confidence interval for that study, and RR_l is the lower bound of the 95% confidence interval for that study

A 95% confidence limit for the estimated relative risk is calculated as

$$95\% \ CI = e^{\ln \ RR_s \pm 1.96 \times \sqrt{\text{variance}_s}}$$

and

$$\text{variance}_s = \frac{1}{\text{sum weight}_i}$$

7.6.2 Application of Confidence Interval Methods

EXAMPLE: A summary estimate of the relative risk of lung cancer and environmental tobacco smoke can be estimated using the confidence interval approach for tha data from Table 7-8. The confidence interval approach is used to estimate a summary relative risk and a 95% confidence interval as follows:

1. Take the natural logarithm of the estimated relative risk for each study:

   Study 1: $\ln RR_1 = \ln 1.31 = 0.270$
   Study 2: $\ln RR_2 = \ln 1.65 = 0.501$

2. Estimate the variance of the relative risk for each based on the estimated relative risk for that study and on the lower bound of the 95% confidence interval for that study where

$$\text{variance RR}_i = \left[\frac{\ln (RR_i \div RR_l)}{1.96} \right]^2$$

$$\text{Study 1: variance}_1 = \left[\frac{\ln (1.31 \div 0.85)}{1.96} \right]^2 = 0.049$$

$$\text{Study 2: variance}_2 = \left[\frac{\ln (1.65 \div 1.14)}{1.96} \right]^2 = 0.036$$

3. Estimate the weight of each study where

$$\text{weight}_i = \frac{1}{\text{variance}_i}$$

Study 1: $\text{weight}_1 = \dfrac{1}{\text{variance}_1} = \dfrac{1}{0.049} = 20.41$

Study 2: $\text{weight}_2 = \dfrac{1}{\text{variance}_2} = \dfrac{1}{0.036} = 27.78$

4. Calculate the sum of the weights:

sum of weights = 20.41 + 27.78 = 48.19

5. Calculate the product of the weight and the natural logarithm of the estimated relative risk:

Study 1: $\text{product}_1 = 20.41 \times 0.270 = 5.511$
Study 2: $\text{product}_2 = 27.78 \times 0.501 = 13.918$

6. Calculate the sum of the products:

sum of products = 5.511 + 13.918 = 19.429

7. Estimate the summary measure of effect where

$\text{RR}_s = e^{(\text{sum of products} \div \text{sum of weights})}$
$\text{RR}_s = e^{19.429 \div 48.19} = e^{0.403} = 1.50$

8. Estimate 95% confidence interval for the summary measure of relative risk where

$\text{C.I.} = e^{\ln\ \text{RR} \pm (1.96 \times \sqrt{\text{variance}_s})}$ and $\text{variance}_s = \dfrac{1}{\text{sum weight}_i}$

upper bound $e^{0.403 + (1.96 \times \sqrt{1 \div 48.19})} = e^{0.685} = 1.98$
lower bound $e^{0.403 - (1.96 \times \sqrt{1 \div 48.19})} = e^{0.121} = 1.13$

The summary estimate of the relative risk of lung cancer based on the Mantel-Haenszel method was 1.49 (95% C.I. 1.13–1.98).

7.6.3   Handling Studies with Missing Confidence Intervals

Sometimes a study will not present an estimate of a 95% confidence interval. A confidence interval can occasionally be estimated from the data provided in the study report. It is sometimes worthwhile to contact the investigator to obtain the information that would allow the confidence interval to be estimated if the data to do so are not provided in the study report. Formulas to estimate confidence intervals for a variety of study designs and data presentations are given by Kleinbaum, Kupper, and Morgenstern (1982).

It is important to be sure that the confidence interval estimated from the raw data presented in a paper is correct. Errors in estimation of confidence intervals can lead to substantial bias in the summary estimate of relative risk.

EXAMPLE: Data from case-control studies of the risk of ovarian cancer in women who had a family history of ovarian cancer were abstracted from case-control studies of ovarian cancer in order to do a meta-analysis (Kerlikowke et al. 1992). The 95% confidence intervals for the estimated relative risk of ovarian cancer in women with a family history of ovarian cancer had not been calculated in some of the studies, but the raw data necessary to make these calculations were presented in all of them. Table 7-11 shows the 95% confidence intervals for the studies as they were originally calculated, based on the raw data. It also shows the summary estimate of the relative risk of ovarian cancer in women with a family history of ovarian cancer based on the estimates shown in the table. The summary estimate is 6.52 (95% C.I. 5.10–8.33). One study, study 3, had a very high weight in the analysis because the confidence interval was narrow. The fact that the study carried so much weight led to recalculation of the 95% confidence interval for the study, and it was found that a mistake in the original calculation had been made. The summary estimate of relative risk based on the correctly calculated intervals, also shown in Table 7-11, is 4.52 (95% C.I. 1.13–3.10).

Greenland (1987) suggests ways to use information on p values to estimate 95% confidence intervals when the p value is the only information available in the study report. These methods are test-based methods and they should be applied recognizing the limitations and problems with test-based methods (Kleinbaum, Kupper, Morgenstern 1982; Greenland 1987). When a p value has been used to estimate the confidence interval for a study, it may be wise to do the meta-analysis with and without the study to determine whether the conclusion is dependent on inclusion, a kind of sensitivity analysis.

7.6.4 Strengths and Limitations

Because the variance estimates are based on the adjusted measure of effect and on the 95% confidence interval for the adjusted measure, the confidence interval methods do not ignore confounding. Since most modern studies present confidence

Table 7-11 Estimated relative risk of ovarian cancer in women with a family history of ovarian cancer based on incorrect calculation of confidence interval for study 3

Study	Estimated Relative Risk	Incorrect 95% Confidence Interval	Correct 95% Confidence Interval
1	9.25	0.49–173.1	0.49–173.1
2	18.20	4.8–59.0	4.8–69.0
3	11.32	8.2–18.3[a]	0.6–211.3
4	3.6	1.8–7.2	1.8–7.2
5	3.3	1.1–9.4	1.1–9.4
6	1.90	1.1–3.6	1.1–3.6

Summary relative risk and incorrect C.I.: 6.52 5.10–8.33
Summary relative risk and correct C.I.: 4.52 1.13–3.10

[a] Incorrect confidence interval.

intervals for estimates of relative risk, or they can be estimated from data in a publication when the authors have not done so themselves, few studies are excluded because of missing data.

7.7 STATISTICAL TESTS OF HOMOGENEITY

The problem of lack of homogeneity was discussed in Section 7.2. Table 7-12 gives the formulas that can be used to calculate a statistic to test the hypothesis that the effect sizes are equal in all of the studies. These tests are variously referred to as tests of homogeneity and tests of heterogeneity. They are called tests of homogeneity here.

All the formulas follow the general pattern of testing the sum of the weighted difference between the summary effect measure and the measure of effect from each study. The statistic calculated by these formulas is referred to the chi-square distribution, although it usually is called Q. The number of degrees of freedom of Q is equal to the number of studies minus one.When the p value for the test of homogeneity exceeds some critical value of alpha (usually 0.05), the hypothesis of homogeneity is rejected. In rejecting the hypothesis that the studies are homogeneous, one can conclude that the studies are not measuring an effect of the same size; that is, the studies are heterogeneous.

> *EXAMPLE:* A statistical test of homogeneity for the studies of stroke and estrogen replacement therapy that were described in Table 6-5 was 17.3 with 9 degrees of freedom (p = 0.044). At a critical value of 0.05, the hypothesis of homogeneity of effects is rejected.

When there is statistical evidence of lack of homogeneity, calculating a summary estimate of effect size is of dubious validity. Attempts to explain the lack of homogeneity based on consideration of study design or other characteristics of the

Table 7-12 Formulas to calculate a statistic for a test of homogeneity of effects

---

Mantel-Haenszel method

$$Q = \text{sum}[\text{weight}_i \times (\ln OR_{mh} - \ln OR_i)^2]$$

where OR_{mh} and the weight_i are estimated as shown in Table 7-7

Peto method

$$Q = \text{sum}[\text{weight}_i \times (O_i - E_i)^2] - \frac{\text{sum}(O_i - E_i)^2}{\text{sum variance}_i}$$

where the O_i, E_i, weight_i, and variance_i are estimated as shown in Table 7-9

General variance-based method

$$Q = \text{sum}[\text{weight}_i \times (\ln OR_s - \ln OR_i)^2]$$

where OR_s and the weight_i are estimated as described in the text

---

Note: Q is referred to the chi-square distribution with degrees of freedom equal to the number of studies minus 1.

studies may be useful (Greenland 1987; Jenicek 1989; Greenland and Salvan 1990; Greenland and Longnecker 1992).

The power of statistical tests of homogeneity is low, and the failure to reject the hypothesis that the studies are homogeneous does not prove that the studies are measuring the same quantity.

7.8 DERSIMONIAN AND LAIRD METHOD

7.8.1 Overview

The DerSimonian and Laird (1986) method is based on the random-effects model. Formulas for applying the DerSimonian and Laird method summarizing studies in the case where effects are measured as odds ratios are given by Fleiss and Gross (1991) as follows:

$$\ln \mathrm{OR}_{dl} = \frac{\mathrm{sum}(w_i^* \times \ln \mathrm{OR}_i)}{\mathrm{sum}\ w_i^*}$$

where OR_{dl} is the DerSimonian-Laird summary estimate of the odds ratio, w_i^* is the DerSimonian-Laird weighting factor for the ith study, and OR_i is the odds ratio from the ith study.

The weighting factors, w_i^*, are estimated as

$$w_i^* = \frac{1}{[D + (1 \div w_i)]}$$

where

$$w_i = \frac{1}{\mathrm{variance}_i}$$

The variance$_i$ for each study is estimated using the Mantel-Haenszel method described previously and:

$$D = \frac{[Q - (S - 1)] \times \mathrm{sum}\ w_i}{[(\mathrm{sum}\ w_i)^2 - \mathrm{sum}\ (w_i^2)]} \text{ and D=0 if Q < S}-1,$$

where S is the number of studies and

$$Q = \mathrm{sum}\ w_i\ (\ln \mathrm{OR}_i - \ln \mathrm{OR}_{mh})^2$$

The OR_i are odds ratios from the ith study, OR_{mh} is the summary odds ratio calculated using the Mantel-Haenszel method, and w_i is the weight of ith study calculated using the Mantel-Haenszel method as described in Section 7.3.

A 95% confidence interval for the DerSimonian-Laird summary estimate of the odds ratio derived from the above equation is estimated as follows:

$$\mathrm{CI} = e^{\ln\ \mathrm{OR}_{dl} \pm 1.96 \times \sqrt{\mathrm{variance}_s^*}}$$

where

$$\text{variance}_i^* = \frac{1}{\text{sum } w_i^*}$$

7.8.2   Application of the DerSimonian-Laird Method

EXAMPLE: The data in Table 7-8 were analyzed using the DerSimonian-Laird method to obtain a summary odds ratio and a 95% confidence interval using the formulas shown above. The summary odds ratio using the DerSimonian-Laird method is 1.50 (95% C.I. 1.13–1.99). Table 7-13 shows the summary odds ratio for the data in Table 7-8 as estimated using the Mantel-Haenszel method, the confidence limit method, and the method of DerSimonian and Laird. In this example, the estimates do not differ much. This is not surprising, since the number of studies is small and there is no evidence of lack of homogeneity.

7.8.3   Strengths and Limitations

If the random-effects model is considered on theoretical grounds to be the appropriate model for meta-analysis, then the method of DerSimonian and Laird (1986) is the appropriate method to use in the analysis. The results of an analysis based on the DerSimonian-Laird method will differ from an analysis based on the fixed-effects model only if there is lack of homogeneity. In this case, calculating a single summary estimate of effect is of questionable validity. Using a random effects model does not account for heterogeneity. It does not correct for bias, failure to control confounding, or for any other cause of lack of homogeneity. In the very situations where application of the method matters, a single summary estimate of effect is inappropriate. Use of a random-effects model should not substitute for exploration of heterogeneity.

Methods based on the random-effects model tend to give high weight to small studies. Since small studies may reflect publication bias, use of the model may emphasize poor evidence at the expense of good evidence (Thompson and Pocock 1991). The computational burden of doing an analysis using the method of DerSimonian and Laird is greater than the computational burden of using any of the other methods.

One approach that has been useful is to calculate effect sizes using both models and to evaluate the dependence of the conclusions of the analysis on the model

Table 7-13   For data shown in Table 7-8, summary estimate of relative risk and 95% confidence intervals from three methods of analysis

Method	Model Assumption	Estimated Relative Risk	95% Confidence Interval
Mantel-Haenszel	Fixed effects	1.49	1.14–1.95
Confidence interval	Fixed effects	1.50	1.13–1.98
DerSimonian-Laird	Random effects	1.50	1.13–1.99

assumption. This is a kind of sensitivity analysis. It is considered further in Chapter 15.

APPENDIX

Formulas to estimate the variance of the Mantel-Haenszel summary odds ratio as described by Robins, Greenland, and Breslow (1986):

$$\text{variance}_{mh} = \left(\frac{\text{sum } F}{2 \times (\text{sum } R)^2}\right) + \left[\frac{\text{sum } G}{(2 \times \text{sum } R \times \text{sum } S)}\right] + \left(\frac{\text{sum } H}{2 \times (\text{sum } S)^2}\right)$$

where

$$F = a_i \times d_i \times \frac{(a_i + d_i)}{n_i^2}$$

$$G = \frac{[a_i \times d_i \times (b_i + c_i)] + [b_i \times c_i \times (a_i + d_i)]}{n_i^2}$$

$$H = \frac{b_i \times c_i \times (b_i + c_i)}{n_i^2}$$

$$R = \frac{a_i \times d_i}{n_i}$$

$$S = \frac{b_i \times c_i}{n_i}$$

The table notation is as follows:

	Exposed	Not Exposed	Total
Diseased	a_i	b_i	
Not diseased	c_i	d_i	
Total			n_i

8

Other Statistical and Methodologic Issues in Meta-Analysis

Studies that measure effects on a continuous scale are often the subject of meta-analysis. The goal of meta-analysis is often not simply to estimate an overall measure of effect, but to estimate the relationship between disease and some measure of intensity of exposure. There are some statistical methods that have been used in meta-analysis that are not recommended. These methods, and the reasons why they are not recommended, need to be understood. Special statistical and methodologic issues arise in cumulative meta-analysis and meta-analysis of individual level data.

Section 8.1 describes statistical methods for meta-analysis of effects measured on a continuous scale. Section 8.2 presents the statistical methods to derive a summary estimate of the trend of effect with increasing level of exposure. Section 8.3 describes some methods for estimating a summary statistic in meta-analysis that are not recommended. Section 8.4 describes several statistical approaches to the problem of publication bias and discusses why these approaches are problematic. Section 8.5 describes cumulative meta-analysis and pertinent statistical methods. Section 8.6 covers meta-analysis of individual-level data.

8.1 MEASURES ON A CONTINUOUS SCALE

8.1.1 Overview

Blood pressure, cholesterol level, hemoglobin concentration, and depression scores are examples of continuous measures that might be outcome measures in experimental or nonexperimental studies. In a meta-analysis of studies in which effect size is measured on a continuous scale, there are two situations to be considered. In the first situation, all of the eligible studies use the same measure of effect. For example, all of the studies may measure the effect of the intervention on diastolic blood pressure measured in millimeters of mercury, serum cholesterol level, or depression as assessed by the Beck depression scale. In the second situation, the eligible studies address the same question, but the measure of effect was made using different instruments and thus different scales. For example, in a series of studies on the effect of the intervention on depression, some studies might have used the CES-D depression scale and some might have used the Hamilton depression scale.

Methods to estimate a summary measure of effect in the first situation are directly related to analysis of variance, and they are described in textbooks, usually under the heading of weighted studies. Most of the statistical writing about meta-analysis of studies specifically dealing with measures of effect on a continuous scale that addresses the second situation appears in the social science literature (Glass, McGaw, Smith 1981; Hedges 1982; Wolf 1986). Methods to handle both situations are described here.

8.1.2   When Outcome Is Measured on the Same Scale

Cochran (1954) comprehensively described methods to combine results from different experiments. These methods are an extension of analysis of variance where the ''groups'' are studies. Using the analysis of variance analogy, application of the fixed-effects model to a continuous measure of effect is application of ''Model 1'' analysis of variance. The application of a random-effects model is ''Model 2'' analysis of variance. Mixed models are also possible. In this book, methods to estimate a summary estimate of effect in a two-group comparison based on a fixed-effects model (Model 1) will be described.

Table 8-1 gives the formulas to carry out an analysis with continuous measures, when all of the outcomes are measured using the same measure. The first step in the analysis is estimating a summary measure of effect, the weighted grand mean. Next, a statistic, Q, referred to the chi-square distribution, is calculated and used to test the hypothesis of homogeneity of effect. If there is no statistical evidence of lack of homogeneity, a 95% confidence limit for the summary estimate of effect is calculated.

8.1.3   Application of the Method

EXAMPLE: Table 8-2 presents data from a meta-analysis of the effect of azathioprine treatment on progression of disability in patients with multiple sclerosis (Yudkin et al. 1991). All of the studies eligible for inclusion in the meta-analysis used the Kurtzke Disability Status Scale to measure the effect of azathioprine. The following are the steps used to calculate a summary estimate of the effect of azathioprine on disability, a statistic to test the hypothesis that effects are homogeneous, and an estimate of the 95% confidence interval for the summary estimate of effect. We begin by estimating the summary mean:

Table 8-1   Continuous measure of effect with all measures on the same scale: formulas to estimate the summary measure of effect, a statistic to test homogeneity, and 95% confidence interval

---

Summary measure of effect size

$$mean_s = \frac{\text{sum (weight}_i \times mean_i)}{\text{sum weight}_i}$$

$$weight_i = \frac{1}{variance_i}$$

where the variance$_i$ are the SD_i^2 as calculated using methods described in introductory textbooks of statistics (e.g., Armitage and Berry 1987)

Test of homogeneity

$$Q = \text{sum [weight}_i \times (mean_s - mean_i)^2]$$

where the weight$_i$ are estimated as described above; Q is referred to the chi-square distribution with degrees of freedom equal to the number of studies minus 1

95% confidence interval

$$95\% \text{ C.I.} = mean_s \pm \left(1.96 \times \sqrt{variance_s}\right)$$

$$variance_s = \frac{1}{\text{sum weight}_i}$$

where the weight$_i$ are estimated as described above

---

1. Estimate the mean difference between treatment and control for each study where

$$mean_i = mean_{ci} - mean_{ei}$$

Study 1: $mean_1 = 0.42 - 0.30 = 0.12$

Study 2: $mean_2 = 0.83 - 0.17 = 0.66$

Study 3: $mean_3 = 0.45 - 0.20 = 0.25$

Study 4: $mean_4 = 0.42 - 0.17 = 0.25$

Table 8-2   Change in Kutzke Disability Status Scale at two years in four randomized trials of the effect of azathioprine treatment in multiple sclerosis

Study	Treated			Control		
	Mean	SD	N^a	Mean	SD	N^a
1	0.30	1.26	162	0.42	1.28	175
2	0.17	0.90	15	0.83	0.98	20
3	0.20	1.10	30	0.45	1.12	32
4	0.17	1.38	27	0.42	1.36	25

[a] Number followed.

Source: Yudkin et al. (1991).

2. Estimate the pooled variance for each study where

$$variance_{pi} = \frac{SD_{ci}^2}{n_{ci}} + \frac{SD_{ei}^2}{n_{ei}}$$

Study 1: $variance_{p1} = \dfrac{(1.28)^2}{175} + \dfrac{(1.26)^2}{162} = 0.019$

Study 2: $variance_{p2} = \dfrac{(0.98)^2}{20} + \dfrac{(0.90)^2}{15} = 0.102$

Study 3: $variance_{p3} = \dfrac{0}{30} = 0.080$

Study 4: $variance_{p4} = \dfrac{(1.36)^2}{25} + \dfrac{(1.38)^2}{27} = 0.145$

3. Calculate a weight for each study where

$$weight_i = \frac{1}{variance_{pi}}$$

Study 1: $weight_1 = \dfrac{1}{0.019} = 52.63$

Study 2: $weight_2 = \dfrac{1}{0.102} = 9.80$

Study 3: $weight_3 = \dfrac{1}{0.080} = 12.50$

Study 4: $weight_4 = \dfrac{1}{0.145} = 6.90$

4. Calculate the product of the weights and the mean difference for each study:

$$product_i = weight_i \times mean_i$$
Study 1: $product_1 = 52.63 \times 0.12 = 6.316$
Study 2: $product_2 = 9.80 \times 0.66 = 6.468$
Study 3: $product_3 = 12.50 \times 0.25 = 3.125$
Study 4: $product_4 = 6.90 \times 0.25 = 1.725$

5. Calculate the sum of the products:

sum of $products_i = 6.316 + 6.468 + 3.125 + 1.725 = 17.634$

6. Calculate the sum of the weights:

sum of $weight_i = 52.63 + 9.80 + 12.50 + 6.90 = 81.83$

7. Calculate the summary mean where

$$mean_s = \frac{sum\ (weight_i \times mean_i)}{sum\ weight_i}$$

$$mean_s = \frac{17.634}{81.83} = 0.22$$

Next calculate Q, a statistic to test the hypothesis of homogeneity of effects:

1. Calculate the square of differences between the mean differences for each study and the summary mean:

   Study 1: $(\text{mean}_1 - \text{mean}_s)^2 = (0.12 - 0.22)^2 = 0.010$
   Study 2: $(\text{mean}_2 - \text{mean}_s)^2 = (0.66 - 0.22)^2 = 0.194$
   Study 3: $(\text{mean}_3 - \text{mean}_s)^2 = (0.25 - 0.22)^2 = 0.001$
   Study 4: $(\text{mean}_4 - \text{mean}_s)^2 = (0.25 - 0.22)^2 = 0.001$

2. Calculate the product of the weight_i and the differences for each study as calculated in step 1:

   Study 1: $\text{weight}_1 \times 0.010 = 52.68 \times 0.010 = 0.527$
   Study 2: $\text{weight}_2 \times 0.194 = 9.80 \times 0.194 = 1.901$
   Study 3: $\text{weight}_3 \times 0.001 = 12.50 \times 0.001 = 0.013$
   Study 4: $\text{weight}_4 \times 0.001 = 6.90 \times 0.001 = 0.007$

3. Calculate Q as the sum of the results of step 2:

   $Q = 0.527 + 1.901 + 0.013 + 0.007 = 2.448$

4. Q is distributed as chi-square with degrees of freedom equal to one less than the number of studies. Based on Q with 3 degrees of freedom, the null hypothesis that the studies are homogeneous is not rejected because $p > 0.05$. There is no statistical evidence of lack of homogeneity and it is appropriate to use the summary weighted mean to estimate effect size.

Finally, we estimate the 95% confidence interval as follows:

1. Estimate a 95% confidence interval for the summary mean where

   $$CI = \text{mean}_s \pm 1.96 \times \sqrt{\text{variance}_s}$$

   and

   $$\text{variance}_s = \frac{1}{\text{sum weight}_i}$$

   $$\text{variance}_s = \frac{1}{81.83} = 0.012$$

   upper bound $= 0.22 + (1.96 \times \sqrt{0.012}) = 0.22 + 0.22 = 0.44$
   lower bound $= 0.22 - (1.96 \times \sqrt{0.012}) = 0.22 - 0.22 = 0.00$

8.1.4   When Effect Size Is Measured on Different Scales

When studies have used different scales to measure effect, the first step is to obtain an estimate of effect size for each study in a common metric. This is generally done as follows:

$$d_i = \frac{(\text{mean}_e - \text{mean}_c)}{SD_{pi}}$$

where d_i is the common metric that measures effect size in the ith study, mean_e is the mean in the experimental (or exposed) group, mean_c is the mean in the control (or unexposed) group, and SD_{pi} is the pooled estimate of the standard deviation of the effect measure for each study. When the study involves a before-after comparison, $mean_e$ and $mean_c$ are mean differences.

Hedges (1982) provides the following formula to estimate a summary effect size for studies that compare two groups taking into account the size of the two groups:

$$d_s = \frac{\text{sum } (w_i \times d_i)}{\text{sum } w_i}$$

where d_s is the summary estimate of the difference in the effect size measured in a common metric, w_i is the weight assigned to each study, and d_i is the effect size, estimated as described previously. This weighted estimator of the summary effect size was shown by Hedges to be asymptotically efficient when sample sizes in the two groups are both greater than 10 and the effect sizes are less than 1.5.

The weight of each study is

$$w_i = \frac{1}{\text{variance}_i}$$

where variance_i is the variance of d_i.

If sample sizes are about equal in the two groups and they are both greater than 10, the weight of each study can be estimated as follows (Hedges 1982; Rosenthal and Rubin 1982):

$$\text{weight}_i = \frac{2N_i}{(8 + d_i^2)}$$

where N_i is the total sample size in the ith study and d_i for each study is calculated as described previously.

A test of homogeneity can be carried out using a Q statistic that is wholly analogous to the Q described above, where

$$Q = \text{sum } [\text{weight}_i \times (d_i - d_s)^2]$$

Q is referred to a chi-square distribution with degrees of freedom equal to the number of studies minus 1.

Analogous to the situation described earlier, a 95% confidence interval for the summary estimate of effect size is estimated as

$$d_s \pm (1.96) \times \sqrt{\text{variance}_s}$$

where

$$\text{variance}_s = \frac{1}{\text{sum weight}_i}$$

Table 8-3 shows these formulas.

8.1.5 Application of the Method

EXAMPLE: Table 8-4 presents data from a meta-analysis of the effect of aminophylline in severe acute asthma that was done by Littenberg (1988).

Table 8-3   Effects are measured as standardized differences: formulas to estimate the summary measure of effect, a statistic to test homogeneity, and 95% confidence interval

---

Summary measure of effect size

$$d_s = \frac{\text{sum (weight}_i \times d_i)}{(\text{sum weight}_i)}$$

$$d_i = \frac{\text{mean}_{\text{experimental}} - \text{mean}_{\text{control}_i}}{\text{SD}_{\text{pooled}_i}}$$

$$\text{weight}_i = \frac{1}{\text{variance}_i}$$

$$\text{variance}_i = \frac{8 + d_i^2}{2N_i}$$

where N_i is the total number of subjects in both groups

Test of homogeneity

$$Q = \text{sum} [\text{weight}_i \times (d_s - d_i)^2]$$

where the weight$_i$ are estimated as described above; Q is referred to the chi-square distribution with degrees of freedom equal to the number of studies minus 1

95% confidence interval

$$95\% \text{ C.I.} = d_s \pm \left(1.96 \times \sqrt{\text{variance}_s}\right)$$

$$\text{variance}_s \quad \frac{1}{\text{sum weight}_i}$$

where the weight$_i$ are estimated as described above

The 13 studies he identified as eligible for the meta-analysis were all studies of the effect of aminophylline on pulmonary function as measured by spirometry. However, the spirometry measures reported were not the same measures in each of the studies. The reported measures were converted to a common metric by dividing the mean difference in the experimental and control groups by an estimate of the pooled standard deviation for each study. The summary estimate of effect size and a 95% confidence interval are calculated as follows:

1. Calculate the weights for each study where

$$\text{weight}_i = \frac{2N_i}{8 + d_i^2}$$

Study 1: $\text{weight}_1 = \dfrac{(2 \times 20)}{(8 + (-0.43)^2)} = 4.89$

Study 2: $\text{weight}_2 = \dfrac{(2 \times 50)}{(8 + (-0.04)^2)} = 12.50$

and continue for all of the studies.

2. Calculate the product of the weight and the estimates of effect size for each study:

Table 8-4   Data from meta-analysis of the effect of aminophylline treatment in severe acute asthma

Reference	Total Number of Subjects	SD[a]	d[b]	Weight	Weight $\times$ d
Beswick et al. (1975)	20	0.76	−0.43	4.89	−2.10
Femi-Pearse et al. (1977)	50	320.00	−0.04	12.50	−0.50
Rossing et al. (1980)	48	0.65	−0.84	11.03	−9.27
Appel and Shim (1981)	24	0.42	−1.67	4.45	−7.43
Sharma et al. (1984)	29	0.22	−1.03	6.40	−6.59
Williams et al. (1975)	20	17.00	−2.41	2.90	−6.99
Tribe et al. (1976)	23	0.62	−0.08	5.75	−0.46
Evans et al. (1980)	13	110.00	0.26	3.22	0.84
Pierson et al. (1971)	23	2.10	2.93	2.77	8.12
Josephson et al. (1979)	51	6.30	0.51	12.35	6.30
Rossing et al. (1981)	61	0.50	0.72	14.32	10.31
Fanta et al. (1982)	66	0.67	0.03	16.50	0.50
Siegel et al. (1985)	40	0.58	−0.02	10.00	−0.20

[a] Standard deviation.

[b] Standardized difference = (improvement in treated group − improvement in control group)/SD.

Source: Littenberg (1988); table references cited there.

$$\text{product}_1 = (4.89) \times (-0.43) = -2.10$$
$$\text{product}_2 = (12.50) \times (0.04) = -0.50$$

and continue for all of the studies.

3. Calculate the sum of the weights:

   sum of weights = 107.08

4. Calculate the sum of the products of the weight and the effect estimates:

   sum of products = −7.47

5. Estimate the summary effect size where

$$d_s = \frac{\text{sum of products}}{\text{sum of weights}}$$
$$d_s = \frac{-7.47}{107.48} = -0.07$$

6. Estimate 95% confidence interval where

   $$95\% \text{ C.I.} = d_s \pm (1.96 \times \sqrt{\text{variance}_s})$$

   and

   $$\text{variance}_s = \frac{1}{\text{sum weight}_i} = \frac{1}{107.48} = 0.009$$
   upper bound $= -0.07 + (1.96 \times \sqrt{0.009}) = -0.07 + 0.186 = 0.116$
   lower bound $= -0.07 - (1.96 \times \sqrt{0.009}) = -0.07 - 0.186 = -0.256$

The method is a method based on the assumptions of fixed effect. Calculations to test for heterogeneity of effect sizes are not shown.

8.1.6 Strengths and Limitations

The use of units of the standard deviation as a measure of the outcome of a comparative study is not accepted by all statisticians, even though the meta-analysis literature in the social sciences has focused on analysis of effect measures of this type. Greenland, Schlesselman, and Criqui (1987) give some examples where studies with identical results can spuriously appear to yield different results when the effect measures are converted to units of standard deviation.

In the social sciences, the effects of interventions are often measured using different instruments and the scales that result from this measurement process cannot be combined directly. It is impossible to do meta-analysis in these situations unless the effect measures are converted to a common metric. The example given in Section 8.1.4, which is from the medical literature, is similar. The effects of asthma treatment were measured using a variety of different measures of lung function derived from spirometry, and the only way to calculate a summary estimate of effect is to first convert the different measures of lung function to a common metric.

When there is no reason to convert the measures of effect to units of standard deviation, natural units should be used. This situation is the most common situation in the medical application of meta-analysis to describe the results of studies where effect size is measured on a continuous scale. Analyses based on units of the standard deviation are widely reported, and their results cannot be dismissed entirely.

8.2 TREND OR "DOSE RESPONSE" ANALYSIS

8.2.1 Overview

For many exposures, the presence or absence of a trend of increasing risk with increasing intensity of exposure, or "dose," is critical to the assessment of the causality of the association. Analyzing data from observational studies in terms only of "ever" and "never" exposed does not make full use of the information that is pertinent to the assessment of causality and it often makes little sense considering biology. For most diseases, it is not reasonable to assume that extremely low-level, short-term exposures will affect risk. Including low-intensity exposures together with high-intensity exposures in a group called "ever use" obscures true associations. Even cigarette smoking, whose causal association with lung cancer is undisputed, does not show an association with risk at very low amounts for short periods of exposure. For example, smoking one cigarette per day for 30 weeks does not measurably increase the risk of lung cancer; if persons with this level of exposure are classified as smokers, a true association with lung cancer will be obscured.

The problems with defining "ever use" and "never use" dichotomies in the analysis of observational studies is especially acute in studies of common drug exposures, where there are many persons who have used a drug at least once. Aspirin, for example, is such a ubiquitous drug exposure that it should be obvious that studying "ever use" of aspirin in relation to almost any condition is a meaningless exercise. It is not much more meaningful to describe associations of disease with ever use of alcohol or caffeine.

8.2.3 Methods

Greenland (1987) and Berlin et al. (1993) describe how to use ordinary weighted least squares regression to estimate beta, the slope of the trend of the odds of disease with dose, and its variance, when information on the number of exposed cases and controls can be extracted from all of the reports in the meta-analysis. An extension of these methods to estimation of beta and its variance when all that can be extracted from the study reports are estimates of effect size (e.g., odds ratios and risk ratios) at various dose levels has also been described (Greenland and Longnecker 1992). In the latter situation, which is the one most commonly encountered when conducting meta-analysis of published studies, estimation of the betas and their variances requires the use of matrix algebra and a computer. The details of these calculations will not be described here. The interested reader is referred to Greenland and Longnecker (1992).

Once the estimates of beta and their variances have been derived, estimating a summary slope and a 95% confidence interval for the summary estimate of it is straightforward. Table 8-5 gives the formulas, which should be familiar by now,

Table 8-5 Formulas to estimate the summary measure of slope, a statistic to test homogeneity, and 95% confidence interval for the summary measure

Summary measure of slope

$$\text{slope}_s = \frac{\text{sum (weight}_i \times \text{slope}_i)}{\text{sum weight}_i}$$

$$\text{weight}_i = \frac{1}{\text{variance}_i}$$

where the variance$_i$ are calculated as described by Greenland and Longnecker (1992) or as described by Greenland (1992) using ordinary least squares regression

Test of homogeneity

$$Q = \text{sum [weight}_i \times (\text{slope}_s - \text{slope}_i)^2]$$

where the weight$_i$ are estimated as described above; Q is referred to the chi-square distribution with degrees of freedom equal to the number of studies minus 1

95% confidence interval

$$95\% \text{ C.I.} = \text{slope}_s \pm \left(1.96 \times \sqrt{\text{variance}_s}\right)$$

$$\text{variance}_s = \frac{1}{\text{sum weight}_i}$$

where the weight$_i$ are estimated as described above

as they have the same general structure as other formulas in this and preceding chapters.

> *EXAMPLE:*   Table 8-6 shows the relative risk estimates for breast cancer in relation to amount of daily alcohol consumption as reported in the 16 studies that were eligible for the meta-analysis of alcohol and breast cancer done by Longnecker et al. (1988). The table also shows beta, which is the estimated increase in the natural logarithm of the relative risk of breast cancer associated with an average daily alcohol consumption of 1 gram per day, along with the weights the studies carry in the estimation of the summary slope. The weight for each study is the inverse of the variance. The betas and their variances were derived using the methods described by Greenland and Longnecker (1992).

A summary estimate of the slope and the 95% confidence interval for the estimate of slope were calculated with the formulas in Table 8-5 using steps that are exactly analogous to the steps given in Section 8.1. The summary estimate of beta is 0.00823. The value of Q, the statistic to test homogeneity, is 75.3. Q is referred to a chi-square distribution with 15 degrees of freedom. The associated probability value is much less than 0.05, and the hypothesis of homogeneity is rejected. This means that the slopes are not the same, and the summary estimate of slope is suspect. Further exploration of the reasons for heterogeneity are in order.

8.2.3   Other Statistical Issues in Analysis of Trend or Dose-Response

Epidemiologic studies that estimate the relative risk of disease in relation to dose generally use a common reference group. The estimates of risk are not, therefore, independent. Methods described by Greenland (1987) and by Berlin et al. (1993) assume independence. Ignoring the lack of independence leads to an underestimate of the variance of the estimate of the slope of the trend, or dose-response, relationship. Greenland and Longnecker (1992) give a method for adjusting the variance of the slope when the slopes are derived from data in tables and Berlin et al. (1993) describe how to adjust the variance in other situations.

The definitions of the categories of exposure usually differ between different studies. The highest category is often open-ended.

> *EXAMPLE:*   In the studies in Table 8-6, there is no consistency in the categories of grams of alcohol per day for which specific estimates of relative risk were derived for the studies in the meta-analysis. In all of the studies, the highest category of dose is open-ended. The value for the highest category of dose is identical for two studies done by the same author (Hiatt) and two other studies by different authors (Rosenberg et al. and Talamini et al.). The lowest dose for some studies is greater than the highest dose for others.

Before estimating a summary slope, the dose data must be expressed in comparable units. The estimate of the slope may be sensitive to the method for assigning these categories.

Table 8-6 Data from studies of association of grams of alcohol per day with breast cancer risk

Reference	Grams of Alcohol per Day	Estimated Relative Risk	Beta[a]	Weight[b]
Hiatt et al. (1984)	≤26	1.0	0.00434	164,000
	39–65	1.4		
	≥78	1.2		
Hiatt et al.(1988)	<13	1.2	0.0109	59,600
	13–26	1.5		
	39–65	1.5		
	≥78	3.3		
Willett et al.(1987)	<2	1.0	0.0284	31,400
	2–5	0.9		
	5–15	1.3		
	>15	1.6		
Schatzkin et al. (1987)	<1	1.4	0.118	441
	1–5	1.6		
	≥5	2.0		
Harvey et al.(1987)	<2	1.1	0.0121	54,200
	2–13	1.0		
	13–26	1.3		
	≥26	1.7		
Rosenberg et al. (1982)	<7	1.5	0.0870	1,860
	≥7	2.0		
Webster et al. (1983)	<7	0.9	0.00311	71,800
	7–21	0.9		
	21–28	1.1		
	29–36	1.1		
	36–43	1.0		
	≥43	1.1		
Paganini-Hill and Funch (1982)	<13	1.0	0.0000	11,300
	≥26	1.0		
Byers and Funch (1982)	<1	1.1	0.00597	23,100
	1–3	1.0		
	4–11	1.1		
	>11	1.1		
Rohan and McMichael (1988)	<3	0.8	0.0479	2,378
	3–9	1.2		
	>9	1.6		
Talamini et al. (1984)	≤7	2.4	0.0389	16,900
	>7	16.7		
O'Connell et al. (1987)	≥2	1.5	0.203	112
Harris and Wynder (1988)	<5	1.0	−0.00673	56,900
	5–15	0.9		
	>15	.9		
Le et al. (1984)	<11	1.0	0.0111	43,300
	11–22	1.4		
	23–34	1.5		
	>34	1.2		
LaVecchia et al. (1985)	≤39	1.3	0.0148	24,800
	>39	2.1		
Begg et al. (1983)	2–13	0.9	−0.000787	13,300
	>13	1.4		

[a] Increase in log relative risk for a gram/day of alcohol.

[b] 1/variance.

Source: Longnecker et al. (1988) and Greenland and Longnecker (1992); table references cited in Longnecker et al. (1988).

EXAMPLE: Table 8-7 shows data from one of the studies of breast cancer in relation to amount of alcohol intake per day that was eligible for a meta-analysis. Three different methods for assigning an average value for dose to the categories of alcohol intake are shown. For each of the three methods, beta, the slope of the relative risk of breast cancer in relation to alcohol intake, the variance of beta, and the weight that the estimate of slope would have in a meta-analysis are shown. The slope of the relation between alcohol and breast cancer ranges from 0.0162 to 0.0487 depending on the method used to assign an average value to categories of alcohol intake.

Berlin, Longnecker, and Greenland (1993) point out that when extreme values are present in the upper end of the exposure distribution, the mean exposure will be higher than the median. This is demonstrated in the data in Table 8-7. Berlin, Longnecker and Greenland (1993) recommend use of the median method because of its reduced sensitivity to the outlying exposure values, which are generally based on small numbers.

In practice, it is unusual to have information on the median value of exposure for each category of dose. In these cases, the mid-point of the interval is generally used for closed intervals (e.g., 3–9 grams).

The choice of a value to assign to dose in the open-ended category is not straightforward.

EXAMPLES: Berlin, Longnecker, and Greenland (1983) assigned a value of 1.9 grams of alcohol per day in the open-ended category of low intake. This value was based on the assumption that the minimum intake of alcohol among drinkers was 0.86 grams per day and the average drinker consumed twice this amount. The open-ended upper category of intake was assigned a value 1.2 times the lower boundary of the interval. The choice of 1.2 was not explained.

Table 8-7 Beta and variance of beta for three different methods for assigning a value to categories of grams of alcohol consumed per day

Category of Grams of Alcohol per Day	Method for Assigning		
	Mean NHIS[a]	Median NHIS[a]	Mid Point[b]
<3	1.5	1.7	1.9
3–9	5.1	5.1	1.2
>9	21.3	16.3	10.8[b]
beta[c]	0.0162	0.0330	0.0487
variance of beta	0.0067	0.0139	0.0208

[a] National Health Interview Survey.

[b] Lower boundary x 1.2 for open-ended category.

[c] Slope of dose-response.

Source: Berlin et al. (1993).

Schesselman (1997) did a meta-analysis of observational studies of oral contraceptives and endometrial cancer. The analysis focused on the relationship risk and the duration of oral contraceptive use. For the open-ended categories of short durations of oral contraceptive use (e.g. < 2 years), the midpoint of the category was used. For the open ended upper category of duration of oral contraceptive use (e.g. 10+ years), 2 years was added to the cut-off point. The latter choice was, Schesselman admitted, "obviously somewhat arbitrary."

In meta-analyses that examine dose-response relationships, the values chosen for the open-ended categories of dose should be subjected to sensitivity analysis. This is discussed in more detail in Chapter 15.

8.3 VOTE COUNTING AND RELATED METHODS

In the most simplistic method of "vote counting," the number of studies with statistically significant positive, negative, and null findings are tallied and the category with the plurality of votes is declared the "winner." There are no advocates of this method, which is naive, has no statistical rationale, and can lead to erroneous conclusions (Hedges and Olkin 1980; Greenland 1987).

More sophisticated uses of vote-counting procedures are discussed in detail by Bushman (1994). The most common one is a vote-counting analysis based on the sign test. The sign test is based on the following reasoning. If the null hypothesis is true (i.e., there is no association between treatment and outcome or between exposure and disease), then one would expect that half of the studies would show a positive association and half would show a negative association.

EXAMPLE: In a meta-analysis of lung cancer and exposure to environmental tobacco smoke by the Environmental Protection Agency, 19 case-control studies were identified as eligible for the meta-analysis. Table 8-8 lists the 19 studies along with the estimated relative risk of lung cancer in women exposed to environmental tobacco smoke. To do the sign test, each study is assigned a plus if the study estimated that the risk of lung cancer in exposed women was increased (i.e., estimated relative risk > 1.0) and a minus if the study estimated that the risk of lung cancer in exposed women was decreased (i.e., estimated relative risk < 1.0). Of the 19 studies, 16 have a plus sign and 3 have a minus sign. The null hypothesis is

H_0: number of studies $+$ = number of studies $-$

Under the null hypothesis, the number of positive studies and the number of negative studies follow a binomial distribution with the probability of occurrence of a positive equal to $1 - \frac{1}{2}$, or $\frac{1}{2}$. The mechanics of the sign test are described in a number of textbooks (e.g., Armitage and Berry 1987). Using the methods described in these texts, one can estimate the probability of observing a 16:3 split strictly due to chance to be 0.002.

Table 8-8   Data from meta-analysis of lung cancer in nonsmoking women exposed to environmental tobacco smoke

Reference	Estimated Relative Risk of Lung Cancer[a]	Sign	S[b]
Akiba, Kato, Blot (1986)	1.52	+	1.48
Browson et al. (1987)	1.52	+	0.61
Buffler et al. (1984)	0.81	−	−0.49
Chan et al. (1979)	0.75	−	−1.02
Correa et al. (1983)	2.07	+	1.52
Gao et al. (1987)	1.19	+	0.91
Garfinkel, Auerbach, Joubert (1985)	1.31	+	1.29
Geng, Liang, Zhang (1988)	2.16	+	2.19
Humble, Samet, Pathak (1987)	2.34	+	1.57
Inoue, Hirayama (1988)	2.55	+	1.50
Kabat, Wynder (1984)	0.79	−	−0.41
Koo et al. (1987)	1.55	+	1.56
Lam et al. (1987)	1.65	+	2.77
Lam (1985)	2.01	+	2.24
Lee, Chamberlain, Alderson (1986)	1.03	+	0.05
Pershagen, Hrubec, Svensson (1987)	1.28	+	0.91
Svensson, Pershagen, Klominek (1988)	1.26	+	0.57
Trichopoulos, Kalandidi, Sparros (1983)	2.13	+	2.55
Wu et al. (1985)	1.41	+	0.70

[a] In women exposed to environmental tobacco smoke compared with nonsmokers.

[b] S is the square root of the Mantel-Haenszel chi-square statistic with a positive sign for relative risk about 1.0 and minus for relative risk less than 1.0.

Source: Environmental Protection Agency (1990); table references cited there.

The sign test is not a recommended way to draw conclusions in a meta-analysis. First, the method yields no estimate of effect size. Second, it does not directly assess homogeneity of effect. Most important, it weights equally studies of all sizes and effects of all magnitudes. Its use should be restricted to situations when effect measures are not presented and cannot be obtained. This situation is very rare in medicine.

8.4   STATISTICAL APPROACHES TO PUBLICATION BIAS

8.4.1   Overview

Chapter 4 described the funnel plot, a quasi-statistical graphical method for assessing whether publication bias exists. Other statistical approaches to publication bias include methods that attempt to estimate the number of studies that would have to exist in order to explain the observed result of a meta-analysis and methods that attempt to adjust for unpublished studies. Some of the methods make untenable assumptions, some are not relevant when estimating effect size, and some have not been subjected to rigorous scrutiny (Begg 1994). None of these methods is recommended. They are described here along with the reasons for recommending against using them.

8.4.2　Estimating the Number of Unpublished Studies

Rosenthal (1979) coined the term "file drawer problem" as a description of the problem of publication bias. According to his widely quoted description, the problem of publication bias arises because there are many studies whose results have been put into a "file drawer" without publication. Rosenthal describes a method for estimating the minimum number of unpublished studies with a null result that must exist in order to make the probability based on the observed (published) studies and the unobserved (unpublished) studies nonsignificant. Gleser and Olkin (1996) expanded on this method.

> *EXAMPLE:*　A meta-analysis of 94 experiments examining the effects of interpersonal self-fulfilling prophecies yielded a probability value of $p <$ 0.001. To reduce the p value to a barely significant level (p = 0.05), Rosenthal (1979) estimated that there would have to exist 3263 other, unpublished studies with an average null effect. The largeness of this number makes a strong intuitive appeal to the contention that unpublished studies do not explain the results of the meta-analysis based only on published studies.

This method is often cited and occasionally used. There are serious problems with the approach. First, in medical applications, one is rarely interested in knowing simply whether the result of the meta-analysis is or is not statistically significant. The approach is inappropriate for studying the effects of publication bias on effect sizes (Gleser and Olkin 1996). Second, the method uses normal theory and the Z statistic, which are not often the main interest in analysis of medical data. Most important, the method assumes that the mean effect size of the unobserved studies is zero. That is, it assumes as true what is in doubt—that the unpublished studies taken together are null.

Orwin (1983) remedies the first problem by suggesting a method similar to Rosenthal's that is based on measures of the standardized difference in effect between a treatment and control group. This method estimates the number of studies whose overall mean is some number, say 0, that would be needed to bring the estimated difference between treatment and control in the observed studies to 0. Again, the estimated number of unobserved studies is sensitive to the assumption about the mean of the unobserved studies (Iyengar and Greenhouse 1988).

The idea of estimating how many unpublished studies there must be to explain the observed results of the meta-analysis as a way of assessing publication bias maintains its intuitive appeal. The statistical theory that would allow this to be done is not well developed. The methods that purport to allow these calculations to be made are all ad hoc, and the approach is not recommended for this reason.

8.4.3　Statistical Adjustment for Publication Bias

Hedges (1984) suggested an approach to publication bias which yields an estimate of a continuous measure "adjusted" for the effect of unobserved studies. The method, like that of Rosenthal (1979), is based on normal theory, and it assumes that errors are all normally distributed. An additional critical assumption, which makes it difficult to apply to the medical literature, is that all statistically significant studies are published and all nonsignificant studies are not published. This method is considered to be an improvement over the method of Rosenthal (see Iyengar and Greenhouse 1988), but it is not widely accepted. It is not recommended.

When sample sizes in each study are similar, Hedges and Olkin (1985) suggest an approach that uses binomial theory to estimate the effect, "adjusted" for unobserved studies. This approach also assumes that all statistically significant results are published and all nonsignificant results are not. This assumption is not tenable for medical applications, and the approach is essentially useless for this reason.

8.4.4 Other Methods

Iyengar and Greenhouse (1988) suggest a maximum-likelihood approach for estimating publication bias. Bayarri (1988) and Rao (1988) suggest that the problem of publication bias might best be dealt with using Bayesian approaches. Development of these methods is incomplete, and they are not covered further in this book.

8.5 CUMULATIVE META-ANALYSIS

In cumulative meta-analysis, studies are sequentially summarized by adding one study at a time in a prespecified order (Lau et al. 1995). In practice, studies are generally added according the dates of conduct or publication. Cumulative meta-analysis is used to assess the robustness of the point estimate of effect size over time and to identify the benefit of an intervention as early as possible (Lau et al. 1992; Antman et al. 1992; Pogue and Yusuf 1998). Trends in the point estimates over time are sometimes readily identifiable using cumulative meta-analysis.

> *EXAMPLE:* In 1992, two publications (Lau et al. 1992; Antman et al. 1992) presented the results of cumulative meta-analysis of randomized trials of a number of different treatments for myocardial infarction. Figure 8-1 shows the results of the cumulative meta-analysis by year of publication for randomized trials of oral beta-blockers for the secondary prevention of mortality following acute myocardial infarction. The figure also shows the recommendations of expert reviewers about the treatment.
>
> The summary estimate of the odds ratio for death from trials of oral beta-blockers was statistically significant ($p < 0.05$) in 1975, at which time four trials involving 3,522 patients had been published. By 1980, none of the expert reviewers recommended oral beta-blockers as routine treatment for patients with acute myocardial infarction. It was not until about 1984, after publication of 15 trials involving 18,348 patients, that virtually all experts recommended oral beta-blockers.

Cumulative meta-analysis of randomized trials is increasingly a planned activity of cooperative groups. One of the main goals of the Cochrane Collaboration, which was described in Chapter 2, is to conduct cumulative meta-analysis and to use the

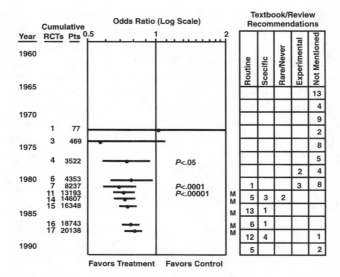

Figure 8-1 Cumulative meta-analysis by year of publication for randomized controlled trials (RCTs) of oral beta-blockers for secondary prevention of mortality following acute myocardial infarction. The number of patients and trials is shown on the left. The recommendations of the clinical expert reviewers are shown on the right. M indicates at least one meta-analysis was published in that year. The numbers in the boxes are the number of expert reviewers that addressed the question of secondary treatments and their recommendation. (Reproduced with permission from Antman et al., *Journal of the Americal Medical Association,* 1992; 268:244.)

resulting information to bring about earlier implementation of changes in clinical practices that are indicated by the body of evidence from randomized trials. Formal interim monitoring of accumulating evidence can be carried out. Pogue and Yusuf (1998) describe methods to do this. These methods are not discussed further in this book.

8.6   META-ANALYSIS OF INDIVIDUAL LEVEL DATA

8.6.1   Overview

In meta-analysis of individual level data, the individual data from participants in a systematically ascertained group of studies are obtained and then analyzed. Meta-analysis of individual level data from multiple studies is conceptually the same as meta-analysis (Friedenreich 1993; Lau, Ioannidis, and Schmid 1998) and has the same aims. It is useful for meta-analysis of both of randomized trials and nonexperimental studies.

EXAMPLES: Chapter 1 described a meta-analysis that assessed the effects of adjuvant tamoxifen and cytotoxic therapy on mortality in early breast cancer. This was a meta-analysis of individual-level data from 28 trials of ta-moxifen and 40 trials of chemotherapy.

The Collaborative Group on Hormonal Factors in Breast Cancer (1997) conducted an individual-level meta-analysis of data from observational studies. It assessed the relationship between a variety of hormonal risk factors, including use of hormone replacement therapy, and the risk of breast cancer, based on data from 51 epidemiologic studies of breast cancer that collected information on use of hormone replacement therapy and factors related to reproduction and the menopause.

8.6.2   Advantages and Disadvantages

Table 8-9 describes the advantages and disadvantages of meta-analysis of individual level data. The main advantages are the ability to create greater comparability between the different studies in definitions of outcomes, coding of covariates, and cut-points. The same variables can be adjusted using the same statistical approach. Effects can be assessed in the same sub-groups, allowing more complete assessment of heterogeneity. The statistical power of sub-group analysis is generally increased because it is based on larger numbers of subjects.

EXAMPLE: The meta-analysis of individual level data from 51 observational studies of breast cancer and hormone replacement therapy assessed the risk of breast cancer in users of hormone-replacement therapy according to time since first and last use of the drug and duration of use (Collaborative Group on Hormonal Factors in Breast Cancer 1997). Examining these data led to a conclusion that the risk of breast cancer increases with increasing duration of use during period of current use but is reduced after cessation of use and then disappears after about 5 years. This conclusion was not apparent from the individual studies and could not easily have been examined using only published data because the cutpoints used to define categories of last use and first use were different in different studies and because information

Table 8-9   Advantages and disadvantages of meta-analysis of individual-level data compared with meta-analysis of study level data

Advantages

Can use common definitions, coding, and cut-points for variables
Allows adjustment for the same variables
Allows estimation of effects in identically defined subgroups
Increases power in subgroup analyses
Can address questions not assessed in the original publication

Disadvantages

More expensive
More time-consuming
Subject to bias due to exclusion because of data unavailability

on the relative risk of breast cancer stratified simultaneously by duration of use within categories of time since first and last use was not presented in all publications.

An advantage of meta-analysis of individual level data is that it can address questions that were not addressed in the publications based on the study.

EXAMPLE: In the meta-analysis of individual-level data of 51 observational studies of breast cancer examining the relationship between hormone replacement therapy and breast cancer (Collaborative Group on Hormonal Factors in Breast Cancer 1997), at least seven published studies were primarily concerned with the risk of breast cancer in users of oral contraceptives. Not all of these studies presented the results of an analysis of hormone replacement therapy in which menopause and hysterectomy were appropriately considered as potential confounders or effect modifiers.

A disadvantage of meta-analysis of individual-level data is the need to exclude studies for which data are unavailable. Exclusion has the potential to create bias, and it may be difficult to assess the amount of bias.

EXAMPLE: In the meta-analysis of individual-level data of breast cancer (Collaborative Group on Hormonal Factors in Breast Cancer 1997), 12 studies were excluded because the individual-level data were not available. The authors stated that excluded studies comprised only 10% of the epidemiologic data on the topic of breast cancer and hormone replacement therapy. The estimated relative risk of breast cancer for ever use of hormone replacement therapy in the excluded studies was 1.0 (95% C.I. 0.9–1.1), and 1.14 (95% C.I. 1.07–1.20 in the included studies. The possibility of bias from exclusion of the 12 studies cannot be ruled out entirely.

The most important problems with meta-analysis of individual-level data are practical. Obtaining individual-level data is expensive and time-consuming. The situations in which individual-level data are available for all the studies that are eligible for the meta-analysis are relatively uncommon.

8.6.3 Steps in Meta-analysis of Individual Level Data

Friedenreich (1993) described eight steps in conducting a meta-analysis of individual-level data. The first two steps—locating all studies on the topic of interest and selecting the studies that should be included—and the last five steps—estimating study-specific effects, assessing heterogeneity, estimating a summary effect size, exploring the reasons for heterogeneity, and conducting sensitivity analysis—are identical to the steps in a meta-analysis of study level data. The second step—obtaining the primary data from the original investigators and preparing the data for the analysis—is unique. The following are recommendations of Friedenreich (1993).

A collaborative project for the meta-analysis of individual-level data should have a lead investigator and a designated center for the collaborative effort. After studies eligible for the meta-analysis have been identified by the lead investigator and the collaborating center, the principal investigators of each eligible study should be invited to participate. They should be asked to help identify other eligible studies based on the study criteria.

When all of the studies to be included have been identified, data on specified variables for each subject in each study are submitted in electronic form to the collaborative center. The data should be submitted based on a set of written specifications for coding each variable and for the kind of electronic file. The specifications can be developed by personnel in the coordinating center for the collaborative project or as a project of the participating principal investigators. Alternatively, the data can be submitted with a detailed data dictionary for each eligible study.

Each of the submitted datasets should be subjected to checks for internal consistency and to identify possible errors in submission. Inconsistencies and errors should be resolved by written queries back to the principal investigators. Either summary tables and listings of the variables or the complete set of edited and cleaned data should be submitted to the principal investigator for a final check prior to conduct of the analysis.

Most successful collaborations involve the principal investigators in decisions about the analysis and in the interpretation of the results and the preparation of material for publication. Written agreements about authorship, manuscript approval, and ownership of data after completion of specified analyses are useful.

9

Complex Decision Problems

Chapter 2 presented a simple decision analysis. The decision analysis was simple because only two alternative interventions were compared, because the events between the intervention and outcome required estimation of only a few probabilities, and because the outcome measure was a simple dichotomous measure—life or death. Decision analysis for most medical problems is more complex because it often involves comparison of more than one treatment or intervention, because the outcomes of interest are not always simple dichotomies, and because the chain from treatment to outcome involves many events, requiring the estimation of many probabilities. This chapter begins the description of decision analysis for more complex situations by showing how to build and analyze decision trees with more complex outcomes and more complex intervening events. Chapter 10 describes the approach to estimating probabilities in a decision analysis. Measuring utilities— the value of various outcomes to patients and society—in order to conduct a utility analysis is considered in Chapter 11. Chapter 13 discusses the incorporation of measures of utility into decision analysis and cost-effectiveness analysis. Sensitivity analysis is covered in Chapter 15.

Section 9.1 describes decision analysis involving comparison of more than two alternative treatments or interventions. Section 9.2 describes decision analysis with more than two outcomes. Section 9.3 describes decision analysis involving many intervening events between intervention and outcome. Section 9.4 shows how to estimate life expectancy, which is commonly used as a measure of outcome in decision analysis, using the declining exponential approximation of life expectancy (DEALE). Section 9.5 discusses the use of Markov models to represent complex, time-related processes in a decision analysis.

9.1   MORE THAN TWO ALTERNATIVE TREATMENTS OR INTERVENTIONS

More than two alternative treatments for a condition may be available, or there may be more than one strategy for addressing a problem. In this case, the decision node of the decision tree has more than two arms. The expected outcome for each arm is calculated by the process of folding back and averaging, and the strategies are compared in relation to one another.

EXAMPLE: Revaccinating children is one strategy for addressing the problem of a measles epidemic. An alternative public health strategy to cope with the epidemic would be a strategy of excluding all children with any rash or fever from school for a two-week period. This "quarantine" strategy would be expected to decrease the likelihood of exposure to measles for children who remain at school and would prevent measles and its consequences for this reason.

Figure 9-1 is a decision tree depicting these three alternative courses of

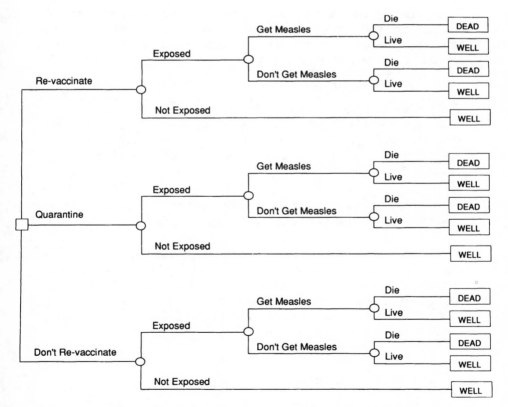

Figure 9-1   Decision tree comparing three strategies for dealing with the measles epidemic: revaccination, quarantine of infectious cases, and no revaccination.

action—revaccination, quarantine, and no revaccination (do nothing). The decision tree has been simplified by removing the branches which have probabilities of 1.0 or 0, a process called "pruning."

Based on review of the literature, it is estimated that quarantine will decrease the likelihood of exposure to measles from 0.20 to 0.15. Table 9-1 shows the three alternatives with the relevant probabilities recorded. A new subtable has been added to represent the new decision alternative—quarantine—and the relevant probabilities are recorded in the table.

The estimates of the expected number of deaths from measles for the revaccination and no-revaccination (do-nothing) strategies do not change. The expected number of deaths from measles for the decision alternative, quarantine, is estimated by the process of folding back and averaging. The products of the probabilities in each row of the subtable are calculated. Then, the expected number of deaths from measles is estimated by adding the entries in the columns corresponding to the rows labeled "die." The expected number of deaths is

$$0.000114 + 0.000000 + 0.000000 + 0.000000 = 0.000114$$

The comparison of the revaccination and no-revaccination strategies does not change. Revaccination is estimated to prevent 12.9 deaths per 100,000 children compared with no revaccination. The strategy of quarantine is compared with the strategy of no-revaccination (do nothing) by subtracting the expected numbers of deaths from measles as follows:

$$0.0000152 - 0.000114 = 0.000038$$

Interpreting these figures from the decision standpoint, the analysis shows that, while quarantine is expected to prevent 3.8 deaths per 100,000 compared with doing nothing, revaccination prevents 12.9 deaths per 100,000. Compared with doing nothing, the strategy of revaccination is superior to the strategy of quarantine.

This was a hypothetical example. In real-life applications, it is also common to compare more than one intervention in a decision analysis.

EXAMPLE: Figure 9-2 shows the graphical representation of the decision options in the decision analysis of warfarin and aspirin for patients with nonvalvular atrial fibrillation that was discussed in Chapter 2. This is an example of a real analysis examining more than two alternative interventions. In this example warfarin, aspirin, and no therapy are examined as alternatives for the management of patients with nonvalvular atrial fibrillation.

9.2 MORE THAN ONE OUTCOME

The outcomes of most medical treatments are not simple dichotomies. Many medical treatments have side effects that need to be taken into account in making

Table 9-1 Calculations to show results of decision analysis comparing three options: revaccination, quarantine, and no revaccination

	Revaccination			
Product	Probability of Exposure	Probability of Getting Measles	Probability of Outcome	
0.000023	0.2	0.05	0.0023	die
0.009977	0.2	0.05	0.9977	don't die
0.000000	0.2	0.95	0.0000	die
0.190000	0.2	0.95	1.0000	don't die
0.000000	0.8	0	0.0023	die
0.000000	0.8	0	0.9977	don't die
0.000000	0.8	1	0.0000	die
0.800000	0.8	1	1.0000	don't die

Sum for deaths
0.000023

	No Revaccination			
Product	Probability of Exposure	Probability of Getting Measles	Probability of Outcome	
0.000152	0.2	0.33	0.0023	die
0.065848	0.2	0.33	0.9977	don't die
0.000000	0.2	0.67	0.0000	die
0.134000	0.2	0.67	1.0000	don't die
0.000000	0.8	0	0.0023	die
0.000000	0.8	0	0.9977	don't die
0.000000	0.8	1	0.0000	die
0.800000	0.8	1	1.0000	don't die

Sum for deaths
0.000152

	Quarantine			
Product	Probability of Exposure	Probability of Getting Measles	Probability of Outcome	
0.000114	0.15	0.33	0.0023	die
0.049386	0.15	0.33	0.9977	don't die
0.000000	0.15	0.67	0.0000	die
0.100500	0.15	0.67	1.0000	don't die
0.000000	0.85	0	0.0023	die
0.000000	0.85	0	0.9977	don't die
0.000000	0.85	1	0.0000	die
0.850000	0.85	1	1.0000	don't die

Sum for deaths
0.000114
Differences
Revaccination compared with no revaccination
0.000129
   12.9 deaths per 100,000
Quarantine compared with no revaccination
0.000038
   3.8 deaths per 100,000

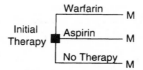

Figure 9-2   Decision tree depicting the choice among three treatment options for patients with nonvalvular atrial fibrillation. (Reproduced with permission from Gage et al., *Journal of the American Medical Association,* 1995; 274:1840.)

decisions about their net benefit and whether or not to recommend them. In addition, the beneficial and adverse consequences of many medical treatments and interventions include outcomes other than life and death.

In the simplest case, there are several mutually exclusive outcomes of an intervention. In this case, the decision tree is modified by including multiple boxes at the terminal or outcome node. This situation is shown for a hypothetical case in Figure 9-3. The probabilities of each outcome are estimated by literature review and recorded on the decision tree and analyzed by the process of folding back and averaging. In this situation, the decision analysis yields separate estimates of the value of each outcome in comparison with each alternative intervention.

EXAMPLE: Measles can cause blindness as well as death. Figure 9-4 shows the decision tree based on the example used in Chapter 1 as modified to

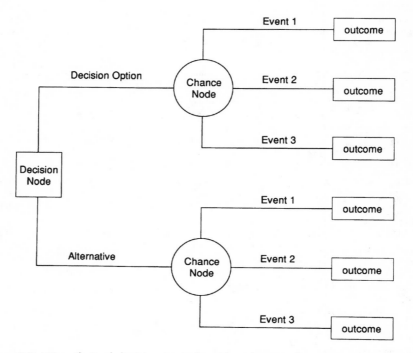

Figure 9-3   Hypothetical decision tree where there is more than one outcome.

include the occurrence of blindness as an outcome. Blindness and death are mutually exclusive outcomes, and it is proper to record them at the terminal node of the decision tree.

Based on review of the literature, it is determined that the likelihood of blindness following measles is 45 cases per 100,000 cases of measles. The likelihood of blindness in the absence of measles is assumed to be 0.0.

Table 9-2 shows the numbers used to analyze the decision tree, again illustrating the analysis as a spreadsheet to simplify understanding of the calculations that are done to analyze the tree. In analyzing the decision tree, for each row, the product of the probability values in each column is computed. The expected number of deaths for the revaccination arm is estimated by summing the entries in the product column for the rows labeled with death in the upper part of the table. The expected number of cases of blindness in the revaccination arm is estimated by summing the entries in the product column for the rows labeled blindness in the upper part of the table. Thus, the expected number of deaths is just as it was in Chapter 2:

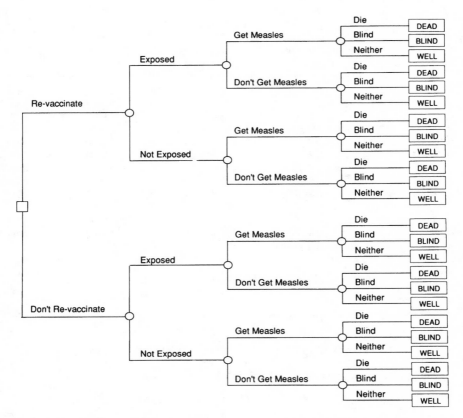

Figure 9-4 Decision tree for the measles problem where the outcomes of interest in the analysis are death, blindness, and remaining well.

Table 9-2 Calculations to show results of decision analysis for revaccination versus no revaccination where measles has three outcomes: death, blindness, well

	Revaccination			
Product	Probability of Exposure	Probability of Getting Measles	Probability of Outcome	
0.000023	0.2	0.05	0.0023	die
0.000045	0.2	0.05	0.0045	blind
0.009932	0.2	0.05	0.9932	well
0.000000	0.2	0.95	0.0000	die
0.000000	0.2	0.95	0.0000	blind
0.190000	0.2	0.95	1.0000	well
0.000000	0.8	0	0.0023	die
0.000000	0.8	0	0.0045	blind
0.000000	0.8	0	0.9932	well
0.000000	0.8	1	0.0000	die
0.000000	0.8	1	0.0000	blind
0.800000	0.8	1	1.0000	well
Sum for deaths	Sum for blind			
0.000023	0.000045			

	No Revaccination			
Product	Probability of Exposure	Probability of Getting Measles	Probability of Outcome	
0.000152	0.2	0.33	0.0023	die
0.000297	0.2	0.33	0.0045	blind
0.065551	0.2	0.33	0.9932	well
0.000000	0.2	0.67	0.0000	die
0.000000	0.2	0.67	0.0000	blind
0.134000	0.2	0.67	1.0000	well
0.000000	0.8	0	0.0023	die
0.000000	0.8	0	0.0045	blind
0.000000	0.8	0	0.9932	well
0.000000	0.8	1	0.0000	die
0.000000	0.8	1	0.0000	blind
0.800000	0.8	1	1.0000	well
Sum for deaths	Sum for blind			
0.000152	0.000297			

Differences between revaccination and no revaccination
Death 0.000129
Blind 0.000252

$$0.000023 + 0.000000 + 0.000000 + 0.000000 = 0.000023$$

The expected number of cases of blindness is

$$0.00045 + 0.000000 + 0.000000 + 0.000000 = 0.000045$$

The expected number of cases of blindness and of death in the no-revaccination arm is estimated by summing the entries in the product columns for the rows corresponding to the relevant outcome entry. The expected number of cases of blindness is

$$0.000297 + 0.000000 + 0.000000 + 0.000000 = 0.000297$$

The expected number of deaths for the no-revaccination strategy is

$$0.000152 + 0.000000 + 0.000000 + 0.000000 = 0.000152$$

The strategies of revaccination and no-revaccination are compared for these two outcomes by subtracting the expected number of deaths and the expected number of cases of blindness. The expected number of deaths from measles is

$$0.000152 - 0.00023 = 0.000129$$

which is the same as in the prior example. The expected number of cases of blindness comparing revaccination with no-revaccination is

$$0.000297 - 0.000045 = 0.000252$$

Translated to numbers per 100,000 persons revaccinated, the revaccination strategy prevents 12.9 deaths from measles and 25.2 cases of blindness.

In practice, the number of outcomes of a particular intervention can be large. Outcomes may be gradations of severity of a single outcome, reflecting the reality of the manifestation of illness in individuals.

EXAMPLE: In the decision model used to compare warfarin and aspirin with no treatment for patients with nonvalvular atrial fibrillation that was discussed in Chapter 2, Gage et al. identified 10 relevant outcomes. These are illustrated in Figure 9-5. They include life and death as well as varying grades of the severity of stroke. Stroke caused by intracranial hemorrhage is distinguished from ischemic stroke as an outcome because the consequences of the two types of stroke are different.

9.3   MANY INTERVENING EVENTS

For most medical problems, the description of the pathway between a decision and its outcome involves many more intervening events than in the example that has been used in this book so far. The decision trees that result from the proper description of medical problems can be very complex. There are often many intervening events that themselves are determined by complex events.

EXAMPLE: Jordan et al. (1991) did a decision analysis to inform clinical decisions about whether or not to give isoniazid prophylaxis routinely to HIV seropositive users of intravenous drugs. Figure 9-6 is the decision tree for this analysis. When the isoniazid arm of the tree is followed along its uppermost branches, the tree includes the occurrence or nonoccurrence of isoniazid toxicity. If isoniazid toxicity occurs, it is either fatal or nonfatal. If

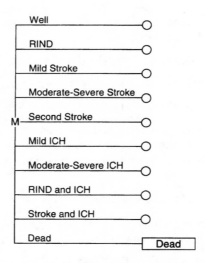

Figure 9-5 Decision tree showing health state outcomes for warfarin and aspirin therapy. RIND refers to reversible ischemic neurologic deficit. ICH refers to intracranial hemorrhage. Modified from Gage et al. (1995). (Reproduced with permission from Gage et al., *Journal of the American Medical Association*, 1995; 274:1840.)

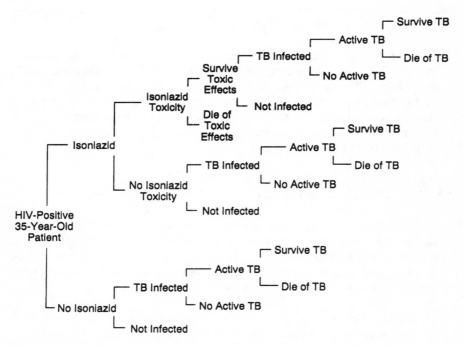

Figure 9-6 Decision tree used for analysis of prophylactic isoniazid versus no treatment in HIV-infected intravenous drug users. (Reproduced with permission from Jordan et al., *Journal of the American Medical Association*, 1991;265:2988.)

toxicity is nonfatal, then infection with tuberculosis either occurs or does not occur. If infection occurs, active tuberculosis may or may not result. If active tuberculosis occurs, it may be either fatal or nonfatal. The other branches of the tree can be similarly described.

Developing a decision tree that properly represents the problem that is posed is one of the most important challenges of decision analysis. The construction of complex decision trees is described in introductory textbooks by Weinstein and Fineberg (1980) and Sox, Blatt, and Higgins (1988), and these descriptions will not be repeated in this book. A software package that helps to construct complex decision trees, Decision Maker, has been developed and can be useful.

The methods for analyzing complex decision trees are a logical extension of the methods that were described in Chapter 2 and in Sections 9.1 and 9.2 and involve the process of folding back and averaging. The introductory textbooks by Weinstein and Fineberg (1980) and Sox et al. (1989) give examples of the analysis of complex decision trees, and such examples will not be provided in this book. For complex decision trees, the challenge of analysis is keeping track of the calculations. Specialized computer software is useful for this purpose. Otherwise, the help of a computer programmer may be necessary.

9.4   ESTIMATING LIFE EXPECTANCY

9.4.1   Overview

The outcome of interest in a decision analysis is often life expectancy and not just life or death. Since everyone must ultimately die, it is obvious that life expectancy is the most appropriate measure of the effect of an intervention whose most important effect is on survival.

Life expectancy is defined by actuaries as the average future lifetime of a person, and it is usually estimated for persons of a specific age, sex, and race. Actuarial methods to estimate life expectancy are based on specialized statistical life-table functions that rely on data on mortality rates specific for age, sex, and race. The age-, sex-, and race-specific mortality rates are based on death certificate data and census data.

Published tables of vital statistics describe the life expectancies of healthy persons. These published life expectancies are often all that is needed in a decision analysis, because the central task of the decision analysis is to estimate the effect of illness, with or without an intervention, on life expectancy.

In very rare cases, life expectancy in persons with an illness who have and have not undergone the intervention and its alternatives has been compared directly in a randomized trial or in a follow-up study. In these rare cases, the information on life expectancy can be used in a decision analysis without modification.

More often, available information on life expectancy in persons with a disease is in the form of overall mortality rates, five-year survival rates, or median survival. In general, the effect of interventions on life expectancy is measured as the relative risk or the odds of mortality in a given interval in those who have the intervention compared with those who do not.

These kinds of information are not easily translated into information about life expectancy. For example, an intervention that halves the relative risk of death in a five-year follow-up interval does not double life expectancy. The effect on life expectancy of a disease that increases five-year survival by 20% is dependent on the age, sex, and race of the person, since life expectancy in the absence of the intervention is also dependent on these factors.

The estimation of life expectancy from information on overall mortality, five-year survival, median survival, and the relative risk of death in a given interval can be done with actuarial methods using information on age-, sex-, and rate-specific mortality. These actuarial methods require complex calculations that will not be described. A method for estimating life expectancy described by Beck, Kassirer, and Pauker (1982) and Beck et al. (1982) that requires only information on the age-, sex-, and race-specific life expectancy from a table of vital statistics and an estimate of the effect of the disease, treatment, or intervention on mortality has been widely used in decision analysis. The method, called the declining exponential approximation of life expectancy (DEALE), is simple to use, and it has been shown to closely approximate estimates of life expectancy based on actuarial methods (Beck, Kassirer, Pauker 1982).

9.4.2   Using the DEALE to Estimate Life Expectancy

Use of the DEALE assumes that survival follows a declining exponential curve. If this assumption is true, then life expectancy for a person of a given age, sex, and race can be estimated as the reciprocal of the mortality rate:

$$\text{life expectancy} = \frac{1}{\text{mortality}}$$

For a person of a specific age, sex, and race, this relationship can be used to estimate mortality from published life tables:

$$m_{asr} = \frac{1}{le_{asr}}$$

where m_{asr} is the average mortality rate of a person of a given age, sex, and race and le_{asr} is the life expectancy of a person of a given age, sex, and race as described in published life tables.

If an intervention decreases mortality by an amount m, then life expectancy for the person who has the intervention l_{ei} is estimated as

$$le_i = \frac{1}{m_{asr} - m}$$

EXAMPLE: Imagine that an intervention decreases the probability of death by 0.001 per year. The problem is to determine the effect of the intervention on life expectancy in a 45-year-old woman.

1. Determine the average life expectancy at age 45 from a table of vital statistics:

$le_{asr} = 37.8$ years

2. Estimate the average mortality rate where

$$m_{asr} = \frac{1}{le_{asr}}$$

$$m_{asr} = \frac{1}{37.8} = 0.026 \text{ per year}$$

3. Estimate the mortality rate in those who have the intervention by subtracting the mortality rate caused by the intervention from the average mortality rate:

$m_i = m_{asr} - m$
$m_i = 0.026 - 0.001 = 0.025$ per year

4. Estimate life expectancy in those who have the intervention where

$$le_i = \frac{1}{m_i}$$

$$le_i = \frac{1}{0.025} = 40.0 \text{ years}$$

5. Estimate the gain in life expectancy in those with the intervention compared with those without the intervention by subtraction:

gain in life expectancy $= 40.0 - 37.8 = 2.2$ years

When the goal of the analysis is to estimate the effect of a disease on life expectancy, the same method can be used. In this case, excess mortality from the disease, m_e, is added to the mortality rate specific for age, sex, and race. That is, in step 3 described above:

$$m_d = m_{asr} + m \quad \text{and} \quad le_d = \frac{1}{m_d}$$

EXAMPLE: The effect of coronary heart disease on life expectancy in 45-year-old white women needs to be estimated. The excess mortality from coronary heart disease is 0.015 per year. The life expectancy of 45-year-old women with coronary heart disease is

$$m_d = m_{asr} + m = 0.026 + 0.015 = 0.041$$

$$le_d = \frac{1}{m_d} = \frac{1}{0.041} = 24.4 \text{ years}$$

Coronary heart disease reduces estimated life expectancy by 13.4 years (37.8 years $-$ 24.4 years).

Excess mortality from various diseases and the effects of interventions on mortality per year are sometimes measured directly, and these equations are then directly applicable. More often, available information consists of overall mortality rate, five-year survival, or median survival in persons with the disease or having the intervention. Only a curve describing the survival of persons with the disease or having the intervention may be available. These measures of observed mortality are compound measures of mortality. All are composed of baseline mortality—the mortality expected in the general population plus either the excess mortality due to the disease or lower mortality due to the intervention. Before applying the DEALE, measures of compound mortality must be decomposed into baseline and excess mortality or baseline and saved mortality. Methods to decompose different kinds of compound measures of mortality so that they can be used to estimate life expectancy using the DEALE are described in detail by Beck et al. (1982), and they will not be described here.

9.5 MARKOV MODELS

9.5.1 Overall Goal

A Markov model is used in decision analysis to try to more accurately represent complex processes that involve transitions in and out of various states of health and risks that change over time (Beck and Pauker 1983; Sonnenberg and Beck 1993). Complex transitions and events that occur more than once or with uncertain timing are difficult to handle with simple decision trees. Markov models are used to attempt to capture the complexity of these transitions and incorporate it into the decision analysis.

> *EXAMPLE:* A decision analysis is being done to try to determine whether to recommend sclerotherapy for men with bleeding esophageal varices. Figure 9-7 is a decision tree drawn to represent this problem. The tree does not accurately represent the complexity of the problem of treating esophageal varices. Thus, a man with bleeding esophageal varices is initially ill and bleeding. He can either recover completely or die from the bleed. If he recovers, he is again at risk of bleeding from the varices. If another bleed from the varices occurs, he may recover or he may die from the bleed. Transitions in and out of states of health occur until the man dies of a bleed or from some other cause. The likelihood of death from other causes is high in men with bleeding esophageal varices. A decision analysis that tries to assess the effect of a treatment for bleeding esophageal varices on life expectancy should take into account the fact that transitions into and out of states of complete health occur and when they occur.

9.5.2 Application of the Method

9.5.2.1 Overview

There are four steps in a decision analysis that uses a Markov model to represent a process between the intervention and outcome. The first step is to determine the

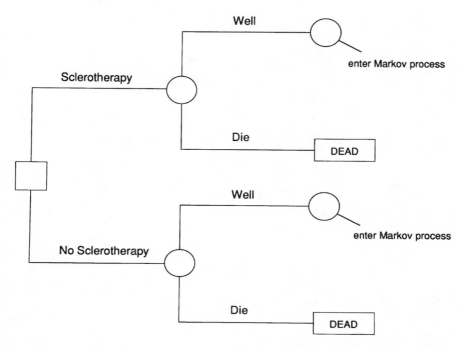

Figure 9-7 Decision tree for comparison of sclerotherapy versus no sclerotherapy for bleeding esophageal varices.

health states that will be modeled and to describe the ways in which transitions into and out of the health states will be allowed to occur in the model. The second step is to choose the length of the cycle that determines when transitions into and out of the various states that will be allowed. Third, the transition probabilities are estimated using the same methods that are used to estimate other probabilities in a decision analysis, as described in Chapter 10. Last, based on the estimates of the transition probabilities, the outcome with and without the intervention is determined by one of several methods.

9.5.2.2 Choose States and Transitions

It is common to represent the Markov process graphically. By convention, the states are defined as ovals or as circles. The time cycles are depicted on the left of the graph, and time runs downward on the graph. Arrows that link one state symbol with another state symbol are used to represent the allowed transitions between states in the model.

EXAMPLE: Figure 9-8 is a graphic representation of the problem of bleeding esophageal varices that was described previously. In the figure, men are assumed to be bleeding from varices at time 0. In the interval from time 0 to time 1, all men with bleeding varices either become well or they die. In the interval from time 1 to time 2, men who were well at time 1 can remain

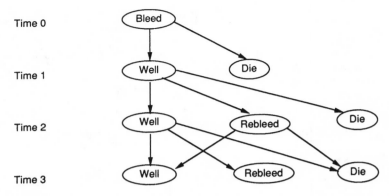

Figure 9-8 Graphical representation of Markov model of rebleeding after an initial episode of bleeding from esophageal varices.

well, bleed again, or die from another cause. In the next interval, from time 2 to time 3, the men who bled again can recover (again) or die; the men who were well can remain well, rebleed, or die of another cause.

9.5.2.3 Choose Cycle Length

The cycle length is the amount of time that elapses between successive evaluations of outcome. It is chosen to reflect the underlying biological process that is being modeled, and it may be short (weeks) or long (years). Computationally, longer cycles are less burdensome than shorter cycles, although the use of a computer program to carry out the Markov analysis makes consideration of the computational burden a relatively unimportant one.

> *EXAMPLE:* The cycle length chosen for the problem of bleeding varices is one year. That is, the outcome in the hypothetical cohort will be evaluated at the end of one-year cycles.

9.5.2.4 Determine Transition Probabilities

The next step is to determine the transition probabilities. The literature is usually the source of information on transition probabilities. Most available information about transitions between clinical states is expressed in the form of a rate and not in the form of a probability. A rate is the number of events per unit time; it can vary from zero to infinity. A probability is a quantity that is unitless (time is built into it); it takes values from zero to one. A rate r can be used to estimate a transition probability p of an event occurring over a time interval t based on the following formula:

$$p = 1 - e^{-rt}$$

where e is the base of the natural logarithm.

EXAMPLE: In studies of men with bleeding esophageal varices, the rate of rebleeding is 51 per 100 per year. The transition probability from being well to rebleeding is

$$P_{rebleed} = 1 - e^{-0.51} = 1 - 0.60 = 0.40$$

This is the probability of a rebleed per year.
The probability of a rebleed per month is

$$P_{rebleed} = 1 - e^{-0.51 \div 12} = 1 - 0.96 = 0.04$$

Table 9-3 shows estimates of mortality at first bleed and subsequent bleeds, mortality from other causes, and the rate of rebleeding for men who do and do not undergo sclerotherapy as determined from a review of the literature. The transition probabilities per year calculated from these annual rates are also presented in the table.

9.5.2.5 Estimate Outcome

There are three main methods that can be used to provide information on life expectancy for the Markov process (Beck and Pauker 1983; Sonnenberg and Beck 1993): Monte Carlo simulation, analysis of hypothetical cohorts of persons (Markov cohort simulation), and matrix algebra. The method for determining life expectancy for a Markov process that is conceptually the easiest is the method in which outcomes in hypothetical cohorts of individuals with and without the intervention are determined iteratively, usually until all members of the hypothetical cohort have "died."

Monte Carlo simulation and the use of matrix algebra are somewhat more complex. The disadvantage of the matrix algebra approach is its restriction to problems with constant transition probabilities. An advantage of Monte Carlo simulation and matrix algebra solutions is that both provide estimates of the variability of the outcome measure. The interested reader is referred to the description by Beck and Pauker (1983) and Sonnenberg and Beck (1993).

Table 9-3 Rates per year and transition probabilities for sclerotherapy versus no sclerotherapy

Event	No Sclerotherapy		Sclerotherapy	
	Rate[a]	Transition Probability[b]	Rate[a]	Transition Probability[b]
Death at first bleed	0.91	0.60	0.69	0.50
Death of subsequent bleed	0.91	0.60	0.91	0.60
Rebleed	0.51	0.40	0.35	0.30
Death from other cause than bleed	0.51	0.40	0.51	0.40

[a] Per 100 per year.

[b] Per year.

The following example uses the hypothetical cohort method (Markov cohort simulation).

EXAMPLE: Table 9-3 gave the estimates of transition probabilities that are used in this example. Using these figures, in a hypothetical cohort of 100,000 men with bleeding esophageal varices at time T_0 who do not undergo sclerotherapy, it is estimated that 60,000 will die in the interval from T_0 to T_1 and 40,000 will be well. In the interval from T_1 to T_2, 16,000 of those who are well at the start of the interval will rebleed, 16,000 will die of other causes, and 8000 will remain well. In the next interval, 9600 of those who bled in the prior interval will die of the rebleed and 6400 will become well; of those well at the end of the last interval, 3200 will rebleed, 3200 will die of other causes, and 1600 will remain well. Calculations are repeated for this hypothetical cohort until all members of the cohort are estimated to have died, as shown in Table 9-4.

In a hypothetical cohort of 100,000 men who undergo sclerotherapy at the initial bleeding episode, sclerotherapy is assumed to decrease the proba-

Table 9-4 Markov process: calculations for hypothetical cohorts of men with bleeding esophageal varices who do or do not have sclerotherapy

	No Sclerotherapy			Sclerotherapy		
Time	Well	Bleed	Dead	Well	Bleed	Dead
0	0	100,000	0	0	100,000	0
1	40,000	0	60,000	50,000	0	50,000
2	8,000	16,000	16,000	15,000	15,000	20,000
3	8,000	3,200	12,800	10,500	4,500	15,000
4	2,880	3,200	5,120	4,950	3,150	6,900
5	1,856	1,152	3,072	2,745	1,485	3,870
6	833	742	1,433	1,417	824	1,989
7	464	333	778	755	425	1,061
8	225	186	386	396	227	557
9	119	90	202	210	119	294
10	59	48	102	111	63	155
11	30	24	53	59	33	82
12	16	12	26	30	18	44
13	9	6	13	16	9	23
14	4	3	8	9	4	11
15	0	0	7[a]	4	3	7
16	0	0	0	0	0	7[a]
Sum	62,495	124,996		86,202	125,860	
Average cycles[b]	0.62	1.25		0.86	1.26	
Life expectancy: no sclerotherapy	$0.62 + 1.25 = 1.87$ years					
Life expectancy: sclerotherapy	$0.86 + 1.26 = 2.12$ years					
Difference	$2.12 - 1.87 = 0.25$ year					

[a] The tail has been truncated.

[b] Sum/100,000.

bility of death at the time of the first bleed from 0.60 to 0.50 and to decrease the probability of rebleeding in each subsequent interval from 0.4 to 0.3, but not to affect either the probability of death given a rebleed or the probability of death from other causes. In this hypothetical cohort, the numbers alive, bleeding, and well are as shown in Table 9-4.

Once the numbers of men in states of being well, rebleeding, and death for each cycle have been calculated, the total number of years spent in the states of well or rebleed is determined by summing the relevant columns. This sum is divided by the size of the hypothetical cohort to determine the average cycle length spent in each of the two living states. Life expectancy is estimated as the sum of the average cycles spent in living states. In the no-sclerotherapy cohort, the average number of years in the well state is 0.62. In the state of bleeding, it is 1.25 years. Both the well state and the bleeding state are living states, and life expectancy is estimated as the sum of the average cycles in these two states, or 1.87 years. In the sclerotherapy cohort, life expectancy is estimated to be 2.12 years, the sum of the average number of years spent in the well state (0.86) and the average number spent in the state of bleeding (1.26). The estimated gain in life expectancy from sclerotherapy is estimated as the difference in these two life expectancies, which is 2.12 − 1.87, or 0.25 year.

9.5.3 Markov Chains Versus Markov Processes

Markov models can assume either that the probabilities of transition are constant over time or that they vary. The first class of models are Markov chain models; the second class are Markov process models. Modeling a problem as a Markov process is required whenever the death occurs remote in time to the intervention, or the cohort "ages." The preceding example used a Markov chain model. In the example, it was not necessary to take age into account because the underlying mortality rate from causes other than bleeding in a cohort of men with bleeding esophageal varices is so high that the increasing mortality rate with age does not come into play in the estimate of life expectancy. Methods for incorporating transition probabilities that vary over time into a decision analysis based on a Markov model are provided by Beck and Pauker (1983) and by Sonnenberg and Beck (1993).

9.5.4 Limitations

Use of a Markov model to represent a process assumes that the behavior of the process in any cycle depends only on that cycle (Sonnenberg and Beck 1993). That is, the transition from a given state is independent of the prior transitions. In the sclerotherapy example, this is equivalent to an assumption that the probability of death from bleeding is independent of the number of times that the person has bled in the past.

The transition state assumption is a fairly tenuous one in many medical applications. The problem can be overcome by creating separate states for subsets of the cohort with different prognoses. This increases the complexity of the analysis and the difficulty of estimating the probabilities.

Additional limitations on the use of Markov models arise because of the unavailability of information that would allow accurate estimation of transition probabilities. Special studies to estimate these are rarely undertaken, and data to derive the estimates may not be easily obtainable.

10

Estimating Probabilities

Proper choice of estimates of the probabilities for a decision analysis is a critically important task. Because decision analytic models are often the basis for cost-effectiveness analysis, the information on estimation of probabilities information in this chapter is directly relevant to cost-effectiveness analysis. This chapter describes how to select probability estimates for a decision analysis and how to justify the choice of probabilities. It presents some of the statistical and quasi-statistical methods for estimating uncertainty in the expected outcome. Estimating utilities is covered in Chapter 11. Estimation of costs is discussed in Chapter 12. Utility analysis is covered in Chapter 13. Sensitivity analysis is considered in Chapter 15.

Section 10.1 describes the overall goals of the process of selecting probabilities for a decision analysis. Sections 10.2 and 10.3 describe the use of published sources to estimate probabilities. Section 10.4 discusses use of expert panels and Section 10.5 the use of subjective judgment and ''guesses'' for this purpose. Section 10.6 describes statistical and quasi-statistical methods that attempt to take the uncertainty in estimates of probability into account in the overall decision analysis.

10.1 OVERALL GOALS

The overall goal of the process of estimating the probabilities for a decision analysis is to obtain valid estimates. There are four important considerations in the gathering of information to fill in the probability estimates for the decision tree. First, identification of information to estimate the probabilities should be systematic. Second, the sources of information used to estimate the probabilities should be documented and, where there are alternative sources of information, a rationale for the choice should be provided. Third, effort should be expended to identify the best available information for each probability as well as for the outcome measures. Last, when information to estimate the probability is generated de novo, by primary data collection or through consultation with experts, the methods used to collect this information should be described in detail.

When published studies are used as sources of probabilities, the validity of the studies that are the source of the probability estimates is a critical consideration. In addition, because complete agreement about the value of a probability is rare and because even probabilities based on large and definitive studies are associated with sampling error, the range of reasonable estimates of the probabilities needs to determined at the same time that the baseline estimate is determined. The upper and lower values of the probability are measures of the uncertainty in the baseline estimate. These values are used in sensitivity analysis. Assumptions about the distribution of the estimates are used in statistical and quasi-statistical analyses that attempt to estimate the uncertainty in the measure of expected outcome. Justification for the choice of values considered to represent the range of reasonable estimates of the probability needs to be rigorous.

The process of selecting probabilities should generate a table that shows the best estimate of the probability, the upper and lower values of the probability that are considered reasonable, and the source of the best estimate of the probability and of the probabilities considered reasonable. The best estimates are called ''baseline'' or ''base case'' estimates. This book will use the term baseline. An analysis that uses the best estimates is called the baseline or base case analysis. This book will use the term baseline.

> *EXAMPLE:* Table 10-1 is a table of the probabilities used in a decision analysis of screening for mild thyroid failure done by Danese et al. (1996) that was first discussed in Chapter 4. This table is an excellent example of the final product of the process of identifying probabilities for a decision analysis.

Probabilities used in decision analysis and cost-effectiveness analysis are usually derived from the published literature. Sometimes there is only one source of information on a particular probability, and this fact is known. Sometimes a source is used to estimate a probability for specific reasons: the source is authoritative, or it is the largest or the best study. In other situations, the literature search procedures described in Chapter 4 can be used to identify systematically information on the probability. If the literature search identifies more than one source of information on the probability, either meta-analysis or ad hoc procedures for aggregating the data can be used to yield probability estimates.

In some cases there is no published source of information on a probability. In these situations the analysis may rely on experts to estimate probabilities. It is possible to use educated ''guesses'' or to rely on subjective judgments. Last, information to estimate a probability can be generated by special studies done specifically for this purpose.

Table 10-1 Initial probability estimates used in decision analysis model of screening for mild thyroid failure

Component of Model	Baseline Probability Estimate	Range of Probabilities		Sources
		Biased Toward Screening	Biased Against Screening	
Prevalence of thyroid failure				
Men, 35 years	0.027	0.054	0.014	
Women, 35 years	0.056	0.112	0.028	Turnbridge et al. (1977)
Reversible symptoms				
Men	0.280	0.50	0.10	
Women	0.280	0.50	0.10	Cooper et al. (1984); Nystrom et al. (1988)
Positive for antithyroid antibodies				
Men	0.400	0.67	0.10	
Women	0.670	0.85	0.33	Turnbridge et al. (1977)
Total cholesterol elevated				
Men	0.250	0.50	0.10	
Women	0.250	0.50	0.10	Bogner et al. (1993); NCHS 1993

Source: Danese et al. (1996); table references cited there.

10.2 RELYING ON SELECTED PUBLISHED SOURCES OF INFORMATION ON PROBABILITIES

10.2.1 Using a Source Because It Is the Only Published Source

Sometimes only one source of information to estimate a probability is available. In these cases, it seems obvious that this source must be used in the analysis.

EXAMPLES: Schrag et al. (1997) did a decision analysis estimating the effects of prophylactic mastectomy and oophorectomy on life expectancy among women with BRCA1 or BRCA2 mutations. To estimate the reduction in the risk of ovarian cancer after prophylactic mastectomy in women known to carry a mutation, they used data from a study by Struewing et al. (1995), which was the only study of the topic that had been completed at the time of their analysis.

Schulman et al. (1991) did an analysis of the cost-effectiveness of low-dose zidovudine (azidothymidine, AZT) therapy for asymptomatic patients with human immunodeficiency virus (HIV) infection. To estimate the effect of low-dose zidovudine on the clinical course of HIV infection, they used data from the AIDS Clinical Trials Group Protocol 019, which was the only study of the topic that had been completed at the time of their analysis.

In the decision analysis comparing prophylactic cholecystectomy with expectant management for silent gallstone disease by Ransohoff et al. (1983)

that was described in Chapter 2, only one study had ascertained gallstones systematically and then followed patients with silent gallstones for a long period of time at the time the study was done.

The availability of only one source of information is usually known to the contemporary readers of the results of the analysis. Other studies may be done after the decision analysis is published, and later readers may not have the time frame of the analysis firmly in mind. For this reason, it is a good idea to mention that the publication has been selected to estimate the probabilities because it is a sole source.

EXAMPLE: Schrag et al. (1997) stated explicitly that the study used to estimate the reduction in the risk of ovarian cancer after prophylactic mastectomy was the only study that had been done.

10.2.2 Using a Source Because It Is Authoritative

Sometimes an information source has been widely used by others and is considered to be authoritative.

EXAMPLES: In the cost-effectiveness analysis of treatment with HMG-CoA reductase inhibitors (e.g., lovastatin) in the primary and secondary prevention of coronary heart disease of Goldman et al.(1991), one goal of the analysis was estimation of the effectiveness of treatment for men and women in several age groups. To make these calculations, estimates of the incidence of coronary heart disease in men and women were required. Data on incidence rates of coronary heart disease in men and women by age derived from the Framingham Heart Study were used because this source is considered authoritative.
  In the decision analysis of screening for mild thyroid failure that was first discussed in Chapter 4, Danese et al. (1996) also used data from the Framingham study to estimate transitions from health to various cardiovascular diseases.
  In their analysis on the effects of prophylactic mastectomy and oophorectomy, Schrag et al. (1997) used data from the SEER (Surveillance, Epidemiology, and End-Results) Program as the basis for their estimate of the stage of diagnosis and survival rate for ovarian cancer in carriers of the BRCA1 or BRCA2 mutation. SEER is the authoritative source of broadly representative information about cancer stage at diagnosis and survival for United States populations.

When a probability estimate is chosen because the source is considered authoritative, this explanation for the choice of the source should be described in the study report. The range should include other studies of the same topic that were not considered authoritative.

10.2.3 Using a Source Based on Its Size or Quality

Sometimes one study is so much larger than any other study that it can be seen a priori that the small studies contribute no useful information. There are instances when one study is so much better than any of the others that it is justified to use the information only from it.

> *EXAMPLE:* Heckerling and Verp (1991) did a decision analysis comparing amniocentesis and chorionic villus sampling for prenatal genetic testing. They used published information from one very large study to estimate the prevalence of a chromosomal abnormality at birth in an infant born to a 35-year-old woman.

When quality or size is the reason for choosing a study, this explanation belongs in the report.

10.2.4 Using a Source Because the Data Are Representative of the Population to Which the Results Will Be Generalized

When results of an analysis will be generalized to a particular population, it is a good idea to use information that is representative of that population in the analysis. When an analysis focuses on a particular intervention and there are studies specifically of that intervention, the analysis should rely on data from studies of that intervention whenever possible.

> *EXAMPLES:* Oster and Epstein (1987) did a cost-effectiveness analysis of cholestyramine for the prevention of coronary heart disease. They used information from the Lipid Research Clinics Coronary Primary Prevention Trial (1984a, 1984b) as the source of their estimate of the amount of reduction in the risk of coronary heart disease associated with use of the drug, because this trial was a study of cholestyramine. This contrasts with the cost-effectiveness of HMG-CoA reductase inhibitors for prevention of coronary heart disease done by Goldman et al. (1991). This group used pooled data from six studies of the effect of cholesterol-lowering drugs to estimate the amount of reduction in the risk of coronary heart disease that would be expected with use of HMG-CoA reductase inhibitors, because no studies estimating the reduction in the risk of coronary heart disease in users of HMG-CoA reductase inhibitors had been done at that time.
>
> In the analysis by Schulman et al. (1991) of low-dose zidovudine therapy for asymptomatic patients with HIV infection discussed earlier, information from the AIDS Clinical Trials Group Protocol 019 was used not only to estimate the effects of zidovudine on outcome in patients with asymptomatic HIV infection, but also to estimate the incremental number of physician visits and tests needed by those treated. The authors reasoned that use of physician services and tests in persons in the study would be representative of use in clinical practice.

10.3 AGGREGATING INFORMATION FROM MULTIPLE PUBLISHED SOURCES

10.3.1 Overview

When there is more than one source of information on a probability, the results of a meta-analysis done by others can be used as the source of the probability estimate, or a formal meta-analysis can be carried out as part of the decision analysis. Information can be aggregated in an ad hoc fashion that falls short of formal meta-analysis.

10.3.2 Meta-Analysis

When multiple studies of a given topic exist, meta-analysis is the preferred method for using the information to derive a probability for several reasons. First, the systematic nature of the information retrieval process for meta-analysis maximizes the likelihood of obtaining an unbiased estimate of the probability. Second, meta-analysis formally takes into account the size of the studies and insulates the decision analysis from criticisms of arbitrariness. Last, use of meta-analysis enhances reproducibility.

The decision analysis or cost-effectiveness analysis may use information from a published meta-analysis.

> *EXAMPLE:* In the cost-effectiveness analysis of aspirin and warfarin for stroke prophylaxis in patients with nonvalvular atrial fibrillation, Gage et al. (1995) used data from a published meta-analysis of individual-level data from five randomized trials of antithrombotic therapy in atrial fibrillation to estimate the rates of stroke without therapy, the percentage reduction in the risk of stroke in users of warfarin, and the percentage of intracranial hemorrhages that were mild, moderate, or severe.

The meta-analysis may be done for the purposes of the decision analysis or cost-effectiveness analysis but might not be formally described as meta-analysis.

> *EXAMPLES:* Oster, Tuden, and Colditz (1987) did an analysis comparing the cost-effectiveness of different methods of prophylaxis against deep vein thrombosis for patients undergoing major orthopedic surgery compared with observation. To estimate the percentage of patients who would experience deep vein thrombosis without any treatment, they did a meta-analysis of 16 randomized trials of prophylaxis that had used a placebo or no-prophylaxis control group. Rates of deep vein thrombosis in the various treatment groups were similarly estimated by meta-analysis of randomized trials that involved the treatment as one of the arms in the trial.

More recently, formal meta-analysis is done as input to the decision analysis of the cost-effectiveness analysis and the results of the meta-analysis makes an independent contribution to the literature.

EXAMPLE: Bennett et al. (1997) did an analysis examining the cost-effectiveness of interferon-alpha 2b in patients with mild chronic hepatitis C. The efficacy of interferon-alpha 2b was estimated based on a meta-analysis of randomized trials of the drug in patients with hepatitis C. The results of the both the meta-analysis and the cost-effectiveness analysis were highlighted in the publication.

10.3.3   Ad hoc Aggregation

The data from a group of studies assembled systematically or informally can be aggregated by averaging or by some ''pooling'' procedure that falls short of formal statistical meta-analysis. Averaging and other nonstatistical methods of pooling are common in decision analysis and cost-effectiveness analysis.

EXAMPLE: In Arevalo and Washington's analysis of the cost effectiveness of prenatal screening and immunization for hepatitis B virus (1988), the efficacy of the hepatitis B vaccine was one of the probabilities in the decision analysis. The rate used in the baseline analysis was taken to be the mean of the rates given in three publications on the topic.

Averaging does not take into account the size of the studies, and all studies are given equal weight in calculating the average. The quality of the studies is also not taken into account.

Although it is not uncommon to average measures from different studies to obtain a probability measure for a decision analysis, this method is not recommended.

10.4   EXPERTS AS SOURCES OF PROBABILITY ESTIMATES

Experts and expert panels are a source of data on probabilities in clinical decision analysis (Weinstein and Fineberg 1980; Sox et al. 1988), and they are used commonly used in decision analysis and cost-effectiveness analysis aimed at formulating policy.

EXAMPLE: Schrag et al. (1997) chose their estimate of an 85% reduction in the cumulative risk of breast cancer following prophylactic mastectomy in women with BRCA1 or BRCA2 mutations after consulting ''experienced clinicians.''

Carefully constituted expert panels may be acceptable as a method for estimating probabilitities, but they should used only when other sources of information on the probabiities do not exist (Gold et al. 1996). If an expert panel is used as the source of information on a probability for a decision analysis or cost-effectiveness analysis, elicitation of information should be structured.

The Delphi method, in which estimates are refined through a process in which the experts review probability estimates and change them based on discussion or feedback, is recommended.

> *EXAMPLE:*   Miller et al. (1996) conducted a cost-effectiveness analysis of incorporation of inactivated polio vaccine into the schedule for routine vaccination of children. This analysis relied on the recommendations of an expert Delphi panel when probability estimates from the published literature were not available.

Any probabilities based on expert judgment should be subjected to sensitivity analysis.

10.5   PERSONAL EXPERIENCE AND "GUESSING" TO ESTIMATE PROBABILITIES

Personal experience and ''guessing'' have been described as methods for deriving probabilities in clinical decision analysis—decision analysis done at the bedside to help guide the management of an individual patient (Weinstein and Fineberg 1980; Sox et al. 1988). Published examples that admitted to the use of subjective experience and guesses in decision analysis aimed at formulation of clinical and public policy could not be identified. Probabilities based on guesses and subjective experience are likely to be criticized in the peer review process, and studies that use such methods probably will not be highly regarded by the scientific community. The use of personal experience and guessing are not recommended approaches to estimating probabilities.

10.6   ACCOUNTING FOR UNCERTAINTY IN PROBABILITY ESTIMATES

Most decision analyses involve estimation of many different probabilities. Errors in these uncertainties propagate when the probabilities are multiplied. When the decision model is complex, small errors in the individual probability estimates can lead to large errors in the final result of the decision analysis.

Sensitivity analysis is the method that is used most often to try to evaluate the effect of uncertainty in the probability estimates on the conclusions of the decision analysis. More generally, sensitivity analysis attempts to evaluate the effect of various assumptions made in an analysis on the conclusions that are reached. Sensitivity analysis is an essential component of both decision analysis and cost-effectiveness analysis. The topic is covered in a separate chapter, Chapter 15, because it is the most commonly used method for assessing uncertainty in decision analysis and cost-effectiveness analysis.

Unfortunately, sensitivity analysis in which three or more probabilities are varied at the same time is difficult to do, and it is difficult to make the results comprehensible. Because of this limitation of sensitivity analysis, statistical and quasi-statistical methods to derive a single summary estimate of the uncertainty in the outcome measure taking into account the uncertainties in all of the probability estimates used in the decision analysis have been developed (Rifkin 1983; Doubilet et al. 1985; Critchfield and Willard 1986). Each of these methods tries to estimate some kind of ''confidence range,'' which is meant to be analogous to the confidence interval that is derived from analysis of data subjected to classical statistical analysis. This estimate is an estimate of the uncertainty in the difference in outcome between the two alternatives examined in the decision analysis. These methods are described and critiqued.

10.6.1   Description of the Methods

For each of the methods, the probability and outcome measures are assumed to be variables with an associated probability density function. The probability density function for each variable has a mean and a standard deviation. The mean of the probability density function for each variable is equal to the probability estimate. The standard deviation is assumed to reflect the degree of uncertainty in the variable. For simple decision trees, the expected outcome of each decision option and a probability density function for the expected outcome are calculated directly using this information.

For complex decision trees, precise calculations of the probability density function for the outcome measure are tedious and often impossible. Thus, in practice, the probability density function of the expected outcome is estimated using Monte Carlo simulation. The decision tree is repeatedly analyzed by picking values of the probabilities and the outcome at random based on the assumed underlying probability density function. At each iteration, the result of the analysis is recorded. The mean of the results of the many iterations estimates the expected outcome. The results of the many iterations are assumed to be normally distributed, and standard normal theory is used to estimate a 95% ''confidence range'' for the expected outcome.

Specifying probability density functions for all of the probabilities and the outcome measure is a critical part of application of these methods. Doing this can be very time-consuming. For many variables, there are no empiric data on the probability density function, and the choice of the probability density function is a guess. Alternatively, the probability is assumed to have a distribution that is convenient.

Doubilet et al. (1985), for example, describe a method for estimating the probability density functions for each of the probabilities in a decision analysis that simplifies application of the Monte Carlo method. They suggest assuming that the probability density function for each probability in the decision analysis follows a log-normal distribution. Details of the method are presented in their publication.

10.6.2   Bayesian Methods

Eddy and colleagues (Eddy 1989; Eddy, Hasselblad, Shachter 1990a, 1990b) described a method for synthesizing evidence that is based on Bayesian statistics. The method is called the confidence profile method. Eddy and colleagues frame the method as a method for estimating uncertainty in a meta-analysis. It is more clearly related to decision analysis and to the broader problem of estimating uncertainty when multiple sources of information are used to estimate the outcome for a clinical problem. Like the methods described previously, the confidence profile method yields a quantity conceptually analogous to the 95% confidence interval based on classic statistics. The methods theoretically can be used to take into account the bias in individual studies as well as the uncertainty in the estimates of individual study parameters.

The full use of these methods requires a fair amount of subjectivity in specifying a prior distribution to represent all of the basic parameters in the model (or to decide to use a noninformative prior distribution). The problem of identifying and measuring bias in individual studies is not addressed by the methods. Adjusting for bias using the methods may require more information from individual studies than is available to the analyst.

10.6.3 Critique of the Methods

None of these statistical and quasi-statistical methods for estimating the uncertainty in the estimate of the expected outcome has been widely applied. The estimation of a probability density function for each probability in the analysis is a formidable undertaking even when an expert panel or a single judge is used for this purpose. The validity and reliability of estimates of the probability density function provided by an expert panel or a single judge are uncertain. The final estimate of the uncertainty of the expected outcome is dependent on the assumptions about the probability density functions of the individual probabilities in the decision analysis.

The suggestion by Doubilet et al. (1985) that probability density functions for all of the probabilities included in a decision analysis be assumed to be log-normal is based on the convenience and mathematical tractability of the log-normal distribution and not on empiric or theoretical data to support its use. The assumption that expected outcome of the Monte Carlo simulation estimating expected outcome follows a normal distribution and that standard normal theory applies is unproven.

The Bayesian approach of Eddy and colleagues (Eddy 1989; Eddy, Shachter 1990A, 1990B) may be useful although the descriptions of the method are difficult to follow. Empirical evaluation is lacking.

Sensitivity analysis is a well-accepted, straightforward method for attempting to assess the amount of uncertainty in a decision analysis. Although sensitivity analysis does not yield a quantitative estimate of the amount of uncertainty in the estimate of expected outcome, the methods that claim to yield such estimates are poorly developed. In the absence of better empirical and theoretical work to support their use, these methods should be used cautiously.

11

Measuring Preferences
for Health States

Decision analysis and cost-effectiveness analysis are increasingly concerned with taking into account the effects of interventions on disability and functional status. Quality-adjusted life years (QALYs), which achieve this goal, are increasingly used as the common metric for decision and cost-effectiveness analysis. When QALYS are the outcome metric, the analysis is a utility or cost-utility analysis.

Section 11.1 discusses the concepts of utility and preferences for health states. It introduces the concept of QALYs. Section 11.2 describes the important conceptual issues in the measurement of preferences for health states. Section 11.3 describes the "traditional" methods for measuring preferences for health states—the standard gamble, time-trade-off, and rating scale methods. Section 11.4 discusses the generic measures of health-related quality of life that can be used as measures of preference in a utility or cost-utility analysis.

Chapter 13 describes how to incorporate preference measures into utility or cost-utility analysis.

11.1 THE CONCEPT OF UTILITY

When an analysis focuses on the difference in the probability of living or life expectancy as outcomes, life and life expectancy are implicitly considered to be valued, and people are assumed to have a preference for longer life expectancy. The need for incorporating measures other than life and life expectancy into a decision analysis and cost analysis follows from the observation that many medical interventions do not affect life or life expectancy and some treatments alter the

169

chances of living or dying but are themselves associated with morbidity. For example, treatments for chronic arthritis, back pain, and headache affect pain and disability but not life expectancy; chemotherapy for acute lymphocytic leukemia in children causes temporarily disabling and unpleasant side effects but increases life expectancy; treatments that save the lives of some persons with stroke may leave some of them in a state of disability.

"Utility" refers to the desirability or preference that individuals or societies have for a given outcome (Torrance 1987). Preferences are the levels of satisfaction, distress, or desirability that people associate with the health outcome (Froberg and Kane 1989A). Decision analysis and cost-effectiveness analysis are increasingly concerned with the measurement of preferences and with the incorporation of utility measures into the analysis.

A decision analysis that incorporates measures of the preferences of individuals or society for health is a utility analysis. A cost analysis that incorporates preferences for health states is a cost-utility analysis.[1]

Measures of preference are incorporated into a decision analysis or cost-effectiveness analysis by using the value of the preference for health to obtain a measure of quality-adjusted life years (QALYs). QALYs attempt to combine expected survival with expected quality of life in a single metric (LaPuma and Lawlor 1990). An analysis that uses quality-adjusted life years seeks to evaluate the trade-off between mortality, morbidity, the preferences of patients and society for various types of morbidity, and the willingness of patients and society to accept a shortening of life to avoid certain morbidities. The concept of the quality-adjusted life year is explicit recognition that in order to achieve certain states of health, people are willing to take a measurable risk of a bad outcome.

11.2 CONCEPTUAL ISSUES IN THE MEASUREMENT OF PREFERENCES FOR HEALTH STATES

11.2.1 Overview

The overall goal of measuring preferences for health states is to construct a reliable and valid numerical representation of preferences for health states. This representation must be put in the form of a numerical scale that ranges from 0 to 1.0, where 0 represents the least preferred health state and 1.0 the most preferred state. The 0 in the scale generally refers to death and 1.0 to perfect health. The scale values assigned to the health states that lie between 0 and 1.0 are the values used to "adjust" life expectancy—yielding a measure of quality-adjusted life expectancy. The incorporation of preference measures scaled from 0.0 to 1.0 into decision analysis and cost-effectiveness analysis (i.e., utility or cost-utility analysis) is covered in Chapter 13.

Measures of health status are often described as measures of health-related quality of life. However, health status and quality of life are distinct concepts. Quality of life encompasses—in addition to physical, mental, and social functioning—environmental quality, subjective well-being, and life satisfaction (McDowell and Newell 1996).

A number of measures of health status attempt to simultaneously assess physical, social, and emotional aspects of health. These measures are often called measures of "general health status," "generic" measures of health status, or measures of "health-related quality of life."

Not all measures that are called measures of health-related quality of life are suitable for use in utility and cost-utility analysis, and not all of them can be used to derive estimates of quality-adjusted life expectancy. Generic measures of health status can be categorized as health profiles or utility measures (Fryback et al. 1997). Health profiles report separate scores for each dimension of health considered. Utility measures are constructed using measurement of preferences for various health states. Only utility measures that are preference-based can be used to estimate quality-adjusted life expectancy.

Preference-based methods are linked with judgments about the *value* placed on a particular health states and yield a single score that is scaled from 0.0 (usually death) to 1.0 (complete health). It is sometimes possible to convert measures made using health profile instruments to preference-based measures of utility by linking the scores derived from them with preferences derived from community-based samples. Some instruments, however, exhibit floor and ceiling effects when used to measure conditions whose associated health states are below or above the scaled range of the profile (Fryback et al. 1997). That is, the instrument does not measure very high and very low levels of health and is insensitive to differences in preferences for these high and low levels of health.

In this chapter, measures of preferences will be conceptualized as direct measures and indirect measures. Direct measures of preferences use a methodology in which community, patient, or physician samples are asked to directly provide information about their preferences for a set of health states. The direct methods include the standard gamble, time trade-off, and direct rating methods. Indirect methods to measure preferences link information from generic or general questionnaires with preferences for health states derived seperately. The goal of both direct and indirect approaches is to derive appropriately-scaled measures that can be used in utility and cost-utility analysis.

11.2.2 Validity and Reliability of Measures of Utility

A measure of preferences for health states (a utility measure) should be reliable and valid. A measure is reliable if the same phenomenon can be measured a second time with the same result. A measure is valid if it measures the phenomenon it claims to measure.

For direct methods to assess preferences for health states, evaluation of three types of reliability is pertinent—internal (intrarater) reliability, test-retest reliability, and interrater reliability. Internal (intrarater) reliability refers to the similarity of replicate measures on the same subject at the same time. Test-retest reliability refers to the similarity of the same measurements made at different times on the same person. Interrater reliability refers to the similarity of the measure made by two or more raters.

Evaluation of two types of validity is pertinent to the construction of measures of preferences for health states: criterion validity and construct validity (Spitzer

1987). Evaluation of criterion validity involves the comparison of the measure with a well-accepted measure of the concept being measured. To evaluate criterion validity, there must be a "gold standard."

Evaluation of construct validity requires relating the measure to a concept or a group of concepts and testing the ability of the measurement to predict events or behaviors that grow out of an understanding of these concepts (Torrance 1976). A measure of preferences for health states would have construct validity if it predicted the actual choices made by individuals or groups of individuals. In practice, construct validity is rarely evaluated in the health preferences literature. Rather, the similarity of scores made using different methods—called convergence—is used as indirect evidence of construct validity.

11.2.3   Level of Measurement

Measurement scales are classified as nominal, ordinal, interval, and ratio. Table 11-1 describes each kind of measurement classification, lists the mathematical operations that can be performed on data from scales that achieve the given level of measurement, and gives an example of a scale of each type. The mathematical and statistical operations required in decision analysis are addition, subtraction, multiplication, and division. To be useful, a scale measuring preferences for health states must achieve measurement on at least an interval scale, because the mathematical operations required in decision analysis are valid only on scales that achieve this level of measurement.

Table 11-1   Measurement scales, permissible mathematical operations, and an example of each scale

Measurement Achieved by Scale	Description	Permissible Operations	Example
Nominal	States are assigned to categories without numerical meaning	None	Religion: Baptist, Catholic, Jewish
Ordinal	States are rank-ordered, but the distance between ranks does not have a numerical interpretation	None	Health status: excellent, good, fair, poor
Interval	States are rank-ordered, and the distance between ranks provides some information on the amount of difference between ranks	Addition, subtraction, multiplication, division	Beck depression scale
Ratio	States are rank-ordered, and the distance between different points on the scale provides information on the amount of difference between ranks	Addition, subtraction, multiplication, division, invariance with multiplication by a constant	Temperature

11.2.4   Strategies for Developing Scales Using Direct Methods

Two different overall strategies for developing scales that measure preference for health states have been described: holistic strategies and decomposed strategies (Froberg and Kane 1989b), which are also called multiattribute strategies (Pliskin, Shepard, Weinstein 1980). Holistic strategies require raters to assign scale values to each possible health state of interest. Decomposed, or multiattribute, strategies use statistical methods to develop a rating scale based on the rating of single attributes of health states or selected combinations of all possible health states.

Holistic strategies can place a heavy response burden on subjects if the number of health states to be rated is large. Decomposed strategies enable the investigator to obtain values for all health states without requiring the raters to assign values to every one. The statistical methods used to derive rating scales from measurements made on decomposed health states are complex, and methods for multiattribute scaling are not considered further in this book. The interested reader is referred to Torrance, Boyle, and Horwood (1982) and to Boyle and Torrance (1984).

11.3   DEVELOPING MEASUREMENT SCALES IN PRACTICE

11.3.1   Overview

The direct development of a scale to measure preferences for health states involves several discrete steps (Torrance 1982; Froberg and Kane 1989a). First, the health states of interest are defined and described. Second, a rater or group of raters provides information on their preferences for each of the health states. Last, the information provided by the raters is used to create the numerical scale.

11.3.2   Defining and Describing the Health States

The health states selected will depend on the topic of the analysis. Usually a health state is defined for every possible distinct outcome of the intervention and its alternatives (Torrance 1982).

In a comparison of different treatments for babies undergoing care in an intensive care unit, the health states that should be defined are all of the possible outcomes of the treatments and of the lack of treatment for the newborn.

The health states that should be defined in a comparison of treatments for cancer should include all of the outcomes of having the cancer and not being treated and all of the outcomes of the treatments for cancer.

After the health states have been defined, they must be described. The descriptions of the health states should be put in functional or behavioral terms (Torrance 1982). Each description should include a statement on the level of physical health, emotional health, and everyday function in social and role activities, and general perceptions of well-being (Ware 1987). Psychological studies suggest that only five to nine separate items can be considered simultaneously (Miller 1956), and each health state description should contain no more than five to nine separate aspects (Torrance 1982; Froberg and Kane 1989A).

EXAMPLE: Table 11-2 presents narrative descriptions of some of the health states describing patients with cancer that Llewellyn-Thomas et al. (1984) used in a study that compared different ways of describing health states. Each description is in functional and behavioral terms, and each one deals with all of the areas described above. There are from seven to nine separate statements about function within each description, and none contains more than nine.

11.3.3 Choosing Raters

Ideally, the raters should be selected according to the purpose of the study (Torrance 1982). For example, when the conclusion of the analysis applies to the society as a whole, a representative sample should be used; when it applies to patients with a given disease, patients should be used. When a cost-utility analysis is done for the societal perspective, representative community samples should be used to assess preferences (Gold et al. 1996).

The published literature on measurement of preferences provides little guidance on the choice of the number of raters to use in a study to measure preferences for health states. It is common to encounter scales of health preferences developed based on the responses of only a handful of raters. It is difficult to apply formulas for formal sample size estimation to the problem of deciding how many raters to use, because a measure of the variation in the scale rating is unavailable. The number of raters used in a study of health preferences should be chosen based on consideration of the variability of the measure, perhaps as measured in a pilot study or in studies by others.

11.3.4 Rating the Health States to Create the Numerical Scale

11.3.4.1 Overview

After the health states have been defined and described and the raters chosen, the health states must be rated. Rating methods fall into three categories: the standard gamble method, the time trade-off method, and direct scaling methods. There is also a set of miscellaneous methods that do not yield numerical scale data, which are described here for completeness.

The standard gamble is conceptually linked with decision theory. The time trade-off method is intuitively appealing and fairly simple to carry out, and it is used with increasing frequency in decision analysis. Direct scaling methods are the most common methods used to create scales, mostly because they are simple for the investigator to develop and for the subjects to understand. Other methods—the willingness-to-pay method and the equivalence method—are of interest because they have been used often in cost-effectiveness analysis.

11.3.4.2 Standard Gamble

The standard gamble is a method of measuring preferences for health states that is directly derived from decision theory. It is considered the ''criterion'' method for obtaining information on preferences (Llewellyn-Thomas et al. 1984), for it incor-

Table 11-2 Descriptions of health status describing patients with cancer

Case 1: I am in the age range 40–64 years. I am unable to work. I am tired and sleep poorly due to discomfort in my back and arm. I am worried about my health and finances. I am able to drive my car and I make an effort to walk about my neighborhood.

Case 2: I am in the age range 40–64 years. Although I worked until recently, I am presently hospitalized and on complete bed rest. A nurse bathes, dresses, and feeds me. I am confused about time and place and have some memory loss. I have vomited and am only able to take clear fluids by mouth. I am dehydrated (lack water) and receive fluids by vein (IV therapy). I am incontinent (unable to control my bowels and bladder). I have low back pain.

Case 3: I am in the age range 40–64 years. I have been tired and weak and unable to work. I have lost 15 pounds in weight. I walk slowly, and travel outside the house is difficult. Much of the day I am alone, lying down in my bedroom. Social contact with my friends is reduced.

Case 4: I am in the age range 40–64 years. I am able to work. Over the past year I have noticed a feeling of tiredness and I have lost 20 pounds in weight. I have little energy and I am unable to keep up with my usual routine. I have made an effort to walk to work but I have let the house and hobbies "slide." I am sleeping poorly. I am maintaining my present weight.

Source: Llewellyn-Thomas et al. (1984).

porates the conceptual framework for decision making under conditions of uncertainty that is at the heart of decision theory.

Application of this method involves having raters choose between two alternatives. One alternative has a certain outcome and one alternative involves a gamble. The certain outcome is the health state to be rated. The gamble has two possible outcomes—the best health state (usually complete health), which is described as occurring with a probability $p;$ or an alternative state, the worst state (usually death), which is described as occurring with a probability of $1 - p$. The probability p is varied until the rater is indifferent between the two alternatives. That is, the rater is indifferent between the alternative that is certain and the gamble that might bring the best health state.

EXAMPLE: Figure 11-1 graphically depicts a hypothetical gamble. Figure 11-2 depicts a gamble where the alternatives are renal transplant surgery and

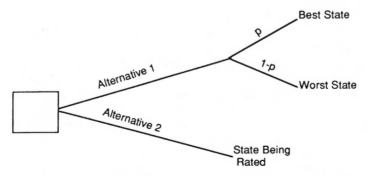

Figure 11-1 Graphical representation of standard gamble.

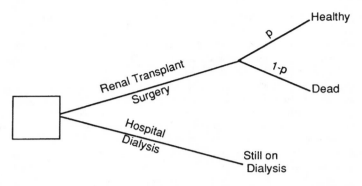

Figure 11-2 Graphic representation of standard gamble for the choice between renal transplant and continued hospital dialysis.

continued dialysis. In the gamble, continued dialysis is the health state that is stated to have a certain outcome, which involves continued poor health and impaired social and role function. Renal transplant is the gamble: it has a probability p of bringing about a state of complete health, but it also is associated with a probability $1 - p$ of death due to surgery. A rater is asked to state at what probability p he or she would be willing to accept the certainty of the state of poor health and impaired social and role function instead of taking the risk of death from surgery as a means of possibly achieving a state of complete health. When p is close to 1.0, meaning that the probability of achieving complete health by gambling on surgery is close to 1, most raters would choose renal transplant surgery. When p is low, meaning that choosing the gamble has a high probability of causing death due to surgery, most raters would choose the certainty of the state of poor health and impaired social and role function.

The gamble is repeated for all of the health states that are to be rated. The points of indifference associated with each health state are the values used in the scale of health preferences.

Torrance (1987) described visual aids that help in the development of a rating scale using the gamble. A probability wheel, or "chance board," consisting of a disk with two movable, different-colored sections, is presented. The alternatives are displayed to the rater on cards, with the two outcomes of the gamble alternative color-coded to the two sectors of the probability wheel. The rater is told that the chance of each outcome is proportional to the similarly colored area of the disk. The rater is asked to adjust the sections to represent the preference for the gamble alternatives.

Even with visual aids, it is difficult for some raters to think in terms of probabilities. The number of health states that must be rated to derive a scale is often large, and resource demands and response burden limit the use of the standard gamble in practice.

The reliability of scales developed from the standard gamble has been evaluated infrequently. Table 11-3 summarizes evaluations of the reliability of the standard gamble and other rating methods. When it has been evaluated, intrarater reliability of the standard gamble has been good (Torrance 1976; Froberg and Kane 1989B). Test-retest reliability was good at one week but poor at one year (Froberg and Kane 1989B).

The ability of scales based on the standard gamble to achieve measurement on an interval or ratio scale has been assumed rather than proven. The standard gamble is considered to be the "criterion" method, but criterion validity has not been evaluated. There is a correlation between measures of preference based on the standard gamble and measures based on the time trade-off and category rating methods ($r = 0.56–0.65$) (Read et al. 1984), but the standard gamble produces consistently higher preference scores. Llewellyn-Thomas et al. (1982) found that small changes in the description of the gamble outcome can affect the value of preferences for health states provided by the same raters, showing internal inconsistency of utility measures based on the standard gamble.

11.3.4.3 Time Trade-Off

The time trade-off method was developed as an alternative to the standard gamble by Torrance, Thomas, and Sackett (1972). The time trade-off method also presents the rater with a choice. The choice is between two alternatives that both have a certain outcome. The choice is how many years of life the rater would be willing to give up to be in the healthier state compared with the less healthy one. Torrance (1987) has also described a useful visual aid for developing scales based on the time trade-off method. It is not described here.

The time trade-off method is easier for raters than the standard gamble. The response burden is about the same as for the standard gamble, but the task is more intuitive both for the rater and for the investigator.

EXAMPLE: Angina pectoris has been shown in several randomized clinical trials to be more common in patients who are managed medically than in patients who undergo coronary artery bypass graft (CABG), even though life

Table 11-3 Reliability of methods for measuring preferences for health states

Measure of Reliability	Method			
	Standard Gamble	Time Trade-off	Rating Scale	Willingness to Pay
Intrarater reliability	0.77	0.77–0.88	0.70–0.94	—
Test-retest reliability				
One week or less	0.80	0.87	0.77	—
One year	0.53	0.62	0.49	0.25
Interrater reliability	—	—	0.75–0.77	—

Source: Froberg and Kane (1989B).

expectancy is not shorter in patients managed medically. Weinstein and Stason (1985) did an analysis of CABG surgery that attempted to incorporate information about the effects of coronary artery surgery on relief from angina into estimates of the effect of CABG on life expectancy. The analysis adjusted for the diminished quality of life that accompanies angina pectoris. Weinstein and Stason used the time trade-off method as a measure of the preferences for health. In the analysis, a patient with mild angina pectoris was willing to accept 9 years of life with no symptoms in exchange for 10 years of life with mild angina.

Scales derived from the time trade-off method have not been routinely subjected to evaluations to determine their reliability. Intrarater reliability was as good or better than the standard gamble when evaluated by the same investigator (Torrance 1976). As shown in Table 11-3, similar to the standard gamble, test-retest reliability has been found to be good at one week or less and poor at one year (Froberg and Kane 1989B).

Whether or not scales derived from the time trade-off method achieve measurement on a ratio or interval scale is unknown. Scales based on the time trade-off method are moderately well-correlated ($r = 0.56$–0.65) with scales based on the standard gamble and category rating methods (Read et al. 1984). The high correlation among scales does not prove that any of the scales measures what it purports to measure. It means that they are the same, not that they are necessarily valid (Read et al. 1984).

11.3.4.4   Direct Rating Scales

Methods for directly constructing a rating scale are the most commonly used methods for measuring preferences for health states. These methods include interval scaling, category-rating, and magnitude estimation (Froberg and Kane 1989B).

Interval scaling starts by depicting the scale as a line on a page with clearly defined endpoints, called anchors. The rater identifies the best and worst health states and places these at the anchor points. The rater then rates the preference for each health state by placing each state at a point on the line between the anchors.

In category rating, raters sort the health states into a specified number of categories, and equal changes in preference between adjacent categories are assumed to exist. In magnitude estimation, the rater is given a "standard" health state and asked to indicate, with a number or a ratio, how much better or worse each health state is compared with the standard. Visual aids—"feeling thermometers," boxes, decks of cards—are useful (Torrance 1987). These methods are the simplest to apply.

Table 11-3 shows that rating scales have good intrarater reliability ($r = 0.70$–0.94) and interrater reliability ($r = 0.75$–0.77) when evaluated. Test-retest reliability is worse than for rating scales developed using the standard gamble and time trade-off methods both in the short term and in the long term.

The level of measurement of scales developed using these methods is assumed to be interval or ratio, but this assumption is unproven. Construct validity has not been evaluated. As noted previously, the scales based on these methods are moderately well correlated with scales based on the other methods ($r = 0.56$–0.65), but this does not assure validity.

11.3.4.5   Miscellaneous

The equivalence method asks the rater to state how many people in one health state are equivalent to a specified number of people in another health state. The willingness-to-pay method asks raters to state what percentage of the family income they would be willing to pay in order to be free of the stated condition. Neither of these methods yields a scale with properties that allow use in a utility or cost-utility analysis.

11.4   USE OF GENERIC MEASURES OF HEALTH-RELATED QUALITY OF LIFE AS PREFERENCE MEASURES

11.4.1   Overview

The Quality of Well-Being Scale (QWB; Kaplan and Anderson 1988), the EuroQol Quality of Life Scale (EuroQol Group 1990; Essink-Bot, Stouthard, Bonsel 1993), and the 36-item Medical Outcomes Study short form (SF-36; Ware and Sherbourne 1992; Ware et al. 1993) are measures of health related quality of life. They are popular instruments in outcomes research. Scores derived from these nonpreference-based generic measures of health status cannot, however, be directly incorporated into utility and cost-utility analysis to estimate quality-adjusted life expectancy. The scores must be linked with data on preferences to create an index, scored from 0.0 to 1.0. The preferences rating for the health states that are based on these instruments need to come from an appropriate population, usually a large and representative sample of the general population.

11.4.2   Quality of Well-Being Scale (QWB)

The Quality of Well-Being Scale (QWB, Kaplan and Anderson 1988) assesses health status by asking about symptoms and level of function in three areas—mobility, physical activity, and social activity. These ratings have been linked with weights that were derived from a general population sample and yield a single index, scaled from 0.0 to 1.0, that represents a judgment about the social undesirability of the overall problem. Thus, information from the QWB is a utility measure, Q, that can be used to adjust life-expectancy in a utility or cost-utility analysis. The actual incorporation of Q into these analyses is described in Chapter 13.

The reliability of the preference weights for the QWB has been shown to be .90 (Kaplan and Bush 1982).

11.4.3   EuroQol Quality of Life Scale (EuroQol)

The EuroQol Quality of Life Scale (EuroQol, EuroQol Group 1990; Essink-Bot, Stouthard, Bonsel 1993) was developed beginning in the late 1980s by a multinational group. The goal was development of a simple measure of general health that would provide a single index preference for health states. The 1993 version of the EuroQol covers five dimensions of health: mobility, self-care, usual activities, pain/discomfort, and anxiety/depression. Respondents rate themselves in each one of three mutually exclusive categories (no problem, some problem, major problem) for each dimension, leading to 243 distinct health states. Two states for death and unconsciousness are added.

The ratings are scored to yield a single index of health status, scaled from 0.0 to 1.0. The scoring algorithm is based on values assigned to each of the 245 health states derived from interviews of a large and representative national sample of adults in Great Britain. Thus, the EuroQol index is a preference measure that can incorporated into utility and cost-utility analysis to estimate QALYs, as described in more detail in Chapter 13.

11.4.4   36-Item Short Form Questionnaire (SF-36)

The 36-item Medical Outcomes Study short form (SF-36, Ware and Sherbourne 1992; Ware et al. 1993) assesses health status by asking respondents to answer 36 questions about their view of their overall health, how well they feel, and how well they are able to perform their usual activities. Thirty-four of the 36 questions are used to calculate scores, scaled from 0 to 100, that assess eight dimensions of health. Two items are used to measure change in health status.

Scores from the SF-36 cannot be used directly in a utility or cost-utility analysis because the scores are not preference-based. Fryback et al. (1997) used information from a population-based study in which participants provided information about health using both the QWB and the SF-36. They compared responses on these two instruments and developed a model that can be used to predict an overall health utility score from the SF-36 scores. The purpose of developing the model was to provide a tool that would allow use of SF-36 scores in utility and cost-utility analysis. Table 11.4 gives the coefficients for their six variable regression models to predict the QWB index from scores from the SF-36.

Table 11-4   Six variable regression model to predict QWB Index from scores on the SF-36

Variable	Coefficient
Intercept	0.59196
Physical function	0.0012588
Mental Health	−0.0011709
Bodily pain	−0.0014261
General health × role function due to physical problem	0.00000705
Physical function × bodily pain	0.00001140
Mental health × bodily pain	0.00001931

Source: Fryback et al. (1997).

This model was cross-validated on an independent sample of 74 persons from the same geographic area and of 57 patients with renal disease. The correlation between the predicted and observed QWB for the population sample was 0.70. It was 0.78 for the renal patients.

11.5 LIMITATIONS OF MEASURES OF PREFERENCES FOR HEALTH STATES

The validity of incorporation of measures of preferences for health states into decision analysis rests on the assumption that preferences are well-defined, consistent, and quantifiable. There are some concerns about the degree to which currently available measures meet these criteria.

The measurement of preferences for health states has been shown to be influenced by the measurement process itself, including the way the information is presented, as well as by the method used to elicit ratings and other circumstances of the rating process (Llewellyn-Thomas et al. 1984). The different scaling methods do not yield identical results even when the same problem is presented (Read et al. 1984; Llewellyn-Thomas et al. 1984), and there is not consensus about which method is the best method. On the conceptual level, Llewellyn-Thomas et al. (1984) have suggested that it might be naive to think of any state of health as possessing a single value.

In practice, measurement of preferences is often based on ad hoc or convenience samples. The methods for making the measurements are often poorly described.

Additional concerns about the use QALYS to set public policy based on considerations of values and ethics are described in Chapter 17.

NOTES

1. Drummond et al. (1997) discuss the theoretical link between classical formulations of the concept of ''utility'' described by Neumann and Morgenstern and the measurement of utility based on this theory. This book assumes that all utility measures, whether or not they are Neumann-Morgenstern utilities, are useful in conducting utility and cost-utility analysis. Calling a measure a utility measure and using it in such an analysis does not, however, guarentee comparability across studies that are labeled as utility or cost-utility studies.

12

Advanced Cost-Effectiveness Analysis

The conceptual model for most cost-effectiveness analyses is a decision analytic model that compares the effectiveness of alternative courses of action. Once the decision analysis has been carried out, costs and outcomes are identified and valued. The cost-effectiveness of the alternatives is then estimated.

This simplistic description of cost-effectiveness analysis belies extraordinary complexity in the definition of the concept of cost-effectiveness and in the identification of valuation of costs and outcomes. Handling of costs and benefits that occur in the future also poses analytic challenges. Cost-effectiveness analysis requires skills in decision analysis and in economics as well as an understanding of study design. Interpretation of the results of economic evaluations often raises complex moral and ethical issues.

It is impossible to cover the topic of cost-effectiveness analysis comprehensively in two or three chapters. There are several excellent textbooks (Drummond et al. 1997; Haddix et al. 1996; Gold et al. 1996) devoted solely to the technical details of economic evaluation of health programs, all emphasizing cost-effectiveness analysis. The book by Gold et al. (1996), based on the deliberations of an expert panel on cost-effectiveness analysis appointed by the U.S. Public Health Service, presents an explicit set of guidelines for the conduct of cost-effectiveness analysis for health and medicine. It is particularly recommended to readers who want in-depth information on how to conduct a cost-effectiveness analysis. The book by Drummond et al. (1997) is recommended as the best single source of information on how to estimate cost for a cost-effectiveness analysis.

Section 12.1 describes the main types of cost analysis used to evaluate health programs, discusses the reasons why cost-benefit analysis is rarely done in health care, and gives the rationale for a focus on cost-effectiveness analysis. Section 12.2 presents key concepts in cost-effectiveness analysis, including descriptions of the various definitions of cost-effective and the distinction between average and marginal cost-effectiveness ratios. This section gives the basic mathematical formulation of cost-effectiveness analysis. Section 12.3 discusses the concept of perspective in cost-effectiveness analysis and its importance. Section 12.4 discusses time horizon. Section 12.5 presents the conceptual basis for estimating cost and describes how cost is most often measured in practice. Sections 12.6 and 12.7 discuss two important issues related to analysis of cost—discounting and inflation.

The incorporation of utilities into a cost analysis is discussed in Chapter 13.

12.1 TYPES OF ECONOMIC EVALUATION

12.1.1 Overview of Main Types of Economic Evaluation

Most authors (O'Brien 1995; Epstein and Sherwood 1996) describe four main types of economic evaluation—cost-minimization analysis, cost-benefit analysis, cost-effectiveness analysis, and cost-utility analysis. The assumptions and questions addressed in these four kinds of economic evaluation are summarized briefly in Table 12-1.

There is substantial overlap between these four types of cost evaluation. Cost-minimization analysis, cost-benefit analysis, and cost-effectiveness analysis all

Table 12-1 Type of health economic evaluations

Type of Analysis	Assumption/Question Addressed
Cost-minimization	The effectiveness (or outcome) of two or more interventions is the same. Which intervention is the least costly?
Cost-benefit	The effectiveness (or outcome) of two or; more interventions differs. What is the economic trade-off between interventions when all of the costs and benefits of the intervention and its outcome are measured in monetary terms?
Cost-effectiveness	The effectiveness of two or more interventions differs. What is the comparative cost per unit of outcome for the intervention?
Cost-utility	The question is the same as for cost-effectiveness analysis. The outcome is a preference measure that reflects the value of patients or society for the outcome. What is the comparative cost per unit of outcome?

compare the cost of alternative interventions. In cost-minimization analysis, the effectiveness of the interventions is assumed or has been shown to be the same, and only the cost difference in the interventions is determined. A cost-minimization analysis asks the question, "which intervention is least expensive given that they are equally effective?" Both cost-effectiveness analysis and cost-benefit analysis compare decision options in terms of their monetary cost assuming that the interventions differ in their non-monetary outcomes.

In cost-benefit analysis, all of the consequences of the decision options are valued in monetary terms. Cost-benefit analysis addresses the question, "what is the overall economic trade-off between the interventions?" In cost-effectiveness analysis, at least some of the consequences of the decision options are valued in non-monetary terms, such as lives saved, years of life saved, or disability avoided. Cost-effectiveness analysis asks the question, "what is the comparative cost of the two interventions per outcome?"

Studies of the cost of interventions per year of quality-adjusted life expectancy (QALYs) are cost-utility analyses. Cost-effectiveness and cost-utility analysis are identical except that the effectiveness measure in a cost-utility analysis is a measure that reflects societal or individual preferences for the outcomes. Some authors (Gold et al. 1996) do not distinguish between cost-utility analysis and cost-effectiveness analysis. Others (Drummond et al. 1997) use a separate label for cost-utility analysis while recognizing that there are many similarities between the two types of analysis. This book considers cost-utility analysis to be a subset of cost-effectiveness analysis but presents many details on cost-utility analysis in a separate chapter, Chapter 13.

Cost-of-illness studies are sometimes identified as a fifth type of economic evaluation study. The goal of a cost-of-illness study is to estimate the total societal costs of caring for persons with an illness compared with persons without the illness without reference to a specific alternative intervention. A cost-of-illness study asks the question, "what is the economic cost of caring for persons with this illness compared with persons free of the illness?" The results of a cost-of-illness study can be used as input to a formal cost-effectiveness analysis.

12.1.2   Cost-Benefit Analysis Versus Other Types of Economic Evaluation

Cost-benefit analysis has the advantage of allowing comparisons of disparate programs, such as programs to vaccinate children and to build highways. These kinds of decisions are important public policy decisions. Cost-benefit analysis is able to make comparisons of disparate programs because, in cost-benefit analysis, all of the consequences of interventions are valued in monetary terms. For example, in a cost-benefit analysis of renal dialysis, a dollar value is assigned to a life saved by providing this treatment. In a cost-benefit analysis of a program to build highways, a dollar value is placed on the benefits to society of improved transportation.

Cost-benefit analysis assigns monetary values to lives and to pain and suffering, which are difficult tasks. There are many methods to do this. These methods can be classified into two groups—human capital approaches and willingness-to-pay approaches. For the human capital approaches, the monetary value of the life of a person who is economically productive, such as a working man, is considered higher than the monetary value of the life of a person who is not economically productive, such as a child, a retiree, or the disabled. Willingness-to-pay approaches do not have this problem.

Cost-benefit analysis is rarely used to address health issues for a number of reasons. Placing monetary values on many of the outcomes of health care is considered immoral by some, even though it is based on rational methods. More important, analysts in health care are rarely deciding whether to vaccinate children or build highways. Rather, they are trying to find ways to maximize health given a fixed number of health care dollars. Because cost-benefit analysis is seldom used in public health and health care settings, it will not be discussed further in this chapter. The interested reader should consult Sugden and Williams (1990) and Warner and Luce (1982) for details on the conduct of cost-benefit analysis.

Cost-effectiveness and cost-utility analysis are used with increasing frequency in public health and health care settings. Most of the important methods and concepts applicable to cost-effectiveness studies are also applicable to cost-of-illness and cost-minimization studies. Cost-utility analysis is essentially a subset of cost-effectiveness analysis, being distinguished only by the use in cost-utility analysis of an outcome that reflects the preferences of individuals and society for the outcomes. Because of the importance of cost-effectiveness analysis and the broadness of the application of the principles of economic analysis illustrated by cost-effectiveness analysis, the remainder of this chapter will address cost-effectiveness analysis. Chapter 13 describes the incorporation of utility measures into a cost analysis in order to conduct cost-utility analysis.

12.2   KEY CONCEPTS

12.2.1   Definitions of Cost-Effective

In medical applications, the term cost-effective is used in many ways, a point made in 1986 by Doubilet, Weinstein, McNeil (1986). Because the implicit goal of cost-effectiveness analysis is the determination of whether a treatment or intervention is or is not cost-effective, an understanding of the various uses and misuses of the term is important. Agreement on how the term should be used is a necessary prelude to meaningful interpretation of claims that an intervention is "cost-effective."

Table 12-2 describes the three ways that the term "cost-effective" is misused in medical applications. First, an intervention is sometimes called cost-effective in the absence of data on both cost and effectiveness. The term cost-effective is meaningless without information both on cost and on effectiveness. The term is also misused as a synonym for effectiveness in the absence of information on cost. Explicit information on cost is a necessary condition for assessing and claiming that an intervention is cost-effective. The term cost-effective is sometimes restricted to situations where the intervention is cost-saving relative to its alternatives. This

Table 12-2 Ways that the term "cost-effective" is misused in medical applications

In the absence of data on both cost and effectiveness
When effectiveness is demonstrated, in the absence of data on cost
In the restricted circumstance where the intervention is cost saving relative to alternatives

Source: Doubilet, Weinstein, McNeil (1986).

restriction stems from the origin of cost-effectiveness analysis in business econom-ics. In business, the ability to reduce everything to a monetary value is easier than it is in medicine, and cost-effectiveness can be based on strict comparison of mon-etary cost. Restricting the term cost-effective to situations where an intervention is cost-saving is considered too narrow a definition of cost-effective in medical ap-plications.

In medical applications the term cost-effective should be used when an inter-vention provides a benefit at an acceptable cost. Within this framework, four criteria for calling an intervention cost effective are generally recognized. These criteria are listed in Table 12-3. First, an intervention is cost-effective when it is less costly and at least as effective as its alternative. Second, an intervention is cost-effective when it is more effective and more costly, but the added benefit is worth the added cost. Third, an intervention is cost-effective when it is less effective and less costly, and the added benefit of the alternative is not worth the added cost. Last, an in-tervention is cost-effective when it is cost-saving, and the outcome is equal to or better than the alternative.

Interventions that are cost-saving fall within the broad framework for calling an intervention cost-effective, but these interventions should be also identified as "cost-saving."

Accepting these criteria as the criteria for calling an intervention cost-effective does not resolve the ethical dilemmas of allocating scarce resources. Except when an intervention is cost-saving, the criteria do not avoid difficult value judgments. Thus, "worth the added cost" is not an economic issue, but an ethical and moral issue. Opinions about whether or not something is "worth" a certain amount of money are subject to variations in the perspective and value structure of the person making the judgment of worth. What is an acceptable cost in one setting may be unacceptable in another. What is acceptable at one time may not be acceptable at another. The limitations of cost-effectiveness analysis as a way to make decisions

Table 12-3 Recommended criteria for calling an intervention "cost-effective" in medical applications

Less costly and at least as effective
More effective and more costly, with the added benefit worth the added cost
Less effective and less costly, with the added benefit of the alternative not worth the added cost
Cost saving with an equal or better outcome

about allocation of resources in situations of scarcity are considered in more detail in Chapter 17.

12.2.2   Average Versus Incremental Cost-Effectiveness

Cost-effectiveness is measured as a ratio of cost to effectiveness. A distinction is made between an average cost-effectiveness ratio and an incremental or marginal cost-effectiveness ratio (Detsky and Naglie 1990). An average cost-effectiveness ratio is estimated by dividing the cost of the intervention by a measure of effectiveness without regard to its alternatives. An incremental or marginal cost-effectiveness ratio is an estimate of the cost per unit of effectiveness of switching from one treatment to another, or the cost of using one treatment in preference to another. In estimating an incremental or marginal cost-effectiveness ratio, the numerator and denominator of the ratio both represent differences between the alternative treatments (Weinstein and Stason 1977):

$$\text{incremental cost effectiveness} = \frac{\text{difference in cost}}{\text{difference in effectiveness}}$$

where

$$\text{difference in cost} = \text{cost of intervention} - \text{cost of alternative}$$

and

$$\text{difference in effectiveness} = \text{effectiveness of intervention}$$
$$- \text{effectiveness of alternative}$$

The average cost-effectiveness ratio and the incremental or marginal cost-effectiveness ratio are identical only in the highly unusual situation where the alternative treatment has a zero cost and no effectiveness (Detsky and Naglie 1990).

> *EXAMPLE:*   Bone marrow transplantation for acute nonlymphocytic leukemia costs $193,000, and its average effect in patients with the disease is to add 3.32 quality-adjusted life years (Welch and Larson 1989). Using this information, it is possible to estimate the average cost-effectiveness ratio of bone marrow transplantation as $193,000÷3.32, or $58,132 per quality-adjusted life year. Imagine for the purpose of illustration that failure to do bone marrow transplantation in a patient with acute nonlymphocytic leukemia always results in death and that patients who do not undergo the procedure incur no costs because the disease is rapidly fatal. The incremental cost-effectiveness of bone marrow transplantation compared with the alternative, doing nothing, is also $58,132 since
>
> $$\frac{\text{cost difference}}{\text{effectiveness difference}} = \frac{\$193,000 - 0}{3.32 \text{ QALY} - 0 \text{ QALY}}$$

Proper cost-effectiveness analysis is always comparative. That is, the average cost-effectiveness ratio is not a useful quantity (Detsky and Naglie 1990). In many cases, the implicit alternative to an intervention is doing nothing. But doing nothing usually has costs and effects that should be taken into account in the cost-effectiveness analysis (Detsky and Naglie 1990). Average cost-effectiveness ratios will be appropriately estimated when decision analysis is the first step in the cost-effectiveness analysis, since decision analysis always compares an intervention with at least one alternative.

12.2.3 The Reference Case

The Panel on Cost-Effectiveness Analysis in Health and Medicine of the U.S. Public Service (Gold 1996) emphasized the importance of conduct of a "reference case" analysis. The reference case analysis is an analysis done according to the standard set of rules. The reference case analysis allows comparison with other cost-effectiveness analyses done using the same set of rules. This greatly enhances the usefulness of information to policymakers.

Other analyses can be done. The analysis that the analyst thinks best characterizes the choices is often called the "base-case" or baseline analysis. The reference case and the base-case are often the same, particularly when the analysis is done from the societal perspective.

12.2.4 Defining the Perspective of the Analysis

One of the key steps in a cost-effectiveness analysis is to define the perspective of the analysis. Costs are seen differently from different perspectives. For example, the cost of vaccinating children against polio from the perspective of a health department or health care organization is the cost of providing the service, which includes the price paid to purchase the vaccine, the labor costs to give the vaccine, the costs of the building in which the services are provided, and other overhead costs. The cost of vaccination from the perspective of the family whose child receives the vaccine is the amount they pay out-of-pocket for the vaccine, the cost of travel to location where the vaccine is given, the cost of parking, and the cost of lost wages because of missed work. The cost of vaccination from the perspective of the child is the "cost" of pain from receiving the injection and the cost of missed day care or school. The societal perspective encompasses all of these costs.

The perspective of a cost-effectiveness analysis should be stated explicitly, because the perspective determines which costs should be included in the analysis and what economic outcomes are considered as benefits. The usual perspectives in cost-effectiveness analysis are the societal perspective and the program perspective. An analysis that takes the societal perspective seeks to determine the total costs of the intervention to all payers for all persons. Analyses that take a program perspective are more heterogeneous in their aims. An analysis that takes the program perspective might, for example, address the question of the immediate cost of an intervention and its outcome in order to compare it with other interventions and outcomes for the same condition. It might seek to determine whether coverage for the intervention would save money for the program in the long run. An intervention might save money for the program but not, in the long run, for society. For example, deciding *not* to provide a costly preventive service for young persons who are insured by a company might save money for the program if the consequence of failing to provide the service is an event that occurs when the person is old and covered by another kind of health insurance.

It is generally agreed that cost-effectiveness studies done by public health agencies to evaluate programs done to affect the health of populations should take the societal perspective (Gold et al. 1996; Haddix et al. 1996). The reference case analysis should take the societal perspective.

> *EXAMPLE:* Both inactivated poliovirus vaccine (IPV) and oral attenuated poliovirus vaccine (OPV) are highly efficacious, although inactivated poliovirus vaccine confers greater immunity to indigenous wild-type poliovirus. The advantages of oral poliovirus vaccine are ease of administration and, because there are no combination vaccines containing inactivated poliovirus vaccine, avoidance of pain from an additional injection. Oral poliovirus vaccine may cause vaccine-associated paralytic poliomyelitis (VAPP), which is sometimes fatal and often disabling. About 10 cases per year of VAPP occur in the United States. In 1995, oral poliovirus vaccine was less costly than inactivated poliovirus vaccine.
>
> Until 1995, the Advisory Committee on Immunization Practices (ACIP) of the U.S. Public Health Service recommended 4 doses of oral poliovirus vaccine. In 1995, the ACIP recommended a change in the poliomyelitis vaccination policy from 4 administrations of oral poliovirus vaccine to a sequential schedule using 2 doses of inactivated poliovirus vaccine followed by 2 doses of oral poliovirus vaccine. In 1996, Miller et al. (1996) published the results of a cost-effectiveness analysis comparing the old and new ACIP recommended poliomyelitis immunization schedules.
>
> Miller et al. (1996) took the societal perspective in their analysis. This is the appropriate perspective for an analysis that informs national policy aimed at maximizing the health and welfare of the total population.

An analysis from the perspective of a health care organization might yield a different estimate of the cost-effectiveness of the new compared with old schedule because the price paid by the organization for vaccine and vaccine delivery might differ from the average societal cost and because the health care organization does not bear some of the costs of the program (e.g., travel costs, the cost of lost productivity).

12.3   TIME HORIZON

The time horizon of an analysis is a time in the future beyond which all costs and benefits are ignored (Sugden and Williams 1990). The time horizon may be short for interventions whose costs and benefits are occur immediately. It may be long for interventions with continuing effects.

EXAMPLES: In the hypothetical cost-effectiveness analysis of measles described in Chapter 2, cost and benefits of measles revaccination in the immediate time period after revaccination were considered. The time horizon was very short.

Chapter 2 and Chapter 9 described a cost-effectiveness analysis comparing aspirin and warfarin for the prophylaxis of stroke in patients with non-valvular atrial fibrillation (Gage et al. 1995). The costs and effects of these interventions were modeled for a period of 10 years.

In their 1997 analysis of the cost-effectiveness of pneumococcal vaccination in the elderly, Sisk et al. (1997) defined the time horizon for the analysis as the time from vaccination until death for cohorts of individuals in three age groups—65–74 years, 75–84 years, 85 years.

The time horizon should extend far enough to capture the major health and economic outcomes of the intervention and its alternatives.

12.4   IDENTIFYING CONTRIBUTORS TO COST

12.4.1   Overview

A key step in cost-effectiveness analysis is to identify and value costs. The economic concept of opportunity cost is central to cost-effectiveness analysis. The opportunity cost of a resource is its total value in another use. When a public health agency spends money to provide health care, this money is not available for housing, education, highway construction, space programs, or as a reduction in income taxes. When a health care organization spends money for bone marrow transplantation, this money is not available for mammography outreach, enhanced prenatal care, or as a reduction in the premium charged to employers or individuals for health care. When an elderly man spends time being vaccinated for influenza, this time is not available to play golf. An overall conceptual goal in cost-effectiveness analysis is comprehensive identification of all of the costs of the intervention and its alternative, including all of the opportunity costs.

12.4.2   Definitions

Contributors to cost must be identified before the costs can be valued. The terms used to describe the contributors to cost (e.g. direct costs, indirect costs, opportunity costs) are used in different ways in different textbooks and in published cost-effectiveness analyses. Although there is increasing consistency in the use of these terms in the past five years, the use is still sometimes confusing and contradictory, and one term may be used for different concepts by different authors. The term ''indirect'' cost is especially troublesome because it has a common meaning as an accounting term which is very different from its use by those who conduct cost-effectiveness analysis.

Table 12-4 gives the definitions of key cost terms in cost-effectiveness analysis as they are used in this chapter. The use of these terms follows the use of the same

Table 12-4 Definition of cost terms as used in this chapter

Opportunity cost	The value of resources in an alternative use
Direct costs	The value of all goods, services, and other resources consumed in the provision of an intervention or in dealing with the side effects or other current and future consequences linked to it
Productivity costs	Costs associated with lost or impaired ability to work or engage in leisure activities and lost economic productivity due to death attributable to the disease

terms by the Panel on Cost-effectiveness Analysis of the U.S. Public Health Service (Gold et al. 1996). In keeping with the recommendations of this group, and in contrast with the prior edition of this book, the term "productivity cost" has been substituted for "indirect" cost to describe the costs associated with lost or impaired ability to work and lost economic productivity due to death. An understanding of the concepts underlying each term is more important than the choice of terms.

12.4.3 Total Direct Cost

Total direct cost includes the value of all goods, services, and other resources that are consumed in the provision of an intervention or in dealing with the side effects of the intervention or other current or future consequences linked to the intervention (Gold et al. 1996). Total direct cost is the numerator in a cost-effectiveness analysis. Identification of the contributors to total direct cost should be exhaustive.

There are several categories of cost that should be considered as possible contributors to total direct cost. These are described in Table 12-5. The first category of total direct cost is direct health care cost. Possible contributors to direct health

Table 12-5 Categories of cost that contribute to total direct cost of a health care intervention

Category	What is Included
Direct health care costs	Tests, drugs, supplies, personnel, equipment
	Rent, depreciation, utilities, maintenance
	Support services
	Costs (savings) due to added (averted) treatments attributable to intervention[a]
Direct non–health care costs	Costs to partake of the intervention
Informal caregiver costs	Monetary value of time of family members or volunteers to provide home care
Cost of patient time	Wages lost to partake of intervention
	Monetary value of time spent to partake of intervention

[a] Induced costs.

care costs include tests, drugs, supplies, personnel, and equipment. Rent and depreciation, space preparation and maintenance, utilities, other support services, and administrative support services needed to produce the intervention should also be counted as a direct health care costs. Induced costs should be counted as direct health care costs in a cost-effectiveness analysis. Induced costs include costs due to added (or averted) treatments or tests attributable to the intervention. For example, the cost of visits to the emergency department to care for children who have fever as a result of being vaccinated for measles are induced costs of a vaccination program.

The second category of total direct cost is direct non–health care cost. These costs include, for example, the cost to patients to partake of the intervention (e.g., transportation, child care, parking). In the example of a polio vaccination program, the cost of travel to the health care facility is a direct non–health care cost that should be included as a contributor to total direct cost.

The third category of total direct cost is the cost of informal caregiver time. This is the monetary value of the time of family members or volunteers who provide home care.

The fourth category of total direct costs is the cost of the use of patient time.

EXAMPLE: In their analysis comparing two different schedules for administering poliovirus vaccine, Miller et al. (1996) included vaccine administration costs, clinic travel costs, and vaccine cost as contributors to direct health care cost. The extra visits generated by the new (2 inactivated poliovirus vaccine, 2 oral poliovirus vaccine) schedule were also considered as direct health care costs. Lost wages for the parent to partake of the program were taken into account in the analysis as direct non–health care costs. There were no caregiver costs attributed to the program. The cost of pain and suffering for the child who undergoes multiple vaccines was not monetarized directly. Rather, it was assumed that multiple injections would lead parents to elect additional visits.

In practice, costs to partake of an intervention are seldom incorporated into cost analyses. These costs can be a high proportion of the total cost of large population screening programs.

EXAMPLE: In the cost-effectiveness analysis comparing two visit schedules for polio vaccination, the estimated private sector cost of oral poliovirus vaccine was $10.18 and the private sector cost of inactivated poliovirus vaccine was $11.55. The cost of administering the vaccines, $9.00, was assumed to be same in both the private and public sector, and the estimated total direct private sector cost of vaccine administration was $19.18 for oral poliovirus vaccine and $20.55 for inactivated poliovirus vaccine. The estimated cost of lost wages for a visit to administer either vaccine, estimated to take an average of 2 hours per clinic visit, was $19.00. Thus, the cost of lost wages for clinic visits accounted for 1/2 of the total cost of vaccine administration. The cost of a program involving the new 2 inactivated poliovirus vaccine and 2 oral poliovirus vaccine schedule was $3.1 million per case VAPP prevented under the base-case assumption that the new but increased to $11.2 million per case of VAPP prevented if 42% of parents would request extra visits to avoid having their children receive more than two injections per visit.

When losses in productivity to partake of the intervention are ignored, the analysis will lead to an overly optimistic view of the societal cost of an intervention (Drummond et al. 1997).

12.4.4 Productivity Costs

Productivity costs are costs associated with lost or impaired ability to work or engage in leisure activities and lost economic productivity due to death from the disease.

Productivity costs are sometimes included in the numerator of a cost-effectiveness analysis. For example, in such an analysis, the "cost" of suffering from paralysis and disability and the monetary value of lost wages from vaccine-associated paralytic poliomyelitis would be considered costs of the vaccination schedule that uses oral poliovirus vaccine and included in the numerator.

The Panel on Cost-Effectiveness Analysis of the U.S. Public Health Service (Gold et al. 1996) argue that productivity costs are encompassed as health effects of the intervention and should not be valued monetarily. They state that a comprehensive measurement of effectiveness (quality-adjusted life years) includes the ability to be productive.

Drummond et al. (1997) consider the issue of whether to directly measure productivity costs and include them in the numerator of a cost analysis to be "contentious." Acceptance of the recommendations of the Panel on Cost-Effectiveness Analysis of the U.S. Public Health Service to exclude productivity costs is not universal.

The arguments for and against including productivity costs in the numerator of the cost-effectiveness equation are complex. They encompass technical problems in measurement of these costs, concerns about double-counting, and ethical issues of equity (Drummond et al. 1997). Detailed consideration of these arguments is beyond the scope of this book. This book recommends acceptance of the suggestion by the Panel on Cost-Effectiveness Analysis of the U.S. Public Service (Gold et al. 1996) that productivity costs NOT be included in the numerator of cost-effectiveness analysis for the reference case analysis.

It is important to recognize that exclusion of productivity costs from the numerator in cost-effectiveness analysis has a large effect on cost-effectiveness analyses that involve interventions for highly disabling conditions in young persons. When the health intervention might result in a return to work or maintenance of the ability to work, the gains in productivity, if considered, would offset the costs of the intervention and may dominate the estimate of the net cost of the intervention.

As described above, costs associated with partaking of the intervention should be considered as direct non–health care costs, and they should included in the numerator in the cost-effectiveness analysis.

12.5 VALUING COSTS

12.5.1 Micro-costing versus Macro-costing Approaches

After the contributors to cost have been identified, they must be valued. Determining the correct monetary value for each contributor to cost can be difficult and time-consuming, especially if micro-costing methodologies are used (Gold et al. 1996; Haddix et al. 1996). Micro-costing involves the direct enumeration and costing out of every input consumed in the intervention. Micro-costing methodologies are described in detail by Gold et al. (1996), by Drummond et al. (1997) and, for prevention programs, by Haddix et al. (1996). Microcosting approaches will not be discussed further in this chapter.

   In practice, gross-costing approaches are used most often in evaluations of health interventions. These approaches use estimates of cost that are large relative to the intervention (e.g., the average cost of a hospital day, the average cost of a physician visit). What is sought in using gross costs is a satisfactory measure of the "typical" cost of the service or its associated health outcome (Gold et al. 1996). When gross-costing methods are used, the amount of "inputs" (e.g., hospital days, physician visits, tests, procedures) are counted, and total costs for the intervention and its alternative are estimated by assigning a cost to each input and then summing.

   EXAMPLE: In the cost-effectiveness analysis of alternative schedules vaccination against poliomyelitis, it was first estimated that 42% of children would require an additional visit to administer the vaccination series. The average cost of a clinic visit, including vaccination administration and clinic travel costs, and the costs of lost wages for the parent, was estimated and used to calculate the extra cost of the new vaccination schedule as a result of the extra clinic visits for the parents who would elect an additional visit.

12.5.2 Using Market Price to Estimate Cost

Market prices (fee schedules or average payment or charges) for various services are often used to estimate gross costs. The Medicare DRG payment is used to estimate the cost of care for a hospitalized condition. The Medicare fee schedule is used as the cost of physician services and procedures. Information for a survey of pharmacies is used to estimate the current price of the drugs. The cost of tests is estimated by surveying commercial laboratories to determine how much they charge for them.

   EXAMPLE: In the cost-effectiveness analysis comparing warfarin and aspirin for the prevention of stroke in patients with non-valvular atrial fibrillation by Gage et al. (1995) that was introduced in Chapter 2 and discussed again in Chapters 9 and 11, the direct medical cost of a transient ischemic attack was estimated as the Medicare payment for DRG 15 (TIA and pre-cerebral occlusion). The cost of an acute neurologic event was estimated as the Medicare payment for DRG 14 (specific cerebrovascular disorders except TIA).

Gage et al. (1995) estimated the cost of warfarin by conducting a tele-phone survey of eight pharmacies in diverse regions of the United States. The cost of warfarin monitoring was estimated based on a survey of eight laboratories in diverse regions of the United States.

Market prices are the sum of the true costs of production of the resource and profit. A cost-effectiveness analysis from the societal perspective seeks to estimate cost free from profit. To more accurately reflect true cost of hospital care, it is a common practice to deflate the Medicare DRG payment by the cost-to-charge ratio. This information is available from the Medicare Cost Reports. Gold et al. (1996, pp. 204–206) describe how to use information on cost-to-charge ratios at both an aggregated and detailed level to deflate payment and charge data to estimate true hospital cost.

The market price for drugs and tests can be similarly deflated to reflect profit, although national sources of data to estimate profit are not readily available.

12.5.3   Limitations of Macro-Costing Approaches Based on Market Price

The Medicare fee schedule for services is based on attempts to relate the service to a standardized scale of input to produce the service—a relative value unit. In-formation on the cost-to-charge ratio is available for hospitalizations, and this in-formation can be used to adjust data on hospital charges when using Medicare DRG payment data to estimate the cost of hospitalized services. The Medicare fee schedule and Medicare DRG payments affect fees and payments for services by other insurers. Thus, it reasonable to use Medicare data to estimate cost in cost-effectiveness analyses, when the analysis takes the societal, and not just the Med-icare, perspective.

Using charge or payment is often correct when the perspective of the analysis is a program perspective, because payments and charges are true costs from the point of view of the program. For example, Medicare would save the amount projected in a cost analysis based on its own payment data. An insurance company would save the amount projected in a cost analysis based on its own payment data.

Using fee schedules and data on payment or charge as a substitute for cost can sometimes lead to unwarranted conclusions (Finkler 1982). Savings projected by using an inappropriate source of cost data may fail to materialize when the costs used in the analysis are not the true costs of the intervention or its consequence in that setting.

12.6 DISCOUNTING

12.6.1 Costs

It is a tenet of economics that the value of a dollar now is greater than the value of a dollar later. The majority of people will prefer to receive $100 today than $100 a year from today. This preference for a dollar today is logical because it would be possible to invest $100 received today in, for example, a savings account that pays 5% interest and receive $105 one year from today. The preference for a dollar today is called the time preference for money. In economic analysis, the time preference for money necessitates discounting future costs. Discounting adjusts future costs and expresses all costs and monetary benefits in terms of their present value.

In most medical situations, not all the costs of an intervention or treatment are incurred at a single point in time. For example, medical treatment of angina pectoris does not cure a patient of coronary heart disease, and so treatment is long term. The costs of treatment are incurred in every year of treatment. Similarly, the effects of a medical treatment or intervention often occur over a long period of time, and the long-range effects of the treatment or intervention may contribute to the total cost and the total cost savings of the treatment or intervention. For example, having coronary artery bypass surgery for an isolated lesion of the left main coronary artery at age 60 affects the likelihood of dying of an acute myocardial infarction in the year of surgery and for 5 to 10 years thereafter. The patient with this condition who undergoes coronary artery surgery is less likely to be hospitalized for an acute myocardial infarction in the years after surgery and will have lower costs of hospitalization for myocardial infarction over the next 10 years compared with a patient who elects medical management.

When costs of treatment or cost savings due to treatment occur over a long period of time, it is necessary to take into account the time preference for money by discounting future costs. Costs can be assumed to occur either at the beginning of the year, at the end of the year, or spread equally throughout the year. The Panel on Cost-Effectiveness Analysis of the U.S. Public Health Service adopted the convention of assuming that costs and benefits occur at the beginning of each year. When costs are assumed to occur at the beginning of the year, the formula for discounting is as follows:

$$c_{\text{present}} = c_0 + \frac{c_1}{(1 + r)^1} + \frac{c_2}{(1 + r)^2} + \cdots + \frac{c_n}{(1 + r)^n}$$

where c_{present} is the cost in current dollars, r is the discount rate, and $c_0, c_1, \ldots,$ c_n are costs in future years.

EXAMPLE: At a discount rate of 5%, the cost, or present value, of an intervention that costs a total of $400 with $200 spent in the first year and $200 in the second year:

present value = $200 + ($200 ÷ (1 + 0.05)^1) = $200 + $190 = $390

At the same discount rate, 5%, the present value of an intervention that costs $600, with $200 spent in the first year and $100 each year of four subsequent years is:

present value = $200 +
$100 ÷ $(1 + 0.05)^1$ +
$100 ÷ $(1 + 0.05)^2$ +
$100 ÷ $(1 + 0.05)^3$ +
$100 ÷ $(1 + 0.05)^4$ =
present value = $200 + $95 + $91 + $86 + $82 = $554

The process of discounting at a positive rate gives greater weight to costs and monetary benefits the earlier they occur. High positive discount rates favor alternatives with costs that occur late.

EXAMPLE: There is an operation for an otherwise fatal disease that costs $10,000 and cures all the patients with the disease. The alternative, a medical treatment, also cures patients with the disease, but the treatments must be given over 5 years. These treatments cost $2,000 per year. Without discounting, compared with doing nothing, the cost of surgery is $10,000 per life saved and the cost of medical treatment is $10,000 per life saved. Neither alternative is cost-effective with respect to the other by any of the definitions of cost-effective given earlier.

Assuming that the discount rate is 5%, the cost of surgery remains $10,000 per life saved. The cost of medical treatment after discounting is

$$\$2000 + \$1905 + \$1814 + \$1728 + 1645 = \$9092$$

After discounting, medical treatment is cost effective relative to surgery, because it is less costly with the same outcome. At any positive discount rate, medical treatment is cost effective relative to surgery.

12.6.2 Benefits

When discounting costs, most economists agree that nonmonetary health benefits (e.g., lives, years of life saved) should be discounted at the same rate as costs, (Weinstein and Fineberg 1980; Drummond et al. 1997; Keeler and Cretin 1983; Gold et al. 1996; Haddix et al. 1996). The topic is not without controversy. The main continuing controversy about discounting benefits relates to the failure of the discounted benefits to reflect individual time preferences for health effects.

When health effects are discounted, the health effects that occur in the future count less than immediate health effects. Discounting health effects at a constant rate assumes implicitly that the discounted health effects continue to represent the preferences of individuals and society for the health outcome. Individuals may have different time preferences for health effects than for costs. Thus, while the preference for more money tomorrow is clear, the preference for more health tomorrow is not certain if additional future health is gained at the expense of current suffering.

Individuals may have a preference for cure now compared with cure later. Healthy years at a young age may be preferred over healthy years at an old age. Discounting health effects at a constant rate fails to capture these preferences.

Gold et al. (1996) counter the arguments against discounting benefits by pointing out that cost-effectiveness analysis is generally a policy tool, not a tool for individual decision-making. Further, in empiric studies, individual time preference for health effects are reflected by a discount rate that is in the range of discount rates used in cost-effectiveness analysis. Other arguments for discounting benefits at the same rate as costs are described in detail by Gold et al. (1996, pp. 219–230) and by Drummond et al. (1997, pp. 107–108). They will not be repeated here. As indicated above, the consensus of experts is that benefits should be discounted at a constant rate. Chapter 13 presents examples of discounting of QALYs.

A sensitivity analysis of the discount rate for benefits should always be done. Sensitivity analysis is discussed in more detail in Chapter 15.

12.6.3 Choice of the Discount Rate

The discount rate reflects the rate of return on investment, or, alternatively the rate of growth of the economy. There is not a single rate of return on investment, and this rate, as well as the rate of growth of the economy, may vary over time. More important, the use of the private sector return on return for public sector program costs, such as the costs of a public health program, may not be correct (Sugden and Williams 1990).

An approach to choice of the discount rate based on the ''shadow-price-of-capital'' has gained support. The expert panel commissioned by the U.S. Public Health Service to make recommendations about the conduct of cost-effectiveness analysis in the evaluation of health care (Gold et al. 1996) based their recommendation on this approach. They present a set of careful arguments for using it. The shadow price of capital approach leads to the use of a discount rate of 3% for economic evaluations involving public investment in health programs. In the past, many important published cost-effectiveness analyses used a discount rate of 5%. In recognition of the use of discount rates of 5% in many published cost-effectiveness analyses, the Panel on Cost Effectiveness Analysis of the U.S. Public Health Service recommended using both a discount rate of 5% and a discount rate of 3% in the reference case analysis.

A second issue with regard to the choice of discount rate is whether to use the same discount rate for benefits as for costs. Gold et al. (1996) review the arguments for and against using the same discount rate for both costs and benefits. These arguments will not be repeated here. The consensus of experts is that costs and benefits should be discounted at the same rate in the reference case analysis.

12.6.4 Effects of the Discount Rate on Estimated Cost-Effectiveness

The choice of the discount rate affects the magnitude of the estimate of the cost effectiveness of an intervention compared with its alternatives.

EXAMPLE: Using a discount rate of 10%, the cost of surgery in the example given above is still $10,000 per life saved. The cost of medical treatment is $8340 per life saved. With a discount rate of 5%, surgery costs $10,000 per life saved, but the cost of medical treatment is $9092 per life saved.

Because the discount rate affects the absolute magnitude of the estimate of costs, it is essentially impossible to compare between interventions examined in different cost-effectiveness analyses done with different discount rates.

EXAMPLE: Consider two treatments for same condition, treatment A and treatment B. Each treatment costs $2000 per year for 5 years. The cost-effectiveness of each treatment was compared with the doing-nothing alternative by two different analysts who used two different rates to discount costs. Assume that both treatment A and treatment B cure all patients and have no other risks or benefits. As shown previously, with a discount rate of 10%, the cost of the treatment A is $8340 per life saved; with a discount rate of 5%, the cost of treatment B is $9092 per life saved. Solely because of the difference in the discount rates, treatment A, which costs $8340 per life saved, would be called cost-effective relative to treatment B because it is less costly and equally effective compared with treatment B. But the cost effectiveness of treatment A is an artifact of the use of a higher discount rate in the analysis that examined its cost-effectiveness.

12.7   INFLATION

Inflation is an issue that is separate from discounting. Available data on cost frequently come from data sources developed in different years. For example, information on the cost of surgery may be available only for the year 1994, whereas information on the cost of medical treatment is available for 1997. Cost data should be adjusted for inflation so that all costs are measured in current dollars at the start of the analysis. The rate of inflation used in this adjustment should be the measured inflation rate in the relevant cost sector. For wages, this would be the consumer price index. If the cost is a medical service cost, the medical component of the consumer price index should be used.

Inflation poses additional problems in estimating the future costs of the intervention. If the inflation rate for medical care costs is the same as for other costs, inflation can be ignored because the payment for inflated future costs will be in dollars that have inflated at the same rate. This can be shown mathematically (Sugden and Williams 1990) as follows.

Assume that the cost of some medical good or service is c_0 in year 0. If the inflation rate is i, then the cost of the medical good or service taking inflation into account is

$$\text{year 1: } c_1 = c_0 (1 + i)$$
$$\text{year 2: } c_2 = c_0 (1 + i)^2$$

The total is

$$c = c_1 + c_2 + \cdots + c_n$$

If the general inflation rate is also i and the discount rate is r, the total cost in current dollars is

$$c_{\text{present}} = c_0 + \left[\frac{c_0 (1 + i)}{(1 + r) (1 + i)} \right] + \left[\frac{c_0 (1 + i)^2}{(1 + r)^2 (1 + i)^2} \right]$$
$$+ \cdots + \left[\frac{c_0 (1 + i)^n}{(1 + r)^n (1 + i)^n} \right]$$

which simplifies to

$$c_{\text{present}} = c_0 + \frac{c_0}{(1 + r)^1} + \frac{c_0}{(1 + r)^2} + \cdots + \frac{c_0}{(1 + r)^n}$$

This amount, c_{present}, is the same as the discounted cost ignoring inflation that was shown in Section 12.6.2.

Inflation in medical care costs has historically not been the same as the general inflation rate. When the inflation rate for a medical care service is different from the general inflation rate, taking the greater inflation rate of medical services into account in a cost-effectiveness analysis may alter conclusions based on it.

EXAMPLE: A health insurance company will decide on the basis of cost-effectiveness analysis whether to pay $100,000 for bone marrow transplant for an advanced cancer or whether to pay for a medical treatment that costs $20,000 per year and lasts 5 years. The treatments are equally effective and, for the purposes of discussion, are assumed to have no other benefits or risks. Thus, the decision on payment is rationally made strictly on the basis of the cost-effectiveness of transplantation relative to its alternative, medical treatment. Assume that the rate of return on investments for the insurance company as a whole is 10%. Using the preceding formulas and discounting at a rate of 10%, the cost of surgery is $100,000. The discounted cost of medical treatment is

$20,000 + $18,181 + $16,529 + $15,026 + $13,660 = $83,396

Based on this analysis, medical treatment is cost effective compared with transplantation, because it is less costly and equally effective.

If the inflation rate for medical services is assumed to be 20%, the cost of transplantation, which is a one-time cost, remains $100,000. The cost of medical treatment after taking inflation into account is

$20,000 + $24,000 + 28,800 + 34,560 + 41,472 = $148,832

Discounting these costs at 10% gives

$20,000 + $21,818 + 23,801 + $25,965 + $28,326 = $119,910

Under these assumptions, transplantation is cost effective compared with medical treatment because it is less costly and equally effective.

Discounting the inflated costs at 20% instead of 10% is equivalent to assuming that the general inflation rate and the rate of inflation of medical goods and services are the same; it would yield the same answer as when inflation is ignored.

If some costs will rise at different rates than others, these costs should be adjusted so that they reflect relative price net of inflation (Gold et al. 1996; Drummond et al. 1997). In practice, differences in the rates of inflation for various kinds of cost are usually ignored in cost-effectiveness analysis. In ignoring inflation, the implicit assumption is that the inflation rate for future medical costs is the same as the general inflation rate. This assumption is rarely made specific, is highly questionable, and may result in unwarranted conclusions about cost-effectiveness. Ignoring the greater inflation of health care costs biases comparisons in favor of future curative over current preventive care (Gold et al. 1996).

13

Utility and Cost-Utility Analysis

In the examples of decision analysis and cost-effectiveness analysis presented so far, the outcome of interest has been life or death, or some measure closely related to life or death, such as years of life lost, years of life saved, or life expectancy. The ability of an intervention to prevent death or to prolong life narrowly frames the goal of many medical treatments and interventions. Many treatments decrease the likelihood of disability but not of death, and many treatments increase life expectancy but cause discomfort or leave the person with impaired function. Attempts to incorporate into the analysis effects of interventions on outcomes other than life or death, and the preferences of individuals or society for these outcomes, is called *utility analysis*. When costs are measured and the utility is the denominator in a cost analysis, the analysis is a *cost-utility analysis*. Quality-adjusted life years (QALYs) are the metric that is used most often in utility and cost-utility analysis.

Section 13.1 is a conceptual overview of utility and cost-utility analysis and a description of the situations in which QALYs are most useful. Section 13.2 gives an overview of the steps in a utility and cost-utility analysis. Section 13.3 is a brief review of approaches to measuring utilities. Section 13.4 illustrates how to do utility and cost-utility analysis by showing the calculations performed in utility and cost-utility analysis for increasingly complex hypothetical problems.

Chapter 11 discussed the concept of utility and the formal methods for measuring utilities in depth. Chapter 12 discussed the measurement of cost.

13.1 QUALITY-ADJUSTED LIFE YEARS

13.1.1 Conceptual Framework

Quality-adjusted life years (QALYs) attempt to combine, in a single metric, expected increments in the quantity of life from an intervention with the effects on quality of life (LaPuma and Lawlor 1990). An analysis that uses QALYs seeks to evaluate the trade-off between mortality, morbidity, the preferences of patients and society for various types of morbidity, and the willingness of patients and society to accept a shortening of life to avoid certain morbidities. It is an integrated measure of outcome.

Although it has become popular to use QALYs as the outcome measure in decision and cost-effectiveness analysis, it is not always necessary to use QALYs as the outcome in a decision or cost-effectiveness analysis. Other outcome measures often suffice for decision making.

> *EXAMPLE:*   Chapter 11 described an analysis by Miller et al. (1996) of the effectiveness and cost-effectiveness of a new schedule for administering polio vaccine in which two administrations of inactivated polio vaccine and two administrations of oral polio vaccine would be substituted for a schedule involving four administrations of oral polio vaccine. The measure of outcome used in the analysis was the number of cases of vaccine-associated poliomyelitis prevented by the new vaccine administration schedule. The analysis estimated that the new schedule would prevent 4.8 cases of vaccine-associated polio and that the cost of the new schedule was $3.1 million per case of vaccine-associated polio averted. No attempt was made to estimate QALYs or cost per QALY for the new vaccine administration schedule. The Advisory Committee on Immunization Practices decided to recommend the new vaccination schedule without information on QALYs or cost per QALY.

Although QALYs are used most often in utility and cost-utility analysis, other metrics could serve the same purpose. The Years of Healthy Life (YHL) measure and healthy-year equivalent (HYE) measures have both been used in place of QALYs. Their advantages will not be reviewed here. The interested reader is referred to Gold et al. (1996) for a thorough review of this topic.

13.1.2 Situations in Which QALYs (Utility and Cost-Utility Analyses) Might Be Useful

Drummond et al. (1997) delineated situations when an analysis using QALYs—i.e., conducting utility or cost-utility analyses—should be used or might be useful. A description of these situations, modified to make them pertinent to both utility and cost-utility analysis, is presented in Table 13-1.

Utility and cost-utility analysis should be done when there is no expected effect of the intervention on mortality and the intervention's effect is on morbidity or physical, social, or psychological well-being. Treatments for arthritis are one example of such an intervention (Drummond et al. 1997).

Table 13-1   Situations when QALYs should be used or might be useful

There is no expected effect of the intervention on mortality; physical, social, and psychological well-being are the expected effects of the intervention
Both morbidity and mortality are affected by the intervention, and a common metric is desired
Interventions with a range of different outcomes will be compared
The intervention being subjected to analysis will be compared with interventions for which utility or cost-utility analysis has previously been done

Source: Modified from Drummond et al. (1997), pp 141–143.

Utility and cost-utility analysis may be useful when an intervention affects both morbidity and mortality and a common metric integrating these effects is needed. This situation occurs often when the effects of the intervention have effects on mortality that are opposite the effects on morbidity.

EXAMPLE: Chapter 2 and Chapter 9 described a decision analysis and cost-effectiveness analysis of warfarin compared with aspirin for the treatment of nonvalvular atrial fibrillation (Gage et al. 1995). Evidence from randomized trials shows that warfarin decreases the overall risk of mortality by 33% in persons with nonvalvular atrial fibrillation, but it almost doubles the risk of intracranial hemorrhage, which is associated with moderate to severe neurologic deficit.

For their analysis, Gage et al. used the time trade-off method to obtain estimates of utilities for neurologic deficit and other health states from 74 patients with atrial fibrillation. Table 13-2 shows the utility measures obtained from these patients. Death and being well and not on any therapy are the anchors and have utility values of 0.0 and 1.0, respectively. The data show

Table 13-2   Utilities for various health states obtained from 74 patients with atrial fibrillation using a time trade-off method

Health State	Utility
Well	
Not on therapy	1.0
Taking aspirin	0.998
Taking warfarin	0.988
Neurologic event with residua	
Mild	0.75
Moderate to severe	0.39
Recurrent	0.12
Other	
Hemorrhage other than intracranial	0.76
Dead	0.0

Source: Gage et al. (1995).

that patients rated quality of life after a stroke that resulted in a moderate to severe residual neurologic deficit (one that resulted in loss of independence for one or more activities of daily living) to be 0.4. Conclusions from this analysis were based on the estimated effect of warfarin and aspirin on quality-adjusted life expectancy in which these utilities were incorporated into the analysis.

Utility and cost-utility analysis is used when the interventions being compared have a range of different outcomes. For example, a program might want to compare outcomes in a new antiarthritic drug with those of warfarin for nonvalvular atrial fibrillation. The new arthritis drug affects joint pain and mobility. Warfarin affects a range of neurologic outcomes.

Utility and cost-utility analysis is also useful when the intervention being studied will be compared with other interventions for which utility or cost-utility analysis has been done.

EXAMPLE: Chapter 10 described a decision and cost-effectiveness analysis that assessed screening for mild thyroid failure (Danese et al. 1996). The analysis estimated that screening 35-year-old patients with a thyroid stimulated hormone assay every 5 years cost $9,223 per QALY for women. Table 13-3 shows how this estimate of cost per QALY compares with the cost per QALY for some widely accepted medical practices based on published cost-utility analyses.

13.1.3 Situations When QALYs (Utility and Cost-Utility Analyses) May Not Be Useful or Should Not Be Used

Table 13.4, also modeled after Drummond et al. (1997), describes situations when QALYs—i.e., utility and cost-utility analysis—may not useful or should not be used. These situations occur for both pragmatic and theoretical reasons.

Table 13-3 Comparison of the cost per QALY of screening for mild thyroid failure compared with other widely accepted medical practices

Medical Practice	Cost/QALY (1994 dollars)
Women	
Breast cancer screening every two years, age 50–70 years	$4,836
Screening for mild thyroid failure every 5 years, age 35–75 years	$9,223
Hypertension screening, age 40 years	$26,130
Men	
Exercise to prevent coronary disease, age 35 years	$13,508
Hypertension screening, age 40 years	$18,323
Screening for mild thyroid failure every 5 years, age 35–75 years	$22,595

Source: Danese et al. (1996).

Table 13-4   Situations when QALYs may not be useful or should not be used

When only intermediate outcome data can be obtained, and these outcomes cannot be converted into
    QALYs
When obtaining utility measures is too expensive or too difficult
When incorporation of utility measures would not change conclusions (e.g. when one intervention is
    both more effective and less costly)

Source: Modified from Drummond et al. (1997), pp 141–143.

QALYs should not be used when only information about intermediate outcomes is available and the intermediate outcomes cannot be directly linked with health status. Sometimes this happens because data to establish this link are not available. In other instances, the link between the intervention and the intermediate outcome is so complex that it cannot be measured. A comparison of the yield of two diagnostic tests is one example of this kind of situation.

The decision to use QALYs must be pragmatic. Thus, QALYs should not be used when the cost and difficulty of estimating utilities is high. This effort and resource consumption associated with it must be weighed against the usefulness of the information about QALYs.

The third situation when QALYS may not be useful applies only to cost-utility analysis. When utility measures will not change conclusions because the intervention is both more effective and less costly, cost-utility analysis is not especially useful.

13.2   STEPS IN A UTILITY OR COST-UTILITY ANALYSIS

Utility and cost-utility analysis involves the following steps. First, the health states pertinent to the intervention and its alternative are defined. Then, the amount of time spent in each health state is estimated for the intervention and its alternatives. The preferences of individuals or society for time spent in each health state (utilities) are assessed and a value for the preferences for each health state is assigned. The difference in quality-adjusted life years in each health state for the intervention and the alternatives is calculated. The number of quality-adjusted life years for the intervention is derived by adding the quality-adjusted life years for all health states for the intervention. The same thing is done for the alternatives. The net number of QALYs for the intervention and its alternative is obtained by subtracting.

The estimate of the gain in quality-adjusted life expectancy is discounted, taking into account the timing of the benefits.

For cost-utility analysis, the last step in the analysis is to take the difference in cost between the intervention and alternative and divide it by the difference in QALYs. This calculation yields the incremental cost of the intervention per QALY gained (or lost).

13.3   REVIEW OF APPROACHES TO MEASURING PREFERENCES (UTILITIES)

Rigorous formal methods to measure preferences for health states in order to estimate utilities were described in Chapter 11. The outcome of a study to formally measure preferences is assignment of a value, usually called Q, to time spent in each health state pertinent to the intervention and its alternative.

The Q values for each health state are often estimated using more ad hoc methods. Q is sometimes assessed by asking experienced clinicians to rate Q for each of the health states. Clinicians are available and willing subjects in such exercises, and the cost and difficulty of measuring Q is greatly reduced. A convenience sample of individuals, drawn from a clinic or some other ready source of willing individuals, may be asked to supply measures of Q in an ad hoc way. The analyst sometimes supplies a value for Q based on experience or simply guesses Q.

The ratings of clinicians and ad hoc samples are not necessarily representative of community preferences, which is the goal of measurement of preferences. Guesses are not easy to justify. Preference measures that reflect community preferences are considered the most appropriate ones for utility and cost-utility analysis (Gold et al. 1996). Preferences measured based on samples of individuals with the condition of interest may be important ancillary information. They should not generally be substituted for preferences measured on representative community samples.

Incorporating Q into a utility or cost-utility analysis is, however, conceptually the same whether Q has been measured by conducting a formal study using the methods described in Chapter 11, using ad hoc samples, or by guessing. Although the practice of using convenience samples, groups of physicians, and guesses is not recommended, it is very widespread and has not made analyses unpublishable.

13.4   INCORPORATING THE PREFERENCE MEASURES INTO THE ANALYSIS

13.4.1   Simple Example

In a simple hypothetical case that will be used to illustrate the principles for incorporating the preference measures in an analysis, assume that the condition of interest does not affect life expectancy at all. Rather, it diminishes function, thus reducing health-related quality of life. Assume further, and again for simplicity, that persons with the condition remain in the diminished health state until they die. The intervention returns function and health to what they would have been in the absence of the condition. The goal of the analysis is to estimate the increase in the number of QALYs for the intervention or the cost of the intervention per QALY compared with doing nothing.

In this simple hypothetical example, life expectancy in those who are candidates for the intervention is estimated as described in Chapter 9. The value of Q for the diminished health state is measured by conducting a study in which a random sample of the general population of a large city rate their preference for life with the condition compared with complete health using a direct rating scale, as described in Chapter 11. The number of quality-adjusted life years for those with the condition who do not have the intervention is estimated by multiplying life expectancy by Q, the measure of the preference for time spent in the diminished health state. The number of quality-adjusted life years in those who undergo the intervention is equal to life expectancy because the intervention returns the person to perfect health.

> *EXAMPLE:* Presbyopia affects most people at about age 40 years. It does not affect life expectancy but diminishes visual function. After vision declines at age 40, it does not (hypothetically) decline more with advancing age. The intervention for presbyopia is a new surgical procedure that restores vision to normal, has no complications, and costs $10,000. The analysis will assess the cost-effectiveness of the intervention compared with doing nothing. Since the procedure does not affect life expectancy, the metric chosen to assess cost-effectiveness is QALYs.
>
> Figure 13-1 depicts the time course of Q for the surgical procedure compared with doing nothing.
>
> Life expectancy at age 40 in the general population is determined to be 42 years based on published actuarial tables. A time trade-off study yields an estimate of Q for presbyopia of 0.999. This can be interpreted to mean that presbyopia reduces health-related quality of life to 0.999 compared with perfect health, which has a Q value of 1.0—death has a Q value of 0.0.

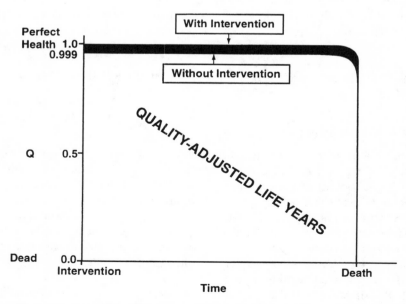

Figure 13-1 Quality-adjusted life years (QALYs) gained from surgery for presbyopia at age 40 compared with wearing glasses. The time horizon is until death. Data are hypothetical.

The number of QALYs in absence of the intervention is:

$$42 \times Q = 42 \times 0.999 = 41.9580 \text{ QALYs}$$

The number of QALYs with the intervention is:

$$42 \times Q = 42 \times 1.000 = 42.000 \text{ QALYs}$$

The difference in QALYs for the intervention compared with no intervention is:

$$42.0000 \text{ QALYs} - 41.9580 \text{ QALYs} = 0.0420 \text{ QALYs}$$

That is, the intervention adds 0.0420 QALYs for a person age 40 who undergoes the procedure.

The cost of the intervention is $10,000. The cost of doing nothing is $0. The net (undiscounted) cost per QALY is:

$$(\$10,000 - \$0) \div 0.0420 \text{ QALYs} = \$238,095 \text{ per QALY.}$$

Discounting

If costs occur at the beginning of the year, the discounted cost of the intervention is the same as the undiscounted cost. Benefits should be discounted.

Spreadsheet programs (EXCEL, LOTUS) have functions that perform discounting. In this simple example, discounting is computationally simple because the increase in QALYs is the same in every year of life. Assuming that benefits, like costs, occur at the beginning of each year, using a discount rate of 5%, and referring to a table of discount rates (see Drummond et al. 1997, Chapter 4, Annex Table 1), discounted QALYs are:

$$0.001 \times (\ 1.0 + \text{sum discount rate}_1 + \text{discount rate}_2$$
$$+ \ldots \text{discount rate}_{41}\ ) = .001 \times 18.2940 = 0.0183 \text{ QALYs}$$

After discounting costs and benefits at 5%, the net cost per QALY for the intervention compared with doing nothing is:

$$(\$10,000 - \$0) \div 0.0183 \text{ QALY} = \$546,448 \text{ per QALY.}$$

Discounting at 3% instead of 5%, the cost of the intervention compared with doing nothing is $409,836 per QALY.

13.4.2 A More Complex Example

In a slightly less simple case, assume that there are no differences in life expectancy between an intervention and its alternative, but the intervention has both beneficial and adverse effects on function and thus on health-related quality of life. The goal of the analysis is to estimate the number of QALYs for the intervention or the cost of the intervention per QALY, compared with its alternative.

In this case, just as in the previous example, life expectancy in those who are candidates for the intervention has been estimated as described in Chapter 9. For this case, Q must be estimated for two health states—the adverse health state and the beneficial state associated with the intervention.

EXAMPLE: In patients with mild angina and three-vessel coronary artery disease, CABG and medical therapy are associated with the same long-term survival, but CABG is better at relieving angina. CABG surgery is, however, associated with a period of increased pain and disability. This is a situation in which estimation of QALYs allows the adverse short-term effects of the surgery to be balanced against the long-term effect in decreasing anginal pain.

Figure 13-2 gives hypothetical data that depicts the time course of Q for CABG and for medical therapy in patients with mild angina.

In this hypothetical example, life expectancy in patients with three-vessel coronary artery disease is determined to be 8 years based on a meta-analysis of data from the placebo arms of randomized trials of treatments for coronary artery disease. A study is done in which the time trade-off method is used in 100 patients who have undergone CABG 4 years ago to obtain measure of preference for various health states that follow CABG surgery using the time trade-off method. The study yields a value for Q of 0.50 for the first month after the surgery, 0.80 for the next 2 months after surgery, and 0.98 for the rest of the first year and 0.99 thereafter. The value of Q for mild angina is obtained from a published time–trade-off study done by Weinstein and Stason (1977). This value is 0.90.

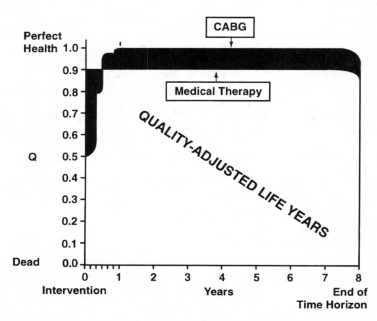

Figure 13-2   Quality-adjusted life years (QALYs) gained from CABG surgery compared with medical therapy for the treatment of angina. The time horizon is 8 years. Data are hypothetical.

The number of QALYs for medical therapy is:

$$8 \times Q = 8 \times 0.90 = 7.2 \text{ QALYs}$$

The number of QALYs for CABG is:

YEAR 1

one month $(1 \div 12) \times (0.5 \text{ QALYs}) = 0.0417 \text{ QALYs}$
two months $(2 \div 12) \times (0.9 \text{ QALYs}) = 0.1500 \text{ QALYs}$
nine months $(9 \div 12) \times (0.98 \text{ QALYs}) = 0.7350 \text{ QALYs}$

Year 1 Total 0.9267 QALYs

YEARS 2–8

$$7 \times Q = 7 \times 0.99 = 6.93 \text{ QALYs}$$

TOTAL FOR YEARS 1–8

0.9267 QALYs + 6.93 QALYS = 7.8567 QALYs

The difference in QALYs for CABG compared with medical therapy is:

$$7.8567 \text{ QALYs} - 7.2 \text{ QALYs} = 0.6567 \text{ QALYs}$$

That is, CABG adds an estimated 0.6567 QALYs compared with medical therapy for a patient with 3-vessel coronary artery disease and mild angina. The cost of CABG is estimated to be $15,000. The cost of medical therapy is $250 per year or $2,000. The (undiscounted) net cost per QALY for CABG compared with medical therapy is:

$$(\$15,000 - \$2,000) \div 0.6567 \text{ QALYs} = \$19,796 \text{ per QALY.}$$

Discounting

If it is assumed that all costs and benefits occur at the beginning of the year, the discounted cost for CABG is the same as the undiscounted cost. The cost of medical therapy discounted at 5% is:

$250 \times (1 + \text{sum discount rate}_1 + \text{discount rate}_2 + \ldots.\text{discount rate}_7) =$
$$\$250 \times 6.7863 = \$1,697$$

Using the same discount rate of 5% and assuming benefits occur at the beginning of each year, the estimated discounted benefit of CABG compared with medical therapy is:

0.10 QALYS $\times$ (1 + sum discount rate$_1$ + discount rate$_2$ +
$\ldots.$discount rate$_7$) = 0.10 QALYs $\times$ 6.7863 = 0.6786 QALYs.

After discounting costs and benefits at 5%, the estimated cost per QALYs for CABG compared with medical therapy is:

$(\$15,000 - \$1,697) \div 0.6786 \text{ QALY} =$
$$\$13,303 \div 0.6786 = \$19,604 \div \text{QALY.}$$

The cost per QALY discounting costs and benefits at 3% is $18,246 per QALY.

Table 13-5 Incorporation of quality adjustment into decision analysis comparing sclerotherapy with no sclerotherapy

	No Sclerotherapy			Sclerotherapy		
	Well	Bleed	Diminished Health	Well	Bleed	Diminished Health
Number of cycles	62,495	124,996	62,498[a]	86,202	125,860	62,930[a]
Quality-adjusted life expectancy: no sclerotherapy						$0.62 + 0.62 = 1.24$ years
Quality-adjusted life expectancy: sclerotherapy						$0.86 + 0.63 = 1.49$ years
Difference						$1.49 - 1.24 = 0.25$ year

[a] After adjustment for diminished quality of life during years where a bleed occurs; $Q = 0.5$.

13.4.3 An Even More Complex Example

Health states may change as a dynamic process. There may be transitions into and out of various health states until death or the end of the time horizon for the analysis. The values of Q for time spent in each health state are then incorporated into the estimate of QALYs.

> *EXAMPLE:* Chapter 9 described a decision analysis that estimated life expectancy in patients with bleeding esophageal varices who did and did not undergo sclerotherapy. This analysis was based on a Markov model. Hypothetical patients with bleeding varices transitioned into and out of varous health states until they died of bleeding or other causes. Each of these periods in a health state is associated with a preference, or quality of life measure.
>
> In the example, life expectancy in the no-sclerotherapy group was estimated to be 1.87 years and in the sclerotherapy group, 2.12 years. The expected effect of sclerotherapy compared with no sclerotherapy is to increase life expectancy by 0.25 years. Years of life when bleeding occurs are not equivalent to years of complete wellness. They are years of diminished health. Imagine that these years in a bleeding state are rated as having a value, Q, of 0.5 relative to complete wellness. To take into account the lower utility of years of life after an initial bleed, the years of life in the states labeled "bleed" in Table 9.4 are multiplied by Q before they are summed. The average cycles based on the quality-adjusted figures are used to estimated quality-adjusted life expectancy, as shown in Table 13.5. For no sclerotherapy, quality-adjusted life expectancy is 1.24 years. For sclerotherapy, quality adjusted life expectancy is 1.49 years. The benefit of sclerotherapy compared with no sclerotherapy is to add 0.25 quality-adjusted life years. This number can be compared with the number of life-years gained with sclerotherapy calculated in Chapter 9—0.25 years.

14

Exploring Heterogeneity

The importance of a careful examination of heterogeneity as a primary goal of meta-analysis is now well established. The examination of heterogeneity only begins with formal statistical tests of heterogeneity. Even in the absence of statistical evidence of heterogeneity (but particularly in its presence), meta-analysis should encompass exploration of the reasons for the statistical heterogeneity. The exploration of heterogeneity includes consideration of the possibility that the effect of the intervention may be different in subgroups of patients or, for observational studies the effect of the exposure may differ in different people. The examination of possible differences in effect in subgroups provides a link between exploration of heterogeneity in meta-analysis and subgroup analysis in decision analysis and cost-effectiveness analysis.

Section 14.1 gives the reasons why exploring heterogeneity is such an important component of meta-analysis. Section 14.2 discusses the distinction between statistical heterogeneity and clinical heterogeneity. Section 14.3 describes some practices to be avoided in exploring heterogeneity. Section 14.4 discusses the limitations of statistical tests of heterogeneity. Section 14.5 provides a framework for exploration of clinical heterogeneity. Sections 14.6 and 14.7 discuss stratification and meta-regression as methods for exploring heterogeneity. Section 14.8 discusses subgroup analysis in decision analysis and cost-effectiveness, providing a linkage between this conceptual component of meta-analysis and conceptual approaches in decision analysis and cost-effectiveness analysis. Section 14.9 discusses the limitations of subgroup analysis.

213

14.1   OVERVIEW

14.1.1   Reasons Why Exploring Heterogeneity Is Important

The early enthusiasm for meta-analysis may have been due in large part to the promise it held as a method for resolving discrepant results. Several influential meta-analyses published in major medical journals appeared, almost miraculously, to permit a strong and credible single conclusion based on a literature that had previously appeared to be contradictory and confusing.

> *EXAMPLE:*   Chapter 2 described a meta-analysis of randomized trials of thrombolytic agents after acute myocardial infarction that was published in 1982 (Stampfer et al. 1982). At that time, eight randomized clinical trials examining the effect of intravenous streptokinase on mortality after an acute myocardial infarction had been done. Chapter 2 presented data from the eight randomized trials that had been published by 1982. Two of the trials found a higher risk of mortality in treated patients, five found a lower risk, and one found essentially identical mortality in treated and untreated patients. The trials were small, and the difference in mortality between treated and control patients was statistically significant in only one trial. Up to 1982, the studies were interpreted as inconclusive about the benefit of intravenous streptokinase in acute treatment of patients with myocardial infarction. The Stampfer et al. (1982) meta-analysis estimated the relative risk of mortality in patients treated with intravenous streptokinase to be 0.80 with 95% confidence limits of 0.68 and 0.95.

The results of this meta-analysis, and others from this era that resolved apparent discrepancies among studies, were influential not only for clinical practice but in creating expectations, and perhaps some misunderstanding, about the capabilities and the most opportune uses of meta-analysis.

The situations in which meta-analysis of many small and consistent studies yields a strong and credible conclusion based on estimation of a single summary measure of effect are the exception, not the rule. Calculation of a single summary estimate of effect size does not resolve the discrepancies among study results when these discrepancies are due to bias, confounding, or to differences in the selection criteria for subjects, treatments, or follow-up.

Exploration of heterogeneity as a formal goal of meta-analysis has replaced the simplistic use of meta-analysis to derive a single summary estimate of effect size. The exploration of heterogeneity presents opportunities to increase the relevance of the conclusions drawn and enhance the scientific understanding of the studies reviewed (Thompson 1994).

14.2   STATISTICAL VERSUS CLINICAL HETEROGENEITY

Thompson (1994) articulates the useful distinction between clinical heterogeneity and statistical heterogeneity. Clinical heterogeneity refers to differences in the characteristics of the studies, such as their designs and the rates of loss to follow-up; differences in the characteristics of study subjects, such as their mean age and the severity of illness; and differences in the intervention, such as the dose or duration of treatment. There may also be differences in the effect of the intervention in different subgroups of patients, and this is also clinical heterogeneity.

Incomparability in the quantitative results of different studies is termed statistical heterogeneity. The presence of statistical heterogeneity is assessed using formal statistical tests. The computational details for statistical tests of heterogeneity are provided in Chapters 7 through 10 for studies of different types. Statistical heterogeneity may arise because of clinical heterogeneity. Statistical heterogeneity, however, could be due to chance.

Exploration of heterogeneity goes beyond the performance of statistical tests. It includes an examination of clinical heterogeneity.

14.3 PRACTICES TO BE AVOIDED

14.3.1 Use of Random Effects Models to "Account For" Statistical Heterogeneity

As discussed in detail in Chapter 7, the results of fixed and random-effects models are essentially identical in the absence of statistical heterogeneity. The arguments for and against the use of fixed versus random-effects models will not be repeated in this chapter. The overall conclusion of Chapter 7 was that the use of random-effects models should not take the place of exploration of the reasons for heterogeneity. That is, random-effects models should not be used in the belief that they "control for," "adjust for," "explain away," or "take into account" heterogeneity (Greenland 1987; Thompson 1991; Thompson 1994; Stroup et al. 1998; Colditz et al. 1995). In the presence of statistical heterogeneity, the main focus should be on trying to understand clinical sources of heterogeneity (Thompson 1994; Colditz et al. 1995; Stroup et al. in press).

14.3.2 Selective Exclusion of Studies to Make the Results Statistically Homogeneous

In the presence of statistical heterogeneity, it is tempting to identify outlier studies and exclude them successively until the statistical test of heterogeneity is no longer statistically significant. Colditz et al. (1995) give several examples of this practice in published meta-analyses. The following example, based on unpublished data, is used to illustrate why this practice should be avoided.

EXAMPLE: Table 14-1 gives the odds ratios and 95% confidence interval intervals for four randomized trials examining the effect of amiodorone on total mortality in patients with myocardial infarction or congestive heart failure. The summary odds ratio for the four studies is 0.72 (95% C.I. 0.49–1.05) based on a fixed-effects model. Q has a value of 7.9. This value is referred to the chi-square distribution with 3 degrees of freedom (the number

Table 14-1 Meta-analysis of four studies to prevent mortality in congestive heart failure

Study	Odds Ratio	95% Confidence Interval	Weight of Study	Contribution to Q
1	0.39	0.15–0.98	−4.2	1.6
2	0.63	0.37–1.08	13.6	0.2
3	0.48	0.16–1.43	3.2	0.5
4	1.94	0.85–4.41	5.6	5.6

All studies
  Summary odds ratio (95% confidence interval) 0.72 (0.49–1.05)
  $Q = 7.9$
  $df = 3$
  p for homogeneity $= 0.04$
Excluding Study 4
  Summary odds ratios (95% confidence interval) 0.55 (0.36–0.84)
  $Q = 0.9$
  $df = 2$
  p for homogeneity $= 0.64$

of studies minus 1), and the associated probability value for Q is 0.04. For these studies, there is evidence of statistical heterogeneity. That is, the hypothesis of homogeneity is rejected.

The table shows the contribution of each study to Q, the statistical test of heterogeneity. Inspection of the data in the table makes it is easy to see that one study, study 4, is the main contributor to Q. The total Q is 7.9 and study 4 contributes 5.6 to the total. If study 4 is excluded, Q becomes 0.9. The number of degrees of freedom is 2, and the associated probability value for the test of homogeneity is 0.64. After excluding study 4, the hypothesis of homogeneity is not rejected.

Post hoc exclusion of study 4 based on inspection of the data is the same as excluding individual values in a clinical trial or a case-control study after inspecting the data. Outlier studies should never be discarded solely on the basis of the results of statistical tests (Stroup et al. in press). Colditz et al. (1995) call the practice "dangerous." Post hoc exclusion is a practice that is especially to be avoided.

14.4 LIMITATIONS OF STATISTICAL TESTS OF HETEROGENEITY

The number of studies eligible for inclusion in a meta-analysis is small for most topics. Meta-analyses of randomized trials typically identify from 5 to 15 eligible studies. A meta-analysis with more than 20 eligible studies is a rarity.

The magnitude of the statistic calculated in a formal test of heterogeneity is dependent on the weight of each study. The weight of each study is a function of its size. When the studies are themselves small or the total number of studies is low, Q will be small (unless, as discussed below, some studies deviate greatly from the summary measure of effect). The smallness of the number of studies in most meta-analyses is one reason that tests of heterogeneity are generally low in their power to reject the null hypothesis of homogeneity.

Because statistical tests of heterogeneity have low power, failure to reject the hypothesis of homogeneity should not preclude examination of the possibility of clinical heterogeneity (Thompson 1994). That is, even if there is no evidence of statistical heterogeneity, one should not accept the null hypothesis and conclude that the study results are homogeneous (Thompson 1994). Some authors (Fleiss 1981) suggest using a significance level of 0.1 instead of the more traditional level of 0.05 to reject the hypothesis of homogeneity.

The magnitude of the statistic calculated in a formal test of heterogeneity is also dependent on the magnitude of the deviation of the study results from the summary estimate of effect size. Because of this, a single outlier study can make a very large contribution to the heterogeneity statistic, resulting in a conclusion that there is heterogeneity in the studies when the studies yield a credible overall conclusion.

EXAMPLE: Table 14-2 shows the odds ratios and 95% confidence intervals from six case-control studies that provide estimates of the risk of ovarian cancer in relation to a history of the disease in a first-degree relative. The summary odds ratio is 3.1 (95% C.I. 2.1–4.5) based on a fixed-effects model. The value of Q is 11.5. This value is referred to the chi-square distribution with 5 degrees of freedom (the number of studies minus 1). The associated probability value for Q is 0.04. For these six studies, there is statistical evidence of heterogeneity.

Table 14-2   Meta-analysis of six studies of family history as a risk factor for ovarian cancer

Study	Odds Ratio	95% Confidence Interval	Weight of Study	Contribution to Q
1	9.3	0.5–173.1	0.4	0.5
2	18.2	4.9–69.0	2.2	7.0
3	11.3	0.6–211.3	0.5	0.7
4	3.6	1.8–7.2	8.0	0.2
5	3.3	1.1–9.4	3.2	0.0
6	1.9	1.1–3.6	12.9	3.1

All studies
  Summary odds ratio (95% confidence interval) 3.1 (2.1–4.5)
  $Q = 11.5$
  $df = 5$
  p for homogeneity $= 0.04$
Excluding Study 2
  Summary odds ratio (95% confidence interval) 2.7 (1.8–3.9)
  $Q = 4.0$
  $df = 4$
  p for homogeneity $= 0.41$

All of the odds ratios are elevated, however, and the results of the test of heterogeneity is counterintuitive. The odds ratio for ovarian cancer in women with a family history of the disease is 18.2 in Study 2. This study accounts for almost half of the Q. The contribution of Study 2 to Q is calculated as:

$$\text{contribution}_2 \text{ to } Q = \text{weight}_2 \times (\ln 3.1 - \ln 18.2)^2$$

Because the value of the odds ratio deviates so much from the summary odds ratio, the magnitude of its contribution to Q is large. This is true even though the odds ratio for the study is in the same direction as the summary odds ratio and the study is consistent with a conclusion that the odds ratio for ovarian cancer in women with a family history of the disease is elevated substantially.

If Study 2 is excluded from the estimation of the summary odds ratio, Q becomes 4.0. Referred to the chi-square distribution with 4 degrees of freedom, the associated p value is 0.41. The hypothesis of homogeneity is not rejected.

14.5 FRAMEWORK FOR EXPLORATION OF CLINICAL HETEROGENEITY

There are many sources of heterogeneity. Studies may differ in their designs (e.g., case-control or cohort; use of community controls or hospital controls; use of internal versus external controls; double-blind or single-blind; placebo-controlled or not placebo-controlled). Studies of the same type may differ in the success with which the study protocol was implemented (e.g., high response rate or low response rate; high follow-up rate or low follow-up rate; high rate of crossover or low rate of crossover).

Even when all studies are randomized, double-blind, and placebo-controlled, within a class of interventions, studies may differ in the exact treatments rendered (e.g., intravenous streptokinase or intravenous tissue plasminogen activator; selective or nonselective beta-blocker). The studies may differ in the background incidence of the outcome being studied, even when they are otherwise identical in their designs and the intervention being examined.

All these differences among studies can cause statistical heterogeneity. They are all candidates for exploration in a comprehensive exploration of clinical heterogeneity.

It is also possible that the effect of the intervention or risk factor is different in different subgroups. For example, amiodarone may be more effective in preventing mortality in patients with more serious arrhythmias. If a treatment has a different effect in different subgroups or a risk factor is a stronger or weaker risk factor in some people, the results of studies with different proportions of people in the subgroups may differ in their estimates of effect for this reason. The studies will be statistically heterogeneous.

More important, meta-analysis presents an opportunity to examine the possibility of differences in treatment effect and the strength of the association of a risk factor for disease in different subgroups. The meta-analysis may have more statistical power to find effects in subgroups than the same examination of effect in subgroups in the original studies because the meta-analysis includes more subjects than any of the original studies.

The exploration of clinical heterogeneity thus has two distinct goals—one methodologic and the second biologic. The overall aim of a comprehensive exploration of heterogeneity is, however, often both to identify methodologic differences that might explain statistical heterogeneity and to assess the possibility of biologic effect modification.

14.5.1   Exploring Methodologic Differences Among Studies

The primary reason for identifying the contribution of methodologic differences between studies to study heterogeneity is to determine whether differences in methodology are a cause of the statistical heterogeneity. Sometimes this can lead to a focus on the studies of a certain type as the basis for a conclusion.

EXAMPLE: Stampfer and Colditz (1991) did a meta-analysis of studies of estrogen replacement therapy and coronary disease. There was strong statistical evidence of heterogeneity (p $<$ 0.001) in the estimate of relative risk derived from the entire group of 31 studies that were eligible for the meta-analysis. When the relative risk of coronary disease was estimated separately by study design, differences were found. Hospital-based case-control studies and prospective cohort studies without internal controls yielded the highest and the lowest estimates of relative risk (Figure 14-1). Estimates derived from prospective studies with internal controls and cross-sectional studies of angiographically determined coronary artery disease were consistent with each other, and, when combined, were not statistically heterogeneous ($p > 0.05$). The hospital-based case-control studies and the prospective cohort studies were judged to have the greatest likelihood of bias, whereas the prospective studies with internal controls and the cross-sectional studies were considered to be least prone to bias. Based on this reasoning and on the homogeneity of results for the prospective cohort studies with internal controls and the cross-sectional studies, Stampfer and Colditz (1991) concluded that estrogen replacement therapy decreases the risk of coronary disease.

Study characteristics other than design can be examined. Assessments of characteristics of study quality can be examined.

EXAMPLE: The question of whether vasectomy increases the risk of prostate cancer is controversial. Vasectomy cannot be assigned at random and information on this association derives entirely from observational studies. Bernal-Delgado et al. (1998) did a meta-analysis of these studies, the main goal being to examine study characteristics, including the quality of the design and execution of the studies, as possible explanations for the discrepancies in the study results. They identified 14 studies that were eligible for the meta-analysis. The estimates of the relative risk of prostate cancer in men with vasectomy ranged from 1.1 (95% C.I. 0.7–1.4) to 6.7 (95% C.I. 2.1–21.6). Table 14-3 shows summary estimates of the relative risk of prostate

Study Type

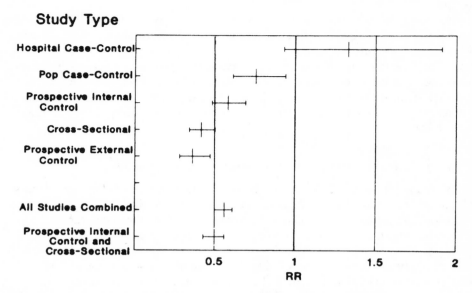

Figure 14-1   Summary estimates of relative risk (RR) and their 95% confidence intervals for studies of postmenopausal estrogen use and coronary heart disease, by type of study design. (Reproduced with permission from Stampfer and Colditz, *Preventive Medicine,* 1991;20:58.)

cancer in relation to various study characteristics and measures of study quality. The summary estimates of the relative risks of prostate cancer in men with vasectomy were higher in case-control studies, in studies done in hospital settings, and in studies rated as having inadequate control selection and detection bias.

14.5.2   Identifying Biologic Effects

The primary reason for exploring heterogeneity of treatment effects in meta-analysis of randomized trials is to identify effect modification for biologic reasons.

EXAMPLE: A large number of randomized trials have examined the relationship between oral potassium and blood pressure. These studies have been mostly small and their results inconsistent. More important, the effect of oral potassium may be different depending on presence of hypertension, race, and background intakes of dietary sodium and potassium. Table 14-4 shows the results of a meta-analysis of a randomized trial of oral potassium and blood pressure by Whelton et al. (1997). The meta-analysis included the examination of blood pressure reduction in subgroups defined by the characteristics of the patients. The purpose was identification of biologic differences in the blood pressure response to oral potassium. The analysis showed that the reduction in systolic blood pressure was greater in hypertensives, blacks, and those with high urine sodium, a measure of dietary intake of sodium.

Table 14-3 Summary estimates of the relative risk of prostate cancer in men with vasectomy according to study characteristics related to study quality

Study Characteristic	Summary Estimate of Relative Risk	95% Confidence Interval
Design		
Cohort	1.1	0.8–1.5
Case–control	1.4	1.0–1.8
Setting		
Population	1.1	1.0–1.3
Hospital	2.0	1.4–2.9
Rating of adequacy of control selection		
Adequate	1.1	0.9–1.3
Inadequate	2.2	1.4–3.5
Rating of presence of detection bias		
None	1.1	1.0–1.3
Possible	1.9	1.4–2.6

Source: Bernal-Delgado et al. (1998).

Table 14-4 Summary estimate of the mean reduction in systolic blood pressure for oral potassium treatment in subgroups defined by patient characteristics

Patient Characteristic	Number of Studies	Mean Reduction in Blood Pressure	p for Difference
Hypertension status			
Hypertensive	20	−4.4	
Normotensive	12	−1.8	0.07
Race			
Black	6	−5.6	
White	25	−2.0	0.03
Net change in urine potassium[a]			
<42	10	−4.3	
42–67	9	−2.9	
≥68	11	−2.2	0.46
Net change in urine sodium[a]			
<5	10	−2.1	
5–12	9	−2.8	
≥13	11	−4.6	0.52
Urine sodium during follow-up[a]			
<140	10	−1.2	
140–164	10	−2.1	
≥165	10	−7.3	<0.001

[a] nmol/day.
Source: Whelton et al. (1997).

Table 14-5   Summary estimates of the odds of end of treatment abstinence from smoking for the nicotine patch by characteristics of other study treatments

Characteristic of Treatment	Number of Studies	Odds Ratio for Abstinence	95% Confidence Interval
Type of Patch			
16 hour	4	3.8	2.7–5.3
24 hour	13	2.5	2.1–2.9
Duration of Treatment			
≤8 weeks	9	2.9	2.2–3.6
≥8 weeks	7	2.4	2.0–2.9
Weaning			
No	6	2.9	2.2–3.8
Yes	10	2.4	2.0–2.9
Counseling Format			
Individual	8	3.4	2.7–4.3
Group	6	3.0	2.3–3.9
Counseling Intensity			
Low	10	2.5	2.0–3.0
High	6	2.8	2.2–3.7

Source: Fiore et al. (1994).

In a related way, subgroups may be defined according to the characteristics of concomitant treatments. The meta-analysis can then attempt to determine whether other treatments provided in the context of the study treatment might modify the effect of the main treatment.

> *EXAMPLE:*   Fiore et al. (1994) did a meta-analysis of randomized trials of the nicotine patch for treating tobacco dependence. The studies differed in the type of patch used and in the duration of treatment. In some studies, treatment with the nicotine patch was part of a comprehensive behavioral smoking cessation program. The question of which kind of patch was more effective and whether the adjunctive behavioral treatments modified the efficacy of the patch arises naturally. Table 14-5 shows the results of their examination of the summary odds ratio for abstinence in subgroups of studies defined according to the characteristics of the patch and adjunctive treatments. The analysis showed that the 16-hour patch was as effective as the 24-hour patch, that treatment beyond 8 weeks did not improve efficacy, and that more intensive counseling was not related to increased efficacy.

14.6   STRATIFICATION AS A METHOD FOR EXPLORING HETEROGENEITY

The method used most often to explore heterogeneity is stratification. Studies are categorized according to the characteristics of the study or the characteristics of the subjects in the study and a summary estimate of effect is estimated in each of the categories.

EXAMPLES: In the example described above of meta-analysis of studies of estrogen replacement therapy and coronary disease (Stampfer and Colditz 1991), studies were stratified according to design—hospital-based case-control, population-based case-control, prospective with internal controls, prospective with external controls. The relative risk and 95% confidence interval for coronary disease in estrogen users was estimated based on all of the studies in each of the four strata of design.

Table 14-6 shows the results of a meta-analysis of the efficacy of screening mammography done by Kerlikowske et al. (1995) that included a comprehensive exploration of heterogeneity using stratification. Studies were categorized by study design, the number of mammographic views, screening interval, duration of follow-up, duration of screening, use of clinical breast examination, and study start date. Within each of these strata defined by study characteristics, estimates of relative risk and 95% confidence intervals were calculated for women of all ages and separately in strata of age (40–49 and 50–74).

Table 14-6 Summary estimates of the relative risk of mortality in women who have undergone screening mammography by study characteristic and in subgroups of age and initial screen

Study Characteristics	Age 40–49		Age 50–74	
	Summary Estimate of Relative Risk	95% Confidence Interval	Summary Estimate of Relative Risk	95% Confidence Interval
Design				
Case-control	1.2	0.3–4.8	0.5	0.3–0.7
Randomized trial	0.9	0.8–1.1	0.8	0.7–0.9
Screening interval				
12 months	1.0	0.7–1.4	0.8	0.6–1.0
18–33 months	0.9	0.7–1.1	0.8	0.7–0.9
Duration of follow–up				
7–9 years	1.0	0.8–1.3	0.7	0.6–0.8
10–12 years	0.8	0.7–1.1	0.8	0.7–0.9
Duration of screening				
3–5 years	1.0	0.7–1.3	0.8	0.6–1.0
8–10 years	0.9	0.6–1.2	0.8	0.7–0.9
Clinical breast exam				
No	0.9	0.7–1.2	0.8	0.7–0.9
Yes	0.9	0.7–1.2	0.8	0.7–1.0
Study start date				
Before 1980	0.8	0.7–1.1	0.8	0.7–0.9
1980 and after	1.2	0.8–1.7	0.8	0.7–0.8

Source: Kerlikowske et al. 1995.

The examination of heterogeneity using stratification can be especially detailed and useful when individual-level data are available.

> *EXAMPLE:*   In the meta-analysis of individual-level data from observational studies of breast cancer and hormone replacement therapy done by the Collaborative Group on Hormonal Factors in Breast Cancer (1997) that was discussed in Chapter 8, stratification was used to examine comprehensively possible differences in the effect of hormone replacement therapy on breast cancer. Estimates of the relative risk of breast cancer in recent hormone users with short and long durations of use and in past users of hormone replacement were made for 14 different strata. Table 14-7 shows the estimates of the relative risk of breast cancer for the recent and long-term users of hormone replacement therapy. The summary estimate of the relative risk of breast cancer in these women was elevated in these women. The stratified analyses show that the effect of long-term use of hormone replacement therapy in increasing the risk of breast cancer in recent and current hormone users occurs in all of the subgroups.

14.7   META-REGRESSION

The term meta-regression (Greenland 1987) refers to analyses in which the characteristics of the studies or of subjects in the studies are used as explanatory variables (covariates) in a multivariate regression analysis with the effect size (or some measure of deviation from the summary measure of effect) as the dependent variable. In meta-regression, the unit of observation is the study or the subgroup. The independent variables could be characteristics of the study defined as categorical variable (e.g,. study design) or a measure of values for subjects in the study (e.g., mean age, percentage of subjects 65+ years).

> *EXAMPLE:*   Phillips (1991) did a meta-analysis of studies of the sensitivity and specificity of tests for HIV seropositivity. There were 26 studies eligible for the meta-analysis. Information on the sensitivity and specificity of the HIV test was abstracted from each study, and each study was abstracted and classified according to year of publication (three categories), whether the test sample was in a population with a low or high prevalence of HIV infection, and by study quality (high, medium, low). Table 14-8 presents the results of the regression analysis in which specificity of the HIV test as measured in each study was the dependent variable, and year of publication, HIV prevalence, and study quality were entered as predictors. The meta-regression analysis showed that low prevalence of HIV was significantly associated with low test specificity.

The number of explanatory variables in a meta-regression analysis should be kept small (Greenland 1987). Meta-regression analysis is exploratory and hypothesis generating.

Table 14-7 Estimates of the relative risk of breast cancer associated with last use of hormone replacement therapy <5 years and duration of use ≥5 years for various subgroups

Subgroup	Estimated Relative Risk	95% Confidence Interval
Age at diagnosis		
<60 years	1.3	1.1–1.5
≥60 years	1.4	1.2–1.7
Family history		
No	1.4	1.2–1.5
Yes	1.1	0.7–1.6
Ethnic group		
White	1.3	1.1–1.4
Other	1.2	0.7–2.2
Education		
<13 years	1.2	1.0–1.5
≥13 years	1.5	1.2–1.8
Body mass index		
<25 kg/m^2	1.5	1.3–1.8
≥25 kg/m^2	1.0	0.8–1.3
Age at menarche		
<13 years	1.2	1.0–1.4
≥13 years	1.4	1.2–1.7
Parity		
Nulliparous	1.4	1.0–1.9
Parous	1.3	1.2–1.5
Age at first birth		
<25 years	1.4	1.2–1.7
≥25 years	1.3	1.0–1.5
Oral contraceptive use		
No	1.4	1.2–1.5
Yes	1.4	0.6–3.3
Alcohol use		
<50 g/week	1.4	1.2–1.7
≥50 g/week	1.6	1.4–1.4
Smoking		
Never	1.3	1.1–1.6
Ever	1.6	1.3–1.9
Type of menopause		
Natural	1.3	1.1–1.6
Oophorectomy	1.3	1.0–1.6

14.8 SUBGROUP ANALYSIS IN DECISION ANALYSIS AND COST-EFFECTIVENESS ANALYSIS

Subgroup analysis is often done in decision analysis and cost-effectiveness analysis. The primary goal of subgroup analysis conducted in the context of decision analysis and cost-effectiveness analysis is to identify groups in whom the treatment is most and least effective or cost-effective. In most instances, the subgroups are defined according to background risk of the main outcome being examined.

Table 14-8   Results of meta-regression analysis for 26 studies: specificity of HIV test in each study is the dependent variable[a]

Variable	Regression Coefficient	T	p
Year of publication	−0.023	−0.90	>0.05
Low-prevalence HIV[b]	0.114	−2.54	<0.05
Study quality[c]			
High	−0.014	−0.20	<0.05
Low	−0.087	−1.38	<0.05

[a] After semi-logarithmic transformation.

[b] High and mixed prevalence is referent.

[c] Intermediate quality is referent.

Source: Phillips (1991).

EXAMPLES: Chapter 10 briefly described a decision analysis done by Schrag et al. (1997) to estimate the effects of prophylactic mastectomy and oophorectomy on life expectancy among women with *BRCA1* or *BRCA2* mutations. Estimates of the gains in life expectancy were made for subgroups of women defined according to their baseline risk of breast and ovarian cancer and age at the time of determination of mutation carrier status. Table 14-9 shows estimates of the gain in life expectancy for immediate prophylactic mastectomy and oophorectomy and for immediate mastectomy only. The analysis shows that 60-year old women gain little in terms of life expectancy irrespective of their risk level. For younger women in the lower two risk levels, immediate oophorectomy adds little to the benefit of immediate mastectomy.

Chapter 2 and Chapter 9 described a cost-effectiveness analysis of war-

Table 14-9   Estimates of the gain in years of life for prophylactic surgery in women with *BRCA1* or *BRCA2* mutations by level of risk and age at determination of carrier status

Risk Level	Surgery Strategy	Age of Carrier			
		30	40	50	60
40% risk of breast cancer, 5% risk of ovarian cancer	Immediate mastectomy and oophorectomy	3.2	2.3	1.1	0.2
	Immediate mastectomy	2.9	2.0	1.0	0.2
60% risk of breast cancer, 20% risk of ovarian cancer	Immediate mastectomy and oophorectomy	5.3	4.0	2.0	0.4
	Immediate mastectomy	4.1	2.9	1.6	0.3
85% risk of breast cancer, 40% risk of ovarian cancer	Immediate mastectomy and oophorectomy	7.6	5.9	3.3	0.9
	Immediate mastectomy	5.3	3.7	2.3	0.5

Source: Schrag et al. (1997).

farin and aspirin for prophylaxis of stroke in patients with nonvalvular atrial fibrillation done by Gage et al. (1995). This analysis assessed the cost-effectiveness of warfarin compared with aspirin and with no therapy in subgroups of patients defined according to their risk of stroke based on six risk factors for stroke (history of stroke or TIA, diabetes, hypertension, congestive heart failure, angina, prior myocardial infarction). Table 14-10 shows the results of the analysis for the comparison of warfarin with aspirin in patients at low, medium, and high risk for stroke. In patients at high risk for stroke, warfarin cost less than aspirin and increased QALYS more. A marginal cost per QALY is not calculated in this situation since warfarin is cost-saving with respect to its alternative. The incremental cost per QALY for warfarin compared with aspirin was $8,000 in patients at medium risk for stroke and $370,000 in patients at low risk for stroke.

Subgroup analysis and sensitivity analysis are closely related. Sensitivity analysis is discussed in more detail in Chapter 15. The computational mechanics of subgroup analysis and one-way sensitivity are essentially indistinguishable in their mechanics. Sensitivity analysis assesses the stability of the conclusions to assumptions about the probabilities used in the analysis and is done as an assessment of the methodology. Subgroup analysis seeks to delineate differences in the effects of the intervention that are biologically based.

14.9   LIMITATIONS OF SUBGROUP ANALYSIS

In meta-analysis, the estimation of effects in subgroups is limited by the lack of uniform reporting of data among studies. Meta-analysis of individual-level patient data mitigates this problem.

Meta-regression is limited by the smallness of the number of studies available

Table 14-10   Estimated QALYs' costs and incremental cost per QALY for warfarin compared with aspirin by level of stroke risk

Stroke Risk Level		QALYs	Cost	Incremental Cost/QALY[a]
High	Warfarin	6.51	$12,500	
	Aspirin	6.27	$13,200	
	Comparison[a]			Warfarin preferred[b]
Medium	Warfarin	6.60	$10,900	
	Aspirin	6.46	$ 9,700	
	Comparison[a]			$ 8,000
Low	Warfarin	6.70	$ 9,000	
	Aspirin	6.69	$ 5,400	
	Comparison[a]			$370,000

[a] Comparing warfarin with aspirin.

[b] Warfarin increases QALY and costs less.

Source: Gage et al. (1995).

for most meta-analyses. When a variable in the regression is one that is defined at the group level, such as percentage of subjects 45 or more years of age or the mean age of subjects in the study, meta-regression is a kind of ecologic analysis and is subject to all of the problems of ecologic analysis (Morgenstern 1982).

Lau, Ioannidis, and Schmid (1997), discussing meta-analysis, point out that subgroup analysis is a post hoc exercise that can turn into a "fishing expedition." This concern applies equally to subgroup analysis done in the context of decision analysis and cost-effectiveness analysis.

Subgroup analysis, in meta-analysis as well as in decision analysis and cost-effectiveness analysis, is always exploratory and hypothesis generating.

15

Sensitivity Analysis

Sensitivity analysis is an essential element of decision analysis and cost-effectiveness analysis. The principles of sensitivity analysis are also directly applicable to meta-analysis. This chapter shows how to do sensitivity analysis for studies using each of the three methods.

Section 15.1 describes the overall purpose of sensitivity analysis. Section 15.2 describes one-way sensitivity analysis as applied to decision analysis and cost-effectiveness analysis. Section 15.3 describes how to do and how to interpret two-way and three-way sensitivity analysis. It discusses n-way sensitivity analysis. Section 15.4 describes the application of the principles of sensitivity analysis to meta-analysis.

15.1 GOALS OF SENSITIVITY ANALYSIS

Sensitivity analysis evaluates the stability of the conclusions of an analysis to assumptions made in the analysis. When a conclusion is shown to be invariate to the assumptions, confidence in the validity of the conclusions of the analysis is enhanced.

Sensitivity analysis also helps identify the most critical assumptions of the analysis. This knowledge can be used to formulate priorities for future research aimed at resolving the problem posed in the analysis.

15.2 ONE-WAY SENSITIVITY ANALYSIS IN DECISION ANALYSIS AND COST-EFFECTIVENESS ANALYSIS

15.2.1 Overview

An implicit assumption of decision analysis is that the values of the probabilities and of the utility measure are the correct values for these variables. In cost-effectiveness analysis, there is a similar implicit assumption that the discount rate and the costs are correct. In one-way sensitivity analysis, the assumed values of each variable in the analysis are varied, one at a time, while the values of the other variables in the analysis remain fixed. One-way sensitivity analysis of a cost-effectiveness analysis should also vary the discount rate for costs and benefits while keeping the values of the other variables in the analysis fixed.

EXAMPLE: A decision analysis comparing radical prostatectomy and external beam radiation with watchful waiting in men with clinically localized prostate cancer was introduced in Chapter 1. The baseline analysis showed that compared with watchful waiting, a 65-year-old man with moderately well-differentiated prostate cancer in average health would have an increase in quality-adjusted life expectancy of 3.1 months for radical prostatectomy and 5.5 months for external beam radiation. Table 15-1 shows the results of

Table 15-1   One-way sensitivity analysis varying probability estimates for treatment-related complications in decision analysis comparing treatments for localized prostate cancer[a]

	Radical Prostatectomy		External Beam Radiation	
Complication	Probability Value	Benefit of Treatment[b]	Probability Value	Benefit of Treatment[b]
Impotence	0.000	5.6	0.000	9.2
	0.310[c]	3.1[c]	0.440[c]	5.5[c]
	1.000	−2.6	0.610	4.1
Incontinence	0.000[b]	6.1	0.000	6.0
	0.060[c]	3.1[c]	0.010[c]	5.5[c]
	0.130	−0.4	0.040	4.0
Bowel injury	0.000	3.3	0.000	5.8
	0.010[c]	3.1[c]	0.010[c]	5.5[c]
	0.040	2.4	0.030	5.0
Bladder outlet obstruction	0.000	3.4	0.000	5.6
	0.090[c]	3.1[c]	0.025[c]	5.5[c]
	0.200	2.8	0.060	5.4

[a] For a 65-year man in average health with moderately well-differentiated cancer.

[b] Quality-adjusted life months compared with watchful waiting.

[c] Baseline value.

Source: Fleming et al. (1993).

a one-way sensitivity analysis in which the probability values for various treatment-related complications were varied while the other probability values for variables in the analysis were held constant. The sensitivity analysis shows that the amount of benefit for radical prostatectomy compared with watchful waiting is sensitive to assumptions about the probability of treatment-related impotence and treatment-related incontinence. At the extreme values of these variables, there is a net loss in quality-adjusted life expectancy for radical prostatectomy compared with watchful waiting.

15.2.2   Interpreting the Results of One-Way Sensitivity Analysis

When the assumed value of a variable affects the conclusion of the analysis, the analysis is said to be "sensitive" to that variable. When the conclusion does not change when the sensitivity analysis includes the values of the variables that are within a reasonable range, the analysis is said to be "insensitive" to that variable.

If an analysis is sensitive to the assumed value of a variable, the likelihood that the extreme value is the true value can be assessed qualitatively. Further research to refine the estimate may be a priority for future studies. The absolute amount of benefit of one strategy over the other under the extreme assumptions can be weighed.

> *EXAMPLE:*   The one-way sensitivity analysis for radical prostatectomy and external beam radiation compared with watchful waiting for 65-year-old men with moderately well-differentiated prostate cancer showed that the increase in quality-adjusted life expectancy was less than 6 months for radical prostatectomy even under the extreme assumption that the probability of treatment-related impotence and treatment-related incontinence are zero. Since it is unlikely that the probabilities of these complications can be reduced to zero, the sensitivity analysis provides a best-case estimate of the benefit of radical prostatectomy compared with watchful waiting.

Sensitivity analysis varying the values of the utilities should always be done. Examination of the sensitivity of the analysis to the utilities can be very useful in formulating recommendations based on the analysis.

> *EXAMPLE:*   Table 15-2 shows the results of the one-way sensitivity analysis of Fleming et al. (1993) in which utility values for treatment-related impotence, incontinence, and bowel injury were varied. The amount of increase in quality-adjusted life expectancy is especially sensitive to the utility for impotence and incontinence. An individual patient's utility for these complications would be relatively easy to elicit. The importance of incorporating individual patient utilities for treatment-related impotence and incontinence into clinical decision making was a main conclusion of this decision analysis.

The sensitivity analysis should vary the discount rate for benefits, holding constant discounting of cost if the analysis is a cost-effectiveness analysis. The analysis should include a discount rate of 0.0. Including a discount rate of 0.0 for benefits

Table 15-2   One-way sensitivity analysis varying utility values for treatment-related complications is decision analysis comparing treatments for localized prostate cancer[a]

Complication	Utility Value	Benefit of Treatment[b]	
		Radical Prostatectomy	External Beam Radiation
Impotence	1.00	5.6	9.2
	0.95[c]	3.1[c]	5.5[c]
	0.90	0.6	1.8
	0.85	−2.0	−1.9
Incontinence	1.00	6.1	6.0
	0.85	4.6	5.8
	0.70[c]	3.1[c]	5.5[c]
	0.55	2.6	5.0
Bowel injury	1.00	3.3	5.8
	0.85[c]	3.1[c]	5.5[c]
	0.70	2.9	5.3
	0.55	1.1	5.2

[a] For a 65-year man in average health with moderately well-differentiated cancer.
[b] Quality-adjusted life months compared with watchful waiting.
[c] Baseline value.
Source: Fleming et al. (1993).

is the equivalent of not discounting benefits. Discounting of benefits values events in the near term more than events that occur in the distant future. The difference between the discounted and undiscounted estimates of outcome may be important.

   EXAMPLE: Table 15-3 shows the results of the one-way sensitivity analysis varying the discount rate for the benefits of radical prostatectomy and external

Table 15-3   One-way sensitivity analysis varying the discount rate for benefits in decision analysis comparing treatments for localized prostate cancer[c]

Discount Rate (%)	Benefit of Treatment[b]	
	Radical Prostatectomy	External Beam Radiation
0	3.3[c]	5.8[c]
5	0.0	1.6
11	−1.1	0.0

[a] For a 65-year man in average health with moderately well-differentiated cancer.
[b] Quality-adjusted life months compared with watchful waiting.
[c] baseline value.
Source: Fleming et al. (1993).

beam radiation compared with watchful waiting for prostate cancer in the decision analysis by Fleming et al. (1993). When benefits are discounted at 5% or more, there is no benefit of radical prostatectomy and the benefit of external beam radiation is reduced from 5.8 to 1.6 quality-adjusted life months. Men with localized prostate cancer are generally free of symptoms, and because prostate cancer is slow-growing, years may pass between discovery of the tumor and progression. The fact that the estimated benefit of treatment is sensitive to discounting may be important information for an individual with prostate cancer who is deciding whether to undergo treatment. Some men might be reluctant to risk years of life with good quality in the near term to avoid an indefinite risk of life with impaired quality in the future (Fleming et al. 1993).

15.2.3 Threshold Analysis

Threshold analysis is an extension of one-way sensitivity analysis. In threshold analysis, the value of one variable is varied until the alternative decision strategies are found to have equal outcomes, and there is no benefit of one alternative over the other in terms of estimated outcome. The threshold point is also called the "break-even" point. At the break-even point, the decision is a "toss-up" (Kassirer and Pauker 1981). That is, neither of the alternative decision options being compared is clearly favored over the other.

EXAMPLE: In the one-way sensitivity analyses of Fleming et al. (1993) comparing treatment options for a 65-year man in average health with moderately well-differentiated prostate cancer that were described in Tables 15-1 and 15-2, treatment was sensitive to the probability of treatment-related impotence, treatment-related incontinence, and the utility value for treatment-related impotence. Table 15-4 shows the results of a threshold analysis for

Table 15-4 Threshold values for sensitive variables for radical prostatectomy and external beam radiation[a]

	Threshold Value[b]	
Sensitive Variable	Radical Prostatectomy	External Beam Radiation
Probability of treatment-related impotence	0.680	—[c]
Probability of treatment-related incontinence	0.120	—[c]
Utility value for impotence	0.89	0.89

[a] For a 65-year old man in average health with moderately well-differentiated cancer.

[b] Value for which expected outcome of treatment is the same as for watchful waiting.

[c] Expected outcome exceeds that of watchful waiting at all values of the variable for external beam radiation.

Source: Fleming et al. (1993).

the values of these three variables. For radical prostatectomy compared with watchful waiting, the threshold probability is 0.68 for treatment-related impotence. This is the value of the probability for this variable at which the expected outcomes of radical prostatectomy and watchful waiting are equal. For the same comparison of radical prostatectomy and watchful waiting, the threshold probability is 0.20 for treatment-related incontinence. The threshold value for the utility of impotence is 0.89.

Threshold analysis is especially useful when the intervention is being considered for use in groups that can be defined a priori based on the values of the variable that is the subject of the threshold analysis.

EXAMPLE: In the decision analysis of isoniazid prophylaxis in HIV-infected intravenous drug users by Jordan et al. (1991) that was discussed in Chapter 9, the overall conclusion was that prophylaxis was beneficial in all groups except black women with negative tuberculin skin tests. One of the key probabilities is life expectancy in the absence of tuberculosis. An analysis was done to determine the threshold for the benefit of isoniazid prophylaxis.

Table 15-5 shows the threshold values. For each of the groups defined in the table, the threshold value is the value of life expectancy at which the strategy of giving prophylaxis would be equal to no prophylaxis in terms of additional life expectancy, considering prevention of tuberculosis. The analysis shows that in all the groups except black women, who had no benefit under baseline assumptions, even persons with a low remaining life expectancy would benefit from tuberculosis prophylaxis with isoniazid.

15.3   TWO-WAY, THREE-WAY, AND n-WAY SENSITIVITY ANALYSIS

15.3.1   Two-Way Sensitivity Analysis

In two-way sensitivity analysis, the expected outcome is determined for every combination of estimates of two variables, while the values of all other variables in the analysis are held constant at baseline. In two-way sensitivity analysis, it is usual to identify the pairs of values that equalize the expected outcome or expected utility of the alternatives and to present the results of the analysis graphically. It is difficult to interpret the results of a two-way sensitivity analysis without the aid of graphs.

EXAMPLE: In the decision analysis comparing the utility of amniocentesis and chorionic villus sampling discussed in Chapter 10 (Heckerling and Verp 1991), a two-way sensitivity analysis varying the estimates of spontaneous abortion following amniocentesis and following chorionic villus sampling was done. Figure 15-1 graphically presents the results of a two-way sensitivity analysis. In the graph, the solid line appears at combinations of the rates of spontaneous abortion that equalize the expected utility of amniocentesis

Table 15-5 Threshold analysis for isoniazid in HIV- infected intravenous drug users: Values of years of remaining life expectancy that would make the decision to use isoniazid a "toss-up"

| | Tuberculin Test Result | |
Patient Description	Positive	Negative
Black men	3.31	5.29
Black women	3.44	No benefit
White men	3.28	4.50
White women	3.27	4.32

Source: Jordan et al. (1991).

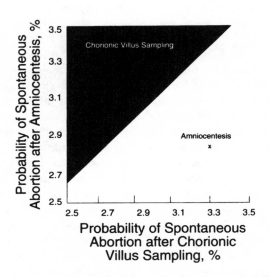

Figure 15-1 Two-way sensitivity analysis from the decision analysis by Heckerling and Verp (1991) comparing amniocentesis and chorionic villus sampling. The probabilities that were subjected to two-way sensitivity analysis are the probability of spontaneous abortion after amniocentesis and the probability of spontaneous abortion after chorionic villus sampling. Other probabilities were held at their baseline values.

The region to the right of the line represents combinations of probabilities of spontaneous abortion for which amniocentesis would be preferred; the region to the left represents combinations for which chorionic villus sampling would be preferred. The baseline combination of values is shown with an x. (Reproduced with permission from Heckerling and Verp, *Journal of Clinical Epidemiology,* 1991;44:663.)

compared with chorionic villus sampling. The combinations of spontaneous abortion rates that would lead to a preference for chorionic villus sampling are shown with dark shading. The combinations that would lead to a preference for amniocentesis are shown with light shading. The baseline estimate is shown with a dot. The two-way sensitivity analysis shows that with the rate of spontaneous abortion after amniocentesis fixed at its baseline rate of 2.8%, amniocentesis is the preferred strategy if the rate of spontaneous abortion after chorionic villus sampling is greater than 2.68%. Amniocentesis is the preferred strategy at all combinations where the spontaneous abortion rate following chorionic villus sampling is greater than the spontaneous abortion rate following amniocentesis. Since chorionic villus sampling is probably inherently more likely to cause spontaneous abortion than amniocentesis, the two-way sensitivity analysis strengthens confidence in the overall conclusion of the analysis favoring amniocentesis over chorionic villus sampling.

15.3.2 Three-Way Sensitivity Analysis

In three-way sensitivity analysis, the expected outcome is determined for combinations of estimates of three variables, while the values of all other variables in the analysis are held constant at baseline. Like two-way sensitivity analysis, it is usual to present the results of three-way sensitivity analysis graphically, and interpretation of the results in the absence of graphical aids is difficult.

EXAMPLE: Heckerling and Verp (1991) did a three-way sensitivity analysis. In it, they varied the probability of spontaneous abortion after chorionic villus sampling, the rate of indeterminate chorionic villus sampling, and the probability of an abnormal amniocentesis after an indeterminate chorionic villus sampling, while holding the values of other variables in the analysis constant at their baseline levels. Figure 15-2 depicts the results graphically. Five lines are shown for five values of the probability of an abnormal amniocentesis following indeterminate chorionic villus sampling. For each of these values, the line shows the combination of values of the rate of indeterminate chorionic villus sampling and probability of spontaneous abortion after chorionic villus sampling that would yield the same expected utility for amniocentesis and chorionic villus sampling. Choosing one line, the combinations of values to the right of the line represent values for which amniocentesis is preferred and the combinations to the left represent values for which chorionic villus sampling is preferred. Figure 15-2 is analogous to Figure 15-1. In fact, the results could have been presented as five figures like Figure 15-1, one for each value of the probability of an abnormal amniocentesis following indeterminate chorionic villus sampling.

The three-way sensitivity analysis shows that amniocentesis is the preferred strategy except if the rate of indeterminate chorionic villus sampling and the spontaneous abortion rate after chorionic villus sampling are implausibly low and the rate of abnormal amniocentesis implausibly high. The sensitivity analysis further strengthens confidence in the conclusion of the decision analysis favoring amniocentesis over chorionic villus sampling.

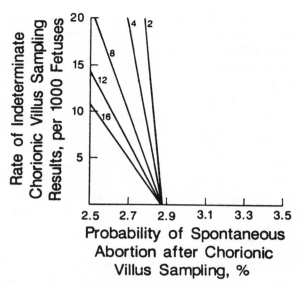

Figure 15-2 Three-way sensitivity analysis from the decision analysis by Heckerling and Verp (1991) comparing amniocentesis and chorionic villus sampling. The probabilities that are subjected to three-way sensitivity analysis are the probability of spontaneous abortion after chorionic villus sampling, the rate of indeterminate chorionic villus sampling results, and the probability of an abnormal amniocentesis after an indeterminate chorionic villus sampling. The other probabilities are held at their baseline values.

For any line, the region to the right represents combinations of the probability of spontaneous abortion after chorionic villus sampling and the rate of indeterminate chorionic villus sampling results for which amniocentesis is preferred; the region to the left represents combinations for which chorionic villus sampling is preferred. (Reproduced with permission from Heckerling and Verp, *Journal of Clinical Epidemiology,* 1991;44: 663.)

15.3.3 *n*-Way Sensitivity Analysis

In *n*-way sensitivity analysis, the expected outcome is determined for every possible combination of every reasonable value of every variable. *n*-way sensitivity analysis is analogous to n-way regression. It is difficult to do and difficult to interpret. *n*-way sensitivity analysis will not be described further in this book.

15.3.4 Choice of Variables for Sensitivity Analysis

It is usual to do one-way sensitivity analysis for each variable in the analysis. The highest and the lowest values within the reasonable range of values are first substituted for the baseline estimate in the decision tree. If substitution of the highest or the lowest value changes the conclusions, more values within the range are substituted to determine the range of values. It is especially important to do one-way sensitivity analysis for the discount rate for cost in cost-effectiveness analysis, because there is generally uncertainty about the correct discount rate. If the conclusion of a cost-effectiveness analysis is shown to be independent of the choice of the discount rate within a reasonable range of estimates of the discount rate, then arguments about the appropriateness of discounting and about the proper discount rate are moot.

> *EXAMPLE:*   Chapter 12 described a cost-effectiveness analysis of bone marrow transplantation in acute nonlymphocytic leukemia. Table 15-6 shows the cost of bone marrow transplantation and the cost of chemotherapy with doing nothing for several estimates of the discount rate. For all of the values from 0 to 10%, bone marrow transplantation costs less than chemotherapy. Thus, bone marrow transplantation is cost-effective relative to chemotherapy by the definition given in Chapter 12. This conclusion does not depend on assumptions about the discount rate.

In an analysis that uses measures of utility derived by any of the methods described in Chapter 11, it is important to do a sensitivity analysis varying the utility. If the analysis is insensitive to assumptions about the utility within reasonable estimates of the utility measure, criticisms of the utility measure itself carry less weight.

In an analysis with many probabilities, there are numerous combinations of two variables and three variables, and the computational burden of doing all possible two-way and three-way sensitivity analyses is large. For this reason, it is not usually feasible to do two-way sensitivity analysis for all combinations of two variables. The choice of variables for two-way and three-way sensitivity analysis requires considerable judgment, and there are no hard and fast rules. The variables that seem the most controversial may be chosen for two-way sensitivity analysis, since the believability of the conclusions of the analysis may hinge on assumptions about these variables.

> *EXAMPLE:*   The rates of spontaneous abortion following chorionic villus sampling and amniocentesis are controversial. However, there is general

Table 15-6   For several estimates of the discount rate, cost per year of life saved for bone marrow transplantation compared with doing nothing and for chemotherapy compared with doing nothing in patients with acute nonlymphocytic leukemia

	Cost per Year of Life Gained	
Discount Rate (%)	Chemotherapy	Bone Marrow Transplant
0	$10,300	$ 6,900
5	22,900	16,600
10	35,500	27,900

Source: Welch and Larson (1989).

agreement that the rate of spontaneous abortion is higher for chorionic villus sampling than for amniocentesis. The two-way sensitivity analysis showed that the rate of spontaneous abortion following amniocentesis would have to be higher than the rate following chorionic villus sampling to alter the conclusion favoring amniocentesis. The confidence in the conclusion is enhanced through this two-way sensitivity analysis.

15.3.5 Linkage of Subgroup and Sensitivity Analysis

Subgroup analysis and sensitivity analysis are closely related. As mentioned in Chapter 14, the computational mechanics of subgroup analysis and one-way sensitivity are essentially indistinguishable. Sensitivity analysis assesses the stability of the conclusions to assumptions about the probabilities used in the analysis and is done as an assessment of the methodology. Subgroup analysis often seeks to delineate differences in the effects of the intervention that are biologically based. In practice, both subgroup analysis and sensitivity analysis are often done and are useful.

EXAMPLE: The cost-effectiveness analysis of Gage et al. (1995) comparing warfarin and aspirin for stroke prophylaxis in patients with nonvalvular atrial fibrillation was discussed in Chapters 2, 9, and 14. Chapter 14 showed the results of the analysis of warfarin in subgroups of patients at low, medium, and high risk of stroke. A sensitivity analysis of warfarin compared to aspirin according to the annual rate of stroke was also done. The results of this sensitivity analysis are shown in Figure 15-3. The sensitivity analysis confirms conclusions based on the subgroup analysis, showing that the incremental cost-effectiveness of warfarin compared with aspirin is very high in patients at low risk of stroke. The sensitivity analysis provides more information than the subgroup analysis. Thus, in all three groups examined (warfarin, aspirin, no therapy), the number of QALYs decreases with increasing stroke rate, whereas the costs increase. The results of the sensitivity analysis also show that cost per QALY for warfarin compared with aspirin decreases sharply when the annual rate of stroke exceeds about 3%.

15.4 APPLICATION OF THE PRINCIPLES OF SENSITIVITY ANALYSIS TO META-ANALYSIS

15.4.1 Overview

The principles of sensitivity analysis are applicable in meta-analysis. The goal of sensitivity analysis in meta-analysis is the same as sensitivity analysis in decision analysis and cost-effectiveness analysis—to assess the stability of conclusions to key assumptions made in conducting the analysis. When overall conclusions based on the analysis are robust—that is, they do not vary when different assumptions are made—confidence in the conclusions is increased.

No firm rules dictate the conduct of sensitivity analysis in meta-analysis, unlike

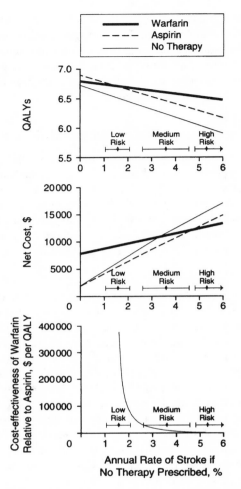

Figure 15-3 Sensitivity analysis showing the estimated number of QALYs and net cost for warfarin, aspirin, and no therapy, and the cost-effectiveness of warfarin compared with aspirin by annual stroke rate. (Reproduced with permission from Gage et al., *Journal of the American Medical Association*, 1995; 274:1842.)

decision analysis and cost-effectiveness analysis. Sensitivity analysis may be underutilized in meta-analysis.

15.4.2   Exclusion of Controversial Studies, Large Studies, or Studies that Might Not Meet Eligibility Criteria

In meta-analysis, sensitivity analysis is often done including and excluding certain studies that are controversial, that are large and thus dominate the analysis, or that cannot be determined to meet the eligibility criteria but whose exclusion may be problematic.

EXAMPLES: Chapter 1 and Chapter 6 described a meta-analysis of randomized trials of primary coronary angioplasty with intravenous thrombolytic therapy for the initial treatment of acute myocardial infarction (Weaver et al. 1997). Weaver et al. (1997) did a sensitivity analysis in which the GUSTOIIb results, which contributed much of the information to the analysis, were compared with the other nine trials for various outcomes as well as analysis comparing earlier and later studies and studies that included only in-hospital deaths compared with studies that included all deaths within 30 days.

Table 15-7 shows the results of the sensitivity analysis. Although there were differences in the estimates of the odds ratio for coronary angioplasty in some of the comparisons, all of the odds ratios were significantly different from 1.0 and all of the analyses suggested that the estimate of the effectiveness of primary angioplasty compared with thrombolysis based on all studies was a conservative estimate of its benefit.

15.4.3   Alternative Estimates of Effect Size

When there is more than one estimate of effect size available from a study, sensitivity analysis can be done using one estimate and then the other.

EXAMPLE: Chapter 8 described a meta-analysis of randomized trials by Saint et al. (1995) that examined the effectiveness of antibiotics in treating exacerbations of chronic obstructive pulmonary disease. Two sensitivity analyses were done. In one, alternative estimates of effect size were used for two

Table 15-7 Sensitivity analysis for meta-analysis of randomized trials of primary coronary angioplasty compared with thrombolysis for myocardial infarction

Outcome	Analysis	Odds Ratio	95% Confidence Internal
Total mortality	All studies[a]	0.66	0.46–0.94[a]
Death plus reinfarction	All studies[a]	0.58	0.44–0.76[a]
Total mortality	GUSTO IIb	0.80	0.50–1.29
	All other trials	0.54	0.33–0.88
Death plus infarction	GUSTO IIb	0.76	0.52–1.11
	All other trials	0.44	0.30–0.66
Total mortality	Trials before GUSTO IIb	0.55	N.R.
	Trials after GUSTO IIb	0.71	N.R.
Death plus reinfarction	Trials before GUSTO IIb	0.44	N.R.
	Trials after GUSTO IIb	0.66	0.48–0.92
Total mortality	In-hospital deaths	0.46	N.R.
	Deaths to 30 days	0.76	N.R.
Death plus reinfarction	In-hospital deaths	0.40	N.R.
	Deaths to 30 days	0.69	0.50–0.95

[a] PCTA compared with thrombolysis.
[b] Baseline analysis.
Source: Weaver et al. (1997).

studies that presented more than one estimate. There was no difference in the results, and confidence in the overall conclusion of the analysis—that antibiotics improve outcomes in patients with exacerbations of chronic obstructive pulmonary disease—is strengthened.

15.4.4 Fixed-Effects and Random-Effects Analysis

The assumptions made in the analytic model used in the analysis can be assessed.

EXAMPLE: The meta-analysis of environmental tobacco smoke and lung cancer discussed in earlier chapters (United States Environmental Protection Agency 1990) used the Mantel-Haenszel method, a method based on the assumption of fixed effect. The estimated relative risk of lung cancer in women exposed to environmental tobacco smoke was 1.42 (95% C.I. 1.24–1.63) when based on this method. A test of heterogeneity yielded a probability value greater than 0.05. As discussed in Chapter 7, when there is no heterogeneity, analyses based on fixed- and random-effects models are not different. As a check, the analysis from these studies can be done using a random-effects model. The analysis based on the assumption of random effects yields an estimated relative risk of 1.35 (95% C.I. 1.18–1.55). The estimates based on the fixed and random effects models do not differ by much, and a conclusion about the statistical significance of the elevation in the relative risk based on inspection of the confidence interval is the same for the analysis based on the fixed-effects model and the random-effects model. The similarity of estimates based on the two models suggests that model choice is not an issue.

15.4.5 Choice of Values for Open-ended Categories

In meta-analyses that examine dose-response relationships, the choice of values for open-ended categories (< 2 years or $10+$ years of duration of use of oral contraceptives; < 3 grams per day of alcohol consumption) should be subjected to sensitivity analysis because, as described in Chapter 8, this choice may be somewhat arbitrary.

EXAMPLE: Chapter 8 described a meta-analysis of observational studies of oral contraceptives and endometrial cancer done by Schesselman (1997). This analysis examined the relationship between duration of oral contraceptive use and the risk of endometrial cancer. In most of the original studies, relative risk estimates in the longest and shortest categories of duration of oral contraceptive user were reported in open-ended categories (e.g. < 2 years, $10+$ years). In this situation, a single value must be assigned to the category, as described in Chapter 8. Schesselman added 2 years to the cut-point for the long, open-ended categories of duration of use.

Schesselman did a sensitivity analysis in which the effects of different choices for the number of years added in the long, open-ended categories of use was assessed. Table 15-8 shows the results of this sensitivity analysis.

Table 15-8 Results of sensitivity analysis assessing the effect of the choice of imputed values of the duration of oral contraceptive use in the high, open-ended category

Imputed Duration for High, Open-ended Category	Estimated Relative Risk of Endometrial Cancer by Duration of Oral Contraceptive Use		
	4 Years	8 Years	12 Years
+2 (base case)	0.44	0.33	0.28
+0	0.42	0.32	0.27
+5	0.46	0.36	0.30

Source: Schesselman (1997).

The summary estimates of the relative risk of endometrial cancer in oral contraceptive users according to duration of oral contraceptive use are essentially the same for analyses that used different values for the high, open-ended duration of oral contraceptive use.

The analysis is not sensitive to the choice of the value of exposure for the open-ended categories. The insensitivity of the conclusion to this choice strengthens the overall conclusion that oral contraceptive use decreases the risk of endometrial cancer in a dose-dependent way.

16

Reporting Results

The published report of the results of a meta-analysis, decision analysis, or cost-effectiveness analysis is usually the only information about the study that is readily available to readers. Most readers do not have the technical expertise to identify all of the assumptions of the study. These methods are complex. For all of these reasons, the description of the study methods and procedures must be comprehensive, and the presentation of the study findings must be clear. Graphs and charts are a useful way to convey the framework for these studies and to present their results.

Sections 16.1 through 16.3 describe the specific information that should be included in the published reports of each of three types of studies. Sections 16.4 and 16.5 describe some of the graphical techniques that can be used to simplify the presentation of results of the studies that use these methods

16.1 META-ANALYSIS

16.1.1 Recommendations of Expert Panels

An expert panel whose work was commissioned by the U.S. Public Health Service has made recommendations about the reporting of meta-analysis (Stroup et al. in press). This panel emphasized the importance of standardization of reporting as a way to enhance the usefulness of information from meta-analysis, to enhance the validity of meta-analysis, and to facilitate the comparison of different meta-analyses of the same topic. The following incorporates the recommendations of this panel wherever possible.

16.1.2   Background and Objectives

The rationale for conducting the meta-analysis should be stated. Other meta-analyses of the same topic should be cited. The main hypotheses to be addressed should be specified.

16.1.3   Information Retrieval

The details of the process that was used to identify studies eligible for the meta-analysis should be given. This should include statements about the qualifications of the searcher, a listing of the databases or registries that were searched, and specification of the exact terms that were used to in the search. If software was used in the search, the name and version should be specified. If there was hand-searching, this should be stated. The approach to retrieval of information from studies published in languages other than English should be specified.

If individuals were asked to furnish information from unpublished studies or to clarify information in published studies, the methods of contact should be described. The response rate to these queries should be given.

16.1.4   Methods

The criteria for eligibility of studies identified in the information retrieval process should be specified, along with the rationale for each criterion, if this is not obvious.

The report should describe the procedures for abstracting data from the study reports. If abstractors were blinded to various aspects of the publication while abstracting other portions, this should be stated.

Steps taken to ensure reliability of data abstraction, such as training of the abstractors or reabstraction of a sample of records, should be described. The results of any formal evaluations of the reliability of data abstraction should be presented, even if reliability was not high.

The rules for choosing among estimates of effect when there is more than one should be stated. The procedures for handling missing data should be described.

If the studies were rated on quality, the methods for obtaining the ratings should be specified. A statement of whether the assessment of quality was done blind to the results or other aspects of the study should be a part of this description. If a scale or checklist was used to rate quality, the items that comprise the scale should be described directly or by reference to publications about the scale or checklist. The results of any assessments of the reliability and validity of the quality rating scale should be presented.

The report should explain the reason for the choice of the effect measure used in the analysis. It should state whether the analysis was based on a fixed-effects or random-effects model. The rationale for the choice of model should be provided. The method for arriving at the summary estimate of effect and its confidence limit should be described either directly or by appropriate citation to the published literature.

16.1.5   Results

The total number of publications or papers retrieved and reviewed should be stated. In many cases, a large number of publications or reports identified in a comprehensive information retrieval process are excluded because they do not present original data, are studies of the wrong intervention, are not of the appropriate study design, or simply do not contain any relevant information. The report should give the number excluded for these broad reasons in a table. Table 16-1 gives an example of such a table from a published meta-analysis.

There are often a small number of publications or reports that are otherwise eligible but cannot be used in the meta-analysis. The report should present detail these. If acceptable to the journal editor, all of the studies with relevant material that were identified should be cited, and minimal information on these excluded studies (author, year of publication, number of subjects) should be presented, preferably in a table. If the journal will not allow presentation of information on the excluded studies with pertinent information, this information should be made available to the reader on request.

Basic descriptive information for each study included in the meta-analysis should be provided in a table. The minimal information that should be included in the table is the first author and year of publication, the study design (when studies other than randomized trials are included), and some indication of the size of the study (number of cases and controls for case-control studies or the number in each treatment group for randomized trials).

The main quantitative results of a meta-analyses are typically presented in a graphic form. The graphic generally displays the effect size measure for each eligible study along with a measure of its precision (e.g., the 95% confidence interval). Later sections of this chapter give a more detailed description of some useful graphical presentations for meta-analysis of studies of several types.

The results of tests of homogeneity should be described. The exact values of the statistics calculated in tests of homogeneity, the number of degrees of freedom, and the exact probability values for each test of homogeneity should be provided.

Table 16-1   Reasons for exclusion from meta-analysis of antibiotics for chronic obstructive pulmonary disease

Primary Reason for Exclusion	Number of Reports
Not original data	76
No control group	61
Main intervention not antibiotic therapy	48
Included non-COPD patients	22
Letter to editor	10
Failure to randomize	6
Antibiotics used for prophylaxis	6
Unable to express outcome as continuous measure	1
Total	230

Source: Saint et al., *JAMA* 1995; 273; 958.

The results of sensitivity and subgroup analyses and other explorations of heterogeneity should be described.

16.1.6   Discussion

The possibility of publication bias should be addressed. If there is any evidence for and against publication bias as an explanation for the results, the evidence should be presented.

16.2   DECISION ANALYSIS

16.2.1   Recommendations of Expert Panels

Published recommendations of expert panels concerning reporting of decision analysis could not be identified.

16.2.2   Background and Objectives

The rationale for conducting the decision analysis should be stated. Other decision analysis of the same topic should be cited. The main hypotheses to be addressed should be specified.

16.2.3   Decision Tree

The decision tree should be presented graphically. Many journals limit the space available for such graphical presentations, which are often very complex. The tree should be presented in as much detail as the journal will allow. All of the symbols used in the tree should be explained in a legend. The tree should be constructed following the conventions that are described in Chapter 4.

16.2.4   Probability Estimates and Utility Values

The source of all the probability estimates should be cited. When data from several studies have been aggregated to obtain a probability estimate, the method for aggregating the data should be described. When there is more than one estimate for a given probability and one estimate is chosen for the decision analysis, the reasons for choosing this estimate should be given in the text. The baseline value for each probability and the range of estimates for each probability in the sensitivity analysis should be presented in a table. This table should also include the utility values used in the analysis. It is useful to indicate whether the upper and lower values used in the sensitivity analysis would be biased toward or against the main outcome.

> *EXAMPLE:*   Chapter 10 discussed a decision analysis of screening for mild thyroid failure. Table 10-1 presented the probability estimates used in the analysis in the recommended format.

16.2.5   Measure of Preference

If the analysis used measures of preference to estimate utilities, the methods for measuring preferences should be described. This description should include the number of subjects, the source of the subjects, and the method for collecting the data. Information on the reliability and validity of the preference measure should be provided, if it is available

16.2.6   Sensitivity Analysis

The variables that were subjected to sensitivity analysis should be identified and the reasons for doing a sensitivity analysis on these variables should be given. The range used for the sensitivity analysis of each variable should be justified. The results of the sensitivity analysis should be presented so that readers can understand them.

16.2.7   Discussion

The discussion section should describe the limitations of the analysis. Critical assumptions and uncertainties should be identified. The importance of the uncertainties and assumptions to the overall conclusion of the analysis should be identified.

If other analyses of the same topic have been done, the differences and similarities between the analyses should be described. An attempt should be made to explain reasons for differences.

16.3   COST-EFFECTIVENESS ANALYSIS

16.3.1   Recommendations of Experts and Expert Panels

The New England Journal of Medicine (Kassirer and Angell 1994) has a published policy with regard to reporting of the results of cost-effectiveness analysis. This policy states that the manuscript reporting on the results of the analysis must include all data used in the analysis and must identify all of the assumptions of the data and the models used in the analysis. Their policy is to require that the model be clearly explained and that it be "sufficiently straightforward and lucid so that ordinary readers can comprehend it."

The Panel on Cost-Effectiveness Analysis in Health and Medicine developed detailed recommendations for reporting cost-effectiveness analyses (Siegel et al. 1996). The Panel emphasized the importance of standardization of reporting as a way to enhance the usefulness of information from cost-effectiveness analysis and to ensure valid comparisons of cost-effectiveness ratios. The following adheres closely to the recommendations of the Panel on Cost-Effectiveness Analysis. If followed, these would fulfill most of the requirements of the editors of the *New England Journal of Medicine.*

16.3.2   Framework of the Study

The reporting of the framework for the cost-effectiveness study explains what motivates the study, gives the objectives of the analysis, and summarizes the design. This section describes to whom the results are to be applied. It should include a statement of the perspective of the analysis, and the reason for the choice of perspective and the time horizon for the study and the rationale for the choice.

Other cost-effectiveness analyses of the same topic should be cited.

16.3.3   Methods and Data

The conceptual model should be described. In this book, decision analysis is used as the main conceptual model for cost-effectiveness analysis. The construction and presentation of the decision tree will identify the "event pathway," which details the progression of the condition being studied, the events associated with the intervention and events following intervention. Assumptions of the model should be given.

Details on the derivation of estimates of effectiveness, cost, and preferences should be provided. For example, if data on cost were collected in a special study, the methods of the study should be described. If charge data are used as a proxy for cost, the source of this information should be cited.

The methods section should state whether costs and benefits were discounted. The discount rates used for costs and for effects should be stated. The rationale for the choice of the discount rate should be provided if a rate other than 3% or 5% will be the basis for conclusions.

All sensitivity analyses performed should be described although not all of the results need to be presented. If subgroup analysis is conducted, the subgroups should be defined.

16.3.4   Results

The results of the base-case analysis—the analysis that the analyst thinks best characterizes the choices—should be described and clearly identified as the base-case results. The results of the reference case analysis—the analysis done according to the standard set of rules laid out in Chapter 12—should be given and clearly identified as the reference case results.

Reporting of the results should include total costs and effectiveness, incremental cost and effectiveness, and incremental cost-effectiveness ratios. (Siegel et al. 1996). These results should be presented in a table.

EXAMPLE: An analysis examining the cost-effectiveness of a change in the poliomyelitis vaccination policy from 4 administrations of oral polio vaccine to a sequential schedule using 2 doses of inactivated polio vaccine followed by 2 doses of oral polio vaccine was discussed in Chapter 12. Table 16-2 gives the main results of the analysis in the recommended format.

Table 16-2   Presentation of the main results of a cost-effectiveness analysis of vaccination schedules for poliomyelitis

Vaccination Schedule	Total Program Cost, $ Million	Cases of VAPP[a] Prevented	Total Benefits, $ Million	Net Incremental Cost, $ Million	Cost per Case of VAPP Prevented, $ Million
4OPV[b]	375.0	0	0	reference	reference
4IPV[c]	414.5	9.50	11.4	28.1[d]	3.0[e]
2IPV[c] and 2OPV[b]	395.4	4.75	5.7	14.7[d]	3.1

[a] Vaccine-associated poliomyelitis.

[b] Oral polio vaccine.

[c] Inactivated polio vaccine.

[d] Total cost minus total benefits minus reference program cost.

[e] Net cost/cases prevented.

Source: Miller et al. (1996).

The results of key sensitivity analyses should be reported in a table or graphically.

16.3.5   Discussion

The baseline results should be summarized. The uncertainties in the analysis should be identified. Limitations and possible biases of the study should be acknowledged. The results should be framed in the context of information about cost-effectiveness from other studies. Any ethical problems arising from assumptions of the analysis should be identified and discussed. The discussion should avoid making any global statement about the ''cost-effectiveness'' of the intervention, except when the intervention is cost saving (Gold et al. 1996).

16.3.6   Technical Appendix

Journals rarely permit full reporting of a cost-effectiveness analysis. It is useful to prepare a detailed technical appendix and submit this with the manuscript so that reviewers can better judge the analysis (Siegel et al. 1996). The technical appendix should be made available on request.

16.4   GRAPHICAL PRESENTATION OF THE RESULTS OF META-ANALYSIS

16.4.1   Overview

The function of a graph is to convey an immediate impression of the relationships among the numbers (Gladen and Rogan 1983). The format of a graph can convey markedly different impressions of the relationships, some erroneous. Attention to the format of graphs used to present the results of meta-analysis is important.

16.4.2 Ratio Measures

Figure 16-1 is an example of the graphic used most frequently to present the results of a meta-analysis of studies where the effect is measured on a ratio scale. Data from the five hospital-based case-control studies of coronary heart disease in estrogen users included in a meta-analysis by Stampfer et al. (1991) are presented. The meta-analysis of studies of breast cancer treatments that was discussed in Chapter 1 was presented in the same type of figure. Each study in the meta-analysis is represented by one horizontal line, whose length is proportional to the length of the 95% confidence interval; the point estimate of effect in the study is indicated with a large dot. The figure also includes a line for the summary estimate of relative risk and its 95% confidence interval. A dashed line is drawn vertically through the summary estimate of relative risk such that it crosses each of the lines representing the individual studies.

Figure 16-1 shows the estimated relative risks and 95% confidence intervals plotted on a linear scale. There are several reasons why plotting ratio measures on a linear scale is unsatisfactory (Gladen and Rogan 1983; Galbraith 1988; Hebert and Miller 1989). First, when plotted on a linear scale, values of the ratio measure and its reciprocal, which are equivalent, are not equidistant from 1.0. Second, a

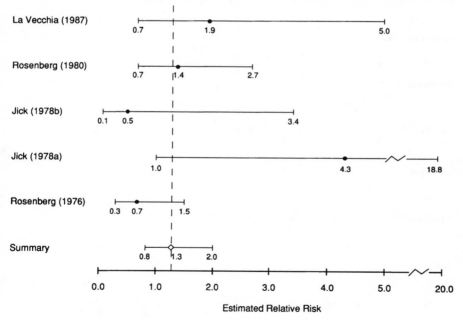

Figure 16-1 Estimated relative risks and 95% confidence intervals for coronary heart disease in estrogen users from hospital-based case-control studies. The relative risk estimates and the 95% confidence intervals are plotted on a linear scale. Data and individual references are from Stampfer et al. (1991).

unit change in the ratio measure does not have the same interpretation at all points of the scale. For example, a change in the estimated relative risk ratio from 2.0 to 3.0 is a 50% increase, whereas a change from 4.0 to 5.0 is only a 25% increase. Third, when plotted on a linear scale, studies with estimated relative risks between 0.0 and 1.0 appear to be less important than studies with estimated relative risk above 1.0 because they take up less visual space on the page. A number of authors have suggested ways to plot ratio measures that remedy these problems (Gladen and Rogan 1983; Greenland 1987; Galbraith 1988; Hebert and Miller 1989; Morgenstern and Greenland 1990).

First, the ratio measure and its confidence interval can be plotted on a logarithmic scale (Gladen and Rogan 1983; Galbraith 1988).

EXAMPLE: In Figure 16-2, the logarithms of data from Figure 16-1 are plotted on a linear scale. The data could have been plotted directly on a logarithmic scale. Plots on a logarithmic scale and plots of the logarithm are superior to plots on a linear scale because the studies that yield estimates of the relative risk of coronary heart disease in estrogen users less than 1.0 and studies that yield estimates greater than 1.0 are equidistant from 1.0, and changes in the estimated relative risk of equal size are represented equally.

Plotting the ratio measure on a reciprocal scale also yields a graph where estimates less than 1.0 and greater than 1.0 are equidistant from 1.0. Morgenstern and Green-

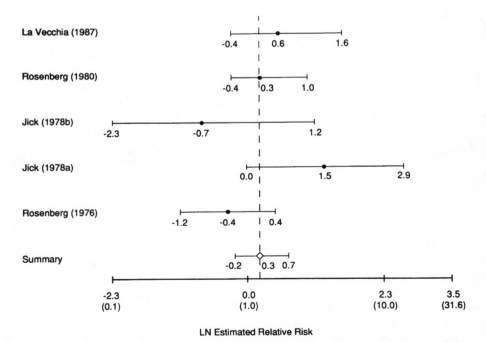

Figure 16-2 Data from Figure 16-1. The natural logarithm of the relative risk estimates and the natural logarithms of 95% confidence intervals are plotted on a linear scale.

land (1990) describe the special advantage of the reciprocal plot as a way to convey proportional impact. Unlike the logarithmic plot, equal ratios between pairs of estimates do not translate into equal distances on a reciprocal plot.

EXAMPLE: Figure 16-3 is a reciprocal plot of the data shown in Figures 16-1 and 16-2.

Plotting the 95% confidence intervals on either a linear or logarithmic scale tends to draw visual attention to the studies that are the least precise and have the lowest weight in the analysis, since less precise estimates have longer confidence intervals and take up more visual space in the plot (Morgenstern and Greenland 1990). To give greater visual prominence to studies with more weight in the analysis, a box that has an area equal to the statistical weight of the study can be drawn around the point estimate of relative risk. In such plots, the eye is drawn to the study with the greatest weight in the analysis.

EXAMPLE: Figure 16-4 shows the data from case-control studies included in the meta-analysis of Stampfer et al. (1991) plotted on a linear scale with the size of box around the point estimate of relative risk equal in area to the statistical weight of the study in the analysis.

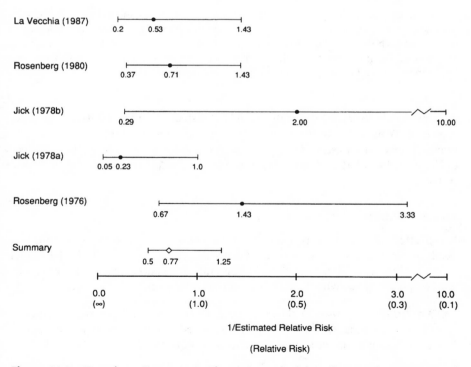

Figure 16-3 Data from Figure 16.1. The reciprocal of the relative risk estimates and the reciprocals of the 95% confidence intervals are plotted on a linear scale.

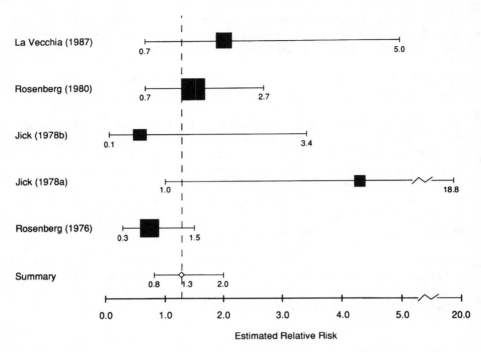

Figure 16-4 Data from Figure 16.1. The relative risk estimates and the 95% confidence intervals are plotted on a linear scale, but the point estimate of relative risk is depicted using a box whose size is proportional to the weight of the study in the meta-analysis. Studies yielding more precise estimates of relative risk are depicted with boxes that are larger than studies yielding less precise estimates of relative risk.

Greenland (1987) suggested that weighted histograms might be useful for some problems. Walker, Martin-Moreno, Artalejo (1988) described the "odd-man-out" graphical method for estimating the confidence interval for a meta-analysis. Neither of these methods has been used much in practice, and they will not be discussed further.

16.4.3 Difference Measures

When effect is measured as a difference between two dichotomous outcomes—death or nondeath, survival or nonsurvival—the graph used to present the results of the analysis is a difference scale. Plotting rate differences on a linear scale does not compress studies with negative differences into a small visual space.

EXAMPLE: Figure 16-5 shows the rate differences in relapse-free survival of postmenopausal breast cancer patients treated or not treated with adjuvant chemotherapy from an analysis by Himel et al. (1986).

As with ratio measures, this visual presentation of the difference measure tends to draw the eye to studies with the widest confidence intervals, which are the least

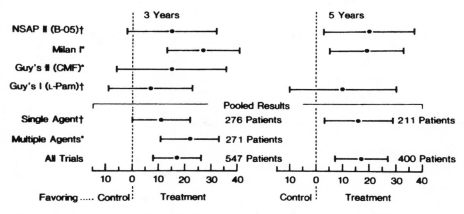

Figure 16-5 Difference in the rate of relapse-free survival at three years and five years among premenopausal women in various trials of chemotherapy for breast cancer. Each line represents one study. The point estimate of the rate difference is depicted with a filled circle; the length of the line is the length of the 95% confidence interval for the rate difference. References to individual studies are as cited in Himel et al. (1986). (Reproduced with permission from Himel et al., *Journal of the American Medical Association,* 1986;256,1157.)

precise. Presenting a box that has an area equal to the statistical weight of the study would mitigate this problem.

16.4.4   Continuous Variables

When a treatment or intervention affects a continuous measure, such as blood pressure or weight, the plot can show effect size as the measured difference between the treated and the control group just as described for differences in a dichotomous measure. If the measures of effect used in different studies are measured on different scales, they can be plotted in units of standard deviation.

EXAMPLES: Figure 16-6 depicts the results of studies of the effect of aminophylline treatment in acute asthma that were included in the meta-analysis of this topic by Littenberg (1988) that was discussed in Chapter 8. Since studies used different measures of pulmonary function, effects were standardized in units of the standard deviation. These have been plotted on a scale whose x-axis is units of standard deviation. The length of the bars is equal to the 95% confidence interval for the measure of standard deviation.

Figure 16-7 is an alternative way to depict these data. It shows the results of randomized trials of the effect of antibiotics in treating exacerbations of chronic obstructive pulmonary disease that were eligible for a meta-analysis of this topic done by Saint et al. (1995) that was described in Section 16.1.4. As in the prior example, the studies eligible for the meta-analysis used different outcomes measures, which were standardized in units of the standard deviation. These have been plotted on a scale whose x-axis is units of stan-

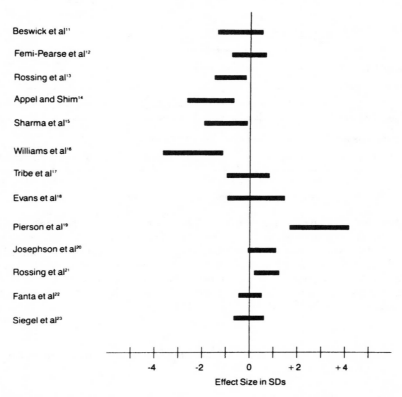

Figure 16-6 Estimated effect of aminophylline treatment compared with control where effect size is expressed in standardized units. Each bar represents one study. Positive effect sizes indicate aminophylline treatment was more effective than control; negative effect sizes indicate the control was more effective than aminophylline. The length of each bar is the length of the 95% confidence interval of the standardized measure for that study. References to individual studies are as cited in Littenberg (1988). (Reproduced with permission from Littenberg, *Journal of the American Medical Association,* 1988; 259,1680.)

dard deviation. In this example, the point estimate of effect is shown with a large dot. The length of the horizontal bars is equal to the 95% confidence interval for the measure of standard deviation. The graphic is labeled so that it is easy to identify studies that favor antibiotic and those that favor placebo. It also shows the summary estimate of effect and its 95% confidence interval.

16.4.5   Box Plots

Williamson, Parker, and Kendrick (1989) have pointed out the usefulness of the box plot in the presentation of the results of meta-analysis. It is not used much in practice but is important because it has the potential to be used for ratio measures, difference measures, and continuous measures.

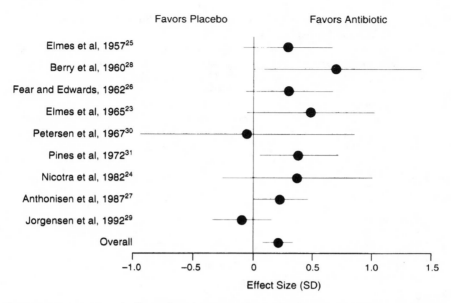

Favors Placebo   Favors Antibiotic

Figure 16-7   Estimated effect of antibiotics compared with placebo for exacerbations of chronic obstructive pulmonary disease where effect size is expressed in standardized units. Dots represent point estimates. Horizontal lines denote 95% confidence intervals for the standardized measure. Studies that favor antibiotic are to the right of the vertical line. Studies that favor placebo are to the left. References to individual studies are cited in Saint et al. (1995). (Reproduced with permission from Saint et al., *Journal of the American Medical Association,* 1995; 273:959.)

The box plot, which is also called a box-and-whiskers plot, plots the median, the approximate quartiles, and the highest and lowest data points as a way of conveying visually the level, the spread, and the amount of symmetry of the data points.

EXAMPLE: Table 16-3 reproduces the data from a meta-analysis of studies of physical activity and coronary heart disease by Williamson, Parker, and Kendrick (1989) to illustrate the presentation of the results of a meta-analysis through a box plot. Figure 16-8 shows box plots of studies in three categories of quality—poor, good, and best quality. The plots are constructed as follows. Within each quality group, the relative risk estimates are ranked from highest to lowest. The median value (the value with an equal number of estimates of relative risk above and below it) is determined. This value is drawn as the horizontal line inside the box. The middle 50% of relative risk values are determined by counting up and down from the median. These values define the ends of the box. A vertical line is drawn from the middle of each of the crossbars of the box to the most extreme upper and lower values of the relative risk.

Table 16-3 Estimates of the relative risk of coronary heart disease and physical inactivity by quality of study

Studies of Poor Quality ($N = 19$)	Studies of Good Quality ($N = 13$)	Studies of Best Quality ($N = 9$)
0.5 Low extreme		
0.5	1.2 Low extreme	1.2 Low extreme
0.9	1.5	1.4
1.1	1.6	1.6
1.1	1.6[a]	1.6[a]
1.1[a]	1.8	1.9 Median
1.1	1.9	2.4
1.1	2.0 Median	2.5[a]
1.5	2.0	2.6
1.5 Median	2.0	3.1 High extreme
1.5	2.0[a]	
1.5	2.3	
1.7	2.3	
1.8	2.5	
1.9[a]	2.8 High extreme	
2.0		
2.2		
2.3		
2.4		
2.5 High extreme [a]		

[a] Values that define 50% of estimates.
Source: Williamson, Parker, Kendrick (1989).

16.4.6   Comprehensive Plots

It has become common to depict the results of meta-analysis in graphics that include information usually presented in a table along with material that is plotted. These graphic presentations attempt to summarize comprehensively the source data and the results of the meta-analysis.

EXAMPLE: Figure 16.9 is from a meta-analysis of health outcomes of antihypertensive therapies done by Psaty et al. (1997). The figure provides information on the effect of four different treatments for five different outcomes. The effects of the first three treatments are based on meta-analysis of placebo-controlled randomized trials, whereas the fourth treatment is stepped care versus referred care from the Hypertension Detection and Follow-up Program. The number of trials and the number of events in treatment and controls groups are displayed. The actual values of the summary estimates of relative risk and their 95% confidence intervals are both presented in text form and as plots that follow the conventions described in sections 16.4.1– 16.4.3. The summary estimate of relative risk and 95% confidence interval from each meta-analysis for each outcome (and separately for the Hyperten-

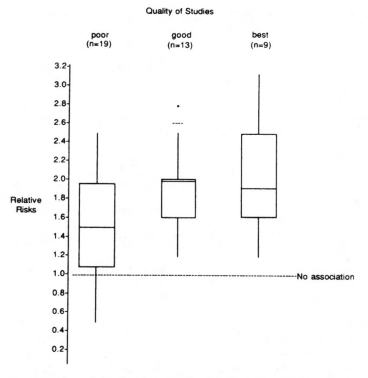

Figure 16-8   Box plots of the distribution of estimates of the relative risk of coronary heart disease in physically inactive compared with physically active men in studies rated as poor, good, and best in quality. The horizontal line inside the box is the median value of the relative risk. The upper and lower ends of the box are the "hinges," the approximate upper and lower quartiles of the distribution of relative risks. The vertical lines from the ends of the boxes connect the extreme data points to their respective hinges. (Reproduced with permission from Williamson, Parker, and Kendrick, *Annals of Internal Medicine,* 1989;110:917.)

sion Detection and Follow-up Program) is plotted on a logarithmic scale. The graphic allows easy identification of studies where treatment was better and control was better.

16.5   GRAPHICAL PRESENTATION OF THE RESULTS OF DECISION ANALYSIS AND COST-EFFECTIVENESS ANALYSIS

16.5.1   Showing the Decision Tree

The decision tree is virtually always presented graphically. The goal should be presentation of sufficient detail so that the reader can understand the main comparisons. Most journals are not able to publish complex decisions trees in all of

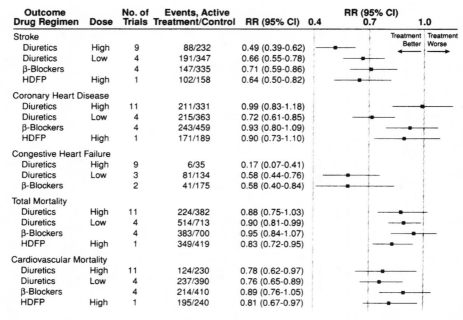

Outcome Drug Regimen	Dose	No. of Trials	Events, Active Treatment/Control	RR (95% CI)	RR (95% CI)
Stroke					
Diuretics	High	9	88/232	0.49 (0.39-0.62)	
Diuretics	Low	4	191/347	0.66 (0.55-0.78)	
β-Blockers		4	147/335	0.71 (0.59-0.86)	
HDFP	High	1	102/158	0.64 (0.50-0.82)	
Coronary Heart Disease					
Diuretics	High	11	211/331	0.99 (0.83-1.18)	
Diuretics	Low	4	215/363	0.72 (0.61-0.85)	
β-Blockers		4	243/459	0.93 (0.80-1.09)	
HDFP	High	1	171/189	0.90 (0.73-1.10)	
Congestive Heart Failure					
Diuretics	High	9	6/35	0.17 (0.07-0.41)	
Diuretics	Low	3	81/134	0.58 (0.44-0.76)	
β-Blockers		2	41/175	0.58 (0.40-0.84)	
Total Mortality					
Diuretics	High	11	224/382	0.88 (0.75-1.03)	
Diuretics	Low	4	514/713	0.90 (0.81-0.99)	
β-Blockers		4	383/700	0.95 (0.84-1.07)	
HDFP	High	1	349/419	0.83 (0.72-0.95)	
Cardiovascular Mortality					
Diuretics	High	11	124/230	0.78 (0.62-0.97)	
Diuretics	Low	4	237/390	0.76 (0.65-0.89)	
β-Blockers		4	214/410	0.89 (0.76-1.05)	
HDFP	High	1	195/240	0.81 (0.67-0.97)	

Figure 16-9 Graphical depiction of meta-analysis of health outcomes of hypertensive therapies. The figure gives information on each of the studies. It includes the exact values of relative risk estimates and their 95% confidence intervals. The plots of the relative risk estimates are on a logarithmic scale that is labeled to indicate the direction of the effect. (Reproduced with permission from Psaty et al., *Journal of the American Medical Association*, 1997; 277:742.)

their complexity, and some simplification will be necessary. It may be necessary to break the decision tree down into several parts.

EXAMPLES: Chapters 2 and 9 gave graphical depictions of simple decision trees. Figures 9-2 and 9-5 are graphical representations of subparts of a decision tree used in an analysis of warfarin and aspirin prophylaxis for patients with nonvalvular atrial fibrillation.

Figure 16-10 is a decision tree from an analysis comparing two approaches to the management of pregnant women with recurrent genital herpes (Binkin and Koplan 1989). The tree is too large to be printed on one page. The terminal nodes depict identical outcomes. The figure thus shows parts of the tree that repeat at the nodes numbered 19 to 33 in a subfigure.

Depiction of a more complicated decision tree may require breaking the tree into even more parts. The challenge in presentation of complex decision trees is to make them small enough so that the journal will publish them. Even if accepted for publication, it is a challenge to make the labels of each element readable. Examples that would reproduce well in a small space could not be identified and are not included here.

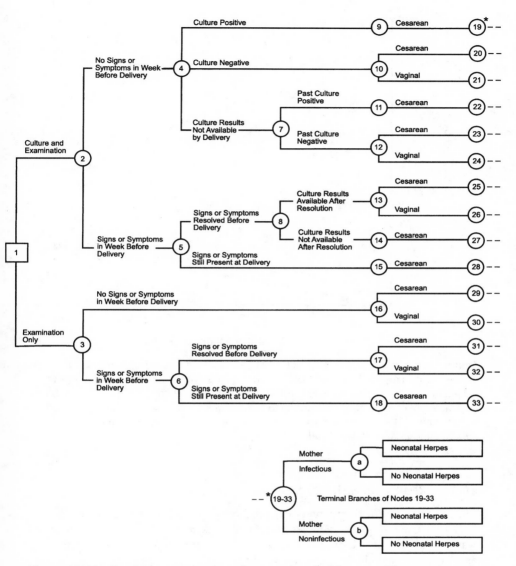

Figure 16-10 Graphic representation of a complex decision tree. The question addressed in the decision analysis is whether to manage recurrent genital herpes during pregnancy by weekly culture and examination or by examination only. The lower right portion of the figure depicts a subtree that represents the outcome at each of the nodes numbered 19–33. (Reproduced with permission from Binkin and Koplan, *Medical Decision Making*, 1989;9:226.)

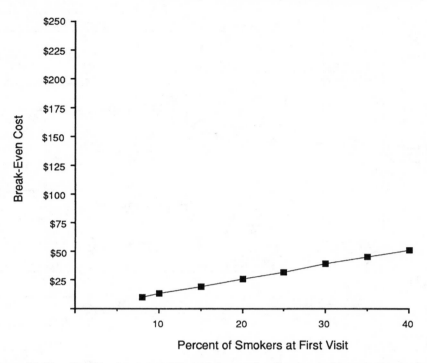

Figure 16-11 Graphical representation of the results of a threshold analysis. The line shows how many dollars could be invested in a smoking cessation program during pregnancy and still "break even" in terms of averted costs of care for sick newborns and maternal complications according to the prevalence of smoking in pregnant women at the time of the first prenatal visit. (Reproduced with permission from Shipp et al., *American Journal of Public Health,* 1992;82:388.)

16.5.2 Results of Sensitivity Analysis

The results of two-way and three-way sensitivity analyses are best presented graphically. Chapter 15 gave examples of graphic presentation of two-way and three-way sensitivity analysis from the study by Heckerling and Verp 1991 comparing amniocentesis and chorionic villus sampling.

When threshold analysis is done, graphic presentation of the results helps the reader interpret the results.

EXAMPLE: Figure 16-11 shows the results of a threshold analysis in which the "break-even" cost of a smoking cessation program during pregnancy was estimated according to the prevalence of smoking at the time of the first prenatal visit. At each estimate of the prevalence of smoking, the line shows the number of dollars that could be invested in a program of smoking cessation and break-even in terms of the averted costs of care for sick newborns and mothers. The higher the prevalence of smoking, the greater the number of dollars that could be invested and still break even.

17
Limitations

This book attempts to show how to maximize the usefulness of meta-analysis, decision analysis, and cost-effectiveness analysis by ensuring that studies that use the methods are rigorous. Throughout the book, important controversies about the statistical and mathematical theories that underlie the methods are highlighted, and key assumptions are identified. The main problems with application of the methods and some ways to overcome these problems are presented. The book advocates the three methods. Having taken a position of advocacy in the first 16 chapters, this chapter identifies the serious limitations of the methods. It summarizes the recommendations of others on how to improve the methods' validity, reliability, and credibility.

Section 17.1 discusses the main criticisms of meta-analysis and reviews empiric studies of the quality, reproducibility, and predictive validity of meta-analysis. Section 17.2 discusses framing and the implications of the existence of framing effects for conclusions based on decision analysis. Section 17.3 discusses the limitation of cost-effectiveness analysis and formal evaluations of the quality of cost-effectiveness studies. Section 17.4 describes the problem of discrimination, which may arise from use of life expectancy (and QALYs) as outcome measures in decision analysis or cost-effectiveness analysis. Section 17.5 discusses ethical concerns about QALYs. Section 17.6 summarizes the situations in which each method is most useful and the situations in which each method may be misleading or wrong. Section 17.7 gives recommendations on how to improve the methods, presenting the opinions of expert groups where available.

17.1 META-ANALYSIS

17.1.1 Overview

Some of the concerns about meta-analysis are broad concerns based on philosophy. Meta-analysis has been subjected to formal evaluations, and the result of these formal evaluations are not all favorable. Moreover, the inability of statistical aggregation methods to overcome problems of bias and uncontrolled confounding is a major problem of meta-analysis of nonexperimental studies.

17.1.2 Broad Concerns About Meta-Analysis

Although the use of meta-analysis is widespread, enthusiasm about it is not universal. Although published in 1978, a letter by Eysenck (1978), titled "an exercise in mega-silliness," is still often quoted when referring to meta-analysis. Eysenck states about meta-analysis: " 'Garbage in—garbage out' is a well-known axiom of computer specialists; it applies here with equal force."

Wachter (1988) identifies four reasons for skepticism about meta-analysis. The first reason is the "garbage-in–garbage-out" criticism. The second reason is the concern that the measurements of outcome in studies that are combined in a meta-analysis are often different measures and that meta-analysis "compares apples and oranges." The third reason for concern about meta-analysis is that the study of previous studies is being reduced to the routinized task of coding relegated to the research assistant. Last, Wachter was concerned that meta-analysis is part of a world in which "bad science drives out good by weight of numbers."

Meta-analytic estimates of effect do appear to be very precise and often carry considerable weight in policy discussions for this reason. The certainty with which the results of meta-analysis are presented might dissuade persons from doing original studies on the same topic. The results of a meta-analysis may limit the availability of funds for additional studies (Shapiro 1994).

Bailar (1995) expressed concern about two other issues after conducting a case studies of the use of meta-analysis in practice. First, Bailar felt that "too rigid and too broad adherence to the principles of meta-analysis could damage progress in science" because meta-analysis is a poor tool for developing new concepts, new hypotheses, and new methods of study. Second, he was concerned that meta-analysis could affect reading of the primary literature, and reduce the likelihood of "serendipitous discovery" that comes of informal browsing of the literature.

The quality of meta-analysis, its reproducibility, and its correlation with the results of "definitive" studies have all been evaluated empirically. The results of these evaluations give a mixed picture of meta-analysis.

17.1.3 Evaluations of Meta-Analysis

17.1.3.1 Assessments of the Quality of Meta-analysis

Sacks et al. (1987) evaluated the quality of 86 published meta-analyses. They found that only 24 of 86 meta-analyses addressed all six major areas that were considered to measure the quality of meta-analysis. Table 17-1 shows the number and the percentage of the 86 studies that were considered adequate for each of the quality features. For 18 of the 23 features, more than 50% of the meta-analyses were rated as inadequate.

Bailar (1995) did five case studies of the use of meta-analysis in practice. He documented major problems with the implementation of the methods of meta-analysis for each case.

17.1.3.2 Comparisons of Meta-Analysis and Large Trials

Four different authors (Chalmers et al. 1987; Villar et al. 1995; Cappelleri et al. 1996; LeLorier et al. 1997) have published comparisons of the results of meta-analysis of small randomized trials with the results of large trials. Chalmers et al. (1987) assessed three topics and found that the results of the meta-analysis and the "gold standard" study were somewhat discrepant for all three. Table 17-2 summarizes the results of more recent studies comparing and the results of large trials.

Table 17-1 Adequacy of 86 meta-analyses published in medical journals in 1966–1986.

Criterion	Studies Considered Adequate	
	N	%
Design	6	7.0
Protocol		
Literature search	30	34.9
List of trials analyzed	81	94.2
Log of rejected trials	11	12.8
Treatment assignment	59	68.6
Ranges of patients	19	22.1
Ranges of treatment	39	45.3
Ranges of diagnosis	34	39.5
Combinability		
Criteria	39	45.3
Measurement	20	23.3
Control of bias		
Selection bias	0	0.0
Data-extraction bias	0	0.0
Interobserver agreement	4	4.7
Source of support	28	32.6
Sensitivity analysis		
Quality assessment	16	18.6
Varying methods	14	16.3
Publication bias	2	2.3
Application of results		
Caveats stated	66	76.7
Economic impact	1	1.2

Source: Sacks et al. (1987).

Table 17-2   Comparisons of meta-analysis with large studies

Author	Definition of Agreement	Number of Meta-analyses and Large Studies Compared	Agreement N	Agreement (%)
Villar et al. (1995)	Total: direction of effect and statistical significance the same		18	60.0
	Partial: direction of effect the same	30	6	20.0
Cappellieri et al. (1996)	Formal statistical test of agreement	79[a]	71	89.9[b]
			65	82.3[c]
		61[d]	50	82.0[b]
			40	65.6[c]
LeLorier et al. (1997)	Total: direction of effect and statistical significance the same	40[e]	25	62.5

[a] Large study defined by sample size ($\geq 1,000$ subjects).
[b] Random-effects model.
[c] Fixed-effects model.
[d] Large study defined by power.
[e] Number of comparisons.

Villar et al. (1995) examined 30 meta-analyses that had one large trial and compared conclusions based on a summary estimate of effect without the largest trials with conclusions based on the largest trial. The percent with complete agreement (direction of effect and statistical significance the same) was 60.0. An additional 20% of comparisons showed partial agreement (the direction of the effect was the same but the meta-analysis and the large trial were not the same in terms of statistical significance). There were no instances where the directions of effect were opposite and both were statistically significant. The meta-analyses tended to show stronger protective effects than the largest trial.

Cappelleri et al. (1996) did a comprehensive search of the medical literature and the Cochrane Collaboration database in order to identify meta-analyses for which there was at least one large trial. Trials were defined as large according to the number of patients and an estimate of the statistical power of the study. Agreement between the meta-analytic estimate of effect and the large trial estimate was assessed using a formal statistical test. The comparison was done separately for estimates done based on fixed-effects and the random-effects models. When based on the random-effects model, agreement was high—almost 90% for the comparison of trials defined as large by number of patients and slightly more than 82% for trials defined as large by power. Agreement was lower with the fixed-effects than the random-effects models. The agreement between the meta-analytic estimates of effect size and the large trial estimate was only 65.6% when based on the fixed-effects model with large trials defined according to statistical power. The meta-analyses tended to show larger treatment effects, just as in the analysis by Villar et al. (1996)

LeLorier et al. (1997) restricted their study to a comparison of trials with more than 1,000 patients that were published in four journals *(New England Journal of Medicine,* the *Lancet,* the *Annals of Internal Medicine,* and the *Journal of the American Medical Association)* and meta-analyses published earlier. Some of the comparisons had also been included in the studies by Villar et al. (1995) and Cappelleri et al. (1996). There was total agreement (the direction of the effect and the statistical significance were the same) between the meta-analysis and the large trial for 25 of 40 comparisons (62.5%) based on fixed-effects estimates of effect size and 26 of 40 comparisons (65.0%) based on random-effects estimates of effect size. For the 14 topics in this study, meta-analysis would have led to the adoption of an ineffective treatment for 4 of 14 (28.6%) interventions and rejection of a beneficial treatment for 1 of 14 (7.1%).

Formal attempts to explain the discrepancies between meta-analysis of small trials and large trials (Borzak and Ridker 1995; Villar et al. 1997; Cappelleri et al. 1996) have focused on examination of use of the fixed-effects versus the random-effects model, publication bias, and differences in event rates in the control population between the small studies and the large study.

Three examples of discrepancies between meta-analysis of small trials and large trials appear repetitively in the formal studies that make this comparison. These examples are magnesium for acute myocardial infarction, nitrates for acute myocardial infarction (Borzak and Ridker 1995; Cappelleri et al. 1996; Lelorier et al. 1997), and antiplatelet agents for prevention of preeclampsia in pregnancy (Cappelleri et al. 1996; LeLorier et al. 1997; Villar et al. 1995; Villar et al. 1997). Table 17.3 summarizes the reasons for discrepancies of the results of the meta-analysis of small trials and the large trial estimate of effect based on these publications.

For nitrates in acute myocardial infarction, both Borzak and Ridker (1995) and Cappelleri et al. (1996) attribute the difference in the results of the early meta-analysis and the large clinical trials to differences in the event rates in controls. Borzak and Ridker (1995) suggest that more widespread use of effective treatments for myocardial infarction accounts for the change in the event rates in the absence of use of nitrates.

There is less consensus about the reasons for the discrepancy between meta-analysis and large trials for magnesium in acute myocardial infarction and for antiplatelet therapy to prevent preeclampsia. For magnesium in acute myocardial infarction, Borzak and Ridker (1995) and Cappelleri et al. (1996) agree that differences in the event rates in controls contributed to the discrepancy between meta-analysis and large trials; they disagree about the contribution of use of a fixed-effects model.

Villar et al. (1997) conclude that there was bias in the publication of studies of antiplatelet drugs in the prevention of preeclampsia and that it may account for the finding of the strong protective effect of antiplatelet drugs for preeclampsia found in the meta-analysis of this topic. Cappelleri et al. did not find statistical evidence of publication bias in the meta-analysis of this topic.

In aggregate, these studies show that, meta-analysis of small trials tends to overestimate treatment effects. The data show that meta-analysis of small trials

Table 17-3 Conclusions about the reasons for the discrepancy between meta-analysis and large study for several topics

	Conclusion		
Topic and Reason for Discrepancy	Borzak and Ridker (1995)	Cappellieri et al. (1996)	Villar et al. (1997)
Nitrates in acute myocardial infarction			
Use of fixed effects model	no	no	N.A.
Publication bias	N.A.	no	N.A.
Difference in event rate in controls	yes	yes	N.A.
Magnesium in acute myocardial infarction			
Use of fixed effects model	yes	no	N.A.
Publication bias	N.A.	no	N.A.
Difference in event rate in controls	yes	yes	N.A.
Antiplatelet agents to prevent pre-eclampsia			
Use of fixed effects model	N.A.	no	N.A.
Publication bias	N.A.	no	yes
Difference in event rate in controls	N.A.	yes	N.A

N.A. = not assessed.

cannot substitute for conduct of large trials. The empiric data suggest that accepting meta-analysis, even meta-analysis of randomized trials, carries a fairly large risk of adoption of ineffective therapies and a small, but not negligible, risk of rejection of effective therapy.

17.1.3.3 Assessments of the Replicability of Meta-analysis

Chalmers et al. (1987) compared the results of independent replications of meta-analyses of the same topic for 18 different topics. Table 17-4 shows the details of their comparisons for the topics where the same endpoint was used in all of the meta-analyses, and Table 17-5 summarizes the comparison. For 12 of the 18 topics (66.7%), all of the replicate meta-analyses agreed both on the direction of the effect of the intervention and on whether or not the effect was statistically significant at a probability level of 0.05. For 3 of the 18 topics (16.7%), at least one of the replicates found an effect opposite in direction to another replicate.

Although not done as a formal comparison of the replicability of meta-analysis, the data presented by LeLorier et al. (1997) are useful. In 8 instances, there were two or more meta-analyses of a topic for which there was also a large randomized trial. For six of the eight topics (75.0%), all of the replicates agreed both on the direction of the effect of the intervention and on statistical significance. For one of the eight topics (12.5%), at least one replicate found an effect opposite in direction from the other replicate.

The findings with regard to the replicability of meta-analysis of randomized trials are only slightly more encouraging than the findings comparing meta-analysis with large trials.

Table 17-4 For 18 topics where two or more meta-analyses have been done, number that agree on direction of effect and statistical significance, on direction of effect but not significance, and number that disagree on direction of effect

Topic	Number of Meta-Analyses of this Topic	Number That Agree on Both Direction of Effect and Significance	Number That Agree on Direction of Effect but Not Significance	Disagree on Direction[a]
Long-term beta blockers post-MI	6	6	0	0
Short-term beta blockers post-MI	4	4	0	0
Intravenous streptokinase post-MI	3	3	0	0
Aspirin post-MI	3	3	0	0
Psychoeducation intervention	2	2	0	0
Patient education	2	2	0	0
Nicotine chewing gum in clinics	2	2	0	0
Nicotine chewing gum in practice	2	2	0	0
Prevention of venous thromboembolism	2	2	0	0
Stimulant therapy for hyperactivity	2	2	0	0
Psychotherapy	5	4	0	1
Steroids in alcohol hepatitis	3	1	2	0
Antidepressant drugs	3	2	1	0
Single-dose TMP-SMZ for UTI	3	1	1	1
Single-dose amoxicillin for UTI	3	0	3	0
Anticoagulants post-MI	3	2	0	1
Radiotherapy after mastectomy	2	2	0	0
Steroids and peptic ulcer	2	2	0	0

[a] Includes studies where one meta-analysis favored treatment or control and the other found no effect.
Source: Chalmers et al. (1987).

Table 17-5 Summary of data on replicates of meta-analysis shown in Table 17-4

Result	Number of Topics
All replicates agree on both direction of effect and statistical significance	12
At least some replicates disagree on direction of effect	3
Other	3

Formal studies of the replicability of meta-analysis of nonexperimental studies could not be identified. The replicability of subgroup analysis also in unproven. Unless there are standards for the conduct of meta-analysis and for judging meta-analysis, it is impossible to know which meta-analysis to believe when the results are discrepant.

17.1.4 Particular Problems with the Meta-Analysis of Nonexperimental Studies

Meta-analysis started as a method to summarize the results of experimental studies. It was a particular response to problems arising from the conduct of small randomized trials that individually showed no effect of the intervention but when combined were statistically significant. In experimental studies, randomization in theory eliminates bias and confounding, and the measure of the effect of the intervention derived from a randomized trial is considered an unbiased and unconfounded measure of the effect of the intervention. Having (theoretically) eliminated bias and confounding as an explanation for the observed differences between the treatment and control groups, the critical remaining issue in a meta-analysis of experimental studies is comprehensive identification of information pertaining to the question addressed in the meta-analysis and unbiased extraction of pertinent data from all of the relevant studies.

Meta-analysis of nonexperimental studies followed on the heels of meta-analysis of experimental studies, until recently somewhat uncritically. Formal consideration of the differences in the most important problems confronting the meta-analysis of nonexperimental and experimental studies has been lacking. Meta-analysis of nonexperimental studies has been conducted often when the results of the individual studies are contradictory, not when they are individually too small to provide an answer to the question addressed. Meta-analysis of nonexperimental studies has been done to "resolve" discrepancies, not recognizing that the method is not up to this task.

> *EXAMPLE:* Four different meta-analyses of estrogen replacement therapy and breast cancer have been published (Armstrong 1988; Dupont and Page 1991; Steinberg et al. 1991; Sillero-Arenas et al. 1992). These meta-analyses were not undertaken to remedy problems due to the small size of studies of breast cancer and estrogen replacement therapy. In fact, each of three different studies of this topic had more than 1000 cases of breast cancer; one study had over 5000 cases; and the total number of cases of breast cancer in all of the studies of the topic combined is more than 10,000. Meta-analysis was used for this topic in an effort to resolve the contradictions between study results.

Unfortunately, meta-analysis is weakest and most controversial when studies disagree. Use of a random-effects model would incorporate the heterogeneity, but statistical analysis will not account for heterogeneity or make the results of contradictory studies agree.

Emphasis on the mechanics of combining estimates of effect from nonexperimental studies of different designs has diverted attention from the more critical question of how to handle studies where there is concern about bias and uncontrolled confounding. In a group of studies where some studies are "positive" and some are "negative," the possibility that the positive ones are due to bias or uncontrolled confounding and the negative ones are free of bias and confounding (or vice versa) is difficult, if not impossible, to rule out. Furthermore, one kind of nonexperimental study design is never inherently superior to another.

Even when the results of virtually all of the studies are consistent, it is still possible that all of them suffer from the same bias.

EXAMPLE: It is argued that studies of lung cancer and passive smoking are flawed by misclassification of active smokers as non-smokers due to underreporting of active smoking. If persons who are truly active smokers are also more likely to be exposed to passive smoke and assuming that active smoking is a very strong risk factor for lung cancer, underreporting of active smoking will bias estimates of the relative risk of lung cancer in relation to passive smoking even if the underreporting is nondifferential. Because it is impossible to validate statements about past active smoking, even with physiologic measures of smoke exposure, this source of bias cannot be eliminated. Underreporting of active smoking may be a relatively universal problem, and the fact that almost all studies of lung cancer and passive smoking are "positive" does not eliminate the possibility that this bias may explain the results of a meta-analysis, since the statistical aggregation of data does not address the possibility of this bias.

17.1.5   Conclusion

Meta-analysis is an observational, not an experimental method (Borzak and Ridker 1995). The main value of meta-analysis, even meta-analysis of randomized trials, is to generate hypotheses, not to test them. All meta-analysis is essentially exploratory analysis.

Meta-analysis can help set the stage for large trials. It may be useful as a guide clinical decision-making until large trials can be completed. It is not a substitute for conduct of large trials and should not be used as such (Peto 1995).

17.2   DECISION ANALYSIS

17.2.1   Overview

Decision analysis rests on the mathematical theory of choice. The existence of framing effects raises serious questions about certain aspects of this fundamental theory. There are no formal evaluations of the reproducibility or quality of decision analysis, and the very absence of critical evaluation of the method is a limitation.

17.2.2   Framing Effects and the Philosophy of Choice

Tversky and Kahnemann (1981) have shown that seemingly inconsequential changes in the formulation of choice problems can cause radical shifts in measured preferences.

> *EXAMPLE:*   Two groups of students in a classroom setting were given the following problem:
>
>> Imagine that the United States is preparing for the outbreak of an unusual Asian disease, which is expected to kill 600 people. Two alternative programs to combat the disease have been proposed.
>
> The two sets of students were asked to choose between two programs. The first set of students ($n = 152$) was given the choice between the following two programs:
>
>> If Program A is adopted, 200 people will be saved.
>> If Program B is adopted, there is a 1/3 probability that 600 people will be saved and 2/3 probability that no people will be saved.
>
> The second set of students ($n = 155$) was given the choice between the following two different programs:
>
>> If Program C is adopted 400 people will die.
>> If Program D is adopted there is 1/3 probability that nobody will die and 2/3 probability than 600 people will die.
>
> In the choice between Program A and Program B, 72% of students chose Program A. In the choice between Program C and Program D, 78% of students chose program D. The only real difference between the two sets of programs is that the first involves the number of lives saved and the second the number of lives lost. Through this and other work, Tversky and Kahnemann (1981) show a consistent pattern in which choices involving certain gains are risk averse and choice involving certain losses are often risk taking.

The influence of the manner in which a problem is presented on choice is an example of a "framing" effect. If changes in "frame" can cause large changes in individual preferences, then choices cannot be assumed to be fixed and stable. If choices are not fixed and stable, then the general theory that is the basis for decision analysis must be questioned (Tversky and Kahnemann 1981).

17.2.3   Formal Evaluations of Decision Analysis

Formal evaluations of the quality and replicability of decision analysis studies could not be identified. Financial support to carry out studies of quality and reliability of these studies is limited, and this may account for the paucity of work on evaluation of the methods. The absence of information proving the quality and the reliability of decision analysis seriously limits the credibility of the method.

17.3 COST-EFFECTIVENESS ANALYSIS

17.3.1 Value Judgments and Politics

Cost-effectiveness and cost-utility analysis do not resolve the ethical dilemmas of allocating scarce resources. Except when an intervention is cost saving, demonstration that it is "cost-effective" does not avoid difficult value judgments. There is no criterion that can be used to say, based on a cost-effectiveness analysis, an intervention should be recommended. A decision to do something because it is "worth the added cost" is an ethical and moral, not an economic, judgment. Opinions about whether something is "worth" a certain amount of money are subject to variations in the perspective and the values of those making the judgment of worth. Judgments about whether added cost is "worth it" are subject to political forces.

EXAMPLES: In their cost-effectiveness analysis of a change to inactivated polio vaccine, Miller et al. (1996) estimated that the new (2 IPV, 2 OPV) schedule would prevent about 5 of 10 cases of vaccine associated polio (VAPP). VAPP cases are compensated, on average, $1,200,000. Miller et al. found that it would cost about $3,100,000 more per VAPP case prevented to implement the new (2 IPV, 2 OPV) schedule. The cost of this program was higher than those of other public health prevention programs. The Advisory Committee on Immunization Practices (ACIP) voted to recommend the new (2IPV, 2 OPV) schedule notwithstanding its high cost compared with other programs, reasoning that public concern about the adverse events from a government-mandated program in a country with no wild type virus outweighed considerations of cost.

In 1990–1991, the state of Oregon attempted to set priorities for the allocation of Medicaid resources for its low income population based on cost-effectiveness analysis. The Oregon Health Services Commission generated a list of condition-treatment pairs ordered by their cost-effectiveness and then attempted to make funding decisions based on this ordering. The sole use of these cost-effectiveness ratios for resource allocation was ultimately rejected by the state of Oregon based on many criticisms (e.g., Hadorn 1991; OTA 1992). In the end, cost-effectiveness analysis was only one of 13 factors used to prioritize funding of services for the poor.

Tengs et al. (1995) compiled information from analyses that assessed the cost-effectiveness of life-saving interventions. Table 17.6 shows the estimated cost per year of life saved for some commonly accepted medical and public health interventions. There are large variations in the amount of money expended per life saved for these accepted interventions. Thus, in practice, society makes decisions to allocate resources in ways that do not reflect their cost-effectiveness.

Ubel et al. (1996) did an empiric study in which prospective jurors, medical ethicists, and experts in medical decision analysis choose between two screening tests for a population at low risk of colon cancer. One test cost $200 per life saved;

Table 17-6　Estimated cost per year of life saved for live-saving interventions

Category	Description	Cost/Life Saved
Safety	Mandatory seat belt use and child restraint laws	$98
	Smoke detectors in airplane lavatories	$30,000
	Flashing lights at rail-highway crossings	$42,000
Toxin Control	Banning asbestos in roofing felt	$550,000
	South Coast of California ozone control program	$610,000
	Radionuclide emission control at Department of Energy facilities	$730,000
Medicine	Mammography every 3 years for women aged 60–65 years	$2,700
	Lovastatin for men aged 45–54 years with no heart disease and cholesterol ≥300 mg LDL	$34,000
	Prophylactic AZT following needle-stick injuries in health care workers	$41,000
	Misoprostol to prevent drug-induced gastrointestinal bleeding	$210,000
	Intensive care for seriously ill patients with multiple trauma	$460,000
	Lovastatin for women aged 45–54 years with no heart disease and cholesterol ≥300 mg LDL	$1,200,000

Source: Tengs et al. (1995).

the other cost $181 per life saved. The second test was, therefore, more cost-effective because it saves more lives for the number of dollars spent. In the example, it would cost $200,000 to offer the first test to everyone—saving 1,000 lives. It would cost $400,000 to offer the second test to everyone—saving 2,200 lives. The subjects were posed with a hypothetical situation in which they could spend only $200,000 for screening. Within this budget, it would be possible to screen all of the population with the first test or half of the population with the second test. Using the first test in everyone would save 1,000 lives. Using the second test in half the population would save 1,100 lives. Fifty-six percent of the jurors, 53% of the ethicists, and 41% of the experts in medical decision analysis recommended offering the less effective screening test to everyone, in spite of the fact that this strategy was less cost-effective and saved 100 fewer lives. The authors concluded that their study illustrated people's discomfort with policies based on cost-effectiveness analysis, in keeping with the Oregon experience.

17.3.2　Data and Models

Data on cost are sometimes obtained in an ad hoc fashion and are not carefully justified.

> *EXAMPLE:*　Danese et al. (1996) estimated the cost of interventions for women with mild hypothyroidism by surveying 10 Baltimore area internists.

The physicians were asked to indicate what interventions they would recommend for women with various symptoms indicative of hypothyroidism. The Medicare fee schedule was used to convert the recommended interventions to a cost per symptom for each physician. The median of the total costs for the 10 physicians was used to estimate cost for the cost-effectiveness analysis.

Measures of utility are sometimes obtained based on convenience samples of patients or are simply the investigators opinions about the utility. In a review of 36 valuations of health states from 15 different published studies, Nord (1993) found that 24 were based on the authors' own judgments. Nord concluded that utility weights seemed "to be used without critical thought and sensible discussion."

The models for complex problems are necessarily complex. The sheer complexity of the models makes them essentially impossible to validate.

17.3.3   Formal Evaluations of Cost-Effectiveness Analysis

Udvarhelyi et al. (1992) did a formal evaluation of the quality of cost-effectiveness analyses published in the medical literature. They identified 77 articles using cost-effectiveness or cost-benefit analysis published in general medical, general surgical, and medical subspecialty journals from 1978 to 1980 and from 1981 to 1987. They assessed the use and reporting of six fundamental principles of cost-effectiveness analysis. The results of their evaluation are summarized in Table 17-7.

Only 3 of the 77 articles on cost-effectiveness analysis adhered to all six fundamental principles of cost-effectiveness analysis. In both periods, more than 50% of articles failed to make an explicit statement of the perspective of the analysis, failed to include the costs of side effects, averted costs, and induced costs, failed to use sensitivity analysis, or failed to use a preferred measure of cost effectiveness. It is possible that more recent cost-effectness analyes are better, but there are no empiric data to support this claim.

It is unusual for more than one cost-effectiveness analysis of the same topic to be done. Whether the rarity of replicate studies of cost-effectiveness analysis reflects an unwillingness of journals to publish replications or of investigators to undertake them is uncertain. The difficulty of carrying out cost-effectiveness analysis, the small number of economists trained in health issues, and the lack of funding for cost-effectiveness analysis probably all contribute to the rarity of replicate studies. Reproducibility is a cornerstone of the scientific method, and the absence of data to establish the reproducibility of cost-effectiveness analysis is a serious limitation of the method.

17.4   LIFE EXPECTANCY

17.4.1   The Problem of Discrimination

Life expectancy is often the outcome measure of decision analysis and cost-effectiveness analysis. Analyses that use QALYs as the outcome are based on

Table 17-7   Nonadherence to six principles of cost-effectiveness analysis for 77 articles published in general medical, general surgical, and medical subspecialty journals

	Articles Not Adhering to Principle			
	1978–1980 (*N* = 31)		1985–1987 (*N* = 46)	
Principle	*N*	%	*N*	%
Perspective explicitly stated	23	74.2	40	87.0
Benefits explicitly stated	5	16.1	8	17.4
Costs				
Cost data provided	11	35.5	2	4.3
Program or treatment costs included	6	19.4	4	8.7
Side effect or morbidity costs included	24	77.4	30	65.2
Averted costs included	23	74.2	35	76.1
Induced costs included	30	96.8	44	95.7
Timing				
Discounting used if timing of costs and benefits are different	$9/15$	60.0	$6/14$	42.9
Sensitivity analysis done	24	77.4	30	65.2
Preferred summary measurement used	24	77.4	34	73.9

Source: Udvarhelyi et al. (1992).

estimates of life-expectancy. Life expectancy in the absence of an intervention is a function of current age and sex and, in most populations, of race. When life expectancy is short, the estimated effect of an intervention will be small even if the intervention has the same absolute effect on mortality per year in every group.

EXAMPLE: Table 17-8 shows estimated life expectancy for 45-year-old white women, 45-year-old black men, and 90-year-old white women. The table also shows the average mortality rate based on these estimates of life expectancy along with the estimated gain in life expectancy from an inter-

Table 17-8   Estimated gain in life expectancy for three groups whose baseline life expectancies differ

Group	Life Expectancy (years)	Average Mortality Rate per Year	Gain in Life Expectancy from Hypothetical Intervention (Years)[a]
45-year-old white women	37.8	0.026	+1.40
45-year-old black man	27.8	0.036	+0.80
90-year-old white women	5.2	0.192	+0.02

[a] For an intervention that decreases mortality by 0.001 per year.

vention that decreases overall mortality by 0.001 per year in each group. These calculations were carried out as described in Section 9.4.2 using the DEALE.

The gain in life expectancy from the hypothetical intervention is 0.02 year in 90-year-old white women, 0.80 year in 45-year-old black men, and 1.40 years in 45-year-old white women. In each group, 1 of 1000 persons alive at the beginning of the year are ''saved'' by the intervention. It is only cumulatively, and because of the lower likelihood of death from other causes, that more persons are saved and more life years are gained in the younger white women.

In general, when life expectancy is used as the measure of effectiveness, an intervention that prolongs life will have the smallest effect on gain in life expectancy in the group with the shortest life expectancy. When a cost-effectiveness analysis is done, the cost per year of life gained will be greatest in the group with the shortest life expectancy in the absence of the intervention.

EXAMPLE: Assume that the cost of the intervention described in the preceding example is $100,000. The alternative intervention is to do nothing, which costs nothing. Assume that the cost of the intervention is a one-time cost and thus discounting of costs does not affect the estimate of cost effectiveness. Table 17-9 shows the estimated cost per year of life gained for the hypothetical intervention for middle-aged white women, middle-aged black men, and elderly white women. For 45-year-old white women, the cost of the intervention is only $71,429 per year of life gained; for 45-year-old black men, it is $125,000 per year of life gained; for 90-year-old white women, it is $5,000,000 per year of life.

Life expectancy and QALYs are used in two ways—to evaluate which of two alternatives is the best for a single patient (or group of patients) and to determine which of several alternative interventions to choose for a population.

EXAMPLES: Weinstein and Stason's (1985) analysis that compared the quality-adjusted life expectancy of CABG and medical management of patients with coronary artery disease is an example of the use of quality-

Table 17-9 Estimated gain in life expectancy and cost per year of life gained for three groups whose baseline life expectancies differ

Group	Gain in Life Expectancy (years)[a]	Cost per Year in Life Gained
45-year-old white women	+1.40	$ 71,429
45-year-old black men	+0.80	125,000
90-year-old white women	+0.02	5,000,000

[a] For an intervention that decreases mortality by 0.001 per year in each group.

adjusted life years in the first way, to inform decisions about how to manage coronary heart disease in individual patients (or groups of patients).

Williams (1985) did an analysis comparing the cost per quality-adjusted life year of coronary artery bypass graft with the cost per quality-adjusted life year of renal transplantation and concluded that bypass grafting for left main coronary artery disease and triple vessel disease should be funded before renal transplantation. This is an example of the use of QALYs used the second way—to decide among different interventions.

When cost-effectiveness analysis is used to guide choices between an intervention for a person with a short life expectancy and similar interventions for persons with a longer life expectancy, use of life expectancy as an outcome will "discriminate" against the group whose life expectancy is shortest (Harris 1987).

17.4.2 Problems With the Magnitude of Gains for Classes of Interventions and Populations

There is no generally agreed on criterion for assessing the value of gains in life expectancy averaged across populations (Wright and Weinstein 1998). The gain in life expectancy from some interventions, (for example, preventive interventions) is small because only a small fraction of the recipients of the intervention receive the benefit, driving down the average gain. Interventions aimed at illnesses that are life-threatening in those who are already ill can yield large gains in life expectancy. The consequence is that strategies aimed at preventing life-threatening illnesses may appear ineffective comparing with treatments in those who are already ill (Wright and Weinstein 1998).

> EXAMPLE: Wright and Weinstein (1998) collected information to estimate gains in life expectancy from data in 83 published sources. They found that for preventive interventions aimed at populations of average risk, a gain in life expectancy of only a month could be considered large when the preventive interventions were compared with each other. In populations at high risk, many interventions were associated with gains in life expectancy of 12 months. For treatments, the gains in life expectancy were highly variable, but some interventions were associated with gains of several years.

These observations highlight the importance of perspective when interpreting gains in life expectancy and, by extension QALYs, which are based on life expectancy.

17.4.3   Ethical Concerns About QALYs

The use of QALYs to help guide choices between alternative interventions for a single patient and investments of society in one intervention in preference to another intervention for the same condition is generally held to be useful (Smith 1987; Harris 1987). The use of estimates of QALYs to make decisions about how to determine which patients to treat and to set priorities to interventions for different conditions has been questioned on ethical grounds. It has been called "positively dangerous and morally indefensible" by one author (Harris 1987) and based on "false premises, faulty reasoning, and unjust principles" by another (Rawles 1989).

Drummond (1987) points out that investing in the interventions that have the lowest cost per QALY ignores the principle of equity (Drummond 1987). The use of QALYs to decide who to treat or what to pay for ignores what might be the choices of individuals, abrogating the ethical principle of autonomy, which is generally most important for individual patients, to the principle of justice or fairness, which is generally most important for a community (LaPuma and Lawlor 1990).

17.5 SITUATIONS WHERE THE METHODS ARE MOST AND LEAST USEFUL

Meta-analysis is most useful when applied to randomized trials. Within this context, it is most useful when the results of the trials are generally consistent. When registries of all trials that have ever been done exist, the usefulness of meta-analysis of experimental studies is especially high. Meta-analysis of randomized trials is least useful when the number of trials is small and when the trials are heterogeneous in the interventions or the outcomes.

Meta-analysis of observational studies is most useful when it used as to identify and explore the reasons for heterogeneity in study results. Meta-analysis is least useful when it used solely to derive a single estimate of effect size. Meta-analysis will not resolve the inconsistencies among the results of nonexperimental studies. Meta-analysis does not eliminate bias in the individual studies.

Both decision analysis and cost-effectiveness analysis are most useful when they are used to try to decide which of two or more alternative treatments to use for a patient or which alternative to prefer for the same condition. Both methods are most useful when information on the probabilities to be estimated is obtained from systematic review of the medical literature or from sources that are reliable, valid, and representative of the population to which results will be generalized.

Cost-effectiveness analysis is most useful when it includes a reference case analysis so that it can be compared with other cost-effectiveness analyses. Cost-effectiveness analysis is most useful when it is used as one of many inputs to decisions about resource allocation and clinical policy (Russell et al. 1996).

Cost-effectiveness analysis is least useful when it is done in an ad hoc way, when it is done from a narrow perspective, and when it done by those who have a financial stake in the results.

17.6 IMPROVING THE METHODS: RECOMMENDATIONS OF EXPERTS

17.6.1 Meta-analysis

A group sponsored by the Centers for Disease Control and Prevention (Stroup et al., in press) developed guidelines for the reporting of meta-analysis of nonexperimental studies, which were described in detail in the Chapter 16. In 1995, a group of 20 scientists from nine countries met to discuss the state of the art of meta-analysis. Out of this meeting came a set of methodologic guidelines for meta-analysis of randomized trials (Cook et al. 1995). This book adheres closely to these recommendations. They will not be repeated here.

17.6.2 Cost-Effectiveness Analysis

In 1994, Kassirer and Angell (1994), the editors of the *New England Journal of Medicine,* described the methods used in cost-effectiveness analysis as "discretionary." Both the perception of arbitrariness and the actual variation in the methods used by different analysts conducting cost-effectiveness analysis are serious issues for cost-effectiveness analysis as a methodology. In response to concern about the inconsistency in methods used and in recognition of the importance of comparability between cost-effectiveness analyses of different topics, expert groups in several different countries and at least three groups in the United States have developed guidelines for economic analysis in the form of regulations, principles, policies, and positions.

Genduso and Kotsanos (1996) compared the recommendations of the expert groups from Australia, Canada, Italy, Spain, the United Kingdom, and two groups from the United States. They identified six recommendations that were common to all of the guidelines. These are shown in Table 17.10.

Because there appears to a broad consensus about these recommendations, they should be adopted for all cost-effectiveness analyses. Doing so would assure adherence to a minimum standards for the conduct of cost-effectiveness analysis and would enhance the comparability between analyses. Unfortunately, the expert groups differed in their recommendations about a number of other important methodologic issues in the conduct of cost-effectiveness analysis.

The Panel on Cost-Effectiveness Analysis in Health and Medicine of the U.S. Public Health Services developed a comprehensive and carefully justified set of recommendations about the conduct of cost-effectiveness analysis. These were published in book form in 1996 (Gold et al. 1996) and in three papers in the *Journal of the American Medical Association* in the same year (Russell et al. 1996; Wein-

Table 17-10 Recommendations common to guidelines on cost-effectiveness analysis from Australia, Canada, Italy, Spain, the United Kingdom, and the United States

---

Use the societal perspective
Justify comparators
Use an appropriate time horizon
Provide information on cost in resource units and as costs, disaggregated and total
Discount costs
Perform sensitivity analysis

Source: Modified from: Genduso and Kotsanos (1996).

stein et al. 1996; Siegel et al. 1996). The recommendations of this panel are becoming widely accepted in the United States. The recommendations shown in Table 17.10 that were common to the guidelines reviewed by Genduso and Kotsanos (1996) are also recommendations of the Panel on Cost-Effectiveness Analysis. This provides further support for adoption of these six recommendations for all cost-effectiveness analyses.

Appendix A of the book by the Panel on Cost-Effectiveness Analysis (Gold et al. 1996, pp. 304–310) summarizes all the panel's recommendations about the conduct of cost-effectiveness analysis. They are presented in less detail in the article by Weinstein et al. (1996). It is not possible to present all of these recommendations in detail here.

Several recommendations of the Panel on Cost-Effectiveness Analysis deserve particular attention. The most important is its recommendation for conduct of a standard reference case analysis. The second is the recommendations from the panel concerning what belongs in the numerator and the denominator of the cost-effectiveness ratio. These are summarized in Table 17-11.

17.6.3 Estimating QALYs

Nord (1993) described seven carefully reasoned suggestions on how to assure quality in the assessment of QALYs. These are summarized in Table 17-12. The Panel on Cost-Effectiveness Analysis made a very strong recommendation that the weights used to estimate QALYs be based on community preferences, rather than those of patients, providers, or investigators. Adopting Nord's recommendations and those of the Panel on Cost-Effectiveness Analysis would enhance the validity, reliability, and believability of measurement and use of QALYs in cost analysis and enhance their usefulness in the formulation of clinical and public policy.

Table 17-11 Highlights of the recommendations of the Panel on Cost-Effectiveness Analysis in Health and Medicine of the United States Public Health Service: what belongs in the numerator and denominator of the cost-effectiveness ratio

---

Include the following categories of resource use in the numerator of the cost-effectiveness ratio:
  Cost of health services
  Cost of patient time to partake of the intervention
  Caregiver costs
  Direct costs to partake of the intervention
  Economic costs born by employers to partake of the intervention
Include effects of the intervention on length of life and morbidity, including the value of improvement in health-related quality of life in the denominator of the cost-effectiveness ratio
Do not impute monetary value for lost life-years and do not include this in the numerator of the cost-effectiveness ratio
Include the costs of related diseases in the original and added life span
Do not include the costs of unrelated diseases in the original life span

---

Source: From: Weinstein et al. (1996).

Table 17-12 Suggestions on how to assure quality in the assessment of QALYs

---

All states of health that are assigned utility weights should be described in terms of concrete symptoms and dysfunctions

The source of each weight should be indicated

Weights should be supported by theoretical arguments and analysts should point out what the weights imply in equivalence terms

The composition of the gain in QALYs in terms of the relative contributions of increased life expectancy and increased quality of life should be given

Sensitivity analysis should be done over a wide range of alternative values of the preference weight

All data, assumptions, and procedures behind each estimate of QALY should be presented

Additional information on the methods for assessing QALYs from the authors should be available

---

Source: Nord (1993).

17.6.4 Reducing the Perception of Bias Due to Financial Incentives in Cost-Effectiveness Analysis

Kassirer and Angel (1994) pointed out that the financial arrangements between those conducting cost-effectiveness analysis and for-profit companies that fund them were ''tangled.'' They, and others, are justifiably concerned about possible bias due to financial arrangements in which analysts are paid large sums of money from companies with a large financial stake in the analysis or where the analysts might themselves profit directly from recommendations made in the analysis. For example, Kassirer and Angell cite a situation in which the author of a cost-effectiveness analysis had a patent pending on an application described in the report on cost-effectiveness.

The perception of bias due to financial incentives would be reduced by following the recommendations of Kassirer and Angell (1994) that cost-effectiveness studies funded by industry should be done by nonprofit entities, such as hospitals and universities. They recommend written assurances of agreements between the analysts and the fundors that ensure the analysts' independence in the design of the study, the interpretation of the data, and the writing and publication of the report. Finally, they point out that analysts who receive a direct salary from the sponsoring company (or its competitors), who have an equity interest in the company that makes the intervention being studied (or its competitors), or who have a patent pending on what is being studied will be perceived as having financial incentives to bias the results of the analysis.

References

Antiplatelet Trialists' Collaboration: Secondary prevention of vascular disease by prolonged antiplatelet treatment. *Br Med J* 1988;296:320-332.

Antman EM, Lau J, Kupelnick B, Mosteller F, Chalmers TC: A comparison of results of meta-analyses of randomized control trials and recommendations of clinical experts: treatments for myocardial infarction. *JAMA* 1992;268:240-248.

Arevalo JA, Washington AE: Cost-effectiveness of prenatal screening and immunization for hepatitis B virus. *JAMA* 1988;259:365-369.

Armitage P, Berry G: *Statistical Methods in Medical Research,* 2nd ed. Oxford, Blackwell Scientific Publications, 1987; pp 409-410.

Armstrong BK: Oestrogen therapy after the menopause—boon or bane? *Med J Aust* 1988; 148:213-214.

Bailar J: The practice of meta-analysis. *J Clin Epidemiol* 1995;48:149-157.

Bailey KR: Inter-study differences: how should they influence the interpretation and analysis of results? *Stat Med* 1987;6:351-358.

Bayarri MJ: Comment on "Selection models and the file drawer problem." *Stat Science* 1988;3:128-131.

Beck JR, Kassirer JP, Pauker SG: A convenient approximation of life expectancy (the "DEALE"): I. Validation of the method. *Am J Med* 1982a;73:883-888.

Beck JR, Pauker SG: The Markov process in medical prognosis. *Med Decis Making* 1983; 3:419-458.

Beck JR, Pauker SG, Gottlieb JE, Klein K, Kassirer JP: A convenient approximation of life expectancy (the "DEALE"): II. Use in medical decision-making. *Am J Med* 1982b; 73:889-897.

Begg CB: Publication bias. In: *The Handbook of Research Synthesis*, Cooper H, Hedges LV (eds). New York, Russell Sage Foundation, 1994; pp 399-409.

Begg C, Cho M, Eastwood S, Horton R, Moher D, Olkin I, Pitkin R, Rennie D, Schulz KF,

Simel D, Stroup DF: Improving the quality of reporting of randomized controlled trials: the CONSORT statement. JAMA 1996;276:637–639.

Begg CB, Berlin JA: Publication bias: a problem in interpreting medical data. *J Royal Stat Soc A* 1988;151:419–463.

Bennett WG, Inoue Y, Beck JR, Wong JB, Pauker SG, Davis GL: Estimates of the cost-effectiveness of a single course of interferon-alpha 2b in patients with histologically mild chronic hepatitis C. *Ann Intern Med* 1997;127:855–865.

Berlin JA: Does blinding of readers affect the results of meta-analyses. *Lancet* 350;1997: 185–186.

Berlin JA, Longnecker MP, Greenland S: Meta-analysis of epidemiologic dose-response data. *Epidemiology* 1993;218–228.

Berlin JA, Laird NM, Sacks HS, Chalmers TC: A comparison of statistical methods for combining event rates from clinical trials. *Stat Med* 1989;8:141–151.

Bernal-Delgado E, Latour-Perez J, Pradas-Arnal F, Gomez-Lopez L: The association between vasectomy and prostate cancer: a systematic review of the literature. *Fertil Steril* 1998;70:191–200.

Bero L, Rennie D: The Cochrane Collaboration. Preparing, maintaining, and disseminating systematic reviews of the effects of health care. *JAMA* 1995;274:1935–1938.

Binkin NJ, Koplan JD: The high cost and low efficacy of weekly viral cultures for pregnant women with recurrent genital herpes: a reappraisal. *Med Decis Making* 1989;9:225–230.

Borzak S, Ridker PM: Discordance between meta-analyses and large-scale randomized, controlled trials. *Ann Intern Med* 1995;123:873–877.

Boyle MH, Torrance GW: Developing multiattribute health indexes. *Med Care* 1984;22: 1045–1057.

Bulpitt CJ: Meta-analysis. *Lancet* 1988;2:93–94.

Bush TL, Barrett-Connor E, Cowan LD, Criqui MH, Wallace RB, Sutchindran CM, Tyroler HA, Rifkind BM: Cardiovascular mortality and noncontraceptive use of estrogen in women: results from the Lipid Research Clinics Program Follow-up Study. *Circulation* 1987;75:1102–1109.

Bushman BJ: Vote-counting procedures in meta-analysis. In: *The Handbook of Research Synthesis,* Cooper H, Hedges LV (eds). New York, Russell Sage Foundation, pp 193–213.

Callahan ML, Wears RL, Weber EJ, Barton C, Young G: Positive-outcome bias and other limitations in the outcome of research abstracts submitted to a scientific meeting. *JAMA* 1998;280:254–257.

Cappelleri JC, Ioannidis JPA, Schmid CH, deFerranti SD, Aubert M, Chalmers TC, Lau J: Large trials vs meta-analysis of smaller trials: how do their results compare? *JAMA* 1996;276:1332–1338.

Centers for Disease Control: Measles—United States, 1989 and first 20 weeks 1990. *MMWR* 1990;39:353–355, 361–363.

Chalmers I, Adams M, Dickersin K, Hetherington J, Tarnow-Mordi W, Meinert C, Tonascia S, Chalmers TC: A cohort study of summary reports of controlled trials. *JAMA* 1990; 263:1401–1405.

Chalmers TC, Block JB, Lee S: Controlled studies in clinical cancer research. *N Engl J Med* 1972;287:75–78.

Chalmers TC, Smith H Jr, Blackburn B, Silverman B, Schroeder B, Reitman D, Ambroz A: A method for assessing the quality of a randomized control trial. *Control Clin Trials* 1981;2:31–49.

Chalmers TC, Berrier J, Sacks HS, Levin H, Reitmen D, Nagalingam R: Meta-analysis of clinical trials as a scientific discipline: II. Replicate variability and comparison of studies that agree and disagree. *Stat Med* 1987b;6:733–744.

Chalmers TC, Levin H, Sacks HS, Reitmen D, Berrier J, Nagalingam R: Meta-analysis of clinical trials as a scientific discipline: I. Control of bias and comparison with large cooperative trials. *Stat Med* 1987a;6:315–325.

Cochran WG: Problems arising in the analysis of a series of similar experiments. *J Royal Stat Soc B* 1937;4:102–118.

Cochran WG: The combination of estimates from different experiments. *Biometrics* 1954; 10:101–129.

Colditz GA, Miller JN, Mosteller F: How study design affects outcomes in comparisons of therapy: I. Medical. *Stat Med* 1989;8:441—454.

Colditz GA, Burdick E, Mosteller F: Heterogeneity in meta-analysis of data from epidemiologic studies: a commentary. *Am J Epidemiol* 1995;142:371—382.

Collaborative Group on Hormonal Factors in Breast Cancer: Breast cancer and hormone replacement therapy: collaborative reanalysis of data from 51 epidemiologic studies of 52,705 women with breast cancer and 108,411 women without breast cancer. *Lancet* 1997;350:1047–1059.

Collins R, Yusuf S, Peto R: Overview of randomized trials of diuretics in pregnancy. *Br Med J* 1985;290:17–23.

Cook DJ, Guyatt GH, Ryan G, Clifton J, Buckingham L, Willan A, McIlroy W, Oxman AD: Should unpublished data be included in meta-analyses? Current convictions and controversies. *JAMA* 1993;269:2749–2753.

Cook DJ, Sackett DL, Spitzer WO: Methodologic guidelines for systematic reviews of randomized control trials in health care from the Potsdam consultation on meta-analysis. *J Clin Epidemiol* 1995;48:167–171.

Critchfield GC, Willard KE: Probabilistic analysis of decision trees using Monte Carlo simulation. *Med Decis Making* 1986;6:85–92.

Danese MD, Powe NR, Sawin CT, Ladenson PW: Screening for mild thryoid failure at the periodic health examination: a decision and cost-effectiveness analysis. *JAMA* 1996; 276:285–292.

De Bruin AF, De Witte LP, Stevens F, Diedericks JP: Sickness Impact Profile: the state of the art of a generic functional status measure. *Soc Sci Med* 1992:35:1003–1014.*

deBellefeuille C, Morrison C, Tannock I: The fate of abstracts submitted to a cancer meeting: factors which influence presentation and subsequent publication. *Ann Oncol* 1992;3: 187–191.

Demets DL: Methods for combining randomized clinical trials: strengths and limitations. *Stat Med* 1987;6:341–348.

DerSimonian R, Laird N: Meta-analysis in clinical trials. *Control Clin Trials* 1986;7:177–188.

Detsky AS, Naglie IG: A clinician's guide to cost-effectiveness analysis. *Ann Intern Med* 1990;113:147–154.

Detsky AS, Naylor CD, O'Rourke K, McGeer AJ, L'Abbe KA: Incorporating variations in the quality of individual randomized trials into meta-analysis. *J Clin Epidemiol* 1992; 45:255—265.

Devine EC, Cook TD: A meta-analytic analysis of effects of psychoeducational interventions on length of postsurgical hospital stay. *Nursing Res* 1983;32:267–274.

Dickersin K, Scherer R, Lefebvre C: Identifying relevant studies for systematic reviews. *BMJ* 1994;309:1286–1291.

Dickersin K, Berlin JA: Meta-analysis: state-of-the-science. *Epidemiol Rev* 1992;14:154–176.

Dickersin K, Hewitt P, Mutch L, Chalmers I, Chalmers TC: Comparison of MEDLINE searching with a perinatal trials database. *Control Clin Trials* 1985;6:306–317.

Dickersin K, Min Y-I, Meinert CL: Factors influencing publication of research results: follow-up of applications submitted to two institutional review boards. *JAMA* 1992; 267:374–378.

Doubilet P, Begg CB, Weinstein MC, Braun P, McNeil BJ: Probabilistic sensitivity analysis using Monte Carlo simulation: a practical approach. *Med Decis Making* 1985;5:157–177.

Doubilet P, Weinstein MC, McNeil BJ: Use and misuse of the term "cost effective" in medicine. *N Engl J Med* 1986;314:253–256.

Drummond MF: Resource allocation decisions in health care: a role for quality of life assessments? *J Chron Dis* 1987;40:605–616.

Drummond MF, O'Brien B, Stoddart GL, Torrance GW: *Methods of Economic Evaluation of Health Care Programmes.* 2nd ed. Oxford, Oxford University Press, 1997.

Dudley HAF: Surgical research: master or servant? *Am J Surg* 1978;135:458–460.

Dupont WD, Page DL: Menopausal estrogen replacement therapy and breast cancer. *Arch Intern Med* 1991;151:67–72.

Early Breast Cancer Trialists' Collaborative Group: Effects of adjuvant tamoxifen and of cytotoxic therapy on mortality in early breast cancer. *N Engl J Med* 1988;319:1681–1692.

Easterbrook PJ, Berlin JA, Gopalan R, Matthews DR: Publication bias in research. *Lancet* 1991;337:867–872.

Eddy DM: The confidence profile method: a Bayesian method for assessing health technologies. *Oper Res* 1989;37:210–228.

Eddy DM, Hasselblad V, Shachter R: A Bayesian method for synthesizing evidence: the confidence profile method. *Int J Tech Assess Health Care* 1990a;6:31–55.

Eddy DM, Hasselblad V, Shachter R: An introduction to a Bayesian method for meta-analysis: the confidence profile method. *Med Decis Making* 1990b;10:15–23.

Egger M, Zellweger-Zahner T, Schneider M, Junker C, Lengeler C, Antes G: Language bias in randomised controlled trials published in English and German. *Lancet* 1997;350: 326–329.**

Elbourne D, Oakley A, Chalmers I: Social and psychological support during pregnancy. In: *Effective Care in Pregnancy and Childbirth,* vol 1, *Pregnancy.* Chalmers I, Enkin M, Keirse MJN (eds). Oxford, Oxford University Press, 1989; pp 221–236.

Essink-Bot ML, Stouthard ME, Bonsel GJ: Generalizability of valuations on health states collected with the EuroQol questionniare. *Heath Econ* 1993;2:237–246.*

EuroQol Group: EuroQol: a new facility for measurement of health-related quality of life. *Health Policy* 1990;16:199–208.

Eysenck HJ: An exercise in mega-silliness. *Am Psychol* 1978;33:517.

Fineberg HV, Scadden D, Goldman: Care of patients with a low probability of acute myocardial infarction: cost effectiveness of alternatives to coronary-care-unit admissions. *N Engl J Med* 1984;310:1301–1307.

Finkler SA: The distinction between cost and charges. *Ann Intern Med* 1982;96:102–109.

Fiore MC, Smith SS, Jorenby DE, Baker TB: The effectiveness of the nicotine patch for smoking cessation: a meta-analysis. *JAMA* 1994;271:1940–1947.

Fisher RA: *Statistical Methods for Research Workers,* 4th ed. London, Oliver and Boyd, 1932.

Fleiss JL: Statistical Methods for Rates and Proportions. 2nd ed. New York, J Wiley, 1981, pp 161–165.

Fleiss JL: The statistical basis of meta-analysis. *Stat Methods Med Res* 1993;2:121–145.

Fleiss JL, Gross AJ: Meta-analysis in epidemiology, with special reference to studies of the association between exposure to environmental tobacco smoke and lung cancer: a critique. *J Clin Epidemiol* 1991;44:127–139.

Fleming C, Wasson JH, Albertsen PC, Barry MJ, Wennberg JE for the Prostate Patient Outcomes Research Team: A decision analysis of alternative treatment strategies for clinically localized prostate cancer. *JAMA* 1993;2650–2658.

Friedenreich CM: Methods for pooled analyses of epidemiologic studies. *Epidemiology* 1993;4:295–302.

Froberg DG, Kane RL: Methodology for measuring health-state preferences: IV. Progress and a research agenda. *J Clin Epidemiol* 1989d;42:675–685.

Froberg DG, Kane RL: Methodology for measuring health-state preferences: III. Population and context effects. *J Clin Epidemiol* 1989c;42:485–592.

Froberg DG, Kane RL: Methodology for measuring health-state preferences: II. Scaling methods. *J Clin Epidemiol* 1989b;42:459–471.

Froberg DG, Kane RL: Methodology for measuring health-state preferences: I. Measurement strategies. *J Clin Epidemiol* 1989a;42:345–354.

Fryback DG, Lawrence WF, Martin PA, Klein R, Klein BEK: Predicting quality of well-being scores from the SF-36: results from the Beaver Dam Health Outcomes Study. *Med Decis Making* 1997;17:1–9.

Gage BF, Cardinalli AB, Albers GW, Owens DK: Cost-effectiveness of warfarin and aspirin for prophylaxis of stroke in patients with nonvalvular atrial fibrillation. *JAMA* 1995; 274:1839–1845.

Garfinkel L, Auerbach O, Joubert L: Involuntary smoking and lung cancer: a case-control study. *J Natl Cancer Inst* 1985;75:463–469.

Genduso LA, Kotsanos JG: Review of health economic guidelines in the form of regulations, principles, policies, and positions. *Drug Information J* 1996;30:1003–1016.

GISSI (Gruppo Italiano per lo Studio Della Streptochiasi Nell'infarto Miocardico): Effectiveness of intravenous thrombolytic treatment in acute myocardial infarction. *Lancet* 1986;1:397–402.

Gladen BC, Rogan WJ: On graphing rate ratios. *Am J Epidemiol* 1983;118:905–908.

Glass GV: Primary, secondary and meta-analysis of research. *Educ Res* 1976;5:3–8.

Glass GV, McGaw B, Smith ML: *Meta-analysis in Social Research.* Beverly Hills, Calif, Sage Publications, 1981.

Gleser LJ, Olkin I: Models for estimating the number of unpublished studies. *Stat Med* 1996;15:2493–2507.

Gold MR, Siegel JE, Russell LB, Weinstein MC: *Cost-effectiveness in Health and Medicine.* New York, Oxford University Press, 1996.

Goldman L, Loscalzo A: Fate of cardiology research originally published in abstract form. *N Engl J Med* 1980;303:255–259.

Goldman L, Weinstein MC, Goldman PA, Williams LW: Cost-effectiveness of HMG-Co-A reductase inhibition for primary and secondary prevention of coronary heart disease. *JAMA* 1991;265:1145–1151.

Grady D, Rubin S, Petitti DB, Fox C, Black D, Ettinger B, Ernster V, Cummings SR. Hormone therapy to prevent disease and prolong life in postmenopausal women. *Ann Intern Med* 1992;117:1016–1037.

Greenland S: Quantitative methods in the review of epidemiologic literature. *Epidemiol Rev* 1987;9:1–30.

Greenland S, Longnecker MP: Methods for trend estimation from summarized dose-response data, with applications to meta-analysis. *Am J Epidemiol* 1992;135:1301–1309.

Greenland S, Rothman KJ: Measures of effect and measures of association. In Rothman KJ and Greenland S. *Modern Epidemiology.* 2nd edition. Lipponcott-Raven, Philidelphia, 1998; pp.47–64.

Greenland S, Salvan A: Bias in the one-step method for pooling study results. *Stat Med* 1990;9:247–252.

Greenland S, Schlesselman JJ, Criqui MH: The fallacy of employing standardized regression coefficients and correlations as measures of effect. *Am J Epidemiol* 1987;123:203–208.

Gregoire G, Derderian F, Le Lorier J: Selecting the language of the publications included in a meta-analysis: is there a Tower of Babel bias? *J Clin Epidemiol* 1995;48:159–163.

Harris J: QALYfying the value of life. *J Med Ethics* 1987;13:117–123.

Hebert JR, Miller DR: Plotting and discussion of rate ratios and relative risk estimates. *J Clin Epidemiol* 1989;3:289–290.

Heckerling PS, Verp MS: Amniocentesis or chorionic villus sampling for prenatal genetic testing: a decision analysis. *J Clin Epidemiol* 1991;44:657–670.

Hedges LV: Estimation of effect size from a series of independent experiments. *Psychol Bull* 1982;92:490–499.

Hedges LV: Combining independent estimators in research synthesis. *Br J Math Stat Psychol* 1983;36:123–131.

Hedges LV, Olkin I: *Statistical Methods for Meta-Analysis.* Orlando, Florida, Academic Press, 1985.

Hedges LV, Olkin I: Vote-counting methods in research synthesis. *Psychol Bull* 1980;88:359–369.

Hedges LV: Estimation of effect size under nonrandom sampling: the effects of censoring studies yielding statistically insignificant mean differences. *J Educ Stat* 1984;9:61–85.

Henschke UK, Flehinger BJ: Decision theory in cancer therapy. *Cancer* 1967;20:1819–1826.

Hillner BE, Smith TJ: Efficacy and cost effectiveness of adjuvant chemotherapy in women with node-negative breast cancer: a decision-analysis model. *N Engl J Med* 1991;324:160–168.

Himel HN, Liberati A, Gelber RD, Chalmers TC: Adjuvant chemotherapy for breast cancer: a pooled estimate based on published randomized control trials. *JAMA* 1986;256:1148–1159.

Hunter JE, Schmidt FL, Jackson BG: *Meta-Analysis: Cumulating Research Findings Across Studies.* Beverly Hills, Calif, Sage Publications, 1982.

Ioannidis JPA, Lau J: Can quality of clinical trials and meta-analyses by quantified? *Lancet* 1998;352:590.

Ioannidis JPA: Effect of the statistical significance of results on the time to completion and publication of randomized efficacy trials. *JAMA* 1998;279:281–286.

Iyengar SI, Greenhouse JB: Selection models and the file drawer problem. *Stat Science* 1988;3:109–117.

Jenicek M: Meta-analysis in medicine: where we are and where we want to go. *J Clin Epidemiol* 1989;42:35–44.

Jenson HB, Pollock BH: The role of intravenous immunoglobulin for the prevention and treatment of neonatal sepsis. *Seminars Perinatol* 1998;22:50–63.

Jordan TJ, Lewit EM, Montgomery RL, Reichman LB: Isoniazid as preventive therapy in HIV-infected intravenous drug abusers: a decision analysis. *JAMA* 1991;265:2987–2991.

Kaplan RM, Anderson JP: A general health policy model: update and applications. *Health Serv Res* 1988;23:203–205.

Kaplan RM, Bush JW: Health-related quality of life measurement for evaluation research and policy analysis. *Health Psychol* 1982;1:61–80.

Kassirer JP: The principles of clinical decision making: an introduction to decision analysis. *Yale J Biol Med* 1976;49:149–164

Kassirer JP, Angell M: The Journal's policy on cost-effectiveness analyses. *N Engl J Med* 1994;331:669–670.

Kassirer JP, Pauker SG: The toss-up. *N Engl J Med* 1981;305:1467–1469.

Keeler EB, Cretin S: Discounting of life-saving and other non-monetary benefits. *Management Science* 1983;29:300–306.

Kerlikowske K, Brown JS, Grady DG: Should women with familial ovarian cancer undergo prophylactic oophorectomy. *Obstet Gynecol* 1992;80:700–707.

Kerlikowske K, Grady D, Rubin SM, Sandrock C, Ernster VL: Efficacy of screening mammography: a meta-analysis. *JAMA* 1995;273:149–154.

Kleinbaum DG, Kupper LL, Morgenstern H: *Epidemiologic Research: Principles and Quantitative Methods.* Belmont, Calif, Lifetime Learning, 1982.

Koren G, Graham K, Shear H, Einarson T: Bias against the null hypothesis: the reproductive hazards of cocaine. *Lancet* 1989;2:1440–1444.

L'Abbe KA, Detsky AS, O'Rourke K: Meta-analysis in clinical research. *Ann Intern Med* 1987;107:224–233.

Laird NM, Mosteller F: Some statistical methods for combining experimental results. *Int J Tech Assess Health Care* 1990;6:5–30.

Lam TH, Kung IT, Wong CM, Lam WK, Kleevens JW, Saw D, Hsu D, Seneviratne S, Lam SY, Lo KK, Chan WC: Smoking, passive smoking and histologic types in lung cancer in Hong Kong Chinese women. *Br J Cancer* 1987;6:673–678.

Lam W, Sze PC, Sacks HS, Chalmers TC: Meta-analysis of randomized controlled trials of nicotine chewing gum. *Lancet* 1987;2:27–30.

LaPuma J, Lawlor EF: Quality-adjusted life-years: ethical implications for physicians and policymakers. *JAMA* 1990;263:2917–2921.

Lau J, Ioannidis PA, Schmid CH: Quantitative synthesis in systematic reviews. *Ann Intern Med* 1997;127:820–827.

Lau J, Antman EM, Jimenez-Silva J, Kupelnick B, Mosteller F, Chalmers TC: Cumulative meta-analysis of therapeutic trials for myocardial infarction. *N Engl J Med* 1992;327:248–254.

Lau J, Schmid CH, Chalmers TC: Cumulative meta-analysis of clinical trials builds evidence for exemplary meta-analysis. *J Clin Epidemiol* 1995;48:45–57.

Lau J, Ioannidis JPA, Schmid CH: Summing up evidence: one answer is not always enough. *Lancet* 1998;351:123–127.

Ledley RS, Lusted LB: Reasoning foundations of medical diagnosis: symbolic logic, probability, and value theory aid our understanding of how physicians reason. *Science* 1959;130:9–21.

LeLorier J, Gregoire G, Benhaddad A, Lapierre J, Derderian F: Discrepancies between meta-analyses and subsequent large randomized, controlled trials. *N Engl J Med* 1997;337:536–542.

Lieu TA, Gurley JR, Lundstrom RJ, Ray GT, Fireman BH, Weinstein MC, Parmley WW: Projected cost-effectiveness of primary angioplasty for acute myocardial infarction. *J Am Coll Cardiol* 1997;30:1741–1750.

Light RJ, Pillemer DB: *Summing Up: The Science of Reviewing Research.* Cambridge, Mass, Harvard University Press, 1984.

Light RJ (ed): *Evaluation Studies. Review Annual,* vol 8. Beverly Hills, Calif, Sage Publications, 1983.

Lipid Research Clinics Program: The Lipid Research Clinics Coronary Primary Prevention Trial results: I. Reduction in incidence of coronary heart disease. *JAMA* 1984a;251:351–364.

Lipid Research Clinics Program: The Lipid Research Clinics Coronary Primary Prevention

Trial results: II. The relationship of reduction in incidence of coronary heart disease to cholesterol lowering. *JAMA* 1984b;25:365–374.

Littenberg B: Aminophylline treatment in severe, acute asthma: a meta-analysis. *JAMA* 1988;259:1678–1684.

Llewellyn-Thomas H, Sutherland HJ, Tibshirani R, Ciampi A, Till JE, Boyd NF: The measurement of patients' values in medicine. *Med Decis Making*1982;2:449–462.

Llewellyn-Thomas H, Sutherland HJ, Tibshirani R, Ciampi A, Till JE, Boyd NF: Describing health states: methodologic issues in obtaining values for health states. *Med Care* 1984; 22:543–552.

Longnecker MP, Berlin JA, Orza MJ, Chalmers TC: A meta-analysis of alcohol consumption in relation to risk of breast cancer. *JAMA* 1988;260:652–656.

Lusted LB: Decision-making studies in patient management. *N Engl J Med* 1971;284:416–424.

Mantel N: Chi-square tests with one degree of freedom: extensions of the Mantel-Haenszel procedure. *JASA* 1963;58:690–700.

Mantel N, Haenszel W: Statistical aspects of the analysis of data from retrospective studies of disease. *J Natl Cancer Inst* 1959;22:719–748.

Mantel N, Brown C, Byar DP: Tests for homogeneity of effect in an epidemiologic investigation. *Am J Epidemiol* 1977;106:125–129.

Mast EE, Berg JL, Hanrahan LP, Wassell JT, Davis JP: Risk factors for measles in a previously vaccinated population and cost-effectiveness of revaccination strategies. *JAMA* 1990;264:2529–2533.

McCormick MC, Holmes JH: Publication of research presented at the pediatric meetings: change in selection. *Am J Dis Child* 1985;139:122–126.

McDowell I, Newell C: *Measuring Health. A Guide to Rating Scales and Questionnaires,* 2nd edition. New York, Oxford University Press, 1996.

McHorney CA: Measuring and monitoring health status in elderly persons: practical and methodological issues in using the SF-36 Health Survey. *Gerontologist* 1996;36:571–593.

Meier P: Commentary on "Why do we need systematic overviews of randomized trials?" *Stat Med* 1987;6:329–331.

Meinert CL: *Trials: Design, Conduct, and Analysis.* Oxford, Oxford University Press, 1986.

Meranze J, Ellison N, Greenhow DE: Publications resulting from anesthesia meeting abstracts. *Anesth Analg* 1982;61:445–448.

Midgley JP, Matthew AG, Greenwood CM, Logan AG: Effect of reduced dietary sodium on blood pressure: a meta-analysis of randomized controlled trials. *JAMA* 1996;275:1590–1597.

Miller GA: The magical number seven plus or minus two: some limits on our capacity to process information. *Psycho Rev* 1956;63:81–97.

Miller JN, Colditz GA, Mosteller F: How study design affects outcomes in comparisons of therapy: II. Surgical. *Stat Med* 1989;8:455–466.

Miller MA, Sutter RW, Strebel PM, Hadler SC: Cost-effectiveness of incorporating inactivated poliovirus vaccine into the routine childhood immunization schedule. *JAMA* 1996;276:967–971.

Moher D, Pham B, Jones A, Cook DJ, Jadad AR, Moher M, Tugwell P, Klassen TP: Does quality of reports of randomised trials affect estimates of intervention efficacy reported in meta-analyses? *Lancet* 1998;352:609–613.

Moher D, Fortin P, Jadad AR, Juni P, Klassen T, LeLorier J, Liberati A, Linde K, Penna A: Completeness of reporting of trials published in languages other than English: implications for conduct and reporting of systematic reviews. *Lancet* 1996;347:363–366.

Moher D, Jadad AR, Nichol G, Penman M, Tugwell P, Walsh S: Assessing the quality of randomized controlled trials: an annotated bibliography of scales and checklists. *Control Clin Trials* 1995;16:62–73.

Morgenstern H: Uses of ecologic analysis in epidemiologic research. *Am J Public Health* 1982;72:1336–1344.

Morgenstern H, Greenland S: Graphing ratio measures of effect. *J Clin Epidemiol* 1990;6: 539–542.

Nord E: Toward quality assurance in QALY calculations. *Inter J Tech Assess Health Care* 1993;9:37–45.

O'Brien B: Principles of economic evaluation for health care. *J Rheumatol* 1995;22:1399–1402.

Office of Technology Assessment (OTA). U.S. Congress. *Evaluation of the Oregon Medicaid Proposal.* OTA-H-531. Washington, DC, U.S. Government Printing Office, 1992.

Orwin RG: A fail-safe N for effect size in meta-analysis. *J Educ Stat* 1983;8:157–159.

Oster G, Epstein AM: Cost-effectiveness of antihyperlipemic therapy in the prevention of coronary heart disease. *JAMA* 1987a;258:2381–2387.

Oster G, Tuden RL, Colditz GA: A cost-effectiveness analysis of prophylaxis against deep-vein thrombosis in major orthopedic surgery. *JAMA* 1987b;257:203–208.

Pauker SG, Kassirer JP: Decision analysis. *N Engl J Med* 1987;316:250–258.

Pearson ES: The probability integral transformation for testing goodness of fit and combining independent tests of significance. *Biometrika* 1938;30:134–148.

Petitti DB, Perlman JA, Sidney S: Noncontraceptive estrogens and mortality: long-term follow-up of women in the Walnut Creek Study. *Obstet Gynecol* 1987;70:289–293.

Peto R, Collins R, Gray R: Large-scale randomized evidence: large, simple trials and overviews of trials. *J Clin Epidemiol* 1995;48:23–40.

Peto R: Why do we need systematic overviews of randomized trials? *Stat Med* 1987;6:233–240.

Phillips K: The use of meta-analysis in technology assessment: a meta-analysis of the enzyme immunosorbent assay human immunodeficiency virus antibody test. *J Clin Epidemiol* 1991;44:925–931.

Pliskin JS, Shepard DS, Weinstein MC: Utility functions for life years and health status. *Oper Res* 1980;28:206–224.

Pogue J, Yusuf S: Overcoming the limitations of current meta-analysis of randomised controlled trials. *Lancet* 1998;351:47–52.

Poole C, Greenland S: Random-effects meta-analyses are not always conservative. in press.

Prentice RL, Thomas DB: On the epidemiology of oral contraceptives and disease. *Adv Cancer Res* 1986;49:285–401.

Psaty BM, Smith NL, Siscovick DS, Koepsell TD, Weiss NS, Heckbert SR, Lemaitre RN, Wagner EH, Furberg CD. Health outcomes associated with antihypertensive therapies used as first-line agents: a systematic review and meta-analysis. *JAMA* 1997;277:739–745.

Radhakrishna S: Combination of results from several 2 × 2 contingency tables. *Biometrics* 1965;21:86–98.

Ransohoff DF, Gracie WA, Wolfenson LB, Neuhauser D: Prophylactic cholecystectomy or expectant management for silent gallstones. *Ann Intern Med* 1983;99:199–204.

Rao CR: Comment on "Selection models and the file drawer problem." *Stat Science* 1988; 3:131–132.

Rawles J: Castigating QALYs. *J Med Ethics* 1989;15:143–147.

Read JL, Quinn RJ, Berwick DM, Fineberg HV, Weinstein MC: Preferences for health outcomes: comparison of assessment methods. *Med Decis Making* 1984;4:315–329.

Rifkin RD: Classical statistical considerations in medical decision models. *Med Decis Making* 1983;3:197–214.

Robins J, Greenland S, Breslow NE: A general estimator for the variance of the Mantel-Haenszel odds ratio. *Am J Epidemiol* 1986;124:719–723.

Rosenthal R: The "file drawer problem" and tolerance for null results. *Psychol Bull* 1979; 86:638–641.

Rosenthal R: Combining results of independent studies. *Psychol Bull* 1978;85:185–193.

Rosenthal R, Rubin DB: Further meta-analytic procedures for assessing cognitive gender differences. *J Educ Psychol* 1982;74:708–712.

Russell LB, Gold MR, Siegel JE, Daniels N, Weinstein MC, for the Panel on Cost-Effectiveness in Health and Medicine: The role of cost-effectiveness analysis in health and medicine. *JAMA* 1996;276;1172–1177.

Sacks HS, Chalmers TC, Smith H Jr: Sensitivity and specificity of clinical trials: randomized v. historical controls. *Ann Intern Med* 1983;143:753–755.

Sacks HS, Berrier J, Reitman D, Ancona-Berk VA, Chalmers TC: Meta-analysis of randomized controlled trials. *N Engl J Med* 1987;316:450–455.

Saint S, Bent S, Vittinghoff E, Grady D: Antibiotics in chronic obstructive pulmonary disease exacerbations: a meta-analysis. *JAMA* 1995;273:957–960.

Schesselman J: Risk of endometrial cancer in relation to use of combined oral contraceptives: a practitioner's guide to meta-analysis. *Hum Reprod* 1997;12:1851–1863.

Schrag D, Kuntz KM, Garber JE, Weeks JC: Decision analysis—effects of prophylactic mastectomy and oophorectomy on life expectancy among women with BRCA1 or BRCA2 mutations. *N Engl J Med* 1997;336:1465–1471.

Schulman KA, Lynn LA, Glick HA, Eisenberg JM: Cost effectiveness of low-dose zidovudine therapy for asymptomatic patients with human immunodeficiency virus (HIV) infection. *Ann Intern Med* 1991;114:798–802.

Schwartz WB, Gorry GA, Kassirer JP, Essig A: Decision analysis and clinical judgment. *Am J Med* 1973;55:459–472.

Shapiro S: Meta-analysis/Shmeta-analysis. *Am J Epidemiol* 1994; 140:771–778.

Shipp M, Croughan-Minihane MS, Petitti DB, Washington AE: Estimation of the break-even point for smoking cessation programs in pregnancy. *Am J Public Health* 1992; 82:383–390.

Siegel JE, Weinstein MC, Russell LB, Gold MR: Recommendations for reporting cost-effectiveness analyses. *JAMA* 1996;276:1339–1341.

Sillero-Arenas M, Delgado-Rodriguez M, Rodriguez-Canteras R, Bueno-Cavanillas A, Galvez-Vargas R: Menopausal hormone replacement therapy and breast cancer: a meta-analysis. *Obstet Gynecol* 1992;79:286–294.

Simes JR: Treatment selection for cancer patients: application of statistical decision theory to the treatment of advanced ovarian cancer. *J Chron Dis* 1985;38:171–186.

Simes JR: Publication bias: the case for an international registry of trials. *J Clin Oncol* 1986; 4:1529–1541.

Simes RJ: Confronting publication bias: a cohort design for meta-analysis. *Stat Med* 1987; 6:11–29.

Sisk JE, Riegelman RK: Cost effectiveness of vaccination against pneumococcal pneumonia: an update. *Ann Intern Med* 1986;104:79–86.

Sisk JE, Moskowitz AJ, Whang W, Lin JD, Fedson DS, McBean AM, Plouffe JF, Cetron MS, Butler JC: Cost-effectiveness of vaccination against pneumococcal bacteremia among elderly people. *JAMA* 1997;278:1333–1339.

Smith A: Qualms about QALYs. *Lancet* 1987;1:1134–1136.

Sonnenberg FA, Beck JR: Markov models in medical decision making: a practical guide. *Med Decis Making* 1993;13:322–338.

Sox HC, Blatt MA, Higgins MC, Marton KI: *Medical Decision Making*. Stoneham, Mass, Butterworth, 1988.

Spilker B (ed): *Quality of Life and Pharmacoeconomic Clinical Trials*. Philadelphia, Pa, Lippincott-Raven, 1995.

Spitzer WO: State of science 1986: quality of life and functional status as target variables for research. *J Chron Dis* 1987;40:465–471.

Stampfer MJ, Goldhaber SZ, Yusuf S, Peto R, Hennekens CH: Effect of intravenous streptokinase on acute myocardial infarction: pooled results from randomized trials. *N Engl J Med* 1982;307:1180–1182.

Stampfer MJ, Colditz GA: Estrogen replacement therapy and coronary heart disease: a quantitative assessment of the epidemiologic evidence. *Prev Med* 1991;20:47–63.

Steinberg KK, Thacker SB, Smith SJ, Stroup DF, Zack MM, Flanders WD, Berkelman RL: A meta-analysis of the effect of estrogen replacement therapy on the risk of breast cancer. *JAMA* 1991;265:1985–1990.

Sterling TD: Publication decisions and their possible effects on inferences drawn from tests of significance—or vice versa. *JASA* 1959;54:30–34.

Stock WA, Okun MA, Haring MJ, Miller W, Kinney C, Ceurvorst RW: Rigor in data synthesis: a case study of reliability in meta-analysis. *Educ Res* 1982;11:10–14, 20.

Stroup DF, Berlin JA, Morton S, Olkin I, Williamson GD, Rennie D, Moher D, Becker BJ, Sipe T, Thacker SB: Meta-analysis of observational studies in epidemiology: summary of a workshop. Am J Epidemiol in press

Struewing JF, Watson R, Easton DF, Ponder RA, Lynch HT, Tucker MA: Prophylactic oophorectomy in inherited breast/ovarian cancer families. In: *Hereditary Breast Cancer, Ovarian and Colon Cancer*. NCI monographs. No. 17. Washington, D.C., Government Printing Office, 1995;33–35.

Sugden R, Williams A: *The Principles of Practical Cost-Benefit Analysis*. Oxford, Oxford University Press, 1990.

Tengs TO, Adama ME, Pliskin JS, Safran DG, Siegl JE, Weinstein MC, Graham JD: Five-hundred life-saving interventions and their cost-effectiveness. *Risk Analysis* 1995;15:369–390.

Thompson SG, Pocock SJ: Can meta-analysis be trusted? *Lancet* 1991;338:1127–1130.

Thompson SG: Why sources of heterogeneity in meta-analysis should be investigated. *BMJ* 1994;309:1351–1355.

Tippett LHC: *The Methods of Statistics*. London, Williams and Norgate, 1931.

Torrance GW: Social preferences for health states: an empirical evaluation of three measurement techniques. *Socio-Econ Plan Sci* 1976;10:129–136.

Torrance GW: Preferences for health states: a review of measurement methods. *Meade Johnson Symposium on Perinatal and Developmental Medicine* 1982;20:37–45.

Torrance GW: Measurement of health state utilities for economic appraisal: a review. *J Health Econ* 1986;5:1–30.

Torrance GW: Utility approach to measuring health-related quality of life. *J Chron Dis* 1987;40:593–600

Torrance GW, Boyle MH, Horwood SP: Application of multi-attribute utility theory to measure social preferences for health states. *Oper Res* 1982;30:1043–1069.

Torrance GW, Thomas WH, Sackett DL: A utility maximization model for evaluation of health care programs. *Health Serv Res* 1972;7:118–133.

Tramer MR, Reynolds DJ, Moore RA, McQuay HJ: Impact of covert duplicate publication on meta-analysis: a case study. *BMJ* 1997;13:635–640.

Tversky A, Kahneman D: The framing of decisions and the psychology of choice. *Science* 1981;211:453–458.

Ubel PA, DeKay ML, Baron J, Asch DA: Cost-effectiveness analysis in a setting of budget constraints: is it equitable? *N Engl J Med* 1996;334:1174–1177.

Udvarhelyi IS, Colditz GA, Rai A, Epstein AM: Cost-effectiveness and cost-benefit analyses in the medical literature: are the methods being used correctly? *Ann Intern Med* 1992; 116:238–244.

United States Department of Health and Human Services: *The Health Effects of Smoking Cessation.*Public Health Service, Office on Smoking and Health. DHHS Publication No. (CDC) 90-8416, 1990; pp 449–453.

United States Environmental Protection Agency: *Health Effects of Passive Smoking: Assessment of Lung Cancer in Adults and Respiratory Disorders in Children.* US EPA Publication No. EPA-600-90-006A, Washington DC, 1990.

Van Agt HM, Essink-Bot ML, Krabbe PF, Bonsel GJ: Test-retest reliability of health state evaluations collected with the EuroQol questionnaire. *Soc Sci Med* 1994;39:1537–1544.

Villar J, Piaggio G, Carroli G, Donner A: Factors affecting the comparability of meta-analyses and largest trials results in perinatology. *J Clin Epidemiol* 1997;50:997–1002.

Villar J, Carroll G, Belizan JM: Predictive ability of meta-analyses of randomised controlled trials. *Lancet* 1995;345:772–776.

Von Neumann J, Morgenstern O: *Theory of Games and Economic Theory.* New York, Wiley, 1947.

Wachter KW: Disturbed by meta-analysis? *Science* 1988;241:1407–1408.

Walker AM, Martin-Moreno JM, Artalejo FR: Odd man out: a graphical approach to meta-analysis. *Am J Public Health* 1988;78:961–966.

Ware JE Jr, Snow KK, Kosinski M, et al: SF-36 *Health Survey: Manual and Interpretation Guide.* Boston, Mass, The Health Institute, New England Medical Center, 1993.

Ware JE, Sherbourne CD: The MOS 36-item Short-Form Health Survey (SF-36). I. Conceptual framework and item selection. *Med Care* 1992;30:473–483.

Ware JE Jr: Standards for validating health measures: definition and content. *J Chron Dis* 1987;40:473–480.

Weaver WD, Simes RJ, Betriu A, Grines CL, Zijlstra F, Garcia E, Grinfeld L, Gibbons RJ, Ribeiro EE, DeWood MA, Ribichini F: Comparison of primary coronary angioplasty and intravenous thrombolytic therapy for acute myocardial infarction: a quantitative review. *JAMA* 1997;278:2093–2098.

Weinstein MC, Siegel JE, Gold MR, Kamlet MS, Russell LB: Recommendations of the Panel on Cost-Effectiveness in Health and Medicine. *JAMA* 1996;276;1253–1258.

Weinstein MC, Stason WB: Cost-effectiveness of interventions to prevent or treat coronary heart disease. *Ann Rev Public Health* 1985;6:41–63.

Weinstein MC, Stason WB: Foundations of cost-effectiveness analysis for health and medical practices. *N Engl J Med* 1977;296:716–721.

Weinstein MC, Fineberg HV: *Clinical Decision Analysis.* Philadelphia, WB Saunders Company, 1980.

Welch GH, Larson EB: Cost effectiveness of bone marrow transplantation in acute nonlymphocytic leukemia. *N Engl J Med* 1989;321:807–812.

Whelton PK, He J, Cutler JA, Brancati FL, Appel LJ, Follmann D, Klag MJ: Effects of oral potassium on blood pressure: meta-analysis of randomized controlled clinical trials. *JAMA* 1997;277:1624–1632.

Williams A: Economics of coronary artery bypass grafting. *Br Med J* 1985;291:326–329.

Williamson DF, Parker RA, Kendrick JS: The box plot: a simple visual method to interpret data. *Ann Intern Med* 1989;110:916–921.

Winkelstein W: The first use of meta-analysis? *Am J Epidemiol* 1998;147:717.

Wolf FM: *Meta-Analysis: Quantitative Methods for Research Synthesis.* Newbury Park, Calif, Sage Publications, 1986.

Wortman PM, Yeatman WH: Synthesis of results of controlled trials of coronary artery bypass graft surgery. In: *Evaluation Studies. Review Annual,* vol 8. Light R (ed). Beverly Hills, Calif, Sage Publications, 1983; pp 536–557.

Wright JC, Weinstein MC: Gains in life expectancy from medical interventions—standardizing data on outcomes. *N Engl J Med* 1998;339:380–386.

Yudkin PL, Ellison GW, Ghezzi A, Goodkin DE, Hughes RAC, McPherson K, Mertin J, Milanese C: Overview of azathioprine treatment in multiple sclerosis. *Lancet* 1991;338:1051–1055.

Yusuf S, Peto R, Lewis J, Collins R, Sleight P: Beta blockade during and after myocardial infarction: an overview of the randomized trials. *Prog Cardiovasc Dis* 1985;27:335–371.

Subject Index

Index of Examples